CULTURAL FOUNDATIONS OF LEARNING

Western and East Asian people hold fundamentally different beliefs about learning that influence how they approach childrearing and education. Reviewing decades of research, Dr. Jin Li presents an important conceptual distinction between the Western mind model and the East Asian virtue model of learning. The former aims to cultivate the mind to understand the world, whereas the latter prioritizes the self to be perfected morally and socially. Tracing the cultural origins of the two large intellectual traditions, Li details how each model manifests itself in the psychology of the learning process, learning affect, regard of one's learning peers, expression of what one knows, and parents' guiding efforts. Despite today's accelerated cultural exchange, these learning models do not diminish but endure.

Dr. Jin Li is associate professor of Education and Human Development at Brown University. Her research examines different cultural learning models and how such culturally based models shape children's learning beliefs and achievement. She collaborates with researchers from Taiwan, Hong Kong, the United Kingdom, Germany, Israel, and the United States. Dr. Li has published in leading journals such as *American Psychologist*, *Journal of Educational Psychology*, *Child Development*, *Developmental Psychology*, *Ethos*, and *Cognition and Emotion*, among others.

Cultural Foundations of Learning

EAST AND WEST

Jin Li
Brown University

CAMBRIDGE UNIVERSITY PRESS
Cambridge, New York, Melbourne, Madrid, Cape Town,
Singapore, São Paulo, Delhi, Mexico City

Cambridge University Press
32 Avenue of the Americas, New York, NY 10013-2473, USA

www.cambridge.org
Information on this title: www.cambridge.org/9780521160629

First published 2012

Printed in the United States of America

A catalog record for this publication is available from the British Library.

Library of Congress Cataloging in Publication data
Li, Jin, 1957–
Cultural foundations of learning : east and west / Jin Li.
    p.   cm.
Includes bibliographical references and index.
ISBN 978-0-521-76829-0 (hardback) – ISBN 978-0-521-16062-9 (paperback)
1. Learning, Psychology of.   2. Learning – Cross-cultural studies.
3. Learning – Western countries.   4. Learning – East Asia.   I. Title.
LB1060.L5   2012
370.15′23–dc23   2011047838

ISBN 978-0-521-76829-0 Hardback
ISBN 978-0-521-16062-9 Paperback

To my late mother Rongzhi Lu and father Duosheng Li who, despite tumultuous times, nurtured in me an insatiable desire to learn

CONTENTS

PREFACE

"Grinding a sword for ten years, but the blade is yet to be tried." These two poetic lines by the Chinese poet Jia Dao (779–843) have come to signify working on something for a long time, hoping the time and labor produce good results. For me, writing this book took not ten years in preparation but much longer. But I did not mind grinding it out slowly, even if what came out was not always to my liking. As the pages of the book will explain, the grinding itself gave me much joy and meaning.

The idea of writing a book like this came to me at the end of my doctoral dissertation in the late 1990s. The original book title had in it the phrase "a heart and mind for wanting to learn" (*hao-xue-xin*, 好學心), as it was the research topic of my dissertation. The phrase is a native Chinese learning concept that my mother suggested to me. When I was exploring a dissertation topic, I asked my mother first, as I always did, to share my learning with her, to brainstorm learning concepts upon hearing the translated term *achievement motivation* (成就動機) from Western psychology. She was puzzled about the Western concept, could not produce a single association in Chinese, and sat there speechless quite some time. Finally, she muttered, "What does learning have to do with motivation?! I only know a motive to murder" (in Chinese, *motivation* and *motive* are translated as the same term 動機. Upon reflection on these two English terms, I, too, failed to discern really meaningful differences!). I knew that if my college-educated mother – who had, in effect, also received a secondhand doctoral education through me – could not make sense of *achievement motivation*, chances are that the people I was going to study in China would not either. I then asked her what Chinese concept captures people's desire to learn. Without any hesitation, she said *hao-xue-xin*. "Yes, you are right! Why didn't I think of it?" I exclaimed and felt that I had just hit the jackpot. When I consulted my Chinese peers at the Harvard Graduate School of Education, they unanimously embraced this concept, to my delight. My peers and I racked our brains to come up with a good translation but failed. We decided to stick to the somewhat awkward English translation, for we felt that the translation is accurate in meaning and feeling and speaks to us: a heart and mind for wanting to learn. Subsequently, this native concept came to stand for the Chinese learning model in my research and writing.

That the Chinese learning model reflects their native ideas, attitudes, passions, and approaches did not surprise me, given that I grew up with them. However, my follow-up comparative research with European-American elite college students, chosen as exemplary learners from the West, did. I was struck by the very fact that both cultures value learning, have a comparably long intellectual history, possess a similarly large repertoire of learning concepts, run the same education system of kindergarten, elementary, secondary, and college education, and above all teach much of the same content (math, science, and also English in Chinese-speaking regions). Yet, the meanings of the found learning concepts differ so markedly that there is very little overlap. I did not know that research could produce such surprising results and wondered how such cultural differences escaped previous researchers' attention. But I must admit that by the time I saw the research results, I had been engaged in learning from the West for more than fifteen years. It was not until I conducted my doctoral dissertation research that I fully realized how large the difference is. My later research on children's developing beliefs also confirmed the shaping power of culture. I reasoned that if I, as a cognizant learner of both Chinese and Western orientations, did not fully grasp the profundity of cultural learning models, then others may not either. Hence, they may appreciate an opportunity to learn about the differences beyond the technical realm of journal articles and specialized academic circles. This realization solidified my decision to embark on this book project. I wanted to piece scattered research together to answer two fundamental questions: (1) What are the two different cultural learning models that produce different learners? (2) Why are the models so different?

My effort in writing this book is descriptive and interpretive rather than prescriptive. My goal is to lay out the basic cultural models by tracing their respective intellectual traditions and by showing how cultural learning models influence children's beliefs and how these beliefs manifest themselves in the learning process. By describing the patterns of cultural learning models and children's learning beliefs, I hope to highlight the idea that cultural models serve as permeating light under which adults guide and children develop. But different cultures have different lights and ways of responding to them. The task of research is to let the lights illuminate and then document their influence.

Years ago when I was still a student of German literature, a Chinese literary critic of German drama lamented that the Chinese have plenty of lived experiences and great art, yet they are poor at turning their experiences and art forms into theories. This provocative claim came from his knowledge that the celebrated German playwright Bertolt Brecht (1898–1956) had an epiphany for his "alienation effect" from watching a performance by the Peking Opera singer Mei Lanfang in Moscow. The fact that Brecht was able to see the abstract but common technique in Peking Opera and then "discovered" the unique effect made this Chinese literary critic realize that Chinese could and should have come up with the theory of their own art. Instead, they had to depend on a Westerner to help "elevate" their art form. In a similar way, researchers do what Brecht did: provide understanding of lived cultural experiences at a theoretical level. This theoretical perspective does not replace thoughts and feelings at the gut level, but it helps us appreciate our own culture in ways lived experiences alone (without reflection) cannot. I hope that this book will stimulate readers in thinking about learning and development under the theorized cultural light.

I wish to make clear that this book focuses on the general cultural orientations of learning instead of on individual differences within East Asia and the West. It is not my intention to generalize the cultural orientations to every individual in these cultures. Even with empirical research that claims to be based on culturally representative samples, the power of generalization is limited. Nevertheless, researchers generally agree that if the same phenomenon has been studied by many from many a different angle and with different methods over a long time, and if similar conclusions are drawn, then chances are that the phenomenon exists. No culturally minded social scientist is seeking across-the-board generalization to all individuals. My own research and that of others are subject to the same inherent limitations. Neither does this book attempt to cover inconsistencies and counterforces that work against the basic cultural orientations. To be sure, these forces abound. Individuals who disagree with or are not served well in either cultural system deserve to be researched and understood, but they are not the focus of this book. I chose to look at the general cultural orientations, instead of the atypical tendencies or discord within each culture, because I am interested in the workings, not anomalies or failures, of culture.

Finally, the slow process of writing this book has enabled me to contemplate freely, broadly, and deeply the various topics written about in this book. This slow grinding afforded me the opportunity to change from a swallow-whole learner of anything that came her way to one that is more observant and questioning, from being an incessant critic of her own culture to one who has discovered its strengths. This transformed intellectual stance has helped me learn from Western masters but also to relearn what I had learned from my own culture. This type of cross-cultural learning and its benefits lie in the process of making the strange familiar (Western) and the familiar strange (Chinese) first, then absorbing both into myself, but at the same time also holding both as objects of continuous contemplation.

I am very grateful to the William T. Grant Foundation for funding my collaboration with Janine Bemperchat and Susan Holloway on Chinese adolescents from immigrant families along with peers from other ethnic groups; to the Foundation for Child Development (FCD) for funding my research on preschool children from Chinese immigrant families; to the Chiang-ching Kuo Foundation for supporting my collaboration with Dr. Heidi Fung; and finally for the Spencer Foundation's support for my early research on preschool children's learning beliefs as well as for the continuation of my longitudinal project started with FCD's funding. Any statements that may appear to be unorthodox and unusual or any failures in this book are not theirs but mine.

To the many research assistants I have had the good fortune to work with at Brown University, in China, and in Taiwan, I owe much gratitude. I thank the hundreds of children, college students, and families in these countries for their participation in my research. It was their permission that allowed me a chance to peek inside cultural learning models and their individual learning beliefs. It was their generous sharing of their thoughts, feelings, upbringing, and their parents' sharing of their childrearing that enabled me to "uncover" what has been flowing for millennia. Reading each parent's interview, each child's story, and each college student's description of learning made me realize what a privilege it is to be a researcher. All the work day and night that I embarked on was, without regret, totally worth it.

The able and professional staff at Cambridge University Press helped craft this book. I would like to thank Simina Calin, the editor of Cambridge's psychology list, for her willingness to consider my book proposal and for her patience with my slow writing. Her successor, Emily Spangler, helped me with the submission of my manuscript. My gratitude is extended to Adina Berk, current editor of Cambridge's psychology and cognitive science list, editorial assistant Amanda O'Connor, and production controller Joshua Penney, as well as many other team members behind the scenes for making this book possible. Jayashree Prabhu, project manager of Newgen Knowledge Works in India, managed all versions of the manuscript skillfully and efficiently. Finally, I would like to thank the professional team at PETT Fox, Inc., in New York, who provided excellent copyediting. Without any doubt, this book is much better as a result of their work.

Thinking back, I would feel that something is amiss if I skipped a number of special people who played a decisive role in shaping this book. These were all of my German teachers, first Herr and Frau Bieg for opening my mind to the German language and culture, to Elizabeth Kurz for her interest in Chinese culture, to Ursula Müller for teaching German literature and Western art history, and to Reneta Bürner-Kotzam and Susanne Günthner for their encouragement and support of my further learning.

I thank Professors Donald Mushalko and Barbara Fredette at the University of Pittsburgh for teaching how to foster children's creativity and their support for my application to Harvard Graduate School of Education. I was very lucky to study with my mentor, Kurt Fischer, who encouraged me to study self-conscious emotions, particularly shame and its significant variations across cultures. This intellectual adventure enabled me to write much of the chapter on learning affect.

To Howard Gardner, also my mentor, I am indebted for life. He took a risk by admitting me as a doctoral student in fear that I might not have sufficient English proficiency to last through the program. He was quite right, given that I studied German rather than English in college. Mentioning this beginning of a cherished mentor–student relationship is to emphasize how much more a European-American doctoral mentor had to do to transform a learning-thirsty but confused foreign student to one who can channel her passion into productivity. There is not enough space for me to enumerate the many and unforgettable ways that Howard mentored me as a student from a different culture and a difficult environment. Suffice it to say that for me Howard served and continues to serve as an exemplar of Western learning. His writing was inspirational to me and his teaching in and out of class was mind-opening. Howard continues to mentor me beyond his call of duty in ways only few match. His insights into research, scholarship, and our world and his wisdom about life continue to amaze me and are among the things I treasure most. I am sure that this book would not have been written if I had not lucked out with Howard.

I would like to thank my dear friend, Heidi Fung, for her moving and beautiful work on Chinese shame as a moral concept and for her willingness to collaborate with me on Taiwanese children's learning beliefs and their parents' guidance. The way she does her work and writes about the people she studies sets an unparalleled example for how a researcher can truly get under the skin of her research subjects. No utterance and no expression could escape her attention. Her research report is so authentic that it speaks to the people whose cultures she studies, and yet at the same time her writing is artful and profound. It was Heidi's example that heartened me to attempt discourse analysis of how mothers talk to their children about learning in both cultures. Heidi was also tremendously encouraging and generous in supplying references from first-rate Taiwanese scholars and writers and for granting me her permission to use a photo that shows how a grandfather demonstrates to his grandson what concentration means in learning for the Chinese.

My admiration also goes to my son, Kylee Hench, who would read drafts of my chapters and offer comments and sonly appreciation, and dutifully and unflaggingly point out awkward expressions and incorrect grammar. His love and help invariably resulted in better thinking and writing on my part. Finally, my gratitude goes to my husband, Michael Hench, my lifelong companion and tireless editor of my writing. His love for theater and spontaneous recitations of great Western writing and poetry permeate my life. But he also appreciates Asian writers and poets, frequently more deeply than I do. It would have been a lot harder for me to make progress in writing, let alone this book, if it were not for Michael's lasting love, support, and literary fondness. My work owes much to him.

1

Faust and the Birth of a Research Agenda

Based on a real person, Dr. Faustus, who lived in Europe in the early sixteenth century, several artistic works combined to build the legend of Faust and the *Faustian Bargain*. Accordingly, Faust came to be known as a man who sought forbidden knowledge and made a bargain with the Devil. In exchange for his immortal soul, Faust would be given the power to know. The two best-known and most acclaimed renditions of the Faust tale were created by English playwright Christopher Marlowe and German poet Johann Wolfgang von Goethe. Marlowe dramatized the irrevocable nature of a pact signed in blood with the Devil, the frivolous and unsatisfying end to which the knowledge was put, and, finally, the passionate and desperate damnation that lay at the end of Faust's search for "illegitimate power through learning."[1] Goethe in his mid-nineteenth-century *geist* modified the bargain and made it contingent on Faust's having a moment of contentment. Goethe allowed the angels to rescue Faust because his search and aspiration never ceased. Faust triumphed in the end. Although these two literary works differ in their emphasis and form, they both kept the Faustian Bargain as the crux of their artistic vision.

Surprisingly, Goethe's *Faust* was also translated, along with other important Western works, into Chinese, and therefore it served as an inspiration for a New Cultural Movement in China during the early twentieth century.[2] My late mother remembered seeing the book as a middle-school girl in the 1930s in her school's library in a rural Chinese town where only a few privileged children could attend school. She did dare to open this book with a strange title, but her desire to read further was put to rest for good because she could understand nothing.

Later, in the 1970s, the first group of Chinese students emerging from the farm labor of Mao Zedong's reeducation program,[3] after ten years of closed schools and condemnation of education, entered college. We woke up from a deep slumber and were shocked to find that China had been left behind. "Economically destitute and culturally barren" (一穷二白) was the general sentiment. The indescribable sorrow that befell everyone was that the Mainland Chinese thought that they had it right, fighting a noble cause to correct a great social wrong, pursuing relentlessly equality, equity, and emancipation from their millennia-long cultural yoke toward some undefined ultimate bliss. But we were wrong (even evil in the world's eye); what was even harder to bear was that we were more pathetic than Don Quixote tilting at windmills mistaken for giants. A hitherto unknown sense of collective shame and anger toward our leadership erupted. A quick reaction was, rightfully, to restore education. All of a sudden, schools were reopened and knowledge, particularly scientific knowledge, prized.

Backed up ten years, millions of students waiting their turn for higher education, still dispersed in the countryside, were urged to hurry to review their book knowledge in order to partake in the first college entrance exam. Many simply gave up because after high school they had trashed or burned their books to display their anti-bourgeoisie resolution, or else they packed their books away, never to touch them again. But many rose to the occasion and gave it their best shot. I was lucky to pass the exam, and the reported ratio of college admissions was 4.7 percent from those who took the exam.[4] Although we were not given much choice of schools and subjects of study (there were few to begin with), most students desired schools and programs that had a reputation of Western disciplines such as natural sciences and technology. However, the most desired subject of study was, perhaps, European languages, with English ranking at the top and French and German next. These languages were especially sought by those who felt not less desirous, but less prepared, to pursue scientific studies. At that time, it was true that few Chinese were fluent in these languages. The Chinese government and people alike had known, since the end of the imperial system at the turn of the twentieth century, that for them to have any chance of making it in the modern world, they had to increase their population's proficiency in Western languages. After all, foreign language is, as Marx asserted, a tool in human struggle – a slogan that every schoolchild could recite, if not comprehend. Studying foreign (really Western) languages became an ever-greater aspiration even when Marx's glow grew dimmer.

The idea that one could be lifted out of the ruins of a collapsed state and learn new things from the advanced human world was analogous to a drowning person holding onto a thread of air. Not only did those who passed the exam harbor the utmost hopes for their own lives, but their government also regarded them as its only hope and epoch-defining fresh blood. These students went to college with all tuition and all study-related fees waived. Moreover, they were not expected to engage in energy-draining work-study to earn extra money. In other words, they were made worry-free, all for one purpose: to devote their time and energy to study, to master what China had lamentably neglected for ten years.

Such was the ethos under which I began my college career. We were an elite group, but not by birth or socioeconomic status; there was no birth class or difference in socioeconomic status. We passed the exam and were chosen; that was the commonality. Before the exam, all exam takers had to declare three schools and three subjects for each school as their preferences. I named English as my first choice of study, followed by French and German, for all three schools. I was admitted into my second-choice college, one of the best schools for foreign languages in the country. The college admissions officer later told me that the reason he placed only me in the German group from all the province's applicants was that I was the only student qualifying for English but also willing to study German. Without any regret and with only gratitude, I welcomed the placement and plunged into my German studies.

To maximize these students' success, the Chinese government contracted with West Germany to send teachers from gymnasiums and universities. As a result, my four years of college were mostly taught, quite unusually, by West German instructors with a curriculum much tuned to their pedagogical theory and design. Although we also had Chinese professors who taught some German classes and other subjects such as history, Chinese literature, economics, and English, German teachers were mostly responsible for what we studied. As far as I can tell, students of my class had a good taste of liberal arts education from the West, understandably with a German bent (the same was true in the French and English departments based on their respective instructors from abroad).

Students exhibited high energy and motivation for learning by any standard. We all got up early in the morning and read our texts aloud. All tried to memorize their vocabulary sheets and related texts. All went to the library to study, and all read into the night in their tent-like mosquito nets until lights went out. No one missed a class unless one was too ill or had an emergency. We did sports and extracurricular activities, but the sight of everyone holding a book in their hand reading, and of a very crowded library, was a daily occurrence. My husband, European American by origin, taught at the same college and to this date attests that he had never – and has never since – seen such a sight on any of the campuses of some twelve American colleges and universities where he has taught. He still could not believe the level of these Chinese students' dedication to their learning.

German is not an easy language for any non-Germanic Westerner, but it was notoriously harder for the Chinese, whose native language does not have conjugations for anything, let alone the three articles, four cases, and endless combinatorial variations. But we absorbed all those mechanical difficulties of the language. We mastered the pronunciation, sentences, comprehension, grammar, even some medieval words and usages. We studied German history and read Goethe, Schiller, Heinrich Heine, Georg Büchner, Gerhart Hauptmann, Thomas Mann, Robert Musil, Franz Kafka, Bertolt Brecht, and the writers after World War II. We listened to Mozart, Beethoven, Schubert, Schumann, Mahler, even Wagner. I loved learning about this important European culture. As this learning deepened, Chinese culture became more and more a distant and vanishing memory. Anything Chinese was scorned. We did not even speak much Chinese on campus because we were busy practicing our German. We also frequently dismissed our German teachers' curiosity about Chinese culture and told them that it was not worth their while because it was the Chinese culture (mistakenly, in hindsight) that brought our country to ashes.

But then came Goethe's *Faust*, a monument of German literature. By then, the knowledge-thirsty students had gained some perspective and had cooled down from the embracing zeal they had cultivated in the revolutionary time. Print materials that revealed unheard-of things were "smuggled in" from Hong Kong, and some classmate even got connected to a Buddhist monk who sent her hand-printed material about Buddhism. We read these things with a flashlight in bed. This exposure and gradual change prepared the students for what might be called a questioning spell. We began questioning everything, not necessarily in open forums but certainly in chats with peers, leisurely strolls, and romantic interactions. We contemplated our existence, our *sein*, our experiences, our society, German culture and people, America, life, death, love, virtually every subject. It was like a mini-renaissance where free spirits roamed outside classrooms. I remember a poem that I wrote in Chinese to share with my peers:

Progress and Regress
The train is dashing through the Yellow Plateau, and I am counting the
    tombs of ancient emperors....

Who says that tombs
Symbolize only death?
I'd say they symbolize immortality and eternity
Who says that the running train
Is progress in our time?
I'd say it's blind curiosity
Like children
Who have to tear into pieces the mushroom
To see what's hidden inside
People on the train are fooled by it
Modernization is not visible in the far end
But tombs are visible right here with us
As if they are reminding us
To contrast, to reason, and to reflect
The train lures us
To follow, to dash, and to blunder

However, despite this vibrant learning, we remained quite "uninterested" in our own culture.

Faust, especially the first parts where the Faustian Bargain took place, was read slowly and discussed line by line. Although the poetic form was no longer daunting, we had difficulty with all the religious tradition and allegories. I remember thinking to myself, tossing ideas to my friends, and hearing their echoes back: Why does Faust have to lose his soul, his life, for wanting to know more? Ignorance was precisely what the Chinese suffered. What's wrong with Faust wanting to be more knowledgeable and wanting to have full human experience? Why did Goethe, the literary giant, write an epic in such a way that seeking knowledge is like committing a crime somehow? Even more, aren't we this guy? Here we are devoting ourselves with all our might and passion, seeking knowledge, resembling in some way Faust's spirit, if not his full scope. We were puzzled. But neither my peers nor I actually raised these questions to our German teacher in fear that we might make fools of ourselves, questioning Goethe. At least for me, I could not abandon these questions until I found their satisfactory answers. But before that happened, I had to come to America to endure more bewilderment and soul searching.

SHOCK IN AMERICA

A few years after college, I gave up my position teaching German and immigrated to America. My first desire was to make myself useful to my newly married life: finding a job. But my English was abysmally poor. This self-assessment was actually not an incidence of the well-known "Asian" self-effacement. My English was abysmal; I had spent all my time perfecting my German. I simply did not spend enough time mastering English. Truth be told, I did not even like English very much because it did not have the complicated articles and cases, or the elegance of the logical combinations of sentence variations. I managed to learn to read and write English at some grade level. But speaking and listening proved to be out of reach. Coming to America was not planned, but I fell in love with a European American. Although I lucked out with this marriage, *Gott sei Dank*, at the time I experienced a profound displacement when I found myself in the United States instead of Germany.

I registered, with my husband's help, as a substitute teacher for German in Burlington, Vermont, where I first landed after immigration. The reason was simple: That was the only thing I could do, short of being a Chinese restaurant kitchen aide. This job did not require a teacher's certificate, and for a while I thought that I could at least teach the fun German language to American students.

Unfortunately, my first teaching assignment at the local high school was English rather than German, which, as confessed previously, I could hardly speak, let alone teach. I had to admit it to the caller just in case she made a mistake. But despite my honesty and insistence that I lacked any qualification for teaching English, I was told that the school needed me, and I had to be there. So I went, in a cold sweat, too scared to face something like an English equivalent of *Faust* – Shakespeare or anything vaguely literary! I wanted to disappear into the ground.

Someone ushered me into the office, trying to calm me down, saying that it would be an easy job, and that the only thing I needed to do was to follow the lesson plan made by the called-in-sick teacher and "to keep the kids out of trouble." "What trouble?" I said to myself, gazing around. I had never seen, not even in my dreams, such a school, with all the brightly lit classrooms, hallways, and all the books in the library. The students were undoubtedly well nourished and well clothed, projecting more self-confidence and happiness than I or any student I had seen back home. This is a learning paradise! What trouble could there be for such blessed lives?

To my shock, those students did not seem to care about maintaining a good learning environment: They chatted freely and giggled and threw things at each other as if I, the teacher, did not exist. What struck me most was that they were not the least bit interested in learning the content of the already minimal English tasks. But my surprise did not lead me to blame the students. Instead, I blamed myself and my poor English. It was then that I vowed to learn English well enough not to let this disappointing situation happen again in my substitute classroom.

As my English and self-confidence improved, sadly, I saw a recurrent, actually more severe, scenario in Pennsylvania. I became, on a *blitz* track, a supervisor for student teaching at the University of Pittsburgh only a year later. I thought that it was strange to bestow such responsibility on me given how little I knew about American education. It was even more bizarre for me to supervise student teachers while struggling through my own student teaching (in German finally) at a high school in a remote town where I provided the only ethnic diversity. Perhaps this was the university's way to kill two birds with one stone. In any event, I was forced to function like a two-headed creature, or else a split personality, while still struggling to improve my English.

My regular visits to five schools across four districts and my daily work in the classroom gave me a pretty good chance to encounter students' lack of interest in learning. This time I could not hold myself responsible because I mostly did not teach. Where I actually taught, I did succeed in boosting their morale for learning from moment to moment, but it often felt like a drop in the ocean of disinterest. In fact, it was this very difficulty that discouraged me once and for all from pursuing my certificate to teach high school in America. Nevertheless, in hindsight, I must say that these Pennsylvanian students were angels. No one really had any "trouble," at least not the type I was aware of: dropping out, drugs, teenage pregnancy, and violence, barring perhaps smoking and other petty offenses. By and large, these students showed up at school on time, remained through the day, and did their assigned work. Not everyone made the best effort, the kind I would have liked to see – certainly not the one that would resemble the by-now already archaic fantasy in my head, the effort worthy of the Faustian spirit. But compared to what I later saw in urban places, these students were any teacher's dream.

Massachusetts students were not better, not even in the supposedly better towns, away from the really troubled inner city. The same lack of enthusiasm in learning continued to shock me as I again endeavored to work more in schools. Of course, the education reform, along with the weekly news reports, drumming up the meager academic performance of American students gave me a clear sense that what I observed was not an isolated phenomenon. My perplexity deepened; the idea of the richest nation on earth inhabited by so many students not wanting to learn really threw me for a loop.

FISH DISCOVERING WATER

At the University of Pittsburgh, I took several courses in educational psychology and child development as required for my teacher certification. The most thrilling course ever was on how to develop children's creativity. I had never studied or even fancied that creativity could be studied, let alone taught. Contemporary Chinese people inherited a long-held (more than a century) belief that their age-old Confucian tradition was the root of all their political, social, and economical ills. Confucianism was even called a culture that "ate people" by radical thinkers such as Lu Xun (1881–1936).[5] In education, the most condemned were children lacking creativity – the sentiment holding strong to the present day. Now, to Chinese people's horror, not only did Marx's dogma and audacious experiment fail to emancipate people into freedom and creativity, but it managed to suck the last breath of human vitality out of their children. Part of my motivation to continue my graduate studies in America was to find ways to help rectify Chinese education problems (another part had to do with my lost confidence that I could ever teach in an American high school). Learning about the teachability of creativity raised hope for me again.

When I inquired where I could study creativity for a PhD, my professors recommended Harvard Graduate School of Education,[6] where Howard Gardner was attracting many students. They gave me his book, *Frames of Mind*, to read, and reading that book made me decide that I wanted to study not just creativity but the whole human potential. I lucked out again with the admissions and began a marathon of doctoral training in human development and psychology. But my single desire to figure out human creativity and potential could not be fulfilled without also studying other important processes that influence child development. Finally and inevitably, I encountered *culture* as a developmental concept. As I delved deeper into my studies, I realized – this time, to my personal astonishment – that I had been blind to culture. I was the fish who was the last to discover water.

Once discovered, I could not see the world without water. Culture soon became the looking glass that was impossible for me to put down, even after all those years of unawareness on my part. Culture, as the largest human-created system (as opposed to our biology), penetrates so profoundly into all spheres of human life that it alters human cognition, emotion, and behavior, setting us apart from the next smartest creatures in the animal kingdom.[7] Culture is like the air we breathe; we are completely dependent on it. Together with our biology, culture produces us, but we also alter culture continuously. This interactive process is the inescapable force underlying child development.

For me, however, the awakening was not about human culture as a whole, but a particular culture, my own culture. Yes, what about my culture? Because I was born into a preexisting world, did my own culture imprint me in any specific way? If so, in what way? I lived my own culture as any anthropologist would attest, but why was I unaware of it for so long? Did Marxism push my culture out of me, or perhaps it buried my culture and pushed something else into me? My questions were endless, and this process was not fun. My peers from China seemed to have gone through a similarly painful process. We shared our identity crises, confusions, and reflections. One friend was already writing her dissertation and introduced me to the writings of Professor Tu Wei-ming (杜維明), an authoritative scholar on Confucianism at Harvard Yenching. I went to the Yenching Library and borrowed his books. He led me to other related books. Now, for the first time, rather late in life, I read, word for word for myself, Confucius's *Analects*, *Mencius*, and other original works. I experienced an intense process similar to when I first peeked into Western cultures through the German gate opened in college, but this time I was gazing into my own soul.

I could not believe the words and passages I was reading from these books. What we as children growing up in China were told[8] (but not allowed to read directly) about Confucius and his ideas and the actual words by Confucius and Mencius were like day and night. I knew that if we had no reason to believe that Chinese people's intelligence is no less than that of any other people on this planet, something must have gone terribly wrong. Why did the Chinese admire Confucius for 2,500 years? Why was he called a sage and an "exemplary teacher for all ages" (萬世師表) even by the powerful (for example, emperors) and smart people (i.e. scholars), and why was his *Analects* required reading of all schoolchildren for millennia?[9] Were all the Chinese who lived before me wrong – stupid even? These questions greatly disturbed me.

Further reading and contemplation led to the realization that the Chinese had gone through a century-long tormented soul searching because they could not defend themselves against the surging Western powers. China was in an all-around steady decline until its eventual defeat and the subsequent chaos, suffering unprecedented humiliation and loss of self-confidence. Intellectuals were the first to turn inward to self-examine, and they came to a devastating verdict: The root cause was the Confucian ideology all ruling dynasties had adopted.[10] It relied on the personal moral cultivation of the ruler to bestow mercy onto his subjects. If a ruler succeeded in cultivating himself, he attracted good and able ministers to manage his dynasty, and people enjoyed peace and prosperity as a result. But if a ruler was ruthless and tyrannical, such as the Qin Emperor who built the Great Wall but caused great suffering to people, then people revolted against the empire, sometimes successfully but oftentimes not. Whenever such a peasant uprising prevailed, another ruler arose and reinstated the same old system with the same old Confucian ideology.[11] Although China was blessed with some good rulers, the bad and incompetent ones outnumbered the more virtuous and able ones.

This cycle of the political process and dynastic ruling lasted for millennia, but its vitality was exhausted when Western powers pounded open China's door.[12] What defeated the Chinese system at the turn of the twentieth century, as intellectuals and politicians agreed, was really not Western troops but their science, which the Confucian ideology clearly lacked. Western science was most admired because it produced "solid ships and effective cannons" (船堅炮利), while the Chinese were still relying on spears, swords, and even martial arts to fight on land and sea. This conclusion led to a whole series of new education policies and political reform. Waves of Chinese students were sent to the West to study science and technology. Moreover, many leaders and scholars attributed Western power to their better democratic governmental systems. China, along with other East Asian nations that suffered a similar fate, began a protracted endeavor of learning from the West (a process that has not yet reached its peak), despite a period of interruption immediately after the communist takeover. I must admit that I myself was also a small element of this massive cross-cultural learning process.

CHINESE CULTURE AND FAUST AGAIN

This grasp of the general historical perspective eased my distress to some extent, but it did not persuade me that Confucius and his ideas were the root cause of, and therefore were to be blamed for, all Chinese political, social, and economic ills. Confucius lived 2,500 years ago and did not have any noted political power. He was a thinker, philosopher, and, most of all, teacher. Students came to him and sought his teaching of their own volition. It would be groundless to blame him or even his ideas for China's later problems. If anyone were to be blamed, it would be those who, under the name of Confucianism, waged unjust wars, conquered land, and established illegitimate dynasties, not to mention those who buried alive Confucian scholars and burned their books,[13] those who ruthlessly oppressed their people and neglected their civil duties, and those who were driven more by power and wealth than by benevolence and virtue. In other words, those who failed to achieve Confucian self-perfection but unfortunately held power. Blaming Confucius is like blaming Jesus for the medieval Inquisition and other immoral acts committed in the name of Christianity.

This new reflection made me finally realize that part of my confusion came from equating a country's political system with its culture. This confusion was the reason why, during my undergraduate years, we thought that anything Chinese was bad. But then, in graduate school, I discovered and began to feel the enormity of culture, thanks to anthropology, Confucian works, and the great body of scholarly interpretations of Ames, de Bary, Fingarette, K. K. Hwang, Ivanhoe, Munro, Rosemont, Wei-ming Tu, C. F. Yang, K. S. Yang, and Ying-shi Yu, among others. Culture is much larger and more long-lasting than any political system. Culture is even larger than the existence of society or nation: Whereas either of the latter is usually bound by a geographical location under a certain political system at a given time, the former encompasses people beyond geographical boundaries, as the case of Jewish culture demonstrates. A given society or nation can witness many political systems come and go even in a short period of time, as is the case with China.[14] But people living in different systems, both successively and simultaneously, such as the Chinese living in the Mainland, Hong Kong, Singapore, Taiwan, the United States, Europe, and other parts of the world, having nothing to do with a particular political system or particular society, still unambiguously identify themselves as Chinese.

This jagged intellectual journey of mine raised the inevitable question for me: Given that I have no doubt that I am Chinese by cultural heritage, what then marks me as such a cultural member, particularly when I am no longer a citizen of Mainland China? As it turns out, this type of question is commonly asked, not just by Chinese, but by anyone who experiences cross-cultural living and the acculturation process. Although commonly asked, answers to this question are not easy to come by. Often one feels that one is different, but articulating such differences proves to be immensely challenging. In a sense, cultural psychologists and anthropologists spend their lives trying to do just that – understanding and articulating such differences among the world's peoples.

Considering the intellectual path by which I encountered two Western cultures, German and European American, it was impossible for me to ignore the topic of learning and knowing. The shadow of the Faustian Bargain still hovered over my head, and American students' indifference toward learning still troubled me. But after I began asking the cultural question about myself, it became clear that I, not Faust or American students, was the cause of my puzzlement and problem. I grew up in a culture that has, despite the apparent political and social upheaval, a very different outlook toward learning and knowledge. That I inherited this outlook (my idiosyncratic characteristics notwithstanding) is, I dare to assert, a result of what anthropologists refer to as the process of enculturation[15] rather than the storm of the Marxist swirl.

The reason, from a developmental perspective, is that the child is cared for, loved, and nurtured day to day by the caregivers. Few caregivers in Mainland Chinese families, during political turmoil or otherwise, and rarely if at all, assigned any kind of priority to delivering political messages to their children (it would be absurd). Even if parents did that, it is highly doubtful that this would have any effect during infancy and subsequent years. Based on anthropological psychology, the overarching political and economic climate is only an indirect factor that influences child development. The local cultural customs, the caregiver's psychological characteristics, and the actual daily interactions are the more direct shaping force on the child.[16] This influence has its most observable effect during the formative years of infancy and early childhood, which is foundational to a person's further development. To the extent that my parents and my nannies inherited from their parents childrearing values and practices of a long-existing culture, it is likely that they adopted these deep-seated cultural frames to care for, to guide, and to discipline their child, rather than using Marxist doctrine to cook, to feed, or to love the child (to my knowledge, Marxism says nothing about human psychology, let lone childrearing routines).[17]

Therefore, I grew up thoroughly Chinese. For learning and education, my parents' voices will probably ring forever in my head. I recall some of their words I heard whenever they tried to encourage and instruct me and my siblings with regard to learning:

- Having studied, to then always practice what you have learned – is this not a pleasure? 學而時習之，不亦說乎？(when we did not want to practice what we learned)
- In strolling with only two people, I am bound to find a teacher. Identifying their strengths, I follow them, and identifying their weaknesses, I correct them in myself. 三人行，必有我師焉，擇其善者而從之，其不善者而改之 (when we failed to see what we could learn from others)

- Continue studying without respite, instruct others without growing weary 學而不厭，誨人不倦 (when we grew tired of studying and of helping others in school)
- Love for learning 好學 (when we talked about going through the motions in learning)
- To know what you know and know what you do not know – this is wisdom 知之為知之，不知為不知，是知也 (when we pretended to know)
- Learn, then you will know your inadequacy 學然后知不足 (when we claimed that we knew enough)
- Do not impose on others what you yourself do not want 己所不欲勿施於人 (when we pushed things we did not like on each other)

These words turned out to be those spoken by Confucius, but I did not know that growing up. My parents began quoting with "the ancient said" (古人說) rather than "Confucius says" because they feared that announcing Confucius's name would bring political persecution during a time when Confucius (and Confucianism) was singled out for criticism.

School learning also instilled much of these same values, norms, and preferences in me, even though schools were under greater pressure to promote Marxist ideology. Consider the following: Any Chinese classroom was, and still is, decorated with a motto "Learn well and make progress everyday" (好好學習，天天向上) – a quote by Mao Zedong. I always found it interesting that out of all of his fierce attacks of traditional education philosophy and pedagogy as expressed in his voluminous writings, this very motto was picked to be posted in every classroom to encourage student learning. Purely in its wording, the message is completely consistent with traditional Chinese learning philosophy. When I visited schools in Beijing, Nanjing, Shanghai, Shandong, Sichuan, and Guangdong during the 1990s and early 2000s, I also saw secondary and college classrooms quite uniformly decorated with these poetic verses among other similar motivational aphorisms:

> Long-term diligence is the road to the mount of knowledge; endurance of hardship is the boat to the boundless sea of learning 書山有路勤為徑，學海無涯苦作舟.[18]

In all my school years, when we had a quiz or exam in class, the teacher frequently asked the most hardworking student, not the highest-achieving one, to stand up to receive applause from peers for his or her great learning virtue. Whenever any student did well in class, teachers would say to them, "don't be too proud but continue to strive to achieve better. There is no end to learning." Whenever a student did not do well, the first line of advising and disciplining was "you did not work hard, you did not concentrate, you did not listen well in class, and you did not practice enough." Sometimes teachers would mention that a student uses his or her mind flexibly (腦筋靈活), but I never heard any teacher, or any peer for that matter, attribute a student's high achievement to his or her born intelligence alone; likewise, no student's low achievement was ever attributed merely to his or her lack of inherited potential.

This unwinding of my childhood experiences has crystallized for me the intellectual tradition that holds the following notions about learning:

1. Learning is the most important thing in life; it is the life's purpose.
2. Learning enables one to become a better, not just smarter, person. The ultimate purpose of learning is to self-perfect and to contribute to others at the same time.
3. Learning is a life-long process. It starts early in life and continues throughout one's life.
4. The kind of knowledge that sets one person apart from another does not come to one automatically. One must seek it. Seeking knowledge requires resolve, diligence, endurance of hardship, steadfastness, concentration, and humility. One must have what the Chinese call "a heart and mind for wanting to learn" (好學心), a passion for learning.
5. Learning does not privilege anyone, and neither does it discriminate against anyone. Everyone is capable of seeking and achieving knowledge regardless of one's inborn capacity and social circumstances.
6. One begins the learning process as a beneficiary from others' dedicated guidance. But one will become a benefactor to others' learning and self-cultivation as one matures, making harmony with the world.[19]

These ideas were (and to a large extent still are) passed down to children through the implicit as well as explicit process of enculturation. As any other cultural process, the deep-seated beliefs were learned and internalized so successfully that hardly any child questioned them and the associated values, preferences, and norms they carried.[20]

As this returning to my own culture took place, my understanding of Western traditions also deepened. Evidently, Faust epitomizes an entirely different way of learning and knowing. Inheriting a long-standing intellectual tradition that originated from Greek antiquity through the Christian scholarship and finally standing at the cusp of modern science, Faust (either the real person or, more likely, the combined figure created by Marlowe and Goethe) represents an approach to learning and knowing that has been essential in the Western world, and this approach still flourishes in the present day and quite possibly will continue for long. This tradition emphasizes the following key themes:

1. Human curiosity about the external world is the inspiration for knowledge.
2. Relentless spirit of inquiry into the universe will lead to knowledge.[21]
3. Mind is the highest human faculty that enables this inquiry.
4. Reason (not heart) is the process by which we know the world.
5. Learning privileges those who have superior ability.
6. The individual is the sole entity for inquiring, discovery, and ultimate triumph.

West

Juxtaposing these two learning traditions, the reason for the difficulties my mother, my college peers, and I had about the Faustian Bargain revealed itself: Learning and knowledge in the Confucian world are *defined* fundamentally differently. Learning and knowing are geared not to the external world, but to one's self as a goal of personal striving. Learning how to perfect oneself and to become a better person morally and socially is never viewed as a cost or liability to oneself or anyone else. As such, it is viewed not just positively, but as an ultimate good.

Apparently, my shock about American students' lack of interest in learning also stemmed from this difference in the learning outlook. My reaction may have appeared judgmental and harsh, and in hindsight was quite regrettable. American students' motivation for learning turned out to be an intricate field of study in itself, but it is no less connected to the Western intellectual tradition, as will be discussed in Chapters 2–8. Still, if not anything else, my initial encounter with the students in Vermont and Pennsylvania stimulated me to look into myself, to discover my own culture, and to peek through the looking glass that has both enabled and constrained my own learning.

This arduous but eventually fruitful search finally gave birth to a research agenda. Now, after a journey on which I myself have inherited some of the Western learning spirit, I could not resist returning to the Faustian quest, but this time with much more grounding and understanding. I wanted to know if these basic learning concepts were still alive today in both cultural worlds. As a developmental researcher, my natural curiosity is directed to children. Assuming the empirical answer would be found affirmatively, how are these beliefs transmitted to children generation after generation? Finally, how do different learning beliefs influence children's learning?

As will be seen in later chapters, I have reviewed and gathered consistent empirical support that, despite much political, social, and economical change and exchange in recent decades, the basic learning models still persist in their respective cultures. They underlie much of thinking, feeling, and behavior of learners as well as actions of their social world, and exert profound influence on their children.

NOTES

1. Quote from Knox, M. M., McGalliard, J. C., Pasinetti, P. M., Hugo, H. E., Spacks, P. M., Wellek, R., Doughlas, K., & S. Lawall (1992) *The Norton anthology of world masterpieces, Vol. 2.* New York: Norton, p. 462.

2. The New Cultural Movement (1915–1923) was a part of China's radical and painful modern history. This movement was launched by intellectuals to reform the political, economic, educational, linguistic, literary, and artistic traditions to embrace Western democratic and scientific spirit. For example, Chinese written language was forced to change from traditional grammar to vernacular grammar across all curricular materials in school. For a comprehensive discussion of the movement, see Yu, Y.-S. (1992). 中國文化與現代變遷 [Chinese culture and modern evolution]. Sanmin Publishing House.

3. Mao Zedong's reeducation program (1968–1978). In the peak of his absolute political power, Mao launched the movement, urging the so-called educated youth from middle and high school to go to the countryside to learn from the farmers. In his espoused radical theory, book knowledge was regarded as divorced from life and therefore useless for his revolution. But his theory in action, according to scholarly analyses, was a strategy to shift the burden of the large unemployment and therefore looming threat of youth unrest to the already destitute but vast farming land. Some 16 million youth were sent down, separated from their families, to work in the fields. In addition to worsening farmers' livelihood, many young people suffered social isolation, displacement, abuse, and emotional disturbances under the conditions of this vast forced-labor camp. For detailed accounts, see Meisner, M. (1999). *Mao's China and after: A history of the People's Republic* (3rd ed.). New York: Free Press; and Chang, T. H. (1999). *China during the Cultural Revolution, 1966–1976: A selected bibliography of English language works.* Westport, CT: Greenwood.

4. The first college admissions rate in 1977 after ten years of Cultural Revolution was 4.7% (27,000 admitted from 5,700,000 who took the exam. However, millions more youth from the ten years of Cultural Revolution did not take the exam. The percentage of successful students entering college that year would be much smaller if all of the potential pool were included). See SSB (State Statistics Bureau). (2005). 新中國55年統計資料匯編 [China's fifty-five years of statistical data]. Beijing, China: China Statistical Press for related statistics.

5. Lu Xun was the most forthright writer, critic of traditional Chinese culture. His novels and essays attacked Confucianism most vehemently. See reference in Note 2 to this chapter for a historical discussion and reevaluation of the anti-tradition writers and other intellectuals in early-twentieth-century China.

6. Finally, I have a chance to express my much belated gratitude to Professors Mushalko and Fredette at the University of Pittsburgh for opening my mind to creativity in children and for mentioning Harvard Graduate School of Education to me. I had no clue that I might not have been qualified to apply. I am forever indebted for their encouragement and confidence.

7. See Tomasello, M. (1999). *The cultural origins of human cognition.* Cambridge, MA: Harvard University Press for his research on the topic of how human culture as a whole has been part of our heritage and how human cognition and social understanding are irreversibly altered.

8. During my formative years, we read nothing by Confucian scholars. But because Mao Zedong liked some writing by Xun Zi (Hsun Tzu 荀子, 325–235 BCE), strangely, the centralized textbook for middle school children during the 1970s contained one of Xun Zi's most famous essay "*Advice on Learning*" (勸學篇), which we were required to memorize. Xun Zi was, with Confucius and Mencius, one of the three early Confucians. However, other than this serendipity, schoolchildren were told that Confucius and his followers were counterrevolutionaries; they disregarded working people; they only valued book knowledge and preached ideas for the ruling class. This vicious distortion and Machiavellian attack of Confucius was the reason why many of my generation felt cheated and lied to about our own culture. These lies become apparent when one opens the *Analects* and *Mencius* and reads for oneself. What a change we witnessed when the 2008 Beijing Olympic Games opened with the second line in Confucius *Analects* "To have friends [who share the goal of self-cultivation] come from distant quarters – is this not enjoyment?" (translated in watered-down English as "Welcome my friends") in front of the 1.3 billion Chinese not just in Mainland China but all Chinese in the world! What a sharp contrast it is for the current Chinese leadership to revamp the fundamental Confucian value of harmony and elevate it to a national agenda for building a harmonious society (although no leader has openly acknowledged its Confucian origin)! All this is signaling to me a cultural awakening, as far as Confucianism is concerned, despite the fast process of Westernization and globalization.

9. *Analects* was a required reading of all schoolchildren since the Han Dynasty (206 BCE–22 CE) until the early twentieth century when the Civil Service Examination system was abolished. But the *Fours Books* and the *Five Scriptures* continued to be taught as the basic texts to schoolchildren until the communists took power in 1945. However, Taiwan, Hong Kong, and Singapore continued (many schools to date still) to require such Confucian books in school; see a review by C.-L. Yang (1995). 論兒童讀經的淵源及從理想層面探討兩種讀經法的功能 [Reciting or listening to the origin and ideal of children's classics training]. 高雄國文學報 [Bulletin of Chinese] (National Kaohsiung Normal University), *8*, 1–50. As such, my mother at age nine in 1930 began her schooling by formally acknowledging Confucius as the "teacher for all ages" and her own private tutor and by

being taught Confucius' *Analects* first. She could still recite much of it well into her late 80s. Likewise, my father at age ten in the 1920s began his schooling with Confucian *Analects* in a village private tutoring school (私塾).

10. See the paragraph on the Civil Service Examination system in the section *Taking the World Upon Oneself* in Chapter 2.

11. See X.-R. Han (2006). *Chinese discourses on the peasant, 1900–1949*. Albany, NY: State University of New York Press; and Gernet, J., Foster, J. R., & Hartman, C. (1996). *A history of Chinese civilization*. New York: Cambridge University Press, for reviews of the dynastic cycle in Chinese history.

12. Western powers opened the door to China. The Opium War and events that followed led to Dr. Sun Yat-sen's revolution in 1911, ending the millennia-long dynastic ruling system in China. The subsequent period was governed by the Nationalist government until the Communist takeover in 1945.

13. Emperor Qin (259–210 BCE) murdered Confucian scholars by burying them alive and by burning their books (213–212 BCE).

14. China for the last century went through dynasty to semi-colony, republic, warlord rule, communist, planned economy, and now market economy. The notion of culture outlasts all of these short-lived governmental forms.

15. See LeVine, R. A. (1990). Enculturation: A biosocial perspective on the development of self. In D. Cicchetti & M. Beeghly (Eds.), *The self in transition: Infancy to childhood* (pp. 99–117). Chicago: University of Chicago Press on the notion of enculturation.

16. See Harkness, S., & Super, C. (1992). The developmental niche: A theoretical framework for analyzing the household production of health. *Social science and Medicine, 38*, 217–226 for their introduction to the notion of "developmental niche." See Trevarthen, C. (1998). The concept and foundation of infant intersubjectivity. In S. Braten (Ed.), *Intersubject communication and emotion in early ontogeny* (pp. 15–46). New York: Cambridge University Press for a review of research on infant-caregiver intersubjectivity.

17. This section was not frivolously written but intended to respond to those who falsely assumed that because the Mainland Chinese lived under a particular political system, somehow they were not normal, worse yet that their parental love and care somehow were subquality, and worse, because they did not receive any cultural heritage.

18. There is little wonder why this set of verses entered the top-twenty list of my learning lexicon study (see more details of the research in Chapter 3).

19. That learning and acquisition of culturally desirable skills also brings practical benefits such as getting a job or supporting oneself or one's family is not a unique Chinese value. It is common value for all humans. Naturally, Chinese people also learn for practical purposes. Chapters 2 and 3 discuss how this part is integrated with the higher purposes of Confucian learning tradition.

20. Yes, Emperor Qin buried Confucian scholars alive and burned their books, and there were other times of persecution of learning, including censored learning in recent history. But these events only proved the Emperor's cruelty and the subsequent times' inhumanity, which faces continuous condemnation. This side of the history, particularly Emperor Qin's tyranny, remains a permanent blemish on Chinese conscience. The learned were and still are the cultural heroes.

Intellectuals during the New Cultural Movement and in a more distorted form throughout recent Chinese history also questioned, attacked, and rejected this learning tradition. However, as will be seen in later chapters, this tradition is not easily done away with. Its power and tenacity are yet to be understood. The fact that only one slogan, "Learn well and make progress everyday," from Mao's voluminous writings got posted in *every* classroom (but no other quote from him enjoyed this persistent popularity) is testimony to the tenacity of this learning tradition. Whenever children see this quote, no specific context in which Mao uttered those words accompanied the sight; nor did any teacher bother to qualify to children that the quote was only for communist purpose. The quote hangs above the blackboard, viewable without failure by anyone entering the classroom. It hangs there, decontextualized forever, as if it is a stand-alone and eternal halo. It is so powerful and enduring that it continues to be the sight in every classroom today. All I had ever heard in China for my twenty-five years of school presence was study hard to contribute to society. Therefore, what message children and teachers receive is the bare meaning of these words, which, as already noted, is but consistent with the enduring Confucian learning tradition. Children study hard regardless of the political system. In a strange way, the very political force that thought itself iconoclastic against tradition ended up promoting and perpetuating the tradition. To me – but to no surprise of any anthropologist – this is but a common manifestation of the enduring power of culture. Viewed from this perspective, this learning tradition transcends time and space and therefore any political system. The claim of this learning tradition meets ample empirical support in and outside China wherever Chinese flourish in the world.

21. However the universe was defined. Faust got himself in trouble because the universe was conceived of, at his time, as God's will and design that was not fully knowable by humans; humans were forbidden from pursuing such knowledge. Although modern philosophy and science no longer treat divinity as the ontological giving of the world, and modern Fausts do not have to give up their lives for their quest, the questions of how the external world is knowable or how certainly it is knowable to humans continue to generate epistemological debates in these fields.

2

Learning to Master the Universe and
to Transform Self

Although many observers of cultures have noted general differences between Western and Confucian philosophy,[1] few have analyzed the differences in learning approaches. The purpose of this chapter is to outline both cultures' foundational outlooks on learning. By tracing leitmotifs of these different intellectual traditions, I hope to establish the basis for examining and interpreting empirical research findings that will be discussed in later chapters.

A brief review of recorded history reveals that both cultures have rich, long-standing, and influential outlooks, *weltanschauung*, on learning. Each outlook is an essential part of their respective philosophy. Both outlooks, by the sheer fact that they are distinguishable from one another, can be analyzed as framed by their fundamental questions about learning. These questions have been guiding their thinkers in pursuing their work. Intellectual pursuit resulted in the generation of schools of thought and theories about the world and human life. In response to changing times, later thinkers modified existing paradigms of thinking and developed new ideas. This pattern of idea production continues and is similar in both cultures' intellectual histories.

Despite these general patterns, the two cultures' intellectual traditions started out with quite different interests and premises and evolved thereafter along their own paths. As such, they did not and are still not likely to intersect or, as has been suggested, to merge in the foreseeable future. The Confucian scholar Shuming Liang,[2] who was also well versed in Western thought, captured this divergence succinctly: If you follow the Western way of knowing and learning, it is unlikely that you will end at the Confucian way. Likewise, if you follow the Confucian approach, you will have little chance of landing in the Western approach. For my purposes, I have identified four themes that I believe are important to consider in the Western intellectual tradition. Each will be discussed in a separate section under the respective headings: know the world, certainty of knowledge, mind and its wonders, and examined life. Likewise, I have also identified four main themes to consider in the Confucian intellectual tradition. These carry the headings of perfect self (完善自我), take the world upon oneself (以天下為己任), learning virtues (學習美德), and action is better than words (行勝於言). Each culture's sections end with a discussion of the concept *learner* in that culture. Let us examine the Western tradition first.

WESTERN INTELLECTUAL TRADITION

Know the World

Opening books on Western intellectual history,[3] one encounters the central focus of learning, from the earliest times to the present, on human epistemology. As an essential philosophical concept in the West, the term *epistemology* is an amalgamation of Greek επιστήμη (*episteme*), meaning "knowledge," and λόγος (*logos*), or "principle," thus creating its current meaning – "theory of knowledge." Epistemology is a branch of philosophy that studies the nature and scope of human knowledge.[4] A textbook definition of epistemological studies includes questions such as what is knowledge, how is knowledge acquired, what do people know, and how do we know what we know.

However, a discussion of Western and Confucian differences cannot proceed with this within-culture frame of questions as a starting point. Clearly, all of these questions already assume an implicit agreement of the legitimacy or validity of the concept of "knowledge." As will be seen later in the chapter, this assumption is not shared when the two cultures' outlooks are set side by side. For the purposes of the present book, but more importantly from a cultural perspective, I start with a question at a more general level applicable to both cultures (or any culture, for that matter). This question does not favor one culture's delineation of knowledge and knowing over that of the other, but rather puts them on equal footing: "*What* are humans to know?" – however the term *know* might be defined. The weight of this question is on the notion of *what*, and it probes the key issue of what is *important* for humans to know or what *ought* humans bother to know first.

The response to the aforementioned question, from what I can gather in reviewing Western intellectual history, is the *external* world. Humans are conceived of as the knowers. Here the notion of *knower* does not address any degree of certainty of knowing. The external world is the object to be known by humans. The notion used here only concerns the observation that humans take mental action to try to know and do end up knowing some things, or at least they believe they do. The concept of the external world has undergone gradual expansion, from a narrower scope of the physical world, to spiritual world, to social world, and finally to the all-encompassing world. Still, all of the versions of the world remain external to the person who does the knowing.

Generally speaking, the external world has been approached from two discernable levels. The first is what meets the eye, the sense-data as philosophers refer to it – that is, things directly sensible and experienced by humans. The interest at this level is to figure out how such things are related and function as a whole. The second level, which assumes much more importance in the Western view,[5] is the underlying, deep forces that cause and drive the surface things; it is uncovering the essence, the stable quality behind the unstable and changing things.

The epistemological frame of the external world as the object of human knowing was first delineated by the Greeks. The early Greek thinkers dealt with both levels. Some tried to link surface things, but those who made a name in history were more interested in knowing the *nature*, the deeper essence of the external world. They wanted to know what the physical world is made of and how it operates. In contemplating the substances of the world, for example, Thales (ca. 640–546 BCE) was recorded to have said that everything is made of water. Anaximander (ca. 611–547 BCE) had his own claim that all things come from a single primal substance, which is infinite, eternal, and ageless. Heraclitus (535–475 BCE) believed that fire is the primordial element out of which everything else arises. Anaximenes (585–528 BCE) declared that the fundamental substance of which the universe is made is air, which was subsequently regarded as a separate substance by Empedocles (ca. 490–430 BCE). More amazing was Anaxagoras (ca. 500–428 BCE) who held that the world is infinitely divisible and that even the smallest part of matter contains each element.

In pondering regularities and laws of the universe, they argued about the shapes of moving bodies, motions, and the temporal nature of the moving world. For example, they conjectured that the celestial bodies moved in perfect circles. Pythagoras (ca. 570–ca. 490 BCE) even discovered that the earth is spherical. At one end, Heraclitus argued that the world is in constant flux as he illustrated with his well-known case: "[Y]ou cannot step twice into the same river; for fresh water is ever flowing in upon you" (and "the sun is new every day"). At the other end, Parmenides (ca. 515–ca. 450 BCE) and Zeno (ca. 490 BC–ca. 430 BCE) contended that the world is eternal and nothing changes, countering Heraclitus' claim.[6]

These Greek thinkers showed an extraordinary attitude and style toward the material world, one that Russell called "disinterested effort"[7] to understand the world. On the one hand, they had profound curiosity about and fascination with the external world, namely displaying childlike innocence that was "imaginative and vigorous and filled with the delight of adventure."[8] They were interested in everything – stars, winds, sea turtles, beans, gods, morality. On the other hand, their contemplation of the world was serene, exhibiting a genuinely scientific spirit, even by today's standards. They hypothesized about the world and argued with each other about their ideas; some even tested their hypotheses. Later Greek thinking was taken up by religious devotion: The object of human knowing was no longer merely the physical world but the divine spirit behind it, conceived of as absolute and perfect. However, modern science in the seventeenth century reclaimed this early Greek stance toward the physical and eventually mechanical world. This stance, as scientists and scientific historians readily agree,[9] ought to be, and has been since, held as the core scientific approach for generations to follow. Needless to say, this model has successfully led great Western scientists to achieve their celebrated breakthroughs.

However, knowing the world is not the only goal of studying and inquiring. Mastering the world in order to control it and to utilize our knowledge to serve human needs has also been a clear goal in the West. Humanity, especially in the West, was slow to accomplish this latter goal during the first several millennia. In time, human knowledge, particularly scientific knowledge, has been used to eliminate deadly diseases, improve health, reduce hunger, provide shelter to large populations, increase efficiency in productivity, generate wealth, and enhance convenience of life in just about every possible way. These achievements notwithstanding, the last two centuries have witnessed unprecedented and ruthless human exploitation of nature. Consequently, more difficult problems have also been created by human activity, with the most serious ones coming as a result of scientific discoveries (e.g., nuclear weaponry and industrial pollution). This trend of destruction is accelerating at such a pace that, if no effective counterforces intervene, the earth's resources will soon be exhausted and real man-made disaster is likely to ensue. However, we remain hopeful that by studying the physical and the human world we will find solutions to these problems.

Certainty of Knowledge

Beyond the basic interest in and stance toward the external world, Western intellectual tradition was further established by its serious pursuit of the key epistemological question: How do we know what we know? This question embeds the related set of questions such as "How does knowledge differ from belief?" and "How certain is human knowledge?"

The basic belief that the external world is knowable to humans also came from Greek antiquity. This belief gave birth to what has been referred to as rationalism, which holds that the world is orderly and that we can comprehend it. Rationalist tendency shaped the approach that values reason, mind, analysis, and abstract thinking more than intuition, emotion, social knowing, and experiential learning.

The Greeks discovered logic (discovered by Parmenides and later formalized by Aristotle, 384–322 BCE), which is the very foundation of reasoning. They favored deduction and used it to prove the existence of physical relationships and forces that the native eye could not see. They believed that they could obtain certainty of knowledge and discover things about the world by first noticing what is self-evident, called the axioms, and then by using deductive reasoning to arrive at theorems or other logical conclusions that are far from self-evident. This method of obtaining knowledge was predominant, and it influenced most Western thinkers.

Perhaps the most significant discovery by Greeks was mathematics, which is even more certain and powerful than logic itself. For this reason, Pythagoras was acclaimed as "one of the greatest men [who] ever lived"[10]; it was he who used mathematics to express the ideal of contemplative life. Russell remarks:

> It might seem that the empirical philosopher is the slave of his material, but that the pure mathematician, like the musician, is a free creator of his world of ordered beauty.... Mathematical knowledge appeared to be certain, exact, and applicable to the real world; moreover, it was obtained by mere thinking, without the need of observation. Consequently, it was thought to supply an ideal from which every-day empirical knowledge fell short. It was supposed on the basis of mathematics, that thought is superior to sense.[11]

Because mathematical knowledge was certain and absolute, it also gave rise to the belief that there was "eternal and exact truth as well as the supersensible and intelligible world."[12] Socrates (469–399 BCE) and Plato (428–348 BCE) were also two advocates for certainty of knowledge and eternal truth. Plato said in his *Republic* that "geometry compels one to look at being.... For geometrical knowing is of what is always."[13] In Greek antiquity, mathematics and logic were also used to glorify gods and the immortal soul, but in subsequent centuries they became the means Christian theologians and scholars used to prove God's existence, His absolute knowledge, His perfectness, and His power. For example, reason and logic were used by St. Thomas Aquinas (1225–1274), based on Aristotle's argument of the unmoved mover, to prove that God is the unmoved mover of all things in the universe.

The edifice of mathematics, deductive logic, and reason ruled and impelled the search for eternity and absolute truth for millennia. For a long time, there was no alternative way to inquire into the external world. Both philosophers and scientists were committed to this search and relied on these tools to pursue their work. Copernicus, Kepler, Galileo, Leibniz, and Newton were the founding giants of modern science in the seventeenth century, and all of their achievements are testimonies to the power of mathematics, logic, and reasoning (along with available but limited observations and facts).

Francis Bacon's inductive method was introduced and accepted as a systematic way of Western scientific inquiry in the seventeenth century. Even though Bacon criticized medieval science and made his great methodological contributions, he did not aim at challenging the search for true knowledge itself. Instead, he energized the inquiry with a more viable method. Neither did John Locke in the eighteenth century abandon reason with his radical idea of all knowledge coming from experience. Quite the contrary, he maintained that rational people should hold their opinions with some measure of doubt and that even religious revelation must be judged by reason. Therefore, reason remained supreme for him.

Reason triumphed again in philosophy. Immanuel Kant (1724–1804), a Western philosophical icon in the eighteenth century and onward, wrote *The Critique of Pure Reason*[14] to distinguish knowledge that is a priori from knowledge that is not. Through pure thinking, Kant arrived at his mental categories, namely quantity, quality, relation, and modality (along with subcategories for each), into which, he claimed, the human mental apparatus was to always filter its experiences rationally (such as permanently wearing rosy spectacles to look at the world). Accordingly, humans have a priori ways of looking at and processing the world. Thus, human knowledge consists not only of mathematics and logic a priori, but also of various other categories a priori, even though this latter kind of knowledge comes from experience first. Moreover, he deduced his well-known "categorical imperative"[15] in his moral theory and argued that all moral concepts originate wholly a priori from reason.

The standard of acceptable knowledge has changed much over the past three centuries. As a result, modern epistemology throws certainty of knowledge into doubt, and absolute truth as a standard has become probabilistic degrees, patterns, and trends in many scientific fields.[16] However, I would argue that the basic question of how certainly we know anything in any scientific field is still a commonly used gauge to evaluate reliable, if not true, knowledge from unreliable information. And no knowledge can be evaluated without sound reasoning. This evaluative frame is applied to social sciences as well as nonscientific fields such as criminal and civil litigation and judgment (e.g., a criminal can be judged guilty beyond reasonable, but not absolute, doubt). Thus, the central role of mathematics and logic reasoning in science and other areas of intellectual pursuit remains unquestioned to date and is likely to last for long in the West.

Mind and Its Wonders

So far I have discussed the questions of what the West regards as important for humans to know and what primary means or methods were developed to obtain reliable knowledge. There is another important question that cannot be ignored in any discussion of knowledge and knowing – and by implication, learning – in the West. This question is "What in us does the knowing?" The discussions in previous sections bear on this very question, but they did not focus on the human knower per se. The part of the human existence in charge of knowing is human intellect, the mind, which is understood as a human faculty, and later in psychology as capacity, and most recently in neuroscience as human brain circuitry. This intellect is endowed with our ability to follow logic, to compare and contrast, to analyze, and to generalize – in sum, to be rational.

What can this human faculty do for us to get knowledge? Again, the Greeks were the first to ponder this question. The best-known thinkers were Socrates[17] and Plato, and their ideas proved to be powerful and long-lasting. Socrates held that human knowledge is not learned but recalled, that the human mind possesses knowledge at birth. One knows without being taught and without learning. He demonstrated his claim by tutoring a slave boy who at the beginning knew nothing about geometry but stated the conclusions correctly himself. Of course, the boy would not have come to the knowledge if Socrates did not guide him question by question with his acclaimed Socratic tutoring method. Socrates maintained that the only skills learned are those that serve mundane functions such as horseback riding, archery, and crafts (including playing music instruments and making statues!). Higher human knowledge, particularly the mathematical and logical kind, is innate.

Plato also advanced his theory of ideas. Accordingly, the human mind has "ideas" or "forms" for all things it knows (a condition that, from our current perspective, has to do with words we use in the language we speak). Our language has words with meanings, some of which denote more concrete ideas (Plato only discussed the notion of "idea" of "form" but not how to abstract concepts from perceived reality) whereas others denote the more abstract category. Take dogs as an example. There are individual dogs, and we can refer to them as "this dog" or "that dog." But all dogs belong to the category "dog." In Plato's theory, this category "dog" is the universal dogginess that is shared by all dogs (today we would just place this species of animals on Linnaeus' biological taxonomy). Therefore, the human mind possesses this kind of abstract idea for all things humans see, hear, and sense in the world. Furthermore, Plato claimed that these universal ideas or forms are also *ideals*, and therefore true knowledge for humans to have. The particular things that we experience are not true knowledge but just appearances. Thus, minds that are not used for seeking true knowledge are satisfied with knowing only beautiful or good things, but wise men, philosophers, use their minds to know beauty or the good *itself*. Socrates and Plato argued that it is our intellect, our mind, that achieves this true and ideal kind of knowledge, and therefore the intellect is superior to our senses.

Jennifer Michael Hecht writes in her book *Doubt* that the Greeks recognized the chaotic nature of the world, but they also recognized the power of human rationality that can achieve human transcendence: "What is fascinating is that Plato's solution is both logical and transcendent. Here one does not use logic to conquer chaos. Rather, one uses logic because the logic itself is beauty, is truth. Plato offers the amazing idea that contemplation of *the way things really are* is, in itself, a purifying process that can bring human beings into the only divinity there is."[18]

Russell points out that because of their abstract nature, mathematics and logic are wholly divorced from the reality that we directly experience. Mathematics and logic happen to be the only kind of knowledge that can be deduced entirely within itself, starting with an axiom, moving lockstepwise to its conclusion. What Socrates proved is not human knowledge per se but our *capacity* to follow logic and proofs. Moreover, I argue that Plato's theory of ideas can be rethought as nothing more than the human cognitive

capacity to classify objects in a hierarchical structure, from concrete inci-
dences to increasingly more abstract categories, and to use words to map
this cognitive structure of our understanding of the world. There is no need
to place one type of cognition as higher or lower, because all humans are
capable of cognizing all levels as they mature developmentally.[19]

Nevertheless, as it turned out, the ideas introduced by Socrates and Plato
about the human mind were not whimsical and short-lived. They resurged
again and again in Western intellectual history, reaching the pinnacle with
Descartes' *cogito* (conventional short form for *cogito ergo sum*, "I think,
therefore I am").[20] Human existence is proved by the person's metacognitive awareness of his or her own thinking. Descartes (1596–1650) set out to
doubt everything, which came to be known as the "Cartesian doubt," and he
eventually succeeded in doing so. He could not even be certain of his own
existence by any other means except one – his *cogito*. It made him certain
that he was thinking; thus he must exist.[21]

It is important to point out that the nativist position of the human mind
and its unmatched capacity in the animal kingdom are still alive and well
today. Chomsky's initial claim that human language is also a manifestation
of this innate capacity, along with subsequent research, has provided hard-
to-refute evidence that human linguistic – particularly our rule-bound and
generative – capacity is endowed to the species, not learned by or taught to
each child after birth.[22] Modern science on human infant cognition added
the final stamp to the conclusion that we are indeed born with amazing
innate capacity to cognize the world.[23]

However, the nativist position is not the only one that declares the
wonders of our mind. Other thinkers disagreed with the nativist view but
savored the mind for other feats nonetheless. Contemporary to Socrates
and Plato, Anaxagoras even suggested that mind is a primary cause of physical changes. The idea (perhaps just as bold as those ideas voiced by Socrates
and Plato) that the mind can make things happen, along with other similar
ideas in later Greek antiquity, may have laid the ground for the eventual
theological position that God is omniscient and omnipotent. It was true
that the highest power imaginable by humans was, owing to Christian the-
ology, the divine mind that not only created the world out of nothing, but
also controls the world and everything in it. Given that humans have been
created by divine power, we are also connected to this power. Although we
may not fully grasp and possess this power, we are able to recognize it, to
hold it in awe, to have faith in it, and to follow it.

Even St. Augustine (354–430), the well-known Catholic bishop in early
Christian history, contemplated the nature of the human mind. He discussed

relativity of time as perceived by the mind and argued that neither past nor future, but only present, is reality because we can sense it as it is passing. He held that past is packed in memory and future in expectation. Hence, time is subjective; it is in the human mind, which expects, considers, and remembers. Of course, in St. Augustine's persuasion, the human mind is created by God to begin with.[24]

The major counterview to the nativist position came from John Locke (1632–1704).[25] Admittedly, this perspective emerged much later in history, but it nevertheless was a radical view that could not be dismissed offhand, either then or now. Locke argued that all our knowledge, perhaps aside from logic and mathematics, comes from our experience. There are no such things as innate knowledge, including the Platonic *ideas* as Socrates, Plato, and others had claimed; our mind is a *tabula rasa*, a blank slate on which we put our knowledge, first through our senses and then through the perception of our mental operation. He further contended that all previously said metaphysical knowledge and concepts of the world were not a priori, but rather owing to the language terms we use. Locke's theory of knowledge opened an alternative inquiry into the nature and the workings of our mind, which calls for analysis of our experience and its impact on our mind and knowing. His theory also gave room for the subjective processes of our mental functioning. However, his theory did not dismiss mind itself, but instead pointed to different ways our mind works its wonders.

Two important philosophers followed up on Locke's theory and offered further arguments about the experiential and subjective nature of our mind. George Berkeley (1685–1753)[26] maintained that all reality, not just discrete things in the world, is mental. We only perceive qualities of things, not things themselves. For instance, heat and cold are only sensations existing in our minds, and things tasting sweet are perceived as pleasure whereas things tasting bitter are perceived as pain. Pleasure and pain are mental, however, not inherent in the food itself. Whatever we know is already filtered through our mental working. Therefore, only minds and mental events can exist, but not the world independently. David Hume (1711–1776)[27] went even further, suggesting that our thinking and reasoning process impressions from our experiences to form simple ideas. Our complex ideas come from both impressions and imaginations. We use language terms to process our ideas. He also contended that much of our knowledge of causality is not from the objects themselves, but from our inference and belief about two things seen constantly conjoined together, with one beginning and the other following. This inference or belief makes us expect the causal relationship. Immanuel Kant, in response to these empiricist challenges and in an attempt to retain human innate capacity, presented his mental categories to reconcile these opposing views. From the perspective of philosophy as a discipline, these later thinkers may have cast much doubt on human rationality, and one may agree with or refute these later arguments. In my view, whether the human mind is rational or subjective and variable to experience is not important, but that the mind as a topic has received so much philosophical thinking resulting in identifying its many remarkable functions is significant.

The mind's wonders have continued to fascinate Western researchers. Modern psychology was built to do just that, studying mental functions and their manifested behaviors. The whole research on human intelligence and its measures and multiple facets has been and still is one of the hallmarks of modern psychology.[28] A century-long research (also from anthropology) involving different peoples across cultures has provided much evidence that human mental processes may share some basic structures such as our beginning capacities to process phonemes, human voices, socioemotional exchange and bonding, and the sequence of language acquisition. But beyond the notion of capacity, human mental processes are, by and large, not uniform, but vary from culture to culture, from ethnicity to ethnicity within diverse cultures, and even from gender to gender. The mind seems to be quite adaptable to the particular cultural and social contexts in which people live. Even for what might appear to be simple categories of color, time, object classification, seeing fish in a tank, looking at a wooden triangle, or weighing contradictions, minds differ across cultural groups and sometimes even between men and women.[29] Regardless of how the human mind has been studied, few in the West would doubt its essential role in human life. Current research in psychology, cognitive science, and neuroscience continues to focus on mapping out the precise functions of our mind. As research deepens, more mind's wonders will surely be revealed.

Examined Life

At least since the time that Socrates lived, the West has valued the idea that one ought to examine life. Socrates is also famous for having said in the *Apology* – his purported self-defense before the Athenian jury who condemned him to death – that "the unexamined life is not worth living."[30] His life is a total embodiment of this very conviction.

In every dialog that Plato wrote, Socrates was portrayed as very steadfast in questioning all conventional concepts that people took for granted. He engaged his interlocutors, particularly those who contended that they were sure of their ideas, to answer questions about the meanings of their familiar concepts. For example, he saw Euthyphro at the court, who was prosecuting his own father for having murdered a laborer who himself was a murderer. Euthyphro told Socrates that his family and friends thought him impious (for a son to prosecute his own father), but Euthyphro found them mistaken and believed that his folks did not understand piety. Socrates took this opportunity to seek the universal definition of piety with Euthyphro as illustrated in the following excerpt between Socrates (S) and Euthyphro (E):

> s: Tell me then, what is the pious, and what the impious, do you say?
> e: I say that the pious is to do what I am doing now, to prosecute the wrong-doer, be it about murder or temple robbery or anything else, whether the wrongdoer is your father or your mother or anyone else; not to prosecute is impious ...
> s: For now, try to tell me more clearly ... you did not teach me adequately when I asked you what the pious was, but you told me that what you are doing now, prosecuting your father for murder, is pious.
> e: And I told you truth, Socrates.
> s: Perhaps, you agree, however, that there are many other pious actions.
> e: There are.
> s: Bear in mind then that I did not bid you tell me one or two of the many pious actions but that form itself that makes all pious actions pious, for you agree that all impious actions are impious and all pious actions pious through one form, or don't you remember?
> e: I do.
> s: Tell me then what this form itself is, so that I may look upon it, and using it as a model, say that any action of yours or another's that is of that kind is pious, and if that is not that it is not.
> e: If that is how you want it, Socrates, that is how I will tell you.
> s: That is what I want.
> e: Well then, what is dear to the gods is pious, what is not is impious.
> s: Splendid, Euthyphro![31]

Although he allowed Euthyphro to respond and to offer counterarguments, Socrates frequently asked sharp questions (disregarding how Euthyphro would feel about being pushed into a corner). He moved forward one step at a time skillfully, leaving Euthyphro no room but to agree with him, thereby arriving at his general definition of piety in the end.

Socrates displayed his commitment and relentlessness in his pursuit of true knowledge. At his trial, he was accused of corrupting youth (as well as not believing in the gods of the city) because he taught them to question everything as he himself did. He refused to escape from prison when it was possible for him to do so and died, calmly and bravely, drinking the poison as his sentence demanded.

Because of the way he lived his life, because of his teachings, and because of how Plato presented that life, those teachings, and that honorable death, Socrates has come to represent not only the "gadfly" prodding the rich and powerful, but also the sage exercising careful judgments and judicious evaluation. Indeed, he is the very embodiment of not just good thinking but *critical* thinking in the West.

Today, in the West, academic freedom is widely respected. Teachers and students are free to inquire, to think, and to challenge old ideas and express new ones. They are also free to some extent, and obligated to some extent, to challenge authority both in the school or university and in the society at large. As a Western cultural ethos, the inquiring and examining spirit in any form (soft or confrontational) is highly prized.

There have been countless thinkers ever since the Greek antiquity who resemble, if not purposefully follow, the critical spirit of Socrates, with the exception of the long, dark Middle Ages (but there was as also the daring image of Faust). All philosophical, scientific, political, and cultural icons who advanced new knowledge or new ways to solve political and social problems challenged existing canons of thought or status quo. Some were more fierce and radical than others, but all inherited this critical inquiring spirit. Take the eighteenth-century Jean Jacques Rousseau (1712–1778) as an example. In his volume *Emile*,[32] Rousseau launched a major attack on educational practice of his day (in addition to his other major attacks on the political and religious system). He claimed that civilization as a whole had done more harm than good to people because it ruins their natural tendencies, which he prized as the ultimate good. In an attempt to radicalize education, he introduced his imaginary and ideal learner, Emile, who has no teachers but only a tutor. Emile is naturally curious about the world, independent in his thinking, innocent in his outlook, and immune to human misery and corruption. Emile learns only according to his inner timetable, and his tutor does not impose anything on the pupil but waits patiently to supply what Emile is ready to learn, to discover for himself. Rousseau's critical charge probably met much resistance in his own culture and abroad. But his ideas proved to enjoy lasting impact on education down to the present time. Progressive educational traditions in Europe and the United States owe inspiration to him, and the currently much celebrated educational model of Reggio Emilia in Italy also retains the kernel of Rousseau's thought.

In today's education, from preschool to university, it remains a central goal to teach students how to think critically. Students are (ideally) encouraged to think for themselves, to raise questions about the subjects they are learning, and to challenge the existing knowledge as well as authority.

An interesting case in point that attests to the enduring nature of the Western intellectual tradition can be offered from the mottos still present in many of the best Western universities' crests in Latin (from a brief Google search): Harvard University's *Veritas* (truth), Yale University's *Lux et veritas* (light and truth), Columbia University's *In lumine Tuo videbimus lumen* (in Thy light shall we see light), University of California, Berkeley's *Fiat lux* (let there be light), University of Oxford's *Dominus illuminatio mea* (the Lord is my light), and University of Cambridge's *Hinc lucem et pocula sacra* ([From] here [we receive] light and sacred draughts). Truth and light convey a similar meaning of the ultimate knowledge. Other universities' mottos stress the mind, the openness, freedom, and critical spirit of inquiry as well as expansion of knowledge: MIT's *Mens et manus* (mind and hand), Stanford University's *Die Luft der Freiheit weht* in German (the wind of freedom blows), University of Chicago's *Crescat scientia; vita excolatur* (let knowledge grow from more to more; and so be human life enriched), University of Heidelberg's *Semper apertus* (the book of learning is always open), and University of Toronto's *Velut arbor ævo* (as a tree through the ages).

One might think that these are vestiges of archaic traditions. However, for each motto found, I saw multiple current discussions linked to it. Students, faculty, administrators, and alumni are actively engaged in interpreting and reinterpreting these crystallized expressions that represent respective universities' fundamental missions. Indeed, each time a new generation of students, faculty, and staff enters the university, the meaning of its motto is reexamined and its spirit revived.

The Western Learner

Within Western intellectual tradition, the concept of the learner did not occupy prominence in philosophical debates. Most thinkers did not write much about the learner as a whole person, but instead focused on the mind. However, despite their primary interest in the nature of knowledge and the mental world, Socrates and Plato (in his *Dialogues*, noticeably his *Republic*) elaborated quite comprehensively on how children should be reared and who among them should be selected to receive the best education (to become the *guardians*) and later to assume leadership as philosopher kings. Some of the later philosophers, namely Locke[33] and Kant,[34] also wrote forcefully on the need to educate people. They also offered proposals on how education should take place. Other important education theorists and leaders in the West, particularly, those since the sixteenth century – Comenius, Pestalozzi, Rousseau, Herbart, Froebel, Montessori, American education theorists Spencer, Dewey, and Kilpatrick, as well as those who have led education reform in the United States in recent decades – have all advocated for the importance of education, with some creating new forms of schooling.

From all of these figures, there seems to be much more suggested for the *provision* of education to children than elaboration on the *learner* him- or herself.[35] Nevertheless, one can still discern key assumptions about the learner or characteristics the learner is ideally to possess, as well as the processes in which the learner is desirably to engage to achieve the envisioned educational goals. For the purpose of conducting cultural comparisons, I have identified the following four characteristics and processes for the learner that in my judgment are most central in Western intellectual tradition.[36]

The first and foremost characteristic of a learner is to have a good mind and to use it well. Individual minds were originally thought to be from the divine source (e.g., Comenius, 1592–1670, took that as a given to launch his education for everyone). Individual minds, therefore, should be enabled to flourish. Later, this divine source was recast into human natural tendency (as advocated by Rousseau and Froebel [1782–1852], the father of the idea and practice of *kindergarten*), and eventually into individual's born potential that needs to be developed fully. The notion of individual potential is still the predominant view held today. It is clear that since Greek antiquity, there has been a strong view that individuals differ in their potential at the outset. Some have greater potential, whereas others may possess ordinary intelligence. Distinguishing the very able learners from the ordinary ones has been important in Western learning tradition.

The mind does not just become great by itself; it needs nurturance to develop fully. For the development of minds, earlier thinkers advocated for strict discipline of children as seen in Plato's *Republic* and the Spartan model.[37] Since the seventeenth century, education theorists and practitioners have increasingly promoted intellectual stimulation, nurturance, experience, and social interaction and participation as the processes by which children develop their minds. The purpose of having a well-developed mind is to use it well. Hence, the learner can seek and ascertain reliable knowledge and truth through critical reasoning, as well as reach sound judgments and make informed decisions.

The second characteristic of the learner is to have natural curiosity, interest, playfulness, and intrinsic enjoyment. This valued characteristic directly reflects the much praised Greek stance toward the world. Since the inception of Froebel's kindergarten, children's innocence as well as natural curiosity about, and interest in, the world have been treasured and held as a central goal for early – and ideally all – formal education. Learners who display curiosity, playfulness, and delight (the notion of *fun* in American preschool and later education) are believed to lead to intrinsic motivation for children to seek knowledge and understand of the world.

The third characteristic of the learner is to inquire into the world. It is important for the learner to maintain an open mind and a free inquiring spirit. A good learner is expected to display his or her intrinsic interest in the world at large on the one hand and to use his or her mind to inquire and to discover on the other. The learner should have what Theodore Sizer calls a "habit of mind"[38] to ponder about essentials of the world, to observe, to ask questions, to argue and debate about issues, to challenge existing canons of knowledge and authority (both teachers and experts), and to self-express.

The fourth characteristic of the learner is to understand and to master the world as the ultimate goal of learning. Such learning is manifested in true personal insights, creativity, discoveries, and problem solving. This type of achievement displays the learner's personal brilliance and calls for reward and celebration. Those achieving the highest level are canonized in the cultural body of knowledge to be transmitted to young generations.[39] All the Western philosophers and scientists that have been mentioned in this chapter and many who have not been presented (who are excellent contributors in other fields of intellectual and artistic pursuit) are clear models of the best images of the Western learning tradition. Even those who achieve lesser degrees of excellence – the ordinary learners in daily classroom settings – are rewarded and celebrated for their fresh ideas, thoughtful questions and answers, novel solutions to problems, and often just any form of self-expression. Figure 2.1 shows a diagram of the Western learner.

CONFUCIAN LEARNING TRADITION

It is not my intention here to provide an account of the intellectual development throughout Chinese – or East Asian – history. What is important in this section is to outline the core values of learning purposes and processes.

Perfect Self

The Confucian learning tradition is the predominant tradition throughout Chinese (as well as much of Japanese, Korean, and Vietnamese) history. The single most important thinker for this tradition is Confucius

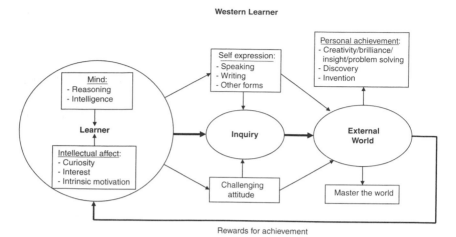

FIGURE 2.1. Western Learner: The basic learning approach is for the learner to study the world out there. In the **Learner**, there are two large components of mind and intellectual affect, with the mind being the most essential. The two most important processes underlying **inquiry** are for the learner to engage in all forms of self-expression on the one hand and challenging authority and the existing canon of knowledge on the other. There are also two outcomes of inquiring into the **external world**: personal creativity and mastery of the world.

(551–479 BCE).[40] According to scholarly accounts, Confucius did not "invent" the core values himself; he inherited a rich culture that had been in existence for several thousand years. However, "it was he who enabled the millennia-long culture before him to be transmitted, and it was also he who charted the path for later cultural flourishing for millennia after him." Indeed, one writer, Yizheng Liu, went so far as to say, "Confucius is the center of Chinese culture. Without Confucius, there would be no Chinese culture."[41] Confucius achieved this impact by compiling the scriptures and texts on religion, philosophy, government, human relations, morality, history, as well as poetry and music. He founded his own school in China and taught some 3,000 students from all walks of life. He was also the first educator in human history to proclaim equality of education for anyone regardless of their social backgrounds and individual differences. If Confucius had only one of the aforementioned accomplishments, his name would remain eternally in the Chinese pantheon. But he achieved all of them. However, the most important legacy that Confucius left is not these compilations, but rather his own teaching on how to be a person, how to learn, and how to achieve human excellence.[42]

Self - perfection

For Confucius, the most important purpose of human life is to self-perfect (自我完善), or self-cultivate (修身, 自我修養), socially and morally. It is the person's self, not the external world, that is the object of his or her intellectual attention, contemplation, practice, and living. The self is the project for the person to work on, to improve, to refine, and to accomplish. Because no one is born with this approach to life, one must *learn* to self-perfect. The sum total of one's lifelong self-perfection constitutes the core meaning of learning. This outline of life's purpose and its process through learning is deeply inspiring to the Chinese and other East Asians (as well as increasingly more non-Asian people in the world).

Counter to the popular belief, the power of Confucius does not focus on the political system, not even political careers of his pupils,[43] but the fundamental question that each human being has to face: How do I live my life? What kind of a person do I want to be? These questions assume personal choices, but they are not framed from the perspective of the individual as a biological entity or as a rights-bearing individual as may be the case in the West. These questions concern the very fact that all humans survive, develop, and flourish in social relationships. A person is not just Jenny (or David), but much more importantly a daughter, a sister, a wife, a mother, an aunt, a teacher, a colleague, and so forth. This means that a person's existence is inevitably enmeshed in profound human relationships. As one develops and ages, one's relationships and roles change. These relationships and their associated social and moral significance – not our biology – define our individual *humanity*. How Jenny goes about her roles and relationships with various people, particularly those who are deeply involved in her life (i.e., parents, siblings, spouse, bosses, and friends), will mold Jenny into the kind of person she is and will be. This basic social nature of her life is the very self-project for Jenny to observe, contemplate, practice, and achieve. This lifelong self-project cannot proceed without learning. Ames and Rosemont state that Confucius' vision of human lives was "not simply one to be *understood*, and accepted, modified, or rejected on the basis of its congruence with the world 'objectively' perceived.... On the contrary, his vision was one that had to be felt, experienced, practiced, and lived. He was interested in how to make one's way in life, not in discovering the 'truth'" (emphasis in the original).[44]

Confucius and later Confucians outlined what have been called the five cardinal human relationships: (1) parent–child relationship, (2) sibling relationships, (3) husband–wife relationship, (4) basic economic relationship (employer–employee or boss/supervisor–subordinate), and (5) friendship.[45] Note that the first three relationships, located within the family, are regarded by Confucius and his followers as the most essential. Without succeeding in the familial relationships, a person is not likely to achieve the other two types of relationship. Since within a family everyone has these relationships, it is then incumbent upon each person to establish and regulate these relationships. Confucius believed that a person who is not able to maintain these fundamental relationships would face difficulties in life. He did not consider such a person to be either able or fit to assume greater responsibilities for the community and society at large.

How then can a person achieve these basic yet very difficult tasks? Confucius taught five virtues corresponding to these relationships for one to learn and four general moral principles for all to strive for. For parent-child relationships, the parent shall show unconditional love (*ai/ciai*, 愛/慈愛) – that is, total commitment to children's welfare – whereas children express what is known as filial piety (*xiao*, 孝). Unconditional love and filial piety are mutually constitutive. Moral obligation lies in this mutuality. Therefore, parental total commitment and children's filial piety are not mere emotions (often determined by momentary spurts of feelings), but rather are anchored in corresponding moral obligations to nurture each other's well-being. So understood and practiced, these obligations shall endure for life.

Confucius talked at great length about the core meaning of filial conduct, for example: "Those today who are filial are considered so because they are able to provide for their parents. But even dogs and horses are given that much care. If you do not have [filial feelings] toward your parents, what is the difference?"[46] Here Confucius emphasizes the genuine human feelings toward parents as the real difference, not the performance of duties as a formality. The appropriate conduct here is to show filial piety willingly, ungrudgingly, and gladly. Thus, to Confucius, filial piety is the very beginning of all human morality (百善孝為先) now. The assumption is that if one cannot even feel filial love and respect toward one's parents who gave birth and, often at great sacrifice, nurtured oneself, how can one show love and care to unrelated people?

For the husband-and-wife relationship, the virtue is respect (*jing*, 敬). Respect here is not simply social etiquette, politeness, or obedience that wives owe to husbands as may be understood in popular parlance. Neither is it the kind that Li and Fischer referred to as *ought-respect*, extended to everyone, based on political and legal rights in the West. Instead, respect in this context is a combination of honoring the other as a full human being and at the same time expressing what Li and Fischer termed *affect-respect* of love and admiration in a marriage.[47]

For sibling relationships, the virtue is sibling love and responsibility (*ti*, 悌). Accordingly, the older siblings care for the younger ones whereas the younger ones remain receptive to and accepting of the care and guidance of the older siblings. *Ti* ensures that siblings continue to stand by one another as a family and look after each other's well-being, prosperity, and moral growth. This is especially important when parents are unable to care for and to guide their children (because of illness, other incapacities, or death).

For the employer–employee (originally king–subject) relationship, the virtue is utmost dedication or loyalty (*zhong*, 忠). This is a basic ethic one has toward work for someone else. The idea is to dedicate oneself to the best of one's ability and without reservation to the cause, the service, or the position. If one agrees to and enters into this relationship, one shall make one's best effort to accomplish the goals. It is simply unethical to cut corners, to provide half-hearted service, to sabotage the work, to engage in conflict of interest, and worse, to betray this relationship. As for many other cultures, this ethical principle is considered very serious.

Finally, for friendship, the principle is trust (*xin*, 信). Although this virtue is also universal across cultures, the Confucian emphasis rests on commitment to friendship and ways that lead to its endurance. Trusting that one's friends will last through good and bad times (同甘苦,共患難) is key to friendship, and such trust is ideally not conditioned to actual time spent together, physical proximity, oscillating emotions, and changing circumstances.

Beyond these five virtues for these cardinal relationships, Confucius articulated four further moral principles that transcend specific relationships, applicable to common life circumstances: propriety (*li*, 禮), rightness (*yi*, 義), integrity (*lian*, 廉), and a sense of shame (*chi*, 恥).[48] Ames and Rosemont, in comparing the Confucian moral concepts with those of the West, offer this explanation of the notion of propriety:

> [*Li*] are a social grammar that provides each member with a defined place and status within the family, community, and polity [at a given time]. *Li* are life forms transmitted from generation to generation as repositories of meaning, enabling youth to appropriate persisting values and to make them approach to their own situations.... What makes propriety profoundly different from laws or rule is [the] process of making the tradition one's own.[49]

The English term *propriety* does not do full justice to the concept of *li*, which is much more encompassing and penetrating into daily life for the Chinese and other East Asians. The idea of *li* extends from the highest level of ritual performance, such as cultural memorial ceremonies, to one's ancestral offerings, and to the most mundane interpersonal interactions such as giving and receiving gifts, praising and accepting praises, serving dinner, and the like. *Li* essentially enables people to acknowledge, to attend or attune to, to connect with, to validate, to honor, and ultimately to care for each other.

Rightness, righteousness, or uprightness (*yi*) refers originally to appropriateness of an act in a given situation. But by extension and lived tradition, the term denotes upholding the right things and a sense of justice in human communities, especially when individuals are confronted with lures of self-interest. For example, self-serving at the cost of others is an incidence of not *yi*. Making a promise without the intent of keeping it or simply breaking one's promise are acts of breaching *yi*. Betrayal of friendship, cheating, fraud, and similar acts are also serious violations of *yi*. Mencius (孟子, ca. 372–289 BCE), a well-known sage and a direct follower of Confucius, said that a great person is one who "will not be led into excesses when wealthy and honored nor deflected from his purpose when poor and obscure, nor will he [bend] before superior force."[50] The moral conviction possessed by such a person is rightness. The specific behaviors and acts of it in concrete life situations are not stated, but each person ought to develop a sense of rightness so that he or she will know right from wrong and act accordingly in any situation.

Of the four moral principles, *shenzheng* or *lian* is readily matched with the English term personal conduct or *integrity*. Similar to the Western concept, it applies mostly to public life or people who hold leadership positions entrusted to them by communities and organizations. Diligence in performing one's work, a sense of duty, honesty, and clean management of funds are hallmarks of personal integrity. Corruption, greed, and embezzlement of public funds are violations of integrity.

The five virtues for relationships and the three general moral principles are stated in the positive. The last one, sense of shame (*chi*), is stated in the negative. However, unlike the sheer negativity associated with shame in the West, Confucius and his followers greatly emphasized the importance and positivity of shame in human lives. As in the West, shame is a self-conscious emotion that occurs when the self fails socially and morally, often in the presence of others. In Confucian teaching, having a sense of shame is equal to having a nagging conscience, therefore a discretional capacity for one to recognize one's own wrongdoing (note that shame and guilt are much more closely related in Chinese culture). The most important function of shame, however, is to urge one to correct oneself. To Confucius, not having a sense of shame is tantamount to losing the very human self-corrective capacity. Shame/guilt thus allows room for personal growth. Should one fail any of the desirable virtues and ethnical behaviors, feeling shame is the first response that enables a person to honestly look inward in order to self-examine, to summon the courage to admit wrongdoing, and then to commit to self-rectification. Mistakes and failures are reasons not to stop self-improving, but to self-perfect further.[51]

However, acquiring these virtues and moral principles is not the ultimate end for human excellence. For Confucius, the highest level of self-cultivation is the larger concept of *ren* (仁). The significance of this concept is evinced in the word *ren* occurring 105 times in only about 55 pages of fragmented passages in the *Analects*. *Ren* has been translated as *human goodness, benevolence, humanity, humanheartedness*, and most recently *authoritative conduct*. There is no precise English concept that captures the full meaning of *ren*. Many of Confucius' students asked him about the meaning as well as conduct of and ways to reach *ren*. Each of them represented an individual personality that purportedly possessed admirable moral qualities and superior intellectual abilities and skills. Confucius acknowledged these students' merits but remained reluctant to claim *ren* in them. Therefore, although foundational, merely possessing some virtues and moral qualities or having a superior mind or knowledge does not suffice for *ren*. To Confucius, a truly *ren* person is one who commits him- or herself to a lifelong striving to become the most genuine, sincere, and humane person he or she can become. This life journey is also referred to as following the Way.[52] This process, Confucius concluded, must be never-ending. It requires that the person charts a path for him- or herself with "vigilant self-watchfulness, in a reverential and respectful spirit, to be exercised in relation to every matter, every action, every thought one becomes engaged in."[53] Because each person's actual living circumstances differ, the process is also open and calls for personal creativity. When engaged in seeking *ren*, the person bears witness to his or her own self-project, moving forward with deep joy, satisfaction, and fulfillment. Thus, *ren* is a personally chosen life path that is simultaneously earthly bound and spiritually transcendent.

Confucius preserved a special term for those who commit themselves to the process of and follow the way of *ren*: *junzi* (君子). *Junzi* has been translated as *gentleman* and *nobleman*, and most recently as *exemplary person* by Ames and Rosemont, which, in my view, conveys the meaning much better than previous terms. According to Rosemont,[54] Confucius spoke of several categories of persons, all of whom display human goodness through dedicated learning. However, the exemplary person is the concept Confucius discussed and savored most (the term *junzi* occurs ninety-one times in the *Analects*). Scholar apprentice (*shi*, 士) is the one who has achieved some virtues and understood the moral principles. This person has also moved beyond the family, kin, and local community, and is committed to pursue *ren*. Still, much learning and self-cultivation remain ahead.

Compared to a scholar-apprentice, *Junzi* is nearer to the ultimate goal of self-cultivation. Rosemont states:

> They have traveled a goodly distance along the way and live a goodly number of roles.... Benefactors to many, they are still beneficiaries of others.... While still capable of anger in the presence of evildoing, they are in their person tranquil.... They ... perform all of their functions not only with skill, but with grace, dignity, and beauty, and they delight in the performances.... Still filial toward parents and elders, they now work on behalf of others ... especially the needy.... [T]heir conduct is not forced, but rather effortless, spontaneous, creative. There is, in sum, a very strong aesthetic and ethical dimension to the life of a *junzi*.[55]

Junzi for Confucius not only cultivate themselves but also help others achieve this height of human excellence. They are viewed as teachers and models for others to emulate; hence, they are exemplary persons. Indeed, *junzi* as described by Confucius is the highest level, and therefore a human ideal, yet it is still possible for most of us to reach.

Confucius did not stop here, however; he pointed to an even "loftier human model," namely the sage (*sheng*, 聖 or later *shengxian*, 聖賢). He identified some historical figures prior to his time, specifically Emperors Yao, Shun, and Yu, King Wen, King Wu, and most of all the Duke of Zhou, who set the highest possible examples of human moral excellence. Even *junzi* stand in awe of them, and the goal of becoming a sage is out of reach for ordinary people. Confucius' own assessment aside, there is no doubt that, despite his own humility, Confucius himself together with Mencius have since been regarded as sages by Chinese people. Sages are those who love, care for, and extend their benevolence to all. "Clearly such persons have extended their human feelings and thoughts to embrace the entire human race."[56]

Ever since Confucius outlined this life purpose and the possibility for humans to reach it, Chinese (as well as other East Asian) people have been inspired by it. Mencius advanced the basic Confucian tenet by arguing that what Confucius promoted presumes human nature to be that which is *not* shared with animals but which is uniquely human (therefore, self-cultivation ought to focus on what is uniquely human). Accordingly, this unique human nature is our moral sense.[57] Mencius highlighted four endowed human capacities, which he termed four germinations of human moral development: (1) ability to have compassion for others' suffering, (2) ability to feel shame, (3) ability for courtesy and modesty, and (4) ability to distinguish right from wrong. He argued that our ability for compassion leads to our *ren*, our ability for shame leads to our sense of rightness, our ability to be courteous and modest leads to our observance of propriety, and our ability to distinguish right from wrong leads to our wisdom (superior knowledge). Mencius' conviction is that moral self-perfection is not reserved to special people or the elite of society, but is available for everyone. By this conviction, Mencius essentially opened the possibility of human excellence to all. However, these human capacities by themselves do not lead to great moral achievement because they are mere germinations. Each individual must make a great effort to *learn* and to self-perfect continuously in order to realize his or her full moral potential.[58]

Elaborating on Confucius' theme of learning for one's self (為己之學, that is, learning to cultivate oneself, not to impress others), Mencius advised learners: "[T]he exemplary person steeps himself in the Way because he wishes to find it in himself (自得之)."[59] For Neo-Confucians in the Song and Ming periods (960–1279 and 1368–1644, respectively), finding *ren* in oneself became the key to repossessing the Way, thereby reclaiming Confucian purpose and process of learning.

After a much diminished role of Confucian learning tradition for nearly a millennium, the early Song Confucians reopened this learning tradition. The first two influential thinkers were Cheng Hao (程顥, 1032–1085) and Cheng Yi (程颐, 1033–1107), brothers who argued that the Way advocated by Confucius represents the heavenly principle (天理) that underlies all matters in the universe, including human moral nature. Following the Way is reaching the highest principle. However, to follow the Way, one must investigate the principle and its particular manifestations (including understanding physical particularities). The Cheng brothers saw this investigative spirit as a necessary step for one's self-cultivation, one's learning, which was new because early Confucians did not elaborate on individuals' investigation of the universe. Nevertheless, the Cheng brothers reaffirmed that the purpose of learning is to become the sage (notice that they did not focus on *junzi*, but rather on sage directly), the loftiest goal as envisioned by Confucius. The Cheng brothers believed not only that sagehood ought to be the ultimate purpose of every learner, but also that it is reachable by everyone. They outlined more concrete learning processes and methods to guide learners in this pursuit. Thus, one needs to begin by investigating things (格物) in order to extend one's knowledge (致知), which enables one to grasp (getting to the bottom of) the principle (窮理).[60]

Zhu Xi (朱熹, 1130–1200), probably the most well-known Confucian thinker after Confucius and Mencius, was profoundly influenced by the Cheng brothers. Zhu Xi's thought carries so much affinity to that of the Cheng brothers that their school of thought is called the Cheng-Zhu School. Continuing the basic tenet of the Cheng Brothers, Zhu Xi provided detailed commentaries to the Confucian texts and compiled the *Four Books* (i.e., *Great Learning,* 大學; the *Doctrine of the Mean,* 中庸; the *Analects,* 論語; and *Mencius,* 孟子). These books became what has been regarded as a must-read for every student and scholar until 1949.[61] In the *Great Learning,* Zhu Xi integrated the Cheng Brothers' argument that investigating things and extending one's knowledge are necessary for grasping the heavenly principle. These learning steps are important for self-cultivation, which is foundational for the life path toward sagehood.

The Cheng-Zhu school strongly emphasized complete personal dedication and commitment to this learning. Neo-Confucian learners had many more books and materials to study than their counterparts in Confucius' time. Therefore, studying books (讀書) was a very serious endeavor (in fact, the term *study books* became a general notion standing for education still commonly used today). Borrowing from the Buddhist method of meditation, Confucian learners also adopted quiet sitting and deep contemplation. All of this was to be geared toward getting it (Confucian Way) for oneself because no one else can learn for another. Without achieving this standard of learning, further learning goals are not likely.

Even though the Cheng-Zhu School dominated Chinese education since then, there were also other Confucians who advocated for different aspects of learning. Notably, Wang Yang Ming (王阳明, 1472–1529) argued that human inborn conscience (良知), rather than heavenly principle, is the real governing power, as first discussed by Mencius (i.e., his four germinations). Therefore, learning to become a sage is not just to follow the moral principle, but to extend what is already there to begin with in each person (致良知). He emphasized that people need to hold on to their innate conscience, not allowing negative life circumstances to taint this innate moral knowing of theirs. Furthermore, continuing the Confucian standard of judging moral achievement by one's action rather than by one's words, Wang Yang Ming held that one must practice tirelessly what one knows in order to achieve sagehood (知行合一). This way of thinking opened the otherwise lofty and hard-to-reach goal of sagehood to all people, including commoners, with no regard for social constraints or scholarship (the latter was emphasized by the Cheng-Zhu School). This tenet greatly encouraged ordinary people to pursue the same moral excellence.

Wang Yang Ming also inspired many followers, who, like Zhu Xi, opened many schools and taught many pupils. Since the Ming time, Wang Ken,

Li Zhi, Huang Zongxi, Gu Yanwu, Wang Chuanshan, and Yan Yuan, among others, have either elaborated on Wang Yang Ming's innate conscience doctrine or adhered to his principle of learning and practicing one's moral knowing. Despite their differences in emphasis, all Confucians still share the fundamental purpose as originally outlined by Confucius himself: learning to self-cultivate.[62]

Take the World Upon Oneself

Confucius' own teaching emphasized personal self-perfection toward *ren* through daily self-examination and practice. Some of his students had ambition to serve the courts (of many small kingdoms). Confucius was very clear that personal gain either for wealth or fame was not part of self-cultivation in his teaching (although he also acknowledged the material need for human survival). The point of serving kings is to ensure *ren* in them. Mencius further clarified the relationship between a *junzi* and a king: The former possesses superior moral power despite lack of political or social power, whereas the latter frequently has the opposite. Therefore, in serving the kings, *junzi* must assume the role of a bearer of moral responsibility as well as a moral teacher/advisor for those in power. Mencius (among other intellectuals of his time) refused to serve any king in any other role or to be "bought" by any of them despite the fact that he was made minister at one court for a few years. Instead, he remained an independent teacher who taught many students and tutored kings and nobles. Moreover, Mencius was exemplary in his insistence on being an independent thinker and voice (not dissimilar to Socrates in this regard). When kings and dukes sought his tutoring, he confronted them critically, urging them to examine their own conduct in order to return to *ren* toward their people. The opening encounter of *Mencius* shows a vivid example:

> Mencius went to see King Hui of Liang. "Sir," said the King, "you have come all this distance, thinking nothing of a thousand li.[63] You must surely have some way of profiting my state?"
>
> "Your majesty," answered Mencius, "what is the point of mentioning the word 'profit?' All that matters is that there should be *ren* and rightness."[64]

Mencius moved on to reason with the king that if profit is the governing principle in the kingdom, then his ministers will seek to profit themselves, and those at lower ranks will do the same for their own self-interest; soon the whole kingdom will see everyone looking after himself. Then who looks after the sick, the poor, and the needy who cannot look after themselves? Therefore, a king should not set profiting himself as a priority, but rather providing care and *ren* to his people.

This kind of upholding the moral principle by a single individual, courageous against the abuse of political power and insisting on reforming the ruler to seek *ren*, is the ultimate task for a Confucian learner, known as *taking the world upon oneself*. Mencius was the first to articulate this idea as "taking on the weight of the world."[65] "Weight" here is one's irrevocable responsibility. De Bary explains:

> This is in accord with voluntarism in the moral life and of action that is in keeping with "learning for one's self – that is, with the idea that one must take full responsibility for one's own actions.... In Neo-Confucianism this is closely associated with the conception of the moral hero.... In turn the idea of taking upon oneself responsibility for the Way, or accepting the duty to uphold it, is predicated on [Zhu Xi's] view of the individual as a self-determining moral agent."[66]

In the *Great Learning*, Zhu Xi expanded the Confucian learning path as starting from the Cheng Brothers' doctrine on grasping the heavenly principle – that is, investigating things (格物) and extending knowledge (致知). He clarified this path to move further to being sincere (誠意) and rectifying the mind (正心) in order to cultivate self (修身), regulate family (齊家), order the state (治國), and ultimately bring peace to the world (平天下). Taking the world upon oneself is reflected in the last two steps. This reformulated path has come down to the Chinese as the process of reaching the sagehood. As pointed out in the previous section, sagehood is not preserved for the privileged elite, but is available to every learner as the ideal and ultimate self. In Zhu Xi's words, "all men should take responsibility themselves for becoming a sage or worthy. Many men think becoming a sage or a worthy is too lofty a goal and regard themselves as unworthy of it. Therefore, they make no effort to advance toward it.... Yet, the natural endowment is the same in all human beings ... how can one not take responsibility oneself for becoming a sage?"[67]

It is thus clear that learning in the Confucian way is not just for personal fulfillment, self-actualization, or personal gain in a practical sense; rather – and more importantly – it moves from an individual starting point and expands gradually to the large spheres of human life as a whole. One begins with a quest for understanding things in the world (note this understanding focuses on the social, not the physical, world). Then one sets one's heart and mind on the path of lifelong self-cultivation. When one achieves maturity, one has the moral strength and practical skill to manage one's family. With the family regulated, one is suited to assume greater responsibility in the community, presumably because one has won trust and respect of the people. If one can lead the community (locally or at higher levels) well, one is fit to lead the world. Thus, one's individual self-perfection is not individualistic but has a strong social component from the very beginning.

This ideal of learning may appear unrealistic. Yet, it has remained a high ideal to date. Against prevailing corruption and decline in any given historical era, the Confucian learning tradition has (and here I paraphrase de Bary's remarks originally on Neo-Confucians because I believe that they apply to the whole Confucian learning tradition):

> upheld a lofty conception of the dignity, integrity, and independence of the individual learner. It has a high estimate of the moral and spiritual resources of humans, and while its celebration of the heroic virtues may seem hopelessly idealistic to modern minds, it aims ... at the moral nobility of humans, judged on the basis of individual worth [cultivation] rather than special rank or social status.[68]

One historical reason that the Neo-Confucians felt strongly about this path toward sagehood (rather than personal achievement of *junzi* per se) was that almost all of them were court officials. They were called *scholar-officials*, literally scholars-turned-into-officials – a uniquely Confucian elite that served the dynastic courts.

Given the learning aspiration to sagehood, how to ensure that the highly self-cultivated and knowledgeable individuals were able to enter the court government became a serious concern, not only for those who took the world upon themselves, but also for the rulers themselves. Starting in the Han Dynasty (206 BCE–220 CE), such individuals were selected based on local recommendations for the court. This system was called *meritorious service*. In the seventh century, this practice was refined and finally institutionalized as the Civil Service Examination system. Young boys from all backgrounds, not nobility alone, were encouraged to begin learning early on and to persist through disciplined studies. All of them were allowed to take the examinations on their understanding of Confucian texts, their literary skills, and their ideas of governance. The successful ones advanced to higher levels and eventually were selected as scholar-officials who assumed leadership positions at the court. At least in principle, a person could make his way from the humblest background to the highest ministerial office in the land, and the motivational impact for individual learners could not be underestimated. This system lasted for more than thirteen centuries until its abolishment in early twentieth century.[69]

This unprecedented coalescence of moral achievement, academic learning, political power, social status, and economic gain led to the suprem-
acy of learning in Chinese culture. Such learning has become cemented as
an unquestionable and nonnegotiable value. Although many scholars were
more motivated by material rewards, they nevertheless had to go through
the ordeal of the same learning process. Willingness to endure this tremendous process, regardless of their original goals, was already testimony
to personal strength and commitment, which was reason for admiration.
Those who could advance all the way to the sage level (great leaders) were
held in awe, and those who tried their best but did not advance far were still
appreciated for their effort. Thus, for Chinese people as a whole, learning
to self-cultivate and learning to receive everything else good in life joined
forces and passed down through history as one and the same path. As
empirical research shows, this way of viewing and engaging in learning has
not changed much since then, despite dramatic political, social, and economic changes in recent times.

What about Chinese students learning in the modern educational curriculum, particularly science? Interestingly, the very acceptance of "taking
the world upon oneself" as a moral duty for Chinese learners can be said
to underlie the massive learning from the West that the Chinese (and other
East Asians) have been undertaking for more than a century. As noted in
the Introduction to this volume, during the mid-nineteenth century, China
encountered the surging powers from the West. The Opium War (1839–
1842), and Sino-Japanese War (1894–1895), the Boxer Rebellion (1898–1901),
and other confrontations forced the last dynasty to open its door and led to
the eventual demise of the dynastic system in 1911. These historical events
also led many Chinese intellectuals to blame Confucian learning as the
cause of their culture's decline, because the Chinese lacked Western learning. Many intellectuals and students regarded themselves as the agents of
change – that is, taking their world upon themselves – and went to Europe
and the United States (as well as Japan for learning how it carried out its
political reform and achieved industrial advancement a step ahead) to learn
science and democratic thought. Many founding leaders of the two major
political parties at that time in China – the Nationalist Party (國民黨) and
the Communist Party (共產黨) – were students returning from the West
and Japan. The motto held by those studying abroad was "saving our nation
and our people" (救國救民). Many other students sought to study science
in the West, among them, notably, future Nobel Prize winners in physics
C. N. Yang, T. D. Lee, and C. C. Ting. Educational reform took place under

the Nationalist government from 1911 to 1945. As a result, the Chinese education system adopted the U.S. system, and the curriculum from elementary school to higher education has kept up to date with Western mathematics and science as the core, in addition to traditional subjects of Chinese and Chinese history.[70] In sum, although the learning content has been broadened and the Western-style schooling established, the value of learning and the ways learners engaged in this process still remained quintessentially Confucian, as will be seen in the empirical research in later chapters.

Learning Virtues

The third characteristic of the Confucian learning tradition is the notion of learning virtues, which is personal agency for Confucian learners. Most Confucian writings discuss the core set of learning virtues that any learner has to develop and to exercise in their learning. Thus far I have identified seven core learning virtues: sincerity (誠心), diligence (勤奮), endurance of hardship (刻苦), perseverance (恆心), concentration (專心), respect for teachers (尊師), and humility (謙虛). These are called virtues for two reasons. First, they have long been part of Chinese moral discourse. As such, they denote personal qualities and dispositions that are regarded as highly positive and desirable for any learner. Second, parents, teachers, and society at large make concerted efforts to foster these learning virtues in children; therefore, they are an integral part of Chinese/East Asian education.

As already alluded to previously, sincerity (*chengxin*) is a key virtue for Confucian learning. It stresses the self-chosen nature of a person's decision to pursue *ren* or even sagehood. It is the honest and authentic commitment that the person makes to him- or herself as the target of learning. An example can illustrate the meaning of sincerity for learning. The Cheng Brothers in the Song period had a student who traveled all the way from the south to study with them. On a cold winter day, this student went with a friend to Cheng Hao's place. Upon arrival, he realized that his teacher was napping. He decided to wait outside. It began snowing. His friend could not endure the cold any longer and pleaded with him to awaken the teacher. But the student insisted on waiting. When the teacher woke up, he saw the two men covered in snow. Cheng Hao was deeply moved by the sincerity of these students.[71] This story has passed down as the epitome of sincerity (as well as respect for teacher, discussed in more detail later). Sincerity is regarded as the starting virtue for Confucian learning and prevails through the process.

The second virtue, diligence (*qinfen*), urges the learner, after a sincere commitment has been made, to come to a course of action so that his or her commitment will be followed through. This course of action requires that one exerts oneself and resists any temptation to stray from the path or simply to give up in the face of obstacles. Diligence, thus, is the virtue that underlies frequent, constant, studious behavior. It emphasizes much time spent on learning. Diligence is also believed to increase familiarity, which in turn opens opportunities for mastery.

The third virtue, endurance of hardship (*keku*), focuses on overcoming difficulties one is bound to encounter in learning. Difficulties in the Chinese context mostly mean lack of resources for learning (e.g., poverty) and lack of time for studying because one needs to make a living, usually via harsh physical labor. A learner may also face intellectual difficulties such as not understanding concepts or lacking natural ability. However, no difficulty, irrespective of type and intensity, is reason for giving up. Instead, one needs to develop the virtue of *keku*, where the learner acknowledges difficulties as an inherent part of learning and must find ways to overcome these hardships. There are many models of *keku* from real learners in history that are still widely read to and by schoolchildren. One of them describes Kuang Heng, a great writer and prime minister of the Han Dynasty, whose childhood was very poor. His family could not even afford light at night. To study, he chiseled a hole in the wall to read. His story is the well-known saying "*chiseling a hole in the wall to borrow the neighbor's light*" (鑿壁偷光), which has inspired later learners.[72] Not only do many Confucian learners not fear hardship, but they actually take pride in meeting the ordeal, thereby displaying their personal strength.

Whereas *keku* is the virtue in the face of difficulties, perseverance (*hengxin*), the fourth virtue, concerns the *lasting* strength for learning from the beginning to the very end. Two key notions are stressed. First is the belief that learning is a long and gradual process; no sudden insight or shortcut can replace this accumulative process. One's willingness to follow through is already testimony to one's attempts to achieve the virtue. Second, the path is full of obstacles and distractions, which demands that one hold fast to the commitment. The following exchange illustrates how a Confucian learner struggles with perseverance: "Ranyou, a student of Confucius, complained that it is not that he did not like Confucius teaching about becoming *ren*, but that he did not have enough strength to follow through with this process. Confucius replied: 'Those who do not have the strength for it collapse somewhere along the way. But with you, you have drawn your own line before you start.'"[73]

Ranyou's problem was not his desire for *ren*, but his inability to follow through with action. Perseverance is the virtue that he lacked for he could not even take the first step, as Confucius pointed out. The central meaning of the well-known phrase, "a thousand-mile journey starts from the first step,"[74] lies in the countless steps it takes to actually cover that "thousand miles." Perseverance is the virtue of holding this long distance in view while taking the first, the second, and all the subsequent steps to reach the end of the journey.

The fifth virtue, concentration (*zhuanxin*), is not exclusive to specific learning tasks, but is rather attributable to any learning. Concentration emphasizes studying with consistent and extended attention and focus. It also includes patience, carefulness, and thoroughness of learning. Concentration is believed to allow the full engagement of one's mind and affect in study. Meditative quiet sitting and retaining a tranquil mind are viewed as conducive for learning.

Respect for teachers (*zunshi*), the sixth virtue, is highly valued in the Confucian tradition. It is closely linked to sincerity and humility (see discussion later). However, respect among East Asian learners has been taken as a sign of obedience, docility, and lack of critical thinking.[75] The need for respect stems from two mutually constitutive sources. The first is from the learner. As a learner, particularly a beginner, one has much to learn. Respect for the teacher makes the learner receptive to the teacher's guidance. One needs to put one's ego aside in order to make a sincere commitment to learning. Respect acknowledges the student–teacher relationship as follows: the teacher will do his best to instruct the learner, and the learner will do his or her best to learn from the teacher. The pupil is not an equal peer to the teacher. This acceptance of the teacher is not regarded as something that causes the pupil low self-esteem. The pupil's submission to the teacher's teaching is similar to Western people going to a religious minister for guidance. One does not approach such a moral guide with the idea of challenging the minister. If one does not like the minister, one simply goes to someone else. Likewise, Western children take sports or music instrument lessons from private teachers, and learners generally do not approach such teachers with arguments and challenges.

The second source for respect is from the teacher. Teachers in this learning tradition are not just hired as employees to fulfill a contractual obligation, namely to teach objective/scientific knowledge. Teachers serve as moral guides, and for this purpose they themselves must embody moral self-cultivation. In other words, they are viewed as the immediate models for students to emulate. The title *teacher/mentor* comes with the assumption that the person has respectable moral and intellectual achievement to warrant respect from pupils. Pupils' respect in turn functions to hold teachers accountable for their own continuous self-cultivation. Therefore, the high esteem granted to teachers does not come free. Moreover, in the Chinese (not just the Confucian) tradition, the teacher–student relationship is likened to that of parent–child. Teachers do not just impart specific knowledge, but also must look after the students' well-being as they do for their own children. Unless one is willing to accept the pupils' expectations and the role of a teacher–parent, one does not take on the heavy responsibility of teaching in the Confucian tradition.

The final learning virtue is humility (*qianxu*), which is closely related but not limited to respect for teachers. Humility directs one to regard oneself as always in need of self-improvement no matter how much one has achieved in life. Humility is believed particularly important when one reaches high levels of achievement. In such situations, the natural human emotion is pride. In Confucian tradition, however, pride is viewed as an emotion that may lead one to develop an inflated sense of self, hence distracting one from self-improvement. Humility is likely to prevent one from developing related problems of arrogance or self-conceit. Confucius offers the advice on how to remain humble: "[I]n strolling with only two people, I am bound to find a teacher. Indentifying their strengths, I follow them, and identifying their weaknesses, I correct them in myself."[76] Humility enables one to want to learn from anyone. Confucius also exemplified humility himself when he acknowledged Xiang Tuo, a prodigious child at age seven, to be his teacher because this child purportedly raised questions to the already well-known Confucius, which he could not answer.[77] Confucius' humility against the background of his own monumental achievement sets a clear example for Chinese learners. Thus, humility is not regarded as a personal weakness but a personal strength because humble individuals are willing to self-examine, admit their inadequacies, and self-improve.

Action Is Better Than Words

East Asian learners have been widely noted to be quiet in school and reluctant to talk in any public forum. This observation applies to learners in East Asia as well as those in the West (foreign students and immigrants). However, labeling East Asian learners as unengaged, unwilling to participate, or simply withdrawn from the classroom is grossly mistaken. To put this matter in a sharper light, the best Chinese science and technology university, Tsinghua, has the aphorism carved on campus in front of its assembly hall – "Action Is Better Than Words" (行勝於言 or *Facta non Verba* in

Latin) – as their university's proud spirit (校風). Thus, what speaking means and how it operates in relation to action in Chinese culture (and other East Asian cultures) is an important, albeit hitherto poorly understood, phenomenon (see a more detailed discussion on this topic in Chapter 8).

Confucius was suspicious and distrustful of glib-tongued talkers. Perhaps for that reason, he did not write anything about his own teaching. He says that "the ancients [great moral leaders] were loath to speak because they would be ashamed if they personally did not live up to what they said," and "the exemplary person wants to be slow to speak yet quick to act."[78] This type of remarks occurs frequently in the *Analects*. To Confucian learners, their words and, for that matter, speaking in general are a very serious matter. There are several clear reasons. First, since the whole point of learning is to cultivate the self morally, the standard of personal progress is one's moral conduct – that is, what one does rather than what one says. One's trustworthiness (*xin*, 信) weighs heavily on one's daily living and conduct. Speaking commits one to the expected action by others, and different types of speaking cause different liabilities for the person. Accordingly, speaking to mislead and deceive deliberately is immoral; speaking without the intention to back oneself up with action is dishonesty; speaking to urge others but not the self to follow through is hypocrisy; speaking without understanding is ignorance; speaking without attending to the context is uncouthness; and speaking to praise oneself is to display self-weakness. None of these consequences reflect well on the person. In sum, speaking in Chinese culture tends to lean toward moral intent and judgment in general. This is why exemplary persons are slow to speak but quick to act. When they speak, they do so with careful words and sincere intentions.[79]

Second, speech is much easier than action; people are more prone to speaking than acting. One area for learners to improve on is to watch out for their tendency to say more than they can deliver. It is believed that one has much to gain by examining one's own actions and interactions and by bettering oneself rather than merely speaking about one's behavior.

Third, this learning tradition also emphasizes the great silent breadth and depth that is the realm of infinite wisdom. Lao Tzu's well-known saying "those who understand are not talkers; talkers don't understand"[80] is a clear expression of this belief. Lao Tzu and Confucius agree on this point about human wisdom being much greater than articulated words. As such, Chinese teachers, be they religious teachers, martial arts masters, craftsmen, or Confucian tutors, tend to speak little or speak just enough, but not exhaustively, to leave room for learners to ruminate, digest, and contemplate. Such a way of speaking and instructing is regarded as conducive to the learners' getting it for themselves (自得). It is rare that the learner and the teacher engage in immediate and lavish verbal exchange. Patience, a virtue related to concentration, is prized in this learning style, whereas impatience is discouraged.

As discussed at the end of the four Western themes, I also performed a Google search for the mottos of iconic Chinese universities in China, Taiwan, Hong Kong, and Singapore. The results revealed sharply contrastive meanings (to those of the Western universities): Tsinghua University's 自強不息, 厚德載物 (strengthen self ceaselessly and cultivate virtue to nurture the world – taken from the *Book of Change*), Beijing University's 勤奮, 嚴謹, 求實, 創新 (diligence, rigor, truthfulness, and creativity – notice the placement of *diligence*); Fudan University's 博學而篤志, 切問而近思 (learn broadly and focus on your purpose, question earnestly and reflect closely – taken verbatim from the *Analects*), Nanjing University's 誠朴雄偉, 勵學敦行 (be sincere and hold high aspirations, learn diligently and practice earnestly – taken from the *Book of Rites*), Jinan University's 忠信篤敬 (utmost dedication, trust, earnestness, and respect), Wuhan University's 自強, 弘毅, 求是, 拓新 (strengthen yourself, carry forward your resolution, seek truth, and create anew), Xiamen University's 自強不息, 止于至善 (strengthen self ceaselessly and strive for the highest good), National University of Taiwan's 敦品, 勵學, 愛國, 愛人 (cultivate virtue, advance intellect; love one's country, love one's people), Hong Kong University's 明德格物 (*Sapietia et virtus* in Latin, cultivate virtue and investigate things – taken verbatim from the *Great Learning*), Hong Kong Chinese University's 博文約禮 (learn broadly of culture and discipline learning with propriety), and National University of Singapore's *per ardua ad alta* in Latin (through hard work, great things are achieved).

Most of these words, as hinted, were taken either directly or condensed from Confucian texts, and they unambiguously and unanimously emphasize the cultivation of one's morals and one's self, which must precede inquiry into the world. Even when truth or fact seeking and creativity are mentioned, it is often the case that they are placed after the Confucian learning purposes and processes are laid down. It is also important to note that the idea of *university* was not a concept of Chinese learning. Most Chinese universities were founded and modeled after Western universities in the late nineteenth and early twentieth centuries, when China was undergoing dramatic political, social, and economic changes. Even so, Confucian learning purposes and processes assumed the first and foremost importance. Again, these mottos enjoy the enduring impact similar to those from Western universities. They, too, convey the central educational missions of their respective universities to the students, faculty, administrators, and staff. Their contemporary relevance is again evident by the many links to lively discussions in the Google search by each university's community.

The Chinese Learner

The foregoing four sections on the Confucian learning tradition offer explicit expectations and characteristics of their learners. Instead of reiterating them here, I provide a summary note: The learner starts learning literacy and numeracy and other basics of the world including Western subjects of modern schooling. Upon reaching the age of maturity (which can vary from individual to individual), the learner ideally makes a commitment to learning. Under the guidance of family and teachers, the learner gradually understands the need and possibility to become *ren* (the modern term for this process is *zuoren*, 做人, to learn how to be a person). This path is both individual and social in nature. As such, one needs to practice in the family what one is learning and to increase one's learning through practice. When this task has been achieved, one aspires to take one's community, country, and finally the world upon oneself. This cultural mandate translates into today's parlance as contributing to society (貢獻社會). From the very beginning, the learner is socialized to develop the seven learning virtues. Once developed, they last for a lifetime. Figure 2.2 shows a diagram of the Chinese learner.

Confucius, as an *exemplary teacher for all ages*, reflected on his own learning path toward the end of his life: "From fifteen, my heart-and-mind was set upon learning; from thirty I took my stance; from forty I was no longer doubtful; from fifty I realized the propensities of [heaven]; from sixty my ear was attuned; from seventy I could give my heart-and mind free rein without overstepping the boundaries."[81] Confucius took ten or fifteen years to reach each milestone of self-transformation. He made his sincere commitment to learning at fifteen, rather late from today's perspective. At thirty, he established himself with recognizable achievement; at forty, he would not doubt the path; at fifty, he was in harmony with the world; at sixty, he could hear all people empathetically; and at seventy he no longer agonized about how to act in any situation.

Indeed, Confucius' teaching mirrors his own life of learning, which projects a profound creative, aesthetic, and ethical quality. He did not need to write books; his whole life, as recorded by his students, was and still remains an open book of inexhaustible inspiration for later generations to read, understand, and emulate.

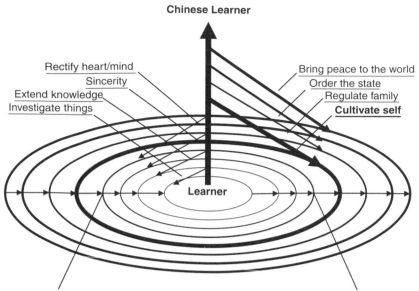

FIGURE 2.2. Chinese Learner: **The four inner circles** have increasing thick lines, representing the first four learning levels. **The fifth circle** has the thickest line, indicating the most important level of self-cultivation as envisioned by Confucius. The circles smaller than the fifth circle do not develop further without self-cultivation, and the larger circles are also not achievable without self-cultivation. The remaining **three circles** have thinner (than the fifth) but still increasingly thicker lines, showing the expansion of one's learning from oneself to one's family, community, and the whole world.

The upward arrow in the center represents the self-perfection process in which the learner engages on the path to becoming a *junzi* and sage, the ideal image of humanity, as held and practiced by Confucians. The upward direction indicates the open-ended and lifelong as well as emotionally uplifting and spiritually transcendent nature of this learning process.

The downward arrows correspond to each level of learning as personal growth in both height and breadth. One's achievement is both individual and social/moral.

The arrows moving away from the learner indicate learning virtues applied to all levels and processes.

The arrows moving toward the learner indicate increasing rewards to the learner as he or he achieves greater levels of learning.

NOTES

1. See Hsu, F. L. K. (1981). *Americans and Chinese: Passage to difference* (3rd ed.). Honolulu: University of Hawaii Press; Ivanhoe, P. J. (2000). *Confucian moral self cultivation* (2nd ed.). Indianapolis, IN: Hackett; Rosemont, H. Jr. (1992). Rights-bearing individuals and role-bearing persons. In M. I. Bockover (Ed.), *Rules, rituals, and responsibility: Essays dedicated to Herbert Fingarette* (pp. 71–101). La Salle, IL: Open Court; Shun, K.-L., & Wong, D. B. (2004). *Confucian ethics.* New York: Cambridge University Press; and Yang, K. S. (Ed.). (1988). 中國人的心理學 [*Chinese people's psychology*]. Taipei, Taiwan: Gwei Gwan Tu Shu for samples of thoughtful discussions of differences in general philosophies and ways of life.
2. Li, Y.-T, & Yan, B.-H. (2003). 梁漱溟先生講孔孟 [*Liang Shuming on Confucius and Mencius*]. Guilin, China: Guangxi Normal University Press.
3. For discussing Western intellectual tradition, I rely mostly on Russell, B. (1975). *A history of western philosophy and its connection with political and social circumstances from the earliest times to the present day.* New York: Simon & Schuster.
4. See Moser, P. K., & Nat, A. V. (2002). *Human knowledge: Classical and contemporary approaches.* New York: Oxford University Press; Williams, M. (2001). *Problems of knowledge: A critical introduction to epistemology.* New York: Oxford University Press for general philosophical discussion on epistemology.
5. See Ames, R. T., & Rosemont, H. Jr. (1999). *The Analects of Confucius: A philosophical translation.* New York: Ballantine for a good discussion on essentialism in Western thought.
6. All sources and quotes are from the reference in note 3 to this chapter.
7. See note 3 to this chapter, p. 72.
8. See note 3 to this chapter, p. 73.
9. Holton, G. (1973). *Thematic origins of scientific thought.* Cambridge, MA: Harvard University Press; and Westfall, R. (1971). *The construction of modern science: Mechanisms and mechanics.* New York: Cambridge University Press.
10. See note 3 to this chapter, p. 29.
11. See note 3 to this chapter, pp. 33–34.
12. See note 3 to this chapter, p. 37.
13. Plato (1991). *The republic of Plato* (2nd ed.). (A. Bloom, Trans.). New York: Basic Books, p. 206.
14. Kant, I. (1787/1999). *Critique of pure reason.* New York: Cambridge University Press.
15. Kant's categories of a priori knowledge and "categorical imperative."
16. See Popper, K. (1972/1989). *Objective knowledge: An evolutionary approach.* Oxford: Oxford University Press for an example.
17. Socrates did not write anything but has come to be known through his student Plato's accounts of his life and thought. Thus, he is commonly referred to as the Platonic Socrates as opposed to another version of Socrates that was portrayed by another, but intellectually much inferior, contemporary, Xenophon. I use the short name Socrates as the Platonic Socrates for convenience.

18. Hecht, J. M. (2003). *Doubt, a history: The great doubters and their legacy of innovation from Socrates and Jesus to Thomas Jefferson and Emily Dickinson*. New York: HarperCollins, p. 20, italics in the original.

19. See Rosch, E. (1978). Principles of categorization. In E. Rosch & B. B. Lloyd (Eds.), *Cognition and categorization* (pp. 27–48). Hillsdale, NJ: Erlbaum for a discussion on human hierarchical categorization of natural objects. See Anglin, J. M. (1977). *Word, object, and conceptual development*. New York: Norton; and Luria, A. R. (1981). *Language and cognition*. New York: Wiley for research on how children have different conceptual understanding of objects and how they acquire the formal structure of word meanings in their language to classify objects.

20. Descartes writes about "Cartesian doubt" in the two books: Descartes, R. (1637/2007). *Discourse on method*. Miami, FL: BN Publishing, and Descartes, R. (1642/2007). *Meditations*. Miami, FL: BN Publishing.

21. In modern views, a person in a vegetative state is biologically alive but unconscious. He or she is certainly not self-aware. Self-awareness necessarily requires thinking of oneself. Therefore, the Cartesian *cogito* is remarkable in that it attaches to human metacognitive thinking, which is thought to be unique in humans and the bare-minimum requirement for us to sense our existence.

22. See Chomsky, N. (1972). *Language and mind*. San Diego, CA: Harcourt; and Pinker, S. (1994). *The language instinct*. New York: Harper for details of how human innate language works.

23. See Piaget, J., & Inhelder, B. (1969). *The psychology of the child* (H. Weaver, Trans.). New York: Basic Books for sample research on human infants' cognitive capacity; second reference in note 16 to Chapter 1 for infants' social engagement with caregivers; and Eimas, P. D. (1985). The perception of speech in early infancy. *Scientific American*, 252(1), 66–72 for infants' phoneme detection.

24. St. Augustine (397/1998). *St. Augustine confessions* (H. Chadwick, Trans.). New York: Oxford University Press.

25. Locke, J. (1690/2008). *An essay concerning human understanding*. Oxford: Oxford University Press.

26. Berkeley, G. (1713/2006). *George Berkeley: Three dialogues between Hylas and Philonous*. Upper Saddle River, NJ: Prentice Hall.

27. Hume, D. (1740/2008). *A treatise of human nature*. Sioux Falls, SD: NuVision.

28. See Gardner, H. (1983). *Frames of mind*. New York: Basic Books; and Sternberg, R. J. (1985). *Beyond IQ: A triarchic theory of human intelligence*. New York: Cambridge University Press for an overview of research on human intelligence.

29. See Nisbett, R. E. (2003). *The geography of thought*. New York: Simon & Schuster for research on these differences between Western and East Asian thinking; Rogoff, B. (2003). *The cultural nature of human development*. New York: Oxford University Press for differences in perceptions of time and age across cultures; Jameson, K. A. (2005). The role of culture in color naming research. *Cross-Cultural Research: The Journal of Comparative Social Science*, 39(1), 88–106 for cultural differences in color perception; and Herlitz, A., & Rehnman, J. (2008). Sex differences in episodic memory. *Current Directions in Psychological Science*, 17(1), 52–56 for gender difference in facial processing.

30. Plato (1981). *Five dialogues* (G. M. A. Gruber, Trans.). Indianapolis, IN: Hackett, p. 41.
31. See note 30 to this chapter, pp. 9–11.
32. Rousseau, J. J. (1762/1979). *Emil, or on education* (A. Bloom, Trans.). New York: Basic Books.
33. Locke, J. (1693/2007). *Some thoughts concerning education*. Sioux Falls, SD: NuVision.
34. Kant, I. (1803/1960). *Kant on education*. Ann Arbor: University of Michigan Press.
35. Modern educational psychology and child development are the only two and closely related areas of empirical research that focus on the learner and the learning process itself. The review of these two areas will be dealt with in Chapters 3, 4, and 5.
36. Although many early educational philosophers advocated for pupils' moral and character development through formal education, the intellectual and academic types of development dominate in formal education in today's Western world. Moral education is left by and large to family and religion.
37. In his *Life of Lycurgus*, Plutarch eulogized the Spartan system, including how children were taught and strictly disciplined. According to Russell, this book strongly influenced Rousseau, Thomas Arnold, and English public school. The idea that children need to be subjected to strong discipline has never disappeared in childrearing and education practices. Much of religiously endorsed schooling still holds it important to discipline children, although perhaps not so strictly as before (see a good discussion in Jackson, P. W., Boostrom, R. E., & Hansen, D. T. [1993]. *The moral life of schools*. San Francisco, CA: Jossey-Bass).
38. Sizer, T. R. (1996). *Horace's hope: What works for the American high school*. Boston, MA: Houghton Mifflin.
39. See Olson, D., & Katz, S. (2001). The fourth folk pedagogy. In B. Torff and R. S. Sternberg (Eds.), *Understanding and teaching the intuitive mind* (pp. 243–263). Mahwah, NJ: Erlbaum for an informative discussion of how great intellectuals, scientists, and artists become canonized and hence perpetuated as the impersonal body of knowledge that is to be transmitted to young generations through formal education.
40. See de Bary, W. T. (1991). *Learning for one's self*. New York: Columbia University Press for a comprehensive treatment of the Confucian learning influence on Japan and Korea, and reference in note 5 to this chapter for Confucian influence on Vietnam. The fact that this learning tradition is named after his profession, *Rujia, 儒家* (not the Latinized name Confucius. During Confucius' time, the term *ru* was used to refer to priests in charge of religious ceremonies for the courts as well as teachers. Because Confucius did such work, his school of thought carries the term *ru*) signifies the important role that Confucius played.
41. Quoted by Shuming Liang, p. 203 in reference in note 2 to this chapter.
42. Despite all the compilations of scriptures and texts, Confucius never wrote anything on his own teaching (much like Socrates). The *Analects of Confucius*, which contains fragmented statements and questions and responses between him and his students, is the primary source from which we glimpse Confucius' thinking and teaching. As many scholars throughout history have argued, some

of the content may have been modified and added by his students. Nevertheless, the first ten chapters are believed to be Confucius' own words. See Fingarett, H. (1972). *Confucius: The secular as sacred.* New York: Harper & Row and reference in note 5 to this chapter for more discussion on the authenticity of the *Analects.*

43. Although Confucianism became the predominant ideology for all dynastic ruling, Confucius' own teaching did not focus on that. When he talked to his pupils about serving kings and dukes in their courts, it was not for career development but to ensure humane ruling in government. See Li & Yan (2003) in note 2 for more comprehensive discussions on these points by Shuming Liang.

44. See note 5 to this chapter, p. 5.

45. To be sure, at the time Confucius lived, the employer–employee relationship was the one between the king and the subject. He also referred to the father-son instead of parent–child relationship given the male-dominant orientation of society at that time. However, this historical condition is less important for our purpose of understanding Confucian teaching of the cardinal relationships as the base for human lives. Today, his teaching is understood as still relevant to the general parent–child and employer–employee relationships.

46. See note 5, 2.7 to this chapter, p. 77.

47. Li, J., & Fischer, K. W. (2007). Respect as a positive self-conscious emotion in European Americans and Chinese. In J. L. Tracy, R. W. Robins, & J. P. Tangney (Eds.), *The self-conscious emotions: Theory and research* (pp. 224–242). New York: Guilford. It is important to point out that even though the roles of husband and wife were delineated at the time, Confucius did not state that women were lower than men in their capacity and moral worth. Gender discrimination against women was more a result of later historical development. During Confucius' time, another great sage, Lao Tzu, argued that femininity was an equal (and often neglected) force in the universe.

48. These four moral principles are carved on the Chinatown gate in Boston, MA. They serve as a monument and reminder of the core Confucian values to Chinese even in a culture vastly different from their own. The term *lian* (廉) was first used not by Confucius himself but by Guanzhong (ca. 723/716–645 BCE), a highly esteemed prime minister of State Qi. Confucius used the term *shenzheng* (身正) to discuss this essential virtue in any government official. *Lian* is the present-day term for integrity.

49. See note 5 to this chapter, p. 51.

50. Mencius (1970). *Mencius* (D. C. Lao, Trans.). Harmondsworth: Penguin Books, p. 107.

51. See Tracy, J. L., & Robins, R. W. (2007). The self in self-conscious emotions: A cognitive appraisal approach. In J. L. Tracy, R. W., Robins, & J. P. Tangney (Eds.), *The self-conscious emotions: Theory and research* (pp. 3–20). New York: Guilford for chapters on the negativity of shame in the West. See Li, J., Wang, L. -Q., & Fischer, K. W. (2004). The organization of Chinese shame concepts. *Cognition and Emotion, 18*(6), 767–797 for research on the meaning of shame in Chinese, and see Fung, H. (1999). Becoming a moral child: The socialization of shame among young Chinese children. *Ethos, 27,* 180–209 for how parents socialize children with a sense of shame in Taiwan.

52. See Tu, W. M. (1979). *Humanity and self-cultivation: Essays in Confucian thought.* Berkeley, CA: Asian Humanities Press for discussions of *ren.*

53. See note 40 to this chapter, p. 342.

54. See Rosemont, Jr., H. (2003). Is there a universal path of spiritual progress in the texts of early Confucianism? In W. M. Tu & M. E. Tucker (Eds.), *Confucian spirituality, vol. 1* (pp. 183–196). New York: Crossroad for an insightful discussion of various kinds of persons talked about by Confucius.

55. See note 54 to this chapter, p. 190.

56. See note 54 to this chapter, p. 191.

57. See note 50 in D. C. Lau for Lau's discussion of Mencius's contribution to Confucianism in the introduction to his translation of *Mencius*. Also see Wilson, J. Q. (1993). *The moral sense*. New York: Simon & Schuster for a review of research on human moral sense. There is strong evidence that very young infants are able to display empathy toward other infants with distress. This supports the Mencian argument for innate human moral sensibilities.

58. See note 50 to this chapter, pp. 82–83.

59. See note 50 to this chapter, p. 130. Note that the Chinese term *junzi* is not gendered, although at that time only men could be educated.

60. The Neo-Confucian movement was in part a response to the prevailing Buddhism and Taoism at that time. Whereas Buddhism advocated eradicating human desires altogether (無欲) to achieve enlightenment, Taoism promoted harmony with nature by avoiding human strife and arduous effort for achievement (無為). Neither doctrine appealed to the Confucians because Confucian teaching encouraged individuals to regulate family, serve the community, and take greater social and moral responsibility for one's society. However, Neo-Confucians incorporated some elements to offer a compromise position (e.g., eliminating human desires in order to uphold the heavenly principle and quiet sitting to study taken from Buddhism and arguing that the enduring human values are consistent with the Taoist tenet of the Supreme Ultimate [太極] – as a normative principle and at the same time the Nonfinite [無極] as an open-ended and flexible principle to guide human lives). See reference in note 40 of de Bary for more discussions on the integration of the three different schools of thought.

61. The *Four Books* along with the other *Five Scriptures* (*Book of Changes, Book of History, Book of Songs, Book of Rites,* and the *Spring and Autumn Annals*) were the core curriculum of any Confucian student and were the content of the Civil Service Examinations. These books continued to be required of and read by students even after the abolishment of the Civil Service Examination system in 1905. When the Communists took power in 1949, these books were no longer part of the school curriculum. But they continued to be taught to and read by students in Taiwan. Interestingly, there has been a new movement to teach children Confucian values since the 1990s in Taiwan, which is now rapidly expanding to Mainland China and other Chinese regions (see a review of this topic in the reference in note 9 Chapter 1).

62. See note 40 to this chapter for a comprehensive account of the Cheng-Zhu school and Yang Ming school and their respective influences. Also see Lee, T. H. C. (1999). *Education in Traditional China: A History*. Boston, MA: Brill Academic for a detailed historical account.

63. A *li* is a little more than 400 meters.

64. See note 50 to this chapter, p. 50.

65. See note 40 to this chapter, p. 29. Also see Yu, Y.-S. (2003). 士與中國文化 [Intellectuals and Chinese culture]. Shanghai: Shanghai People's Press for a historical account of the role of Confucian intellectuals.

66. See note 65 to this chapter.

67. See note 40 to this chapter, p. 30.

68. See note 40 to this chapter, p. 37.

69. See Lee, W. O. (1996). The cultural context for Chinese learners: Conceptions of learning in the Confucian tradition. In D. A. Watkins & J. B. Biggs (Eds.), *The Chinese learner* (pp. 45–67). Hong Kong: Comparative Education Research Centre for a discussion on meritorious service; and Lee, T. H. C. (1985). *Government education and examinations in Sung China, 960–1278*. Hong Kong: Chinese University Press for a historical account of the Civil Service Examination system.

70. See Su, Y.-F., & Wu, J.-Y. (2005). 中國新教育的萌芽與成長 *(1860–1928)* [The emergence and development of new Chinese education (1860–1928)]. Taipei, Taiwan: Wunan Publishing; and Wu, J.-Y. (1990). 中華民國教育政策發展史 *(國民政府時期 1925–1940)* [History of the development of education policy during 1925–1940 under the China's Nationalist government]. Taipei, Taiwan: Wunan Publishing for a thorough treatment on the modern history of Chinese education.

71. Wang, T., et al. (1985). 中國成語大辭典 [Dictionary of Chinese idioms]. Shanghai: Shanghai Dictionary Press, pp. 166–167.

72. See note 71 to this chapter, p. 1816.

73. See note 5 to this chapter, p. 106.

74. Lao Tzu (1992). *The Tao of the Tao Te Ching* (M. LaFargue, Trans.). Albany: State University of New York Press, p. 156.

75. See Pratt, D. D., Kelly, M., & Wong, K. M. (1999). Chinese conceptions of "effective teaching" in Hong Kong: Towards culturally sensitive evaluation of teaching. *International Journal of Lifelong Learning, 18*, 241–258; and Tweed, R. G., & Lehman, D. R. (2002). Learning considered within a cultural context: Confucian and Socratic approaches. *American Psychologist, 57*(2), 89–99 for general discussions on obedience and docility of East Asian students. See also Flowerdew, J., & Miller, L. (1995). On the notion of culture in L2 lectures. *TESOL Quarterly, 29*(2), 345–373, and McGuire, J. (1997). English as a foreign language in China. *Occasional Papers, 48*. University of Southhampton: Centre for Language in Education for similar observations in Chinese students.

76. See note 5 to this chapter, p. 116.

77. Huang, D. Y., & Peng, H. J. (1992). 三字經 [Three character classic]. Taipei, Taiwan: Ruisheng Book & Magazine Publishing House, p. 90.

78. See note 5 to this chapter, pp. 93–94.

79. See Chang, H. C. (1997). Language and words: Communication in the *Analects* of Confucius. *Journal of Language and Social Psychology, 16*, 107–131 for a comprehensive discussion on Confucius' treatment of speaking.

80. See note 74 to this chapter, p. 66. Also in Japan, a talkative person, particularly a man, is regarded as unintelligent according to Doi, T. (1981). *The anatomy of dependence* [J. Bester, Trans.]. New York: Kodansha International.

81. See note 5 to this chapter, pp. 76–77.

3

Time Past and Time Present

With the core values of each culture's learning tradition having been out-lined, I now turn to the central question of this book: Do these respective learning traditions still influence the present-day learners? In this chapter, I present empirical research that gives an affirmative response to the question. Research for the past several decades documents specific ways the present-day learners' beliefs and actual learning processes reflect their respective cultural learning traditions. However, before I present that empirical research, it is necessary to address some important questions about current education practice in China (and by extension, in East Asia as a whole) that may lurk in the minds of readers.

CHANGED CURRICULUM AND INCREASED COMPETITION

No one disputes that times have changed and that ancient values have undergone significant changes in much of the world. East Asia and the West are no exception. Yet, at least with regard to intellectual pursuit, the West has not undergone changes as radical as East Asia has, as noted in Chapter 1. In fact, there is little regarding approaches to learning that the West has adopted from other cultures. Admittedly, educational con-tent in the West – that is, what children learn about – has opened up to knowledge of other cultures and ethnic groups. Clearly, the most notable changes the West has witnessed are the broadening of compulsory educa-tion to all and the elevation of achievement standards for all.[1] Yet, we do not have evidence that any Western country has put in the core of their curriculum to teach children, for example, how to study as a Confucian or a Buddhist learner does. By contrast, education in China (and East Asia in general) has been fundamentally altered as a result of Western influence, ranging from its system (i.e., at what age children attend school, move to the next level, etc.) to the very curricular content.[2] Thus, I focus more on the changes in China in this section.

Peculiarly, media and even some researchers have asserted that perhaps the present-day Chinese learners are no longer influenced by the Confucian learning tradition but have instead become more Westernized. I had a recent personal encounter that drives this perception home. I met a Mainland Chinese graduate student in sociology in Germany, who came to my research presentation on Chinese versus Western learning beliefs. During the break, we chatted. He asked me, "Do you really think that we have anything to do with Confucian values? I think that we are more Westernized." I had a *deja vu* lapse. His question and remark were incredibly reminiscent of questions I asked during my undergraduate years. However, many Westerners with whom I have spoken view not only Mainland Chinese but all East Asians (including Asian immigrants with generations behind them in their host countries) as *very* different. Quite a bit of cross-cultural research demonstrates that Confucianism is largely responsible for that difference.

To be sure, educational curriculum, as noted previously, has changed in such a way that Western mathematics and science (and English at an increasing rate) have become the required core. The case can be made that learning fundamentally different subjects in school is bound to alter the learner's approach to learning. After all, it is presumed that to succeed in learning math and science, learners must develop logical reasoning, causal inference, scientific methods, and objectivity in looking at the world. Furthermore, such learners need to adjust their purposes of learning as well. That Asian students have been documented to achieve well in these subjects adds more weight to the argument that East Asians must have changed or ought to have changed their approach to learning.

Moreover, the social conditions have changed dramatically, which increases demands on education. China has the largest population on earth, and since 1986, under their compulsory education law, every child must receive nine years of education.[3] Population growth and compulsory education are similar in other Chinese and East Asian regions. These changes have resulted in a much greater need and pressure on the governments to educate people. Exacerbating this social burden is the fact that the world has been witnessing an explosion of knowledge, which also demands prolonged learning to ensure mastery. From the perspective of individual learners, competition for higher education, especially for the highly selective universities, is becoming more and more fierce as both the population and knowledge continue to grow. If desirable employment opportunities do not grow proportional to the highly educated workforce, the workforce may have to retrain or upgrade skill sets. Thus, Chinese and other East Asian learners' learning beliefs and achievement may well be a direct response to these social changes, having nothing to do with Confucian learning tradition.

These arguments are well taken. However, with regard to the contention about learning Western subjects, the fact remains that before entering formal schooling, children have lived some five-to-six years under the intimate care of their families – in the Asian case, frequently of not just parents but the grandparents and extended kin. Although nuclear families are becoming the norm, they still remain more or less a living arrangement rather than a true nuclear structure as defined in the West. It is still very common for grandparents and even relatives to co-parent children; this pattern applies, surprisingly, also to Chinese immigrants who live in the United States.[4] According to developmental research, the first few years are essential to children's later development.[5] Therefore, during these very important formative years, Chinese children, as children from any culture, develop many important culturally informed beliefs and behavioral tendencies regarding learning,[6] and they come with these beliefs and behavioral tendencies to the first day of school. As alluded to in Chapter 2, the teacher–child relationship is modeled after the parent–child relationship in the Confucian tradition (more detailed empirical research on this topic will be discussed in later chapters). There is much more home-school coherence than may be the case in an ethnically diverse culture.[7] Although children begin learning math and science, sometimes even during preschool, the social environment in which learning takes place is still fundamentally Confucian. Therefore, it is quite likely that while children learn math and science as subjects, the way they engage in learning may be different from their Western peers.[8]

With regard to social changes, Asia is not unique; most developed and developing nations also face similar educational challenges. However, nowhere is competition for education as intense as in East Asia. Pressure for children to achieve highly in school seems to be particularly pronounced. Again, this pattern also applies to East Asians living outside Asia in many societies where the mind, creativity, and intrinsic motivation are more prized than in East Asia. Moreover, although Western societies provide more educational opportunities and longer compulsory education than many Asian countries, competition for the best schools is just as fierce among Asian immigrants.[9] Becoming the best in education seems to be the guidepost for Asians regardless of where they live. When asked "as a parent, what expectations do you have for your child's future?" one parent responded, "Magnet High, Harvard, and Heaven!" (Magnet High is a pseudonym for one of the most competitive public high schools in the United States.) Desiree Qin, the researcher, describes this kind of desire for their children to go to the very best schools and universities as very common among immigrant Chinese parents whether they are from well-to-do or humble backgrounds.[10]

At this juncture, it is also important to acknowledge that popular press has portrayed Asian students' achievement as coming at a high price of their psychological well-being.[11] While comparable data are difficult to obtain from the Asian countries because of unclear reporting procedures and methods, available data do not support this view. A study comparing Chinese, Japanese, and American high school students' psychological adjustment in relation to parental and school pressure found that despite their reports of higher parental expectation and lower parental satisfaction with their achievement, Japanese students indicated fewer, not more, adjustment problems than their American peers. Chinese students also reported less stress, academic anxiety, and aggressive feelings than the Americans, although they did reveal higher frequencies of depressive mood and somatic complaints. Moreover, high achievement was not correlated with these adjustment problems for Asian students, but it was for American high achievers. Another recent study from Korea shows that parental pressure had positive, not negative, influence on adolescents' effort and achievement motivation.[12] The most recent data on suicidal thoughts among youths with major depressive episode (MDE, a strong predictor of suicide) from the U.S. Department of Health and Human Services show a lower rate of MDE among Asian youth than European-American youth aged twelve to seventeen.[13] Finally, nationally representative data on Asian Americans' mental health indicate that as a whole, they suffer less, not more, mental problems than European-Americans.[14] If parental pressure for school achievement truly causes these problems (because most Asian parents exert such pressure), Asian-American population as a whole should have a higher proportion of mental problems. The data, however, do not support this conclusion.

Recent research does indicate that Asian immigrant children in the United States display adjustment problems, particularly among adolescents. This issue merits our attention. However, academic pressure may be the easy scapegoat. If the Asian-American youth as a group do not show a higher rate of mental illness, and if some Asian immigrant children in the West show adjustment problems, then the *immigrant context* and the interactions between the home culture's childrearing values and practice and those of the mainstream culture may need to be studied in order to explain the true causes. Unfortunately, little research exists in this area. A few pioneering studies shed light on some key factors, such as cross-language use (parents talk in their native language, but children respond in English, which leads to the breakdown in parent–child communication), the gap between desired parental warmth and the actual received warmth, decreasing time together, parents not understanding children's changed worldviews, and children not understanding parents' perspectives from their native culture all predict adjustment problems. But pressure to achieve has yet to be shown to be a direct cause of Asian immigrant children's mental health problems.[15]

EXAMINATION HELL

The most astonishing part of the current Asian education system is its infamous examination system. That East Asian education system is examination-driven is no secret to the world. Any discussion of Chinese and Asian learning without acknowledging this condemned side is bound to face skepticism. This system has been accused of doing everything bad compared to the known good education practices from the West. The system, it is claimed, is notoriously teacher-centered and authoritarian, favors learning by rote, fosters extrinsic motivation, and stifles creativity.

As such, this system has been, quite unsurprisingly, under fierce criticism for quite some time (in fact, for more than a century). To express the aversion toward this system, Ishisada used the phrase "examination hell."[16] This loathing is echoed not only by non-Chinese researchers and educators, but also by many East Asian researchers and educators themselves. Nevertheless, anyone with some degree of sanity must ask the obvious question of why this notorious system still remains, is even flourishing today, and why Asians do not seem inclined to abandon it in spite of its having received such condemnation for so long. To be sure, many attempts to change the system have been made across East Asia (e.g., Japan and Taiwan). Yet, the system is no more likely to disappear than it ever was. Even more bizarre is the fact that most education policy makers in these societies are familiar with the "better" practices in the West, and many of these leaders were themselves trained in Western educational fields.

This fact is unsettling and demands some explanation. To my knowledge, no one has explained the legitimacy and vitality of this "examination hell" better than Samuel Peng.[17] According to him, East Asian societies are "stuck" with the exam system because it is the only solution to a predicament with which East Asian cultures are faced. As stated previously, the Confucian tradition regards respect for and honoring of one's family as the most important moral foundation for oneself. At the same time, Chinese people and societies uphold the moral principle also espoused by Confucius: equality of education for all regardless of their backgrounds (有教無類). However, those holding power over educational access (e.g., college admissions officers) face a serious moral dilemma when their family members request favorable treatment (consider the case of a relative who just missed a few points on the college exam, which, in all likelihood, indicates only a trivial difference between students). If the request is denied, the person with institutional power violates the familial moral code; if the request is granted, the person violates public ethical standards. Alternative means of evaluating students, such as teacher recommendations and interviews, are all subject to the same dilemma. There is no other solution but to resort to the impartial test score. The only person responsible for advancement in education then is the student him- or herself. Viewed from this perspective, the examination hell may not be as hellish as it first seems.

This predicament would not exist in the first place if Chinese/East Asians as a whole, regardless of their socioeconomic status, did not desire and actually study to advance in learning. The real question here is why the Chinese/East Asians feel that they must pursue learning. Do they have nothing else meaningful in life to pursue other than academic learning?

A very well-established theoretical outlook among contemporary Western or Asian researchers alike is that school learning has one overwhelming purpose: providing an individual with knowledge and skills to make a good living and increasing opportunities for social mobility. Although researchers may not set out to study learning for social mobility, much of the actual research tends to focus on products of learning such as academic achievements and practical gains that reflect utilitarian purposes. Admittedly, economic survival goals may be valued by most, if not all, learners from any culture.[18] However, if making a living were the only raison d'être for learning, we would not care about children's natural questions about the world, such as "why do maple leaves turn golden in the fall?" or "why is the sun bigger but colder in the morning but smaller yet hotter at noon?" Neither would we admire adolescents who engage in philosophical debates about, for example, the meaning of justice. Nor would we continue to read Socrates' demonstration of human innate knowledge in his tutelage of an uneducated slave boy, or Confucius' words about commitment to self-perfection in learning. But we do, and we do so diligently.

Making a living may be the convenient reason for pursuing academic learning among people at lower socioeconomic status. It does not, however, explain learning behaviors of affluent people. I happen to teach at a university where there is a mixture of affluent and low-income but very bright

European-American, as well as quite a few Chinese/East Asian and Asian-American students from both affluent and humble backgrounds. It is my observation that regardless of their socioeconomic status, the European-American students engage in learning with similar attitudes and behaviors – that is, emphasizing personal curiosity, inquiry, verbal communication, and individual insights and brilliance. Likewise, it is also common to see many Chinese/East Asian students from affluent homes study just as hard as their peers from low-income backgrounds. These students do not need to make a living by studying hard; their families can ensure them a comfortable life. But they go through the ordeal of hard work willingly or feel they need to honor their parents by dedicating themselves to study even if they would not take on the ordeal so willingly for themselves. Chinese immigrant learners throw this issue in an even sharper light. These learners enjoy freedom, choice, and creative environments available to them at U.S. schools. Yet, they consistently display the same degree of seriousness and achievement as their peers in East Asia, which cannot be attributed to the pressures of the examination system. Thus, we are compelled to think that learning for the present-day European-Americans and Chinese/East Asians has to serve other purposes as well. As it turns out, the compelling forces behind their respective learning approaches are still their own cultural traditions.

EXPLAINING ASIAN STUDENTS' ACHIEVEMENT IN EARLIER RESEARCH

There was virtually no research on comparative learning beliefs or the related area of achievement motivation between Western and East Asian learners prior to 1960. In 1963, David McClelland published a paper on the motivational pattern of Chinese, in which he declared that traditional Chinese lacked achievement motivation, but thanks to the communist ideological spirit, Chinese people gained revolutionary zeal and became more motivated.[19] After this publication, there was a long silence on the subject until the late 1970s, when international assessment of educational achievement revealed that Japanese students outperformed their counterparts in many Western countries in math and science, with the United States falling behind other developed countries.[20] This rather unexpected outcome suddenly spawned an interest in understanding East Asian schools and children's learning. Herald Stevenson and James Stigler launched a decade-long landmark research that compared American (mostly European-American) and Asian elementary school students from Japan, Taiwan, and China. Their central objective was to find out the causes of Asian children's higher academic achievement. The researchers overcame great challenges to conduct this multination, multilingual research. They ensured that elementary school students were representative in their own countries. They constructed their own achievement tests in math to control for bias, collected surveys from children and parents on their views of achievement, observed classroom teaching, and interviewed teachers.[21]

The results were quite startling. They found that whereas American children, parents, and teachers explained children's achievement based on the notion of ability, their Asian counterparts attributed children's achievement to their effort. They dubbed this learning difference the "learning gap." They also found this major distinction of beliefs to be linked to how schools and the school day were organized. American children attended school for fewer days and shorter time daily than Asian children. Asian teachers assigned more homework, and parents expressed dissatisfaction with their children's achievement even when the achievement was already very high. Teachers were not reluctant to display and correct children's mistakes publicly and even to make children's achievement public in the classroom (i.e., everyone knew how everyone else did on any test). American teachers assigned less homework, and parents showed more satisfaction with their children even when the achievement was mediocre. American teachers would not do what Asians teachers did to expose children's mistakes and weaknesses in public. Quite the contrary, they would keep children's achievement confidential to protect their self-esteem.[22]

This research occupied the center stage and generated much more research interest. For example, American researchers studied American and Japanese concepts that learners used to describe their ability and effort, and their analysis yielded that Japanese learners display culturally specific dispositions such as *seishin*, the mental attitude that helps one tackle a task, and *gambaru*, a "positive orientation toward the intrinsic benefits of ... persistence."[23] Researchers in Hong Kong took the concept of *effort* to study Chinese students. Effort had been defined, in Western motivation literature, as an internal but unstable factor (meaning that a person may or may not exert effort depending on the achievement task). They found that effort was not situationally unstable but, in fact, a stable factor across time and situations for the Chinese learners. In other words, Chinese students believed that they need to make an effort all the time for all learning tasks.[24]

Others also focused on U.S. and Asian curricular and classroom differences within school and found that Japanese schools provided more opportunities for children to learn math and that their curriculum was more differentiated and better sequenced in intensity according to the advancement of grades.[25] Joseph Tobin, David Wu, and Dana Davidson observed and videotaped the routines of a preschool in the United States, Japan, and China for one day. They showed the representative footages to the teachers, administrators, and parents of each school as well as those of the other two participating schools. Their video-ethnography captured details of how children's daily activities were organized and guided, how they were instructed in class, and how they interacted with peers. This research revealed that the U.S. preschool education emphasized children's self-expression, free exploration, enjoyment, smooth peer interaction, and enforcement of social and moral rules of school. Chinese preschool stressed nutritional care, collective activities under teachers' close supervision, disciplined learning in class, and following social and moral rules strictly. Japanese preschool exhibited yet another feature: fostering children's learning among themselves. Teachers were mostly hands-off, leaving children to play, fight, and resolve their conflicts on their own. Quite surprisingly, there was little academic learning.[26] Similarly, Catherine Lewis documented Japanese elementary school teaching and learning in an in-depth ethnography. She further showed that Japanese schools organized instructions and activities in a way that engaged not only children's minds but also children's affect in learning.[27] Finally, Robert Hess and Hiroshi Azuma studied teaching styles in classrooms of U.S. and Japanese young children and discovered that whereas U.S. teachers preferred an efficient, well-paced style of instruction, their Japanese counterparts used a slow but thorough style. These different styles predicted children's working habits and achievement in their respective cultures.[28] More researchers also documented effective teaching strategies in math and science in Japanese elementary classrooms, which promoted student achievement.[29] The best-known effort was, however, the video-study led by James Stigler to compare classroom teaching in the United States, Japan, and Germany. The study concluded that Japanese pedagogy indeed had advantages compared to its Western counterparts.[30]

Research attention was also paid to the familial factors. Researchers investigated European-American and East Asian parents and found that although parents in both cultures valued education highly, they differed in several areas. Asian parents expressed higher expectations of their children's achievement (usually straight A's compared to A's and B's by European-American parents). Asian parents also engaged their children in more structured learning activities such as enrolling them in afterschool or weekend enrichment programs. Asian parents also monitored their children's home learning more closely than European-American parents did.[31]

Meanwhile, achievement in math and science by East Asian students from Singapore, Korea, Japan, Hong Kong, and Taiwan continues to rank at the top of the global rankings for the past three decades, as again confirmed by the more recently published results from the Trends in International Mathematics and Science Study (TIMSS) and the Programme for International Student Assessment (PISA) results. It seems that regardless of how the students are tested, they remain at the top. Furthermore, they show larger improvements even in reading (e.g., Korea ranked sixth and Japan eighth in PISA, 2003). Asian immigrant students in North America, Europe, Australia, New Zealand, and other parts of the world also consistently show higher achievement. Note that all of these TIMSS and PISA assessments did not involve China until 2009 (when China's Shanghai participated in PISA) probably because of China's (then) lagging economic development. Given their first placement in their only participation in one 1990 international assessment, they were unsurprisingly placed in 2009 PISA as first with 17 points for reading, 54 points for math, and 37 points for science above the second-place Korea, followed by Finland and other East Asian countries who differed by only a few points (all these scores are based on a mean score of about 500).[32]

THE PARADOXICAL CHINESE LEARNER

Against this international backdrop, somewhat detached from U.S. interest in East Asian learning, a group of researchers from Australia, the United Kingdom, and Sweden working in Hong Kong wrestled with a phenomenon that they termed the paradox of the Chinese learner. The basic problem is that whenever Westerners teach Chinese students or visit Chinese schools, they are disappointed with, if not outraged by and condemnatory toward, Chinese learning. As noted previously, the Chinese educational system consists largely of old-fashioned teaching and learning. On the one hand, pedagogy is teacher-centered, authoritarian, with a centralized curriculum (implying inflexibility and lack of attention to individual children's learning needs). On the other hand, students are docile, obedient, and uncritical; they learn by rote, lack intrinsic motivation, and aim only for exams. In other words, everything known about good educational practice is violated in the Chinese/Asian educational system. I also remember attending a graduate course at Harvard Graduate School of Education. When I tried to share with the instructor that practicing writing Chinese characters or calligraphy really helps the child learn how to concentrate, the instructor dismissively said "All Chinese students do is rote learning! That is not what we are dealing with in this course." These remarks shut me up for the rest of the course. Indeed, at that time, I did not even know how to respond. It was clear to me, however, that Chinese learning was regarded as a negative model. As it turned out, my personal experience was not unique. There are plenty of articles, books, and popular press that have criticized East Asian learning.[33]

Yet, time and again – and by now it is quite unambiguous – Chinese/ Asian learners achieve well in comparison with students from other developed countries. They continue to do well when they come to the West for advanced studies, and more, their immigrant children in the West are also highly achieving. All these findings indicate to me that Chinese/East Asian children achieve well no matter how they have been (often quite exhaustively) assessed. This stark contrast between poor learning approaches and high achievement has led keen observers of Chinese learning such as John Biggs and David Watkins to regard the whole phenomenon as begging for a new explanation. Indeed, how could such an educational system with such learners produce any meaningful achievement?

Watkins and Biggs assembled a team of researchers who contributed to their influential volume, *The Chinese Learner*, in which they posited the phenomenon as a paradox.[34] Because most East Asian learners are under the influence of the Confucian learning tradition, Watkins and Biggs used the term *Confucian heritage cultures* (CHC) to include countries of China, Hong Kong, Taiwan, Singapore, Japan, Korea, and Vietnam. The contributors presented empirical research that documented basic beliefs and learning processes observed in learners that are distinctly CHC. In 2001, Watkins and Biggs published a sequel of their first book, *Teaching of the Chinese Learner*.[35] Despite the focus on teaching, most research was conducted in close relation to learning. Alongside these volumes, other researchers also collected telling data that added weight to the needed explanation of the paradox. In the next section, I present the research findings from these efforts.

Learning Beliefs

With regard to cultural beliefs, Wing On Lee provided a historical account of core Confucian values concerning learning and argued for their enduring impact on Chinese learners today. Accordingly, most essential is the Confucian belief in human self-perfection pursued as the highest purpose of life through personal commitment to learning. This belief is also linked to other beliefs such as one's social contributions in the form of meritorious service and practical concerns for honoring their families as well as enhancing their own social status and mobility.[36] Lee's argument is coherent with the Confucian learning tradition reviewed in Chapter 2. In support of Lee's argument, Kai-ming Cheng collected data on people's beliefs about learning in a comprehensive ethnographic study on one Chinese province's primary education. He concluded that Chinese parents, whether well off or destitute, send their children to school not to learn literacy and numeracy skills, but to become a person who is knowledgeable of the world, able to function well in social relations, and, most important of all, morally cultivated.[37] Similarly, An Ran's qualitative research examined how Chinese parents in Britain and British teachers clashed on the purpose of learning. Whereas British teachers focused on acknowledging and expressing satisfaction with Chinese children's apparent high achievement, Chinese parents were discontented, emphasizing more demanding learning materials and their children's continuous effort to self-improve regardless of their accomplishments.[38]

Related to these studies, Lixian Jin and Marin Cortazzi found that the image of a good teacher as described by British students is one who is able to arouse students' interest, explain clearly, use effective instructional methods, and organize activities. However, the image of a good teacher offered by their Chinese peers is one who has deep knowledge, is able to answer questions, and is a good moral model.[39] Similarly, Lingbiao Gao and David Watkins used both qualitative and quantitative methods to identify different goals of teaching held by Chinese science teachers. They emphasized cultivating students' adaptive attitudes toward learning and moral guidance in addition to other cognitive goals.[40] Irene Ho interviewed Hong Kong and Australian teachers and found that Australian teachers viewed their teaching within the framework of professional responsibility with clearly defined roles and boundaries. As such, they would notify the families if students failed or misbehaved, but they did not see as their responsibility to teach morals to their students. Instead, the family was more responsible for moral instruction. In comparison, Hong Kong teachers stressed their moral charge of guiding students on the "right path and were prepared to go all the way to rectify misbehaviour, spending as much time as they could and often getting personally involved." They attributed students' academic failure and misbehaviors more to their own inadequacy than to students themselves or their families.[41] Finally, Thomas Tang used qualitative methods to study Hong Kong teachers' conceptions of learning and teaching and found that moral development is the highest learning as well as highest teaching conception beyond the more cognitively oriented conceptions.[42]

In the studies where comparative perspectives were taken, Chinese students and teachers, but not their Western counterparts, emphasized moral and personal growth as a central purpose of learning and teaching.

Learning Processes

With regard to the learning process itself, Ference Marton, Gloria Dall'Alba, and Lai Kun Tse tackled rote learning and memorization, the notoriously Chinese/Asian style of learning that has received much criticism from the West as well as from Chinese educators themselves. However, it turned out that Chinese rote learning was not an end in itself but was used as the first step of a larger strategy for achieving deeper understanding.[43] In a related study comparing British and Chinese students' use of memorization and repetition, Bo Dahlin and David Watkins further found significant cultural differences. Whereas British students used repetition to check if they really remembered something, Chinese students used it to create "deep impressions" to lay a foundation for developing understanding. Moreover, British students viewed understanding as a process of sudden insight, whereas Chinese students believed understanding to be a long process that required extensive mental effort.[44]

In exploring perceptions of effective teaching by Hong Kong college students and faculty (both Chinese and Western expatriate), Daniel Pratt, Mavis Kelly, and Winnie Wong found that Chinese students and faculty held different views of learning from those of Western teachers. Western teachers often characterized Chinese students "as not knowing how to think, having only short term goals ... wanting to be spoon-fed, needing too much structure ... taking a quiet, receptive, and deferential attitude during class, and [unwillingness to] challenge or question ... authority."[45] However, Chinese students believed that learning is a gradual process that requires tremendous dedication and methodical steps (similar to Japanese learning and teaching style as documented by Robert Hess and Hiroshi Azuma).[46] Generally, they engage in four distinct steps to accomplish any learning task. Upon encountering new materials, Chinese students initially commit the material to memory; next they seek to understand the intention, style, and meaning of the material. They then try to apply their understanding to situations that call for use of such knowledge, and finally they enter a deeper level of questioning and modification of the original material. Whereas the last step in their approach is verbally interactive by nature, the first three steps may call for more solitary learning and contemplation (which is an important aspect of Chinese intellectual tradition[47]). Clearly, this style is not bound by the immediate verbal exchange at the moment but can extend over a period of days, weeks, months, and in some cases even several years (as a doctoral student may publish a paper to challenge his or her mentor's ideas with which the student disagreed several years earlier)! Thus, these researchers observed that Chinese students often feel frustrated and bewildered when they are confronted with a Western teacher "whose expectations and forms of assessment thrust them immediately to the far end of this chain (questioning and analysis)."[48]

With regard to Asian learners being driven by extrinsic instead of the more desirable intrinsic motivation, one study shed some important light on this topic: Sheena Iyengar and Mark Lepper examined how personal autonomy and choice functioned among Asian-American and European-American schoolchildren in learning and achievement situations. Personal autonomy and choice are hallmarks of intrinsic motivation, whereas social influence and determination (such as choice made by others) are forms of extrinsic motivation. It has long been assumed that personal autonomy and choice are conducive to learning and performance, whereas the lack of such personal freedom is detrimental.[49] However, these researchers demonstrated that this assumption held true for European-American children but not for their Asian-American counterparts. The former enjoyed learning and performed better when given personal choices (of what to learn and how to learn it), whereas the latter enjoyed the learning just as much and did better when their task was chosen by significant others (e.g., mothers or trusted peers). More recent research further documents that Asian children learn well and enjoy learning activities chosen by others with whom they have good relationships. Thus, Asian learners' need for personal choice may not play as essential a role as for Western learners.[50]

FURTHER RESEARCH: DIGGING INTO CULTURAL
LEARNING BELIEFS

More than two decades of research has greatly enhanced our understanding of Chinese/East Asian learners. Notably, most of recent research has been done with impressive qualitative methods designed to uncover valid cultural meanings behind the observed differences in learning processes and outcomes. Although small in size, Hong Kong offers a unique research ground for such truly cross-cultural research because of its unique free-trade status. Researchers in Hong Kong from both CHC and Western cultures interact with each other frequently, and more importantly, many Western teachers interact with CHC learners and schools directly. This research has indeed charted new grounds for further research.

Mapping Cultural Learning Models

Although learning research by the 1990s had made significant advancement, the accumulated knowledge as a whole remained quite discrete and lacked a systematic approach to learning from a *cultural* perspective. There was no comprehensive description of learners in the West and Asia, or, for that matter, in any other culture. The separate pieces of information may have represented fragmented learner images, but this information explained neither learners' culturally based beliefs nor the underlying reasons and processes that produce such learner beliefs. If our goal was to understand human learning from all perspectives, a comprehensive documentation of cultural learning models – the missing link – was in order.

I began researching this topic by adopting what is called an *emic* perspective. An emic perspective is the insider perspective, originating with the people being studied, as opposed to the one originating with the outside observer/researcher, which is called an *etic* perspective.[51] Scholars have advocated for the inclusion of both emic and etic views in any research on human cultures (or else cross-cultural understanding would be impossible). However, traditional research has been dominated by the etic perspective, particularly in the form of theory-driven and hypothesis-testing research modeled after the Western scientific paradigm. Anthropological research was the avant-garde in introducing the emic perspective and has helped us achieve a great deal of understanding of the world's cultures. Research from the emic perspective tends to have high validity and is preferable to the etic perspective in uncovering native concepts and the beliefs that underlie observed behaviors of people.

I also explored this research topic from the framework of *cultural models*, again an anthropological insight. Cultural models are established by historical processes of the culture and continue to be revised as the culture evolves further. They are conceptual frames that shape members' experiences by supplying the group's shared ways of explaining, predicting, and interpreting people's thoughts, feelings, and behaviors. These frames also guide people in forming their goals and motivate them toward obtaining their goals.[52] An example of a cultural model is the image of a teacher in the United States. Anyone who has gone through school from K to 12 in the United States probably knows what a teacher does, what power and responsibilities he or she has, what students ought to do in relation to the teacher, and what happens when a student fails to do what the teacher is charged to demand from the student. Similarly, Western and Chinese learning beliefs can be studied as such cultural models.

I conducted two studies comparing Chinese and European-American learning models. The specific empirical methods I used are called *prototype* methods. These methods are based on the theory and empirical evidence that much of human understanding of the world consists of categorizations of objects, activities, and experienced events. For example, furniture as a higher-order abstract category contains functional categories of sofas, tables, chairs, and so forth, which people use for daily life. With each sub-category, there are finely differentiated types such as couch, bench, and stool for people to sit on. Humans achieve this categorization system with the aid of language by giving objects names and labels. Once these categorical structures exist, they become prototypes of objects, models, or scripts of human activities and events, according to which people categorize new objects, activities, and events. For example, when we see a chair-like object, we are likely to use the prototypical chair to conceptualize the object and subsequently categorize it as chair.[53] Thus, the language of a given culture has these prototypes for people to use and to organize their understanding of the world. Prototype methods lent themselves to the study of learning as conceptualized by humans living in specific cultures.

To access the language that contains learning conceptions in each culture, we asked three native-speaking students from selective universities in each culture to free-associate the Chinese term *xuexi* (學習) and *learn/ learning* in English, respectively.[54] To ensure that the Chinese and English terms were equivalent in meaning, several steps were taken. First, we consulted the word frequency dictionaries in both Chinese and English. Word frequency is a standardized linguistic index for how frequently a word is used in a natural language. The higher the frequency, the faster and more accurately the word is recognized by the users of that language.[55] We chose the Chinese term *xuexi* (*learn/learning*) because it occupies a word frequency of 679, the highest of all the Chinese learning synonyms. Similarly, we identified *learn/learning* because its word frequency of 254 was the highest among its synonyms.[56] Then, we asked twenty fluent bilingual adults, with half native-speakers and the other half non-native-speakers who had acquired high fluency with the other language, from each culture to translate the Chinese term into English and also translate the English term into Chinese. The cross-translation and a rating procedure (see more discussion later) led to the conclusion that *xuexi* and *learn/learning* were the closest equivalents among synonyms in both languages.[57]

The three college students in each culture respectively wrote down common words and phrases denoting aspects of learning that came to mind when they heard the word *xuexi* and *learn/learning*. This step resulted in an initial list of 242 in English and 145 in Chinese. Next, we presented each list to twenty more college students from similar backgrounds in each culture and asked them to add any items they thought referred to learning. This step was necessary to cast the nest wide so that important cultural learning concepts were not left out. We obtained an expanded list of 496 in English and 478 in Chinese. Finally, it was quite likely that these lists contained items that might not have been shared by most cultural members, but instead represented idiosyncratic ideas of individuals. To obtain a core list likely shared by most cultural members, we asked sixty more participants in each culture to rate each item on a four-point scale according to its relation to learning with, "1" meaning no relation and "4" a definite relation to learning.

Following research conventions, we used the median number 2.72 as a cut-off line in order to select a core list from all the rated items.[58] We carefully examined each item and selected a final core list of 203 English and 225 Chinese items, representing a reasonable degree of relevance to learning as determined by group consensus. Table 3.1 shows the top English and Chinese terms referring to learning.

As can be seen in Table 3.1, there are striking differences in these two lists of learning terms. Table 3.2 summarizes four types of differences immediately observable by glancing at Table 3.1. With regard to purely linguistic features, English terms are mostly single and regular words. By contrast, Chinese terms typically have multiple words with many modifiers. Many terms are idiomatic expressions in the form of proverbs and sayings. Regarding the conceptual features, English terms have references to external factors such as resources, institutions, and teacher. The highest-rated items on the Chinese list have no such references (although there were such references with lower-rated items). Interestingly, among the nearly 500 initial English terms, there were no terms referring to hard work. In sharp contrast, many Chinese terms refer to hard work and related learning attitudes (this finding does support the research by Stevenson and Stigler as reviewed earlier). Neither does the English list contain terms on life-long learning, but the Chinese list has several terms including the very top item ("keep on learning as long as you live"). There is one category that has the reversed trend: The English list has many terms denoting thinking and mental processes (61 terms, or 30% of the entire list of 203 terms), but only one such term appears on the Chinese list of the top 20 terms (and only 14

TABLE 3.1. *Top twenty learning-related terms nominated and rated by U.S. and Chinese adults*

English	English Translation (Chinese)
1. Study	Keep on learning as long as you live (life-long learning) (活到老, 學到老)
2. Thinking	Read extensively (博覽群書)
3. Teaching	Learn assiduously (刻苦學習)
4. School	Read books (看書)
5. Education	Diligent (in one's learning) (勤奮(學習)
6. Reading	Extensive knowledge and multifaceted ability (博學多才)
7. Teacher	Study (讀書)
8. Books	Make a firm resolution to study (發奮讀書)
9. Critical thinking	Study as if thirsting or hungering (如飢似渴地學習)
10. Brain	There is no boundary to learning (學無止境)
11. Discovery	Concentrate on learning (專心學習)
12. Understand	Eager to learn (好學)
13. Information	Take great pains to study (苦心攻讀)
14. Knowledge	Seek knowledge (求知)
15. Motivation	The learned understands reasoning (讀書人明理)
16. Library	Study abroad (留學)
17. Students	Do one's utmost to self-study (勤勉自學)
18. Learn by doing	Learning without thinking is labor lost; thinking without learning is perilous (Confucius) (學而不思則罔, 思而不學則殆 [孔子])
19. Applying ideas	After learning, one understands that one's knowledge is inadequate (Confucius) (學然后知不足 [孔子])
20. Communication	Long-term diligence is the road to the mount of knowledge; endurance of hardship is the boat to the boundless sea of learning (書山有路勤為徑, 學海無涯苦作)

terms overall, or 6% of the entire list of 225 terms, with the remainder having no reference to either logic or analysis).

With respect to affective features, the English terms lack affect. The Chinese terms, in contrast, express strong affect, showing desire, passion, and intensity. Finally, in reference to behavioral features, there is no clear call for action in the English terms. The Chinese terms exert a strong call for action.

The significance of these noted differences in the learning vocabulary becomes quite clear when we consider the process by which children develop their learning beliefs in these two cultures. In Chapter 7, I present data on how the two cultures' mothers converse with their children about learning. Mothers use many of the words and phrases captured in my initial

TABLE 3.2. *Linguistic, conceptual, affective, and behavioral differences in English and Chinese learning lexicon*

English	Chinese
Linguistic features	
Single words	Multiple words with many modifiers
Regular words	Idiomatic expressions including proverbs and sayings
Conceptual features	
Reference to external factors (e.g., resources and institutions)	No such reference
No references to hard work	Many references to hard work and learning attitudes
No references to life-long learning	Several such references
Many references to thinking/ mental processes	Only one such reference
Affective features	
Affectively neutral	Strong affect (desire/passion/intensity)
Behavioral features	
No clear call for action	Clear call for action

studies to guide their children in their discussions of their offspring's good and poor learning attitudes and behavior. Children develop their own learning beliefs by hearing and using these terms. Thus, the learning vocabulary plays an important role in child development.

To map out the relationships among various conceptions for each culture, we asked 100 college students from similar backgrounds to sort their culture's core list into groups according to similarity in meaning. There sortings were then submitted to the statistical analysis called *cluster analysis*, which resulted in two conceptual maps of learning, one for English and another for Chinese as shown in Figures 3.1 and 3.2.[59]

Both maps contain much detailed information, showing the magnitude and complexity of each culture's learning model. There are two dimensions on each map: levels and clusters. Levels refer to the hierarchical structure of categorization as discussed previously in the section on prototype methods. As can be seen, both maps consist of four levels. At the very top is the Superordinate Level, below it is the Basic Level with two further levels, called Basic Level I and Basic Level II. Further down is the Subordinate Level, which has the most divisions. It is this level that contains the actual learning terms. The clusters show similarities and differences in learning conceptions as sorted by the participants. They are found at the Subordinate Level that

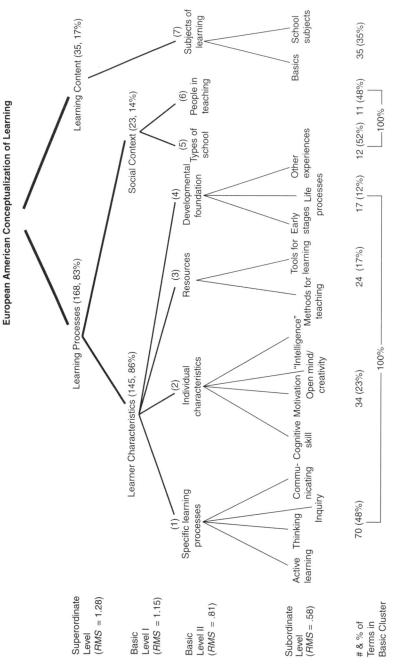

FIGURE 3.1. Diagram for a European-American hierarchical structure. From J. Li (2003). "European-American conceptualization of learning," *Journal of Educational Psychology*, 95, p. 261. Copyright 2003 by the American Psychological Association. Adapted with permission.

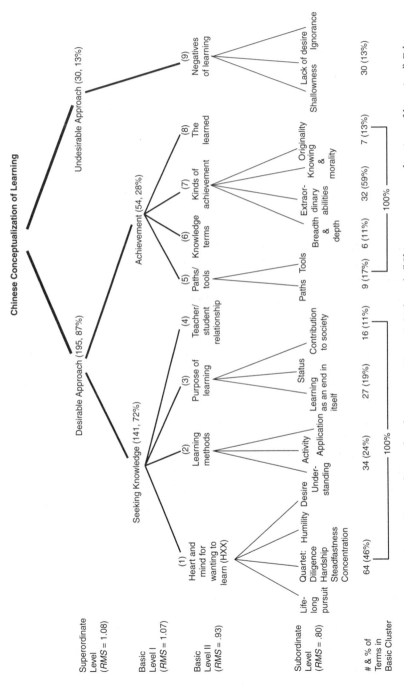

FIGURE 3.2. Diagram for a Chinese hierarchical structure. From J. Li (2001). "Chinese conceptualization of learning," *Ethos, 29*, p. 123. Copyright 2001 by the American Anthropological Association. Adapted with permission.

literally "clusters" words and phrases from the lexicons into the various divisions. How many clusters there are and how large each cluster is are determined by how many people sorted how many learning concepts into various groups. Based on the assumption of prototype methods, a greater number of items indicate greater awareness/emphasis of the conceptions in that culture.[60] Because these maps are empirically derived with group consensus, they are the *culture-level* learning beliefs, which are taken to represent a form of cultural learning models as accessed through language usage.

For our present purpose, it suffices to highlight the most relevant features. The U.S. map (Figure 3.1) focuses on learning processes (with the majority of terms) on one side and learning content (with fewer terms) on the other. Within the learning processes, a great many more terms fall within learner characteristics than within social context. The two most significant dimensions are under learner characteristics: (1) specific learning processes elaborating on (a) thinking, (b) inquiry, (c) active learning, and (d) communicating; and (2) individual characteristics stressing (a) cognitive skills, (b) motivation, (c) open mind, and (d) intelligence.

The Chinese map (Figure 3.2) displays desirable versus undesirable approaches to learning with a preference/value at the top. The majority of terms fall on the desirable side, which contains two further distinctions: seeking knowledge and achievement standards. Under seeking knowledge, the most significant groups are: (1) heart and mind for wanting to learn (in Chinese, *hao-xue-xin*, 好學心), which includes (a) life-long pursuit, (b) a set of learning virtues (diligence, endurance of hardship, steadfast perseverance, and concentration), (c) humility, and (d) desire; and (2) purpose of learning, containing three essential ideas: (a) learning as an end in itself, (b) status, and (c) contributions to society. Under achievement there is one significant dimension: kinds of achievement emphasizing breadth and depth of knowledge, abilities, unity of knowing and morality, and originality.

In the second study, we asked 62 college students for each culture to describe their ideal learners in their respective cultures (124 in the sample).[61] We targeted ideal-learner images instead of average learners because they provide what developmental researchers term the "optimum" of developmental outcome. Accordingly, cultures have preferable "endpoints" or "optimal ways of being" toward which younger members of a culture are enculturated.[62] Although no two children will achieve identical outcomes in the enculturation process because of diversity in individual characteristics and contextual influence, it is important to describe the ideals because they exist in people's minds and guide people's behavior.[63] The ideal-learner image, as opposed to words and phrases in the first study, would also compensate for the limitations inherent in the lexicon from which I derived culture-level learning beliefs. Ideal images are thus also culture-level, but not individual-level, learning models.

We probed four specific dimensions of the ideal learner: (1) thinking on the nature of knowledge, purposes and processes of learning, and views of intelligence and excellence; (2) understanding of the relationship between learning and one's moral development; (3) learning behaviors in routine situations any learner is likely to encounter, such as high achievement, high intelligence, failure, not understanding concepts, inability to learn despite effort, and boredom; and (4) emotional patterns associated with good or poor learning. The written descriptions of each of these dimensions were analyzed both qualitatively and quantitatively.[64] These procedures yielded four profiles corresponding to the four probed dimensions of the ideal learner for each culture.

The basic findings from the two studies converge to two comprehensive pictures of the two cultures' learning models. Table 3.3 summarizes the components and dimensions of these two belief systems. As can be seen, there are at least four large common component headings across the two cultures: purpose, agentic process, affect, and achievement. The specific items within each component were determined by the number of each culture's respondents who referred to these ideas as well as the presence of these components on the two cultural maps of learning concepts as derived from the first study of learning terms. Below I discuss each culture's model while highlighting similarities and differences between the European-American and Chinese models.

European-American Learning Model

Purpose of Learning

As indicated in Table 3.3, three main purposes emerged: (1) cultivate the mind/understand the world, (2) develop one's ability/skill, and (3) reach personal goals. The most frequently mentioned associations with the idea of the purpose of learning are to cultivate one's mind and to understand the world. The mind enables one to learn, but it also develops or becomes sharpened as a result of exposure to a stimulating environment that demands its proper use for understanding the world.

The second learning purpose is to develop the ability/skills that one needs to be a fully functioning member of one's society. Important skills include those for a successful career, for one's self-sufficiency and independence, as well as knowledge that enables one to solve problems and to

TABLE 3.3. *Components and dimensions of European-American and Chinese learning models*

EA	Chinese
Purpose of Learning	
Cultivate mind/understand world	Perfect self morally/socially
Develop ability/skill	Acquire knowledge/skills for self
Reach personal goals	Contribute to society
Agentic Process of Learning	
Active engagement	Diligence
Thinking	Self-exertion
Inquiry	Endurance of hardship
Communication	Perseverance
	Concentration
Kinds of Achievement	
Understanding of essentials/expertise	Breadth-depth/mastery of knowledge
Personal insights/creativity	Application of knowledge
Being the best one can be	Unity of knowledge and moral character
Affect	
Positive	
Curiosity/interest	Commitment ("establish one's will")
Intrinsic enjoyment	Love/passion/thirst
Challenging attitudes	Respect/receptivity
Pride for achievement	Humility for achievement
Negative	
Indifference/boredom	Lack of desire
Extrinsic motivation	Arrogance
Disappointment/low self-esteem for failure	Shame/guilt for failure

Source: Li, J. (2011). Cultural frames of children's learning beliefs. In L. Arnett Jensen (Ed.), *Bridging cultural and developmental approaches to psychology: New syntheses in theory, research, and policy* (pp. 26–48). New York: Oxford University Press; p. 30. Copyright 2011 by Oxford University Press. Reprint with permission. Originally adapted from table 14–1 in Li, J. & Fischer, K. W. (2004). Thoughts and emotions in American and Chinese cultural beliefs about learning. In D. Y. Dai & R. Sternberg (Eds.), *Motivation, emotion, and cognition: Integrative perspectives on intellectual functioning and development* (pp. 385–418). Mahwah, NJ: Erlbaum.

take control of one's life and surroundings. The third learning purpose is to reach one's personal goals (beyond ability/skill). This purpose includes finding self-fulfillment, achieving personal happiness, becoming a well-rounded person, embarking on a spiritual quest, or reaching any personal goals individuals may desire.

These three types of purposes are inherently related. While the mind plays a central role in learning, it also needs cultivation. This very process is also one by which a person develops various abilities and skills in order to reach personal goals in life.

Agentic Process of Learning

The features under this heading are called *agentic* because they are personal actions directed at achieving desirable goals. In other words, these are the processes in which people engage in order to learn, given their purposes and goals.[65] Four main agentic processes were found. First is active engagement, centering on the notion that a person needs to be actively involved in learning. This active nature emphasizes learning by doing and life experiences, both inside and outside the classroom. The second process is captured in the idea of "thinking/critical reasoning," which is what the mind does or ought to do. Thinking concerns the whole spectrum of mental processes involved in learning. For example, one could move from lower-order differentiations of objects to higher-order synthesis of relations, or one could engage in rigorous deductive logic or inductive reasoning, or one is free to reflect, introspect, or contemplate on anything of personal interest.

Inquiry, the quintessential process and agency underlying Western scientific development, is the third kind that stresses discovering the unknown and inventing the new. In this process, one seeks to find out about things in the world through a variety of research activities such as gathering data, experimentation, observation, analysis, and drawing conclusions. Key to this process is one's engagement in challenging existing canons of thought, finding new problems, and searching for creative solutions.

Finally, the fourth process, communication, serves both as learning itself and a form of dissemination of one's knowledge and discoveries. For learning itself, one participates in oral as well as written forms of social interactions. In these communications, one not only exchanges ideas with others, but also discusses, debates, critiques, or argues with others in order to achieve better understanding of a subject, using tools such as logic, evidence, and devil's advocacy. For dissemination purposes, one presents, explains, articulates, and demonstrates one's views, positions, or research findings, often using visual forms and technical devices to reach audiences and readers.

Like the purposes, these four agentic processes in learning are also linked coherently, even though they each have distinct emphases. Active learning ensures fuller engagement of the mind, which promotes thinking at all levels, forms, and dimensions in inquiry. Communication is a natural part of active learning given its interactive nature, which in turn facilitates more active engagement, thinking, and inquiry.

Kinds of Achievement

Three kinds of achievement were most frequently identified (Table 3.3): (1) understanding of essentials/expertise, (2) personal insights/creative problem solving, and (3) being the best one can be. Understanding of essentials is not limited to a particular field of study but includes anything deemed worthy of learning by the person. Expertise is a notion that applies only to an area of study, such as math or art. Given that the purpose of learning is to understand the world, the standard for gauging achievement is sensibly the extent to which a person gains better understanding of a subject. Many respondents asserted that excellence of learning does not rest just on knowing facts but on knowing the deeper underlying principles of things – that is, the essence of the phenomenon. Personal insight and creative problem solving, the second standard, displays one's brilliance and creativity. The third kind of achievement addresses being the best one can be in learning. Whereas the first two standards imply less social recognition, the third standard is a more subjective and intrapersonal delineation of "being one's best." One sets his or her own goal of achievement and strives for it.

Of these three kinds of achievement, the first two are more closely related with one another than with the third one, although when striving to be one's best is aligned with understanding the world, developing expertise in a field, and applying one's knowledge/skill creatively to solving problems, the three kinds are synergistically linked and inform each other.

Affect

Affect is an integral part of learning beliefs and processes. Whenever human beings pursue their goals with any degree of effort, they experience related emotions and feelings. Whereas emotions typically involve physiological responses such as heartbeat, muscle tension, facial expressions, and bodily gestures, feelings may not involve such.[66] For example, if we feel strange in a situation, we may not experience bodily change. Nevertheless, our feeling strange is part of our affective system that allows us to detect noteworthy changes in our environment.[67] Affect in our research refers to all emotional responses as well as longer-term feelings toward learning and self-engagement in the learning process as has been defined and used in the research on human motivation.[68]

We found both positive and negative affects in our research on European-American learning model (Table 3.3): For positive affects there were (1) curiosity, interest, and motivation for learning, (2) intrinsic enjoyment, (3) challenging attitudes, and (4) pride in achievement. For negative affects there were (1) indifference and boredom, (2) extrinsic motivation, and (3) disappointment/low self-esteem for failure.

Curiosity, interest, and motivation were the most often mentioned positive affect for purposes. Intrinsic enjoyment was named as the affect that accompanies the learning process. Attitudes that challenged existing canons of knowledge and authority were greatly prized. The general positive affect associated with achievement was pride – an expression for self-confidence and self-esteem. These positive feelings about oneself in turn motivated the person to learn further.

Negative affects occur when the learning task is perceived as uninteresting or boring. When this happens, ideal learners were described usually as not giving up, but continuing to learn the materials, especially if the materials were still required or were important knowledge. Still, they would not display intrinsic motivation and enjoyment. Instead, they would persist with some level of indifference, boredom, even dread. Many respondents also acknowledged that these learners would stop investing time and effort into the materials if they were deemed less essential. Relatedly, respondents referred to extrinsic motivation as antithetical to natural curiosity, interest, and enjoyment.

When experiencing failure, ideal learners were described to feel a number of related negative emotions: disappointment, lack of confidence, low self-esteem, and inferiority. Naturally, these emotions stand in sharp contrast to those associated with high achievement.

European-American Learning Model Echoes
Western Intellectual Tradition

Taken together, it is remarkable that the findings regarding purposes and agency of learning reflect well the four key dimensions of the long-standing Western intellectual tradition since Greek antiquity as discussed in Chapter 2. The purpose of learning remains to understand the external world. Although this external world has expanded to the social world, human psychology, the fictional world, the brain, and even the self, the approach to these worlds is to treat them as *objects of analysis* rather than as a process of personal transformation by the learner him- or herself. Mind still remains supreme as a human capacity to crack the worlds, and the process of obtaining verified, objective, and reliable knowledge is still prized. A critical attitude toward existing knowledge and inquiry into all phenomena is still essential in any course of learning and research. The achievement standards are by and large framed also within the Western intellectual tradition. Individual learners' achievement is judged by how well they understand their chosen world of study. Their personal excellence is intimately tied to the ultimate purposes and goals on the one hand and the learning processes on the other.

Similarly, their affects mirror the fascination, wonder, and intrinsic passion about the world as well as the inquisitive and critical spirit that characterize Western scientists since the Greeks first displayed such affective tendencies. Although historical materials typically do not elaborate on affective responses to failure by the Greeks and subsequent scientists, the findings of our research on negative affects about personal failures were sensible, given the emphasis on those positive affects.

Chinese Learning Model

Purpose of Learning

Similar to the European-American model, there are also three main purposes: (1) perfect oneself morally/socially, (2) acquire knowledge/skills for self, and (3) contribute to society (Table 3.3). The first, the most significant one, was described as a need to perfect oneself in the moral and social realm. It is important to point out that some European-American respondents also mentioned self-fulfillment and self-actualization as their ideal-learner's purposes. However, they emphasized being one's best through learning academic subjects rather than cultivating themselves morally as defined in Confucian terms. Interestingly, the term *learning* was left open for respondents to construe. Whereas European-Americans interpreted it as understanding the world, their Chinese peers took it to connote moral and social self-perfection in addition to academic learning.[69]

The second purpose, acquiring knowledge/skills for self, is reminiscent of the European-American second purpose, developing one's ability and skill. Chinese respondents stressed mastery of knowledge whereas European-Americans emphasized developing ability. Chinese ideal learners also needed knowledge/skill for leading a good life. They, too, must have those skills for survival, self-sufficiency, and successful careers. Finally, these skills were seen as enabling and empowering them to solve problems, maintain satisfying social relations, and reach their personal goals.

The third purpose is contributing to society, which reflects directly the core Confucian value. As Rosemont suggests, Chinese children are beneficiaries of their social world's love, care, and teaching, but they gradually become benefactors as they gain knowledge, skill, and moral maturity.[70]

Individual learning is not divorced from contributing to community as an ultimate purpose.[71]

These Chinese purposes are also inherently related. They have been explicitly part of Confucian values regarding learning and are actively promoted by families, communities, schools, and society at large.[72] Therefore, one needs to engage in personal skill learning and moral development before one can meaningfully contribute to society. However, one's moral self-perfection and skill acquisition are not conceptualized as separate or sequential processes. They take place simultaneously from early on and continue throughout life. Many European-American ideal learners also desired to make a difference in the word, relieve suffering, and help others. However, this purpose was not as strongly or prevalently expressed as by their Chinese peers.

Agentic Process of Learning

When asked to describe how their model learners learn (i.e., what they do, what steps they take, how they behave when they encounter difficulties such as failure or boredom), Chinese respondents did not, surprisingly, describe much that would be considered learning processes per se as seen in European-American descriptions. Instead, they wrote extensively about the learning virtues, as discussed in Chapter 2. These learning virtues also appeared in my study on Chinese learning terms (see "quartet" in Figure 3.2).

Five such virtues emerged. The first, the notion of earnestness/sincerity (*renzhen*, 認真/誠意), a variation of the ancient spirit of sincerity in learning (as discussed in Chapter 2), stresses the seriousness that one needs to bring to learning. The seriousness is sensible given that Chinese learning is centered around one's moral self-perfection. As respondents described, earnestness is the predecessor of dedication, which is the long-lasting virtue all learners are urged to develop.

The second virtue, diligence/self-exertion (*qinfen*, 勤奮/發奮), refers to frequent studying behavior after the person has made a resolve to pursue learning. The emphasis falls on the actual learning behavior, therefore much time spent on learning, following the person's resolve.[73] *Qinfen* as a behavioral manifestation of self-exertion is believed necessary to ensure one's clarification of goals; the course of action one must take to realize them; and a way to hold oneself accountable for any temptation to stray from one's resolve. Frequently, upon making the resolve, the person shares his or her learning goal with his or her family, close friends, or teachers, who serve as witnesses to monitor, to watch for, and even to demand consistency between one's resolve and follow-up action.

The third virtue, endurance of hardship (*keku*, 刻苦), focuses on overcoming difficulties and obstacles one is bound to encounter in learning. Respondents described three kinds of difficulties: (1) physical drudgery and poverty, (2) difficult knowledge, and (3) lack of natural ability. First, physical drudgery and poverty are considered hardships because they have been an unavoidable living condition throughout Chinese history (see Chapter 2 for an account of this virtue as part of Chinese learning tradition). Even though living standards have improved in recent decades, physical labor and poverty remain the harsh reality for many. Difficulty in understanding particular academic subjects or concepts is a routine hurdle for any learner. Finally, respondents were very clear about individual differences in their natural capacity and acknowledged the associated impact on people's learning. However, there was also consensus that these obstacles are not reasons for not learning. Instead, ideal learners developed endurance of hardship, which would enable them to face and combat these particular obstacles.

The fourth virtue, perseverance (*hengxin*, 恒心), addresses a general attitude toward learning and a behavioral tendency in learning. Perseverance is valued because of the belief that there is no shortcut to learning. Knowledge does not come about overnight, but through a bit-by-bit, accumulative process over a long period of time, a process fraught with obstacles and distractions.[74] Perseverance is believed potent in helping one stay on the task from the beginning to the very end. It is a virtue required to achieve any serious learning.[75]

The final virtue, concentration (*zhuanxin*, 专心), is used in Chinese more often to describe a general learning behavior, not necessarily related to specific tasks. Concentration emphasizes studying with consistent focus and unswerving dedication. It also includes carefulness and thoroughness of learning.[76] Concentration is believed to be an essential quality of the learner because this disposition allows the full engagement of one's mind and heart in study.[77]

These five learning virtues are clearly related and form a whole. They all presume a desire to learn because without it, these learning processes and behaviors cannot be sustained. Without resolve and its resultant commitment, diligence, endurance of hardship, and persistence may be limited to sheer situational factors. Likewise, if concentration can be halted by "hardship" or if one lacks perseverance, one's resolve may be aborted halfway.

Chinese respondents also revealed other learning processes and activities similar to those revealed by their European-American peers, such as thinking, observation, participation in social activities, and talking to people. However, compared to their European-American peers, they mentioned those categories significantly less. Similarly, European-American respondents also acknowledged their ideal-learner's hard work and persistence, but their reference to these learning virtues was less central and consistent.

Kinds of Achievement

There were also three general kinds of achievement similar to the European-American achievement (Table 3.3), but the two sets of achievement standards convey very different meanings. The first one, depth and breadth and/or mastery of knowledge, is also captured in Figure 3.2 under "kinds of achievement." Whereas breadth refers to one's extensive knowledge of different disciplines or subjects, depth concerns one's profound understanding of one subject. Moreover, the integration of breadth and depth is also emphasized. Mastery may not highlight breadth and depth, but it nevertheless stresses possession of knowledge, and by implication, the broader and deeper such possession, the better. Mastery together with breadth/depth is sensible considering that the ultimate goal is self-perfection, which is open-ended and life-long in nature.

The second standard, application of knowledge, is reminiscent of the European-American personal problem solving. However, the Chinese emphasis falls on the *use* of what one has learned in real-life situations. The conceptual distinction lies in book knowledge versus knowledge in use. Whether such use is personal or social in origin matters less. This standard thus includes applications that may not be deemed as creative or insightful in any sense (e.g., use math to verify a bank transaction). The third standard is unity of knowledge and moral character, also shown as one kind of achievement in Figure 3.2. Consistent with the purposes of moral and social self-perfection, acquisition of knowledge for self, and contribution to society, achieving the unity of the cognitive/intellectual with the social/moral makes the elements compatible and harmonious.

These achievement standards are inherently related to each other. Acquisition of depth and breadth of knowledge can enable the person to better apply such knowledge, which in turn can broaden and deepen one's knowledge. So long as the learner also continues to self-perfect morally and socially, he or she will likely continue to seek breadth and depth of learning, which loops back to his or her ability to use his or her knowledge in life.

Affect

Chinese affect also contained both positive and negative types. Four positive affects emerged: (1) commitment ("establish one's will"), (2) love, passion, and thirst for learning, (3) respect and receptivity, and (4) humility for achievement. There were three negative affects: (1) lack of desire, (2) arrogance, and (3) shame/guilt for poor learning.

The notion of commitment, establishing one' will (*lizhi*, 立志), is part of one's learning purpose. This concept aims at helping the learner, often during secondary school, start pondering his or her life's purposes in order to come to a clear personal vision (*zhixiang*, 志向 or *baofu*, 抱負). In doing so, Chinese learners believe that they will not only find a more specific path to focus on (e.g., I want to be an engineer), but also know to what path to attach their energy and dedication (e.g., therefore I will study math, physics, and engineering). Therefore, the process of *lizhi* is a spiritually very uplifting and emotionally positive process.

Some European-American respondents also touched on personal ambitions. However, such cases were not described consistently as a deliberate and socially concerted process where the learner is urged to search for a purpose and to establish commitment to reaching it.

Love, passion, and thirst were described similarly as enjoyment among European-American ideal learners. However, a significant difference lies in the source of such affect. Whereas for the European-American learners, intrinsic enjoyment, curiosity, and interest were described as essential, this intrinsic source was not emphasized by Chinese respondents. In fact, many acknowledged that their ideal learners were initially not motivated or interested in learning at a young age, but they developed love and passion once they realized the importance of learning, or once their parents and teachers guided them into the process. This kind of formation of love and passion as cultivated and fostered by one's social world parallels the recent work on intrinsic motivation as less essential for Asian-American children for school learning.[78]

Respect/receptivity is another distinct affect that Chinese ideal learners express toward knowledge and teachers.[79] Because learning in the Confucian persuasion is not limited to academic learning but also includes social and moral learning, respect toward knowledge and teachers (that ideally embody the self-perfecting process) is sensible and expected. However, this general attitude of respect/receptivity among Asian learners has been taken as a sign of docility, obedience, and lack of critical thinking.[80] This is a misunderstanding. Asian learners' deference toward knowledge and teachers does not stem from their fear or blind acceptance of authority, but from their deep sense of humility. Instead of treating humility as a personal weakness, they regard it as personal strength and courage, because those who are humble are willing to self-examine, admit their inadequacies, and self-improve. Therefore, respect/receptivity and humility go hand in hand. When experiencing feelings of inadequacy, one's ego or self-esteem is not seriously threatened and in need of protection as may be the case among European-American learners.[81] Chinese learners believe that one can always self-improve so long as one learns humbly and respectfully from others.[82]

As alluded to earlier, Chinese learners' receptivity and humility may be very different from European-American learners' challenging attitude, especially in the form of immediate verbal exchange in the midst of a class or a discussion. It was generally the case that Chinese respondents made few references to such challenging attitudes toward teachers, even though their ideal learners did engage in debates with their peers. However, this does not mean that Chinese learners do not challenge. In fact, many respondents wrote that challenging old knowledge or advancing new knowledge was an important goal for learners in the end. But one is reluctant to engage in challenges until one has thoroughly understood the knowledge in question or mastered one's field.[83]

For achievement, Chinese learners generally display less pride even if they may be happy themselves.[84] This tendency is different from their European-American peers who usually feel proud of themselves and like to share their joy with others.[85] Chinese ideal learners were described as feeling a need to remain calm and humble. Relatedly, the need to be humble comes from the same recognition that learning is a life-long journey. Although others may acknowledge one's achievement publicly, focusing on celebration for oneself may be perceived as a negative tendency that pulls one away from further self-perfection.

The two negative affects are lack of desire and arrogance. The former shows some affinity to the European-American indifference and boredom. Lack of desire is the opposite of a heart and mind for wanting to learn.[86] Many Chinese learning-related terms refer to this state as being at the heart of any motivational problem. By using or hearing these words, learners sense disapproval and concern from their social world. Arrogance is also an affect that is the opposite of humility. Learners who achieve highly are believed to be particularly vulnerable to this inflated sense of self. Given the importance of humility in the Chinese learning model, there is little wonder why pride/arrogance is a great concern among learners.

Similar to their EA peers, Chinese-model learners were described as feeling a number of related negative emotions such as sadness and pain when they experience poor learning. The most frequently revealed emotions are shame and guilt both for themselves as well as their families.[87] Shame is a powerful and prevalent emotion in Chinese culture and is an emotion of disgrace or humiliation as in most cultures. However, it is also a moral discretion and sensibility that people desire to develop.[88] Thus, the meanings of shame and guilt shade into each other. Together they function to direct people into self-examination in order to recognize their own wrongdoings as well as to motivate people to mend and to improve themselves. Given that learning is geared toward self-perfection for Chinese lives, feeling shame/ guilt in poor learning is to be expected.

Chinese Model and Its Confucian Lineage

As alluded to throughout the preceding section, the key components as found in the research also reflect well the four key themes of the Chinese learning tradition as outlined in Chapter 2. Perfecting self, as the most important purpose of learning, continues to inspire Chinese learners as a whole. Although few college students in my study used the expression "taking the world upon oneself (以天下為己任), they unequivocally named contribution to society as a major purpose of their learning. This latter expression is the modern manifestation of the ancient "take the world upon oneself." They convey the same meaning by linking individuals' learning to a larger social and therefore moral purpose beyond personal benefits from learning.

With regard to learning virtues, the empirical findings virtually match the traditional phrases and expressions. In fact, learning virtues may be the most intact and potent survival of this Chinese learning tradition. Perhaps this is because learning virtues are more an individual psychological matter, and their cultivation and maintenance are not readily subject to political changes. The process of forming such learning virtues takes place via family socialization and teacher–student interactions modeled after parent–child relationships, rather than in receiving or embracing political ideologies. So long as the political and large social movements do not vehemently attack these learning virtues, they have little reason to change (e.g., consider the possibility that the emancipation of women from homes to schools and workplace may have intensified the transmission of these learning virtues instead of destroying them – there are now twice as many people developing and exercising the learning virtues in school as both genders are schooled).

Finally, none of the learning virtues and purposes of learning empha-size self-expression and verbal communication. Chinese learners appear to think and behave in accordance with the principle of "action is better than words." They prefer showing by doing over speaking about what they know.[89]

CULTURE-LEVEL VERSUS INDIVIDUAL-LEVEL BELIEFS

The aforementioned research that I conducted provides descriptions of the European-American and Chinese learning models at the cultural level, which is not to be taken as a model of individuals. These learning mod-els are considered as cultural models for two reasons. First, the models are derived from learning-related lexicons that are the properties of the two cultures, the languages that belong to the cultures, not to specific individu-als. Second, the derived ideal-learner images are not specific real persons, but rather two generalized ideal images, despite the fact that a sample of participants, taken as representative of each culture's learners, described their ideal image.

Each cultural learning model is recognizable by the members of the cul-ture. It also serves to influence and guide (but not determine) the mem-bers' thinking and action in learning. Individual learning beliefs are not termed as models because they are specific to individuals. Their own beliefs may differ from their cultural model as a function of social categories such as gender, socioeconomic status, and region of residence, by context (e.g., political turmoil and increased educational opportunities), as well as by other changing factors such as age and role (e.g., parent versus student). Although cultural models do evolve over time, they tend to be stable rela-tive to individual-level beliefs, which can change more rapidly as a result of changed circumstances or development of the person.

NOTES

1. See Mangan, J. A. (Ed.). (1994). *A significant social revolution: Cross-cultural aspects of the evolution of compulsory education.* London: Woborn for a com-parative account of compulsory education in the West; and see Toch, T. (1991). *In the name of excellence.* New York: Oxford University Press for an account of how the educational standard of excellence for all emerged in recent years in the United States.
2. See reference in note 70, Chapter 2 for details. Also see Wong, N.-Y., Han, J.-W., & Lee, P.-Y. (2004). The mathematics curriculum: Toward Globalization

or Westernization? In L.-H. Fan, N.-Y. Wong, J.-F Cai, S.-Q. Li, & T.-Y. Tso (Eds.), *How Chinese learn mathematics: Perspectives from insiders* (pp. 27–64). Singapore: World Scientific for a comprehensive review of the similarity in current East Asian and Western mathematics curriculum.

3. See National Center for Education Development Research (2001). *2001 年中國 教育綠皮書* [2001 green paper on education in China: Annual report on policies of China's education]. Beijing, China: Educational Science Publishing for information on China's compulsory education law and its implementation.

4. See Chen, F.-N. (2005). Residential patterns of parents and their married children in contemporary China: A life course approach. *Population Research & Policy Review, 24*(2), 125–148 for research on how grandparents still care for their grandchildren and married children still care for their ailing parents. See Li, J., Holloway, S. D., Bempechat, J., & Loh, E. (2008). Building and using a social network: Nurture for low-income Chinese American adolescents' learning. In H. Yoshikawa & N. Way (Eds.), *Beyond families and schools: How broader social contexts shape the adjustment of children and youth in immigrant families* (pp. 7–25). New Directions in Child and Adolescent Development Series. R. W. Larson & L. A. Jensen (Series Eds.). San Francisco, CA: Jossey-Bass for research on extended family's co-parenting of Chinese American children.

5. See Coley, R. J. (2002). *An uneven start: Indicators of inequality in school readiness.* Princeton, NJ: ETS for the differences in school readiness as a function of the first few years of home life.

6. See Li, J. (2004). Learning as a task and a virtue: U.S. and Chinese preschoolers explain learning. *Developmental Psychology, 40*(4), 595–605; and Li, J., & Wang, Q. (2004). Perceptions of achievement and achieving peers in U.S. and Chinese kindergartners. *Social Development, 13*(3), 413–436 for research reports on differences in learning beliefs between EA and Chinese preschoolers.

7. See Kim, U., & Park, Y. S. (2008). Cognitive, relational and social basis of academic achievement in Confucian cultures: Psychological, indigenous and cultural perspectives. In R. Sorrentino and S. Yamaguchi (Eds.), *Handbook of motivation and cognition across cultures* (pp. 491–515). New York: Elsevier for a discussion on home-school compatibility in East Asian societies. See Hill, N. E. (2009). Culturally based world views, family processes, and family-school interactions. In S. L. Christenson & A. Reschly (Eds.), *Handbook of School-Family Partnerships* (pp. 101–127). New York: Routledge for a review of home-school incompatibility among U.S. ethnic groups.

8. See An, S.-H. (2004). Capturing the Chinese way of teaching: The learning-questioning and learning-reviewing instructional model. In L.-H. Fan, N.-Y. Wong, J.-F Cai, S.-Q. Li, & T.-Y. Tso (Eds.), *How Chinese learn mathematics: Perspectives from insiders* (pp. 462–482). Singapore: World Scientific; and Wong, N.-Y. The CHC learner's phenomenon: Its implications on mathematics education (same book, pp. 503–534) for reasons Chinese learners and teachers still use long-standing Confucian learning methods to learn and to teach math.

9. See The Economist (2008, September 11). Huddled classes: How migrants fare in school, and what schools can learn from them (print ed.). http://www.economist.com/world/international/displaystory.cfm?story_id=12208631 for the most recent report by Programme for International Student Assessment (PISA)

of the Organization for Economic Co-operation and Development (OECD) on immigrant children from and to different countries. Among the four sending countries – Turkey, former Soviet Union, ex-Yugoslavia, and China – the first three showed large variability with regard to where the students came from, where they landed, what language they spoke at home, and what SES their families had. However, Chinese immigrant children achieved highest irrespective of these factors. That Chinese children in Macau, Hong Kong, New Zealand, and Australia continue to achieve well cannot be attributed to the particular regions they came from, their host countries, schools they attended there, and their SES levels. The head of OECD, Andreas Schleicher remarked: "[I]n general, socio-economic status has less impact in East Asian countries than in Western European ones." If these key factors did not impact Chinese learners, then we are compelled to look somewhere else to explain their learning. I suggest that the way in which Chinese parents socialize their children and the way Chinese learners engage in learning may be crucial. See also Ran, A. (2001). Traveling on parallel tracks: Chinese parents and English teachers. *Educational Research, 43*, 311–328 for clashes between immigrant Chinese parents and British teachers' expectations of children's learning. See Zhou, M., & Kim, S. S. (2006). Community forces, social capital, and educational achievement: The case of supplementary education in the Chinese and Korean immigrant communities. *Harvard Educational Review, 76*, 1–29 for manifestations of Confucian learning values among Chinese and Korean immigrant families in the United States.

10. Qin, D. B. (2008). The other side of the model minority story: Understanding psychological and social adjustment of Chinese American students. In G. Li & L. Wang (Eds.), *Model minority myths revisited: An interdisciplinary approach to demystifying Asian American education experiences* (pp. 133–156). Charlotte, NC: Information Age.

11. Holman, R. L. (1991, December 21). Exam hell linked to depression. *Wall Street Journal*, (*Eastern ed.*). New York: Dec. 26, p. 4.

12. Crystal, D. S., Chen, C.-S., Fuligni, A. J., Stevenson, H. W., Hsu, C. –C., Ko, H.-J., Kitamura, S., & Kimura, S. (1994). Psychological maladjustment and academic achievement: A cross-cultural study of Japanese, Chinese, and American high school students. *Child Development, 65*, 738–753. Also see first reference in note 7 to this chapter for empirical findings on Korean adolescents.

13. See U.S. National Survey on Drug Use and Health (2005). *The NSDUH report*. Retrieved July 8, 2009 from http://www.oas.samhsa.gov/2k5/suicide/suicide. htm for the data provided by the Office of Applied Studies of Substance Abuse and Mental Health Services Administration, U.S. Department of Health and Human Services.

14. See the second reference in note 4 to this chapter for research reporting that 95% of low-income Chinese immigrant students indicated that their parents regard learning as the *only* way to a good life. Most of these students acknowledged pressure from their parents. While some did not like the pressure, none disagreed with their parents' emphasis on education. Also see, for example, Takeuchi, D. T., Chung, R. C. Y., Lin, K. M. et al. (1998). Lifetime and twelve-month prevalence rates of major depressive episodes and dysthymia among Chinese Americans in Log Angeles. *American Journal of Psychiatry, 155*,

1407–1414 for a research report on lower rates of mental illness among Asian Americans in the United States.

15. See Qin, D. B.-L. (2008). Doing well vs. feeling well: Understanding family dynamics and the psychological adjustment of Chinese immigrant adolescent. *Journal of Youth and Adolescence, 37*(1), 22–35 for a qualitative study on socioemotional adjustment problems of some immigrant adolescents. Qin compared those who adjusted well with those who did not. See also Tseng, V., & Fuligni, A. J. (2000). Parent–adolescent language use and relationships among immigrant families with East Asian, Filipino, and Latin American Backgrounds. *Journal of Marriage and the Family, 62,* 465–476; and Wu, C.-X., & Chao, R. K. (2005). Intergenerational cultural conflicts in norms of parental warmth among Chinese American immigrants. *International Journal of Behavioral Development, 29*(6), 516–523 for attempts to explain factors related to Asian immigrant youth adjustment problems.

16. Ishisada, M. (1974). The civil service examination: China's examination hell. *Chinese Education, 7,* 1–74.

17. Peng, S. (1998, July). Communication at Meeting of Chinese American Educational Research and Development Association, Chicago, IL.

18. LeVine, R. A. (1974). Parental goals: A cross cultural view. In H. J. Leichter (Ed.), *The family as educator* (pp. 52–65). New York: Teachers College Press.

19. McClelland, D. C. (1963). Motivational pattern in Southeast Asia with special reference to the Chinese case. *Journal of Social Issues, 19*(1), 6–19.

20. Medrich, E. A., & Griffith, J. E. (1992). *International mathematics and science assessment: What have we learned?* Washington, DC: U.S. Department of Education. Note that other than Japan and Hong Kong, other East Asian countries did not participate in the studies until later in the 1990s.

21. Their results were summarized in their influential book: Stevenson, H. W., & Stigler, J. W. (1992). *The learning gap.* New York: Simon & Schuster. Interested readers may look at the empirical details in their references.

22. See note 21 to this chapter.

23. White, M. I., & LeVine, R. A. (1987). What is an "ii ko" (good child)? In H. Stevenson, H. Azuma, & H. Kenji (Eds.). *Child development in Japan* (pp. 55–62). New York: Freeman; and Holloway, S. D. (1988). Concepts of ability and effort in Japan and the US. *Review of Educational Research, 58,* 327–345.

24. Hau, K. T., & Salili, F. (1991). Structure and semantic differential placement of specific causes: Academic causal attributions by Chinese students in Hong Kong. *International Journal of Psychology, 26,* 175–193; and Salili F., & Hau, K. T. (1994). The effect of teachers' evaluative feedback on Chinese students' perception of ability: A cultural and situational analysis. *Educational Studies, 20,* 223–236.

25. McKnight, C. C., Crosswhite, F. J., Dossey, J. A., Kifer, E., Swafford, J. O., Travers, K. J., & Cooney, T. J. (1987). *The underachieving curriculum: Assessing U. S. school mathematics from an international perspective.* Champaign, IL: Stipes.

26. Tobin, J. J., Wu, D. Y. H., & Davidson, D. H. (1989). *Preschool in three cultures: Japan, China, and the United States.* New Haven, CT: Yale University Press.

27. Lewis, C. C. (1995). *Educating hearts and minds: Reflections on Japanese preschool and elementary education.* New York: Cambridge University Press.

28. Hess, R. D., & Azuma, H. (1991). Cultural support for schooling: Contrasts between Japan and the United States. *Educational Researcher, 20*(9), 2–8.
29. Kobayashi, Y. (1994). Conceptual acquisition and change through social interaction. *Human Development, 37*, 232–241; Matsushita, K. (1994). Acquiring mathematical knowledge through semantic and pragmatic problem solving. *Human Development, 37*, 220–232; and Inagaki, K., Hatano, G., & Morita, E. (1998). Construction of mathematical knowledge through whole-class discussion. *Learning and Instruction, 8*, 503–526.
30. Stigler, J. W., & Hiebert J. (1999). *The teaching gap: Best ideas from the world's teachers for improving education in the classroom.* New York: The Free Press.
31. Au, T. K. F., & Harackiewicz, J. M. (1986). The effects of perceived parental expectations on Chinese children's mathematics performance. *Merrill-Palmer Quarterly, 32*(4), 383–392; Hess, R. D., Chang, C.-M., & McDevitt, T. M. (1987). Cultural variations in family belief about children's performance in mathematics: Comparisons among People's Republic of China, Chinese American, and Caucasian-American families. *Journal of Educational Psychology, 79*, 179–188; and Yao, E. (1985). A comparison of family characteristics of Asian-American and Anglo-American high achievers. *International Journal of Comparative Sociology, 26*(34), 198–208.
32. Gonzales, P., William, T., Jocylin, L., Roey, S., Kastberg, D., & Brewalt, S. (2008). *Highlights from TISMM 2007.* Washington, DC: National Center for Education Statistics; Organization for Economic Co-operation and Development (OECD) (2003). *Education at a glance: OECD indicators 2003.* Paris, OECD; OECD (2006). *Education at a glance: OECO indicators 2006.* Paris: OECD. In the study entitled *International Assessment of Educational Progress (IAEP)* as conducted by the Education Testing Service in 1990–1991, China did participate. Their students were ranked first in their math achievement; see Lapointe, A. E., Mead, N. A., & Askew, J. M. (1992). *Learning mathematics.* Princeton, NJ: Educational Testing Service. See OECD (2009). *PISA 2009 results: Executive summary.* Retrieved January 5, 2011 from http://www.pisa.oecd.org/dataoecd/34/60/46619703.pdf for the most recent PISA results.
33. See Gardner, H. (1989). *To open minds.* New York: Basic Books; and Ginsberg, E. (1992). Not just a matter of English. *HERDSA News, 14*(1), 6–8 as examples for such reactions to Chinese learning from the West.
34. Watkins, D. A., & Biggs, J. B. (Eds.) (1996). *The Chinese learner: Cultural, psychological, and contextual influences.* Hong Kong: Comparative Education Research Centre.
35. Watkins, D. A., & Biggs, J. B. (Eds.) (2001). *Teaching the Chinese learner: Psychological and pedagogical perspectives.* Hong Kong: Comparative Education Research Centre.
36. See first reference in note 69 to Chapter 2.
37. Cheng, K.-M. (1996). *The quality of primary education: A case study of Zhejiang Province, China.* Paris: International Institute for Educational Planning.
38. See second reference in note 9 to this chapter.
39. Jin, L., & Cortazzi, M. (1998). Dimensions of dialogue: Large classes in China. *International Journal of Educational Research, 29*(8), 739–761.

40. Gao, L.-B., & Watkins, D. (2001). Identifying and assessing the conceptions of teaching of secondary school physics teachers in China. *British Journal of Educational Psychology, 71*, 443–469.

41. Ho, I. T. (2001). Are Chinese teachers authoritarian? In D. A. Watkins & J. B. Biggs (Eds.), *Teaching the Chinese learner: Psychological and pedagogical perspectives.* (pp. 99–114). Hong Kong: Comparative Education Research Centre, p. 102.

42. Tang, T. K. W. (2001). The influence of teacher education on conceptions of teaching and learning. In D. A. Watkins & J. B. Biggs (Eds.), *Teaching the Chinese learner: Psychological and pedagogical perspectives* (pp. 221–238). Hong Kong: Comparative Education Research Centre.

43. Marton, F., Dall'Alba, G., & Tse, L. K. (1996). Memorizing and understanding: The keys to the paradox? In D. A. Watkins & J. B. Biggs (Eds.), *The Chinese learner* (pp. 69–83). Hong Kong: Comparative Education Research Centre.

44. Dahlin, B., & Watkins, D. (2000). The role of repetition in the processes of memorizing and understanding: A comparison of the views of Western and Chinese secondary school students in Hong Kong. *British Journal of Educational Psychology, 70*, 65–84.

45. See first reference in note 75 to Chapter 2, p. 250.

46. See note 28 to this chapter.

47. See note 40 to Chapter 2.

48. See first reference in note 75 to Chapter 2, p. 253.

49. See Conti, R., Amabile, T. M., & Pollack, S. (1995). Enhancing intrinsic motivation, learning, and creativity. *Personality and Social Psychology Bulletin, 21*, 1107–1116; Deci, E. L., & Ryan, R. M. (1985). *Intrinsic motivation and self-determination in human behavior.* New York: Academic Press; and Hennessey, B. A., & Amabile, T. M. (1998). Reward, intrinsic motivation, and creativity. *American Psychologist, 53*, 674–675 for a sample of this well-established line of research in psychology.

50. Iyengar, S. S., & Lepper, M. R. (1999). Rethinking the value of choice: A cultural perspective on intrinsic motivation. *Journal of Personality and Social Psychology, 76*, 349–366; and Bao, X.-H., & Lam, S.-F. (2008). Who makes the choice? Rethinking the role of autonomy and relatedness in Chinese children's motivation. *Child Development, 79*, 269–283.

51. See Berry, J. W. (1969). On cross-cultural comparability. *International Journal of Psychology, 4*, 119–128 for a more comprehensive discussion of the emic versus etic distinction in cross-cultural research.

52. D'Andrade, R. G. (1992). Schemas and motivation. In R. G. D'Andrade & C. Strauss (Eds.), *Human motives and cultural models* (pp. 23–44). New York: Cambridge University Press; D'Andrade, R. G. (1995). *The development of cognitive anthropology.* New York: Cambridge University Press; Harkness, S. & Super, C. M. (1999). From parents' cultural belief systems to behavior: Implications for the development of early intervention programs. In L. Eldering & P. Leseman (Eds.), *Effective early education: Cross-cultural perspectives* (pp. 67–90). New York: Falmer; Quinn, N., & Holland, D. (1987). Introduction. In D. Holland & N. Quinn (Eds.), *Cultural models in language and thought* (pp. 3–40). New York: Cambridge University Press; and Shweder, R. A. (1991). *Thinking through cultures.* Cambridge, MA: Harvard University Press.

53. Rosch, E. (1975). Cognitive representations of semantic categories. *Journal of Experimental Psychology: General, 104*, 192–233; and Shaver, P., Schwartz, J., Kirson, D., & O'Connor, C. (1987). Emotion knowledge: Further exploration of a prototype approach. *Journal of Personality and Social Psychology, 52*, 1061–1086.

54. See Li, J. (2001). Chinese conceptualization of learning. *Ethos, 29*, 111–137; and Li, J. (2003). U.S. and Chinese cultural beliefs about learning. *Journal of Educational Psychology, 95*(2), 258–267 for details of these studies.

55. Forster, K. I. (1976). Accessing the mental lexicon. In R. J. Wales & E. Walker (Eds.), *New approaches to language mechanisms* (pp. 257–287). Amsterdam: North Holland; and Morton, J. (1969). Interaction of information in word recognition. *Psychological Review, 76*, 165–178.

56. See Wang, H., Chang, B.-R., Li, Y.-S., Lin, L.-H., Liu, J., Sun, Y.-L. et al. (1986). 現代漢語頻率詞典 [Dictionary of the frequency of vocabulary in modern Chinese]. Beijing, China: Beijing Languages Institute Press for the Chinese term, and see Francis, N. W., & Kucera, H. (1982). *Frequency analysis of English usage: Lexicon and grammar*. Boston, MA: Houghton Mifflin for the English term.

57. See note 54 to this chapter.

58. See second reference in note 53 to this chapter.

59. See note 54 to this chapter.

60. See second reference in note 53 to this chapter.

61. Li, J. (2002). A cultural model of learning: Chinese "heart and mind for wanting to learn." *Journal of Cross-Cultural Psychology, 33*(3), 248–269; and Li, J., & Fischer, K. W. (2004). Thoughts and emotions in American and Chinese cultural beliefs about learning. In D. Y. Dai & R. Sternberg (Eds.), *Motivation, emotion, and cognition: Integrative perspectives on intellectual functioning and development* (pp. 385–418). Mahwah, NJ: Erlbaum.

62. Bruner, J. S. (1986). Value presupposition of developmental theory. In L. Cirillo & S. Wapner (Eds.), *Value presuppositions in theories of human development* (pp. 19–28). Hillsdale, NJ: Erlbaum; Rogers, C. (1969). *Freedom to learn*. Columbus, OH: Merrill; and Csikszentmihalyi, M., & Rathunde, K. (1998). The development of the person: An experiential perspective on the ontogenesis of psychological complexity. In R. M. Lerner (Ed.), *Handbook of child psychology. Vol 1: Theoretical models of human development* (5th ed., pp. 635–684). New York: Wiley, p. 639.

63. See first reference in note 52 to this chapter.

64. See first reference in note 61 to this chapter.

65. Bandura, A. (2001). Social cognitive theory: An agentic perspective. *Annual Review of Psychology, 52*, 1–26.

66. Brown, T. (1994). Affective dimensions of meaning. In W. F. Overton & D. S. Palermo (Eds.), *The nature and ontogenesis of meaning* (pp. 167–190). Hillsdale, NJ: Erlbaum.

67. Buck, R. (1999). The biological affects: A typology. *Psychological Review, 106*(2), 301–336.

68. Atkinson, J. W., & Rynor, J. O. (1978). *Personality, motivation, and achievement*. New York: Wiley; and Ryan, R. M., & Deci, E. L. (2000). Self-determination theory and the facilitation of intrinsic motivation, social development, and well-being. *American Psychologist, 55*(1), 68–78.

69. See note 61 to this chapter.
70. See the third reference in note 1 to Chapter 2.
71. See note 54 to this chapter as well as Wu, S.-P., & Lai, C.-Y. (1992). 白話四書五經全譯本 [Complete translations of the four books and five classics into modern Chinese]. Beijing, China: International Culture Press.
72. See note 69 to Chapter 2.
73. See the first reference in note 54 to this chapter.
74. See note 44 to this chapter for related research on Chinese students in comparison with British students.
75. See the first reference in note 54 to this chapter.
76. See note 28 to this chapter for similar research findings on Japanese children.
77. See note 54 to this chapter.
78. See note 50 to this chapter.
79. See note 47 to Chapter 2 for research on Chinese respect as a positive self-conscious emotion.
80. See the second and third references in note 75 to Chapter 2.
81. Brickman, P., & Bulman, R. J. (1977). Pleasure and pain in social comparison. In J. M. Suls & R. L. Miller (Eds.), *Social comparison processes: Theoretical and empirical perspectives* (pp. 149–186). Washington, DC: Hemisphere; and Ruble, D. N., Eisenberg, R., & Higgins, E. T. (1994). Developmental changes in achievement evaluations: Motivational implications of self-other differences. *Child Development, 65,* 1095–1110.
82. See the first reference in note 61 to this chapter. Also see Tangney, J. P. (2002). Humility. In C. R. Snyder & S. J. Lopez (Eds.), *Handbook of positive psychology* (pp. 411–419). New York: Oxford University Press; and Exline, J. J., & Geyer, A. L. (2004). Perceptions of humility: A preliminary study. *Self and Identity, 3,* 95–114 for recent writings on similar concepts of humility in the West and related research.
83. See the third reference in note 29 to this chapter and also see first reference in note 75 to Chapter 2.
84. See the first reference in note 61 to this chapter and Stipek, D. (1998). Differences between Americans and Chinese in the circumstances evoking pride, shame, and guilt. *Journal of Cross-Cultural Psychology, 29*(5), 616–629.
85. Mascolo, M. F., Fischer, K. W., & Li, J. (2003). The dynamic construction of emotions in development: A component systems approach. In N. Davidson, K. Scherer, & H. Goldsmith (Eds.), *Handbook of affective science* (pp. 375–408). New York: Oxford University Press.
86. See the first reference in note 54 to this chapter.
87. See the first reference in note 61 to this chapter.
88. See the second and third references in note 51 to Chapter 2; and Fung, H., & Chen, E. C.-H. (2001). Across time and beyond skin: Self and transgression in the everyday socialization of shame among Taiwanese preschool children. *Social Development, 10*(3), 420–437.
89. See Chapter 8 for a presentation of the most recent research on speaking versus action among EA and Chinese people.

4

Mind-Oriented and Virtue-Oriented
Learning Processes

Given the cultural learning models, an important question to consider is how these cultural models may influence the *actual* learning process in which the members of each culture engage. I attempt to address this question in this chapter. Before proceeding, however, it is important to lay out different kinds of human learning and clarify to what kind of learning the cultural models are most relevant.

KINDS OF HUMAN LEARNING

It is a well-established scientific fact that human beings are capable of learning virtually unlimited things. Human learning takes place in many ways, and it starts even before birth. For the most part, infants and young children learn much about the world without being specifically taught; for example, they acquire vocabulary of their native tongue and social norms of behavior without deliberate adult instructions.[1] However, because it proceeds more or less without the need for effort on the part of young children or deliberate instructions on the part of adults, this kind of individual learning is not directly influenced by culture. It is instead testimony to the human capacity to learn.[2]

However, the emergence of human culture led to the accumulation of knowledge and skill, including all the tangible and intangible cultural artifacts (e.g., tools and symbols). This cultural development demanded a totally different kind of learning, one that requires effort from the learner and effort from the person who can impart the knowledge/skill. This kind of learning can still be seen widely in informal settings in today's world, such as a mother teaching her child how to feed pigs, or an older brother showing his younger siblings how to shoot a jump shot.

As knowledge and skills continued to accumulate and division of labor widened during the long preliterate human history, most cultures relied on *apprenticeship* as a form of learning. In this system, most learners went to a master to learn a craft or trade such as blacksmithing or pottery making. Apprenticeship learning took an extended period of time to complete before the apprentice could be regarded as having mastered the trade. The typical learning process was one-on-one teaching, with the apprentice observing the master intently and starting with low-levels of tasks and gradually taking on higher levels of tasks. Most skills were not explicitly explained by the master but were embedded in the activities. It was the apprentice's responsibility to learn the skill. Apprenticeship learning was also part of productive labor, producing tangible products such as tailoring and carpentry that contributed to the livelihood or the business of the master.[3]

While apprenticeship learning continued, human cultures also developed literacy, arithmetic, and other higher-level and specialized knowledge/skills. Such new forms of knowledge/skill enabled better human productivity and survival; therefore, transmitting such knowledge/skill became necessary. These new forms of knowledge/skill differed fundamentally from previous forms in that they could be written down on material (clay, stone, bronze, bark, cloth, and later paper) for preservation, unlike the previous reliance on human memory and oral transmission. This advancement of knowledge preservation also eased transmission of knowledge. This development ushered in formal schooling where such knowledge could be systematically transmitted to the young. The earliest formal schooling begun in the Middle East around 4000 BCE and in China during the Xia Dynasty around 2000 BCE, where young boys were taught literacy and other important skills (poetry, music, and rites, among others). However, before modern time, formal schooling existed only for the ruling class and the elite in the West and aristocracy in China.[4]

The learning that formal schooling demanded was yet a shift in kind. Reading, writing, and arithmetic lay in the heart of schooling, and they were encoded in intangible symbols that were abstract by nature. Learning such things was different not only with regard to content, but more importantly to the great *mental* effort that was required from the learner. Yet, learner's effort alone was no guarantee for mastery; a specialist, the teacher, was needed for ensuring such learning. The teacher had to achieve the intended knowledge in the first place, usually demonstrating superior mastery before he could be acknowledged and granted the privilege to teach the young.

When teaching, the teacher had to continue to exert sustained mental effort to ensure his pupils' successful learning.

With industrialization came mass education. For the first time in human history, formal schooling was not controlled by the powerful and the elite but extended to every child wherever the compulsory education law exists. Compulsory education is still expanding, and it is quite possible that such education will be realized across the globe in the foreseeable future.[5]

As knowledge grew more extensive, it also grew more abstract. Both the quantity and increasingly abstract nature posed great challenges to learning. How best to teach and to learn given the specific cultural heritage became important questions for many cultures. Western and Chinese/East Asian learning traditions were developed in response to these questions and concerns. As discussed in Chapter 2, the different paths that the West and East Asia followed resulted in quite different approaches to learning.

However, present-day formal schooling shares some common characteristics regardless of the culture in which education takes place. Two such commonalities are particularly noteworthy. First, the world has been witnessing convergence of knowledge, mostly because of Western contributions. Such knowledge has become the common human heritage regarded as important for any child to learn. Mathematics and science are such knowledge. There is hardly any current formal education system in any culture that does not include math and science in their curriculum. Second, formal schooling proceeds uniformly inside the classroom with additional learning assigned outside the classroom. This kind of learning aims at mastery in the most efficient way by the greatest number of learners. Regardless of how much inherent ability an individual learner has, any given learner is likely to spend much more time and to exert much more effort to acquire currently desirable knowledge than the same learner would have a century or two ago, regardless of the culture.

Still, as research documents, individual culture's ways of learning (and teaching) as formed in their long histories are unlikely to disappear even for cultures that have incorporated other cultures' bodies of knowledge and pedagogy. Instead, these culturally formed ways of learning may continue to shape how learners actually engage in their learning. What seems to emerge is that cultures retain the best of their own practices as a more basic learning approach while assimilating elements from other cultures in order to respond to new challenges of learning. It is therefore important to describe each culture's basic learning process. This understanding could help us appreciate the more complex process of borrowing and incorporation of new elements from other cultures.

LEARNING PROCESS IN WESTERN AND CHINESE CULTURES

In this section, I describe how each culture's learners typically engage in the learning process. These portrayals of the respective learning processes are based on empirical research on learners' self-descriptions and reflections, observations of academic learning inside and outside school, as well as observations of other but equally effortful types of learning such as painting, dance, martial arts, and playing musical instruments. Although some examples come from specific individuals, particularly the cultural icons of learning, I do not suggest that these portrayals represent the learning processes that *every* individual of the culture follows. The discussion is only meaningful with regard to general cultural trends and patterns as found by research, not processes that are undertaken by specific individuals. Neither are these portrayals about pedagogy and teaching – that is, how school curriculum is organized and executed and how teachers teach in the classroom. These portrayals are about learning.

Mind-Oriented Learning Process in the West

In describing Western learners' process of learning, I highlight the processes of active engagement, exploration and inquiry, thinking and critical thinking, and self-expression and communication (see Figure 4.1).

Active Engagement

From my study of the English lexicon of learning,[6] active learning emerged as the very first major category of specific learning processes.[7] It has the following typical words and phrases: *active learning, acquainting/familiarizing oneself with something, competition, experience, getting the hang of it, hands-on, learn by doing, learning it the hard way, practice, study, training, trial and error, and work.* As can be seen clearly, these are the actual activities in which learners engage. They are behaviors that can also be observed. What is emphasized in these expressions is the active nature of learning, not what is being learned or even what strategies are being used. When learners are said to be actively engaged, they are physically present, frequently with their hands and bodies, not just their minds, fully involved.

Descriptions of European-American ideal but real learners that I collected also confirm the active nature of learning. Many respondents wrote of active involvement in the learning process, for example, reading all kinds of books and newspapers, browsing the Internet, writing papers, performing observations, trying out ideas, and getting involved in activities.

Aside from these words and descriptions, it is a common scene in most Western schools that learners are highly encouraged to go to the library and get on the Internet to research topics of interest, to read books, to write essays and reports of their discoveries, to construct objects (e.g., a papier-mâché model of a volcano), to make models to demonstrate their understanding (e.g., a cardboard box showing the terrain and animals of the tundra), to do scientific experiments (e.g., lab experiment or following a hurricane's movement over time), and to document their observations.

Another common form of active learning is taking children out on fieldtrips. Entire classes of students go to real-life settings such as museums, aquariums, observatories, historical sites, power plants, and factories. Students take notes on site and discuss and write about what they have learned. A third form of active learning is the kaleidoscopic afterschool program. Many public and private schools offer many different kinds of programs that are, by nature, learning by doing (activities). Children learn crafts, such as how to draw, sculpt, play musical instruments, make books, make jewelry, dance, and play various sports. Finally, during the summer break, students also join camps and organized trips to other places within their country and abroad. Many such camps and trips are for fun, but many have a strong component of learning by doing.

The best cases can be found in many Western preschools such as Montessori schools, schools inspired by John Dewey's philosophy such as Shady Hill School in Cambridge, Massachusetts and Putney School in Vermont, and without doubt the much admired preschools of Reggio Emilia, Italy. What strikes visitors not from the West (and even from the West) is how much emphasis is placed on the active nature of children as learners. Sitting in a classroom to be instructed day in and day out is not the mode of these exemplary learners. They engage in learning with their senses, curiosities, experiences, and questions about their surroundings, human or physical, real or imagined. They draw, build, investigate, and design things in order to learn and to study them. For example, stepping into a puddle after rain leads to children's study of how water and mirrors reflect things. Children draw their images standing by the puddle or on top of a mirror, learning and thinking about what they discovered. These young learners also study man-made modern environments such as supermarkets by gathering information, by talking to store managers and shoppers, and by making suggestions on how to improve the stores.[8]

Children also have plenty of opportunities to be active in learning out-side school. Many museums are interactive just for that purpose. In other words, children are welcome to visit museums where they can touch things, take things apart and put them together, play, experiment, and explore. In Philadelphia, there is even a children's museum called the "Please Touch Museum" where young children are invited to start touching and playing with their exhibits as soon as they enter the museum. Children's museums in the West are exemplary in their effort to actively involve children in learning and exploration.

In addition to and oftentimes embedded in the observable active learn-ing engagements, there are a host of what is called *learning strategies* or *self-regulated learning strategies* that Western learners employ in their learning. These may not always be observable, but they are nonetheless very active processes. In general, learners use three kinds of strategies: cognitive strat-egies, metacognitive strategies, and support strategies as Paul Pintrich and colleagues labeled them. The first kind, cognitive strategies, are more basic. They include three specific processes: (1) processing of information from written material and lectures such as rehearsal (e.g., repeating words over and over and using flash cards to recall information); (2) elaboration such as paraphrasing concepts and summarizing readings; and (3) organization such as outlining, grouping, and combining previously unorganized mate-rial. The second kind, metacognitive strategies, also include three specific processes: (1) planning (e.g., setting goals and steps), (2) monitoring (e.g., one's own progress and understanding), and (3) regulating (e.g., allotting and adjusting one's review according to one's understanding). The third kind, resource strategies, include (1) one's time management (e.g., prioritizing one's competing tasks), (2) maintaining a conducive study environment, (3) regulating one's effort (e.g., increasing effort for more challenging work), (4) peer learning (e.g., forming study groups), and (5) seeking help when one needs it. These strategies have indeed been found to be commonly used by Western learners (more than Asian).[9]

Exploration and Inquiry

As detailed in Chapter 2, inquiry is of central importance to Western learn-ing. What then does the learner do when he or she is said to engage in the process of inquiry? The learning terms that were sorted into the concep-tual group *inquiry* in my lexicon study contained these typical expressions: *visual intake, visualization, questioning, brainstorming, exploring, breaking things down, experimenting, applying ideas, relating ideas, analyzing, problem solving, putting things together,* and *synthesizing.* These terms emphasize the mental activities in the process of inquiry that learners carry out.

There are many facets of the notion of inquiry, and all are important. First, our most common human experience in daily life enables us to notice discrepancies between our current beliefs or knowledge about things in the world and those of others, or discrepancy between our self-derived beliefs and those of authority (i.e., parents, teachers, scientists, politicians, media, and government). For example, as a case for the first kind of discrepancy, a child has learned how to swim and believes that everyone can learn how to swim, but her friend tried to learn and failed. The friend told her that she cannot learn how to swim. The child is likely to be in a state of realizing that her own belief and her friend's are different. As an example of the second kind of discrepancy, an elementary school student thought that lobsters were gigantic bugs when his parents first brought them home. He therefore did not believe that lobsters were edible, and in fact the idea of eating bugs was scary and turned him off. But his parents kept inciting him into tasting the delicious "bug." If the child were an inquisitive learner, he would likely wonder why a bug could be delicious as claimed by his parents, and perhaps he would want to find out why his parents did not think lobsters were bugs.

In situations like this, most people raise questions. When Western learners find themselves in this state, they are not only admired but highly encouraged to express their questions (not just keep the questions to themselves) and to look for answers on their own. Thus, being observant about existing beliefs and knowledge in oneself and in others and recognizing discrepancies are the first step in order for one to raise questions. Questions carrying the potential of prompting an inquiry are necessary before the learner can continue. This is why in Western intellectual tradition and pedagogy, asking questions is so prized. Being able to pose good research questions is the high point for graduate training, dissertation writing, and ultimately a successful academic life.

Curiosity and interest are similar mental states conducive to asking questions. A learner who is not curious and not interested in a topic is not believed to be able to raise questions, certainly not good and worthy questions for inquiry. When a learner is curious about something, he or she wants to know more about it. When a learner is interested in something, he or she moves beyond the momentary spurt of attention to which curiosity may be closely linked. For example, a learner with an interest in math is someone who likes math and is eager to learn more on that subject. The fine distinction between curiosity and interest in motivating the learner is not the focus here (the affective dimensions will be discussed in Chapter 5).[10] Suffice it to say that both of these mental activities and attentional states are likely to generate questions similar to noticing discrepancies. Curiosity and interest frequently do result in good and worthy questions that can lead to inquiry. In Western learning, curious and interested learners are in some ways more prized than the discrepancy-dependent questioners because their curiosity and interest are indicative of an enduring and highly valued disposition in the learners: inquisitiveness.

After raising questions, the learner may begin the process of *exploration*. This process for children, particularly toddlers and preschool children, is usually, barring any endangerment, unrestricted. Children are ensured freedom to explore anyway they prefer, be it something that happens to draw their attention or something that is their "obsession" such as a child being completely enamored with dinosaurs. Adults and teachers are deliberately hands-off, leaving children to wander off, to take apart or put together objects (and many do break objects), to ask questions endlessly, to make noise, even to make mistakes and get frustrated. Adults and teachers are reluctant to spoon-feed children with the "right" ways to do things or the "correct" answers to their questions because they believe that children's natural curiosity and interest need to be protected and promoted. Overly involved adult teaching in this process is considered as "interfering" and therefore stifling children's sense of wonder about the world, which is regarded as the most precious quality in children.

Spontaneity in children's learning is synonymous with their exploration. Children, particularly preschool children, are believed to possess a spontaneous thirst for learning. This belief rests largely on the scientific fact that children's rapidly developing brain and body enable them to perform many cognitive and social feats such as inventing words and other symbols and to imagine social scenes in their pretend play without the apparent need for heavy-handed instructions from adults. Preschool children are also admired for their innocence from conventional constraints. This is one reason why children's thoughts, expressions, drawings, and behaviors seem inherently creative to adults.[11] Some world-renowned artists – for example, Picasso, Klee, and Miro – were so fascinated with children's drawings that they imitated them and perhaps discovered their essence. Constraining young children in the classroom and subjecting them to the strong discipline of studying are considered inappropriate because this type of adult control makes children passive. Passivity in children is the death of exploration and inquiry. Passivity, therefore, is to be prevented as much as possible.

If a preschool in the West wants to be successful, the best way to achieve that goal is to make children spontaneous, lively, and exploratory learners.

A vivid example offered by Howard Gardner in his book *To Open Minds* can illustrate this precious process of exploring by their toddler son Benjamin and their strong effort to protect the child from being "interfered" with by well-intentioned but not so inquiry-oriented Chinese adult helpers:

> When Howard Gardner and his wife Ellen Winner spent a month in Nanjing in the late 1980's for studying Chinese children's arts education, they stayed in a hotel. There was a key slot for guests to insert their keys before leaving the hotel. Their one-year-and-half-old son Benjamin enjoyed playing with the key. He also tried to put the key into the key slot. But because the slot was narrow and rectangular, it was hard for the toddler to succeed. Since he seemed to have so much fun with this key and the key slot, the parents did not intervene, leaving him alone to engage in his exploration. But the Chinese hotel attendants and passers-by would watch the child, then show and even help him put the key into the key slot.[12]

One repeated reason that the preschools in Reggio Emilia are regarded as the champion of Western preschool education is that children are truly allowed to explore themselves and their worlds. These Italian children enjoy complete freedom of exploration. But unlike the incident described in Gardner's book, these children's explorations – including their movements, activities, questions, conversations, and other utterances – as well as their detours and setbacks are recorded, analyzed, and revisited. In other words, their explorations are valued so much that the skillful teachers actively follow up, support, and guide these children's explorations to the next level, bearing intellectual and artistic fruit. These children's drawings, sculptures, and other constructed objects as well as their conversations with peers stun the world with their spontaneity, sophistication, and beauty, yet show no trace of adult educators' interventions and impositions. Reggio Emilia once again demonstrates that there is no limit to how much children can explore and inquire even at preschool age.[13]

The inquiry process involving older children and college students is somewhat different. Older learners, too, are encouraged to explore and ask questions, but the actual process is not purely self-initiated and spontaneous with parents and teachers staying hands-off. School-aged learners attend compulsory education in most Western countries. This means that they must receive either a certain number of years of education (typically nine or more years) or they must attend school up to a certain age (e.g., sixteen in most U.S. states). Schools are usually charged to teach a curriculum of government-mandated content (e.g., subject matters), pedagogy (e.g., there must be instructions and feedback given to students), and achievement standards (e.g., passing statewide or national tests). Completely free exploring by students alone cannot guarantee the attainment of such a curriculum.

However, compared to Asian learners, Western schoolchildren still have much more freedom to inquire into many topics. Beyond sitting in the classroom listening to the teacher, children are often asked to build models. For instance, in learning about atoms, middle school children may be asked to learn the basic structure of atoms, and then go home and find household materials (e.g., yarn, cloth, dried noodles, plastic, and crayons) to build a model of an atom. Each child then brings a model built with different material back to school. This is a typical process of engaging schoolchildren in the process of inquiry. Without such personal exploration, children may not be able to gain such clear understanding of what atoms are and how they function. The diverse approaches by different children also serve to inform each of them that there are many ways to achieve understanding and discoveries.

Children also frequently replicate scientific experiments in class that were done by the original scientists who discovered the laws. By going through the experiments, children learn step by step how such laws were discovered. Oftentimes, children are given opportunities to vary from the original experiments in order to formulate their own hypotheses, gather genuinely new data, and draw informed conclusions. In other words, this learning process models after the real scientific inquiry. Moreover, children participate in science fairs in most schools, where they must come up with their *own* research topics without any teacher input and follow the inquiry process to complete their projects.[14] At the science fairs, they present their discoveries and the steps they took to make their discoveries.

In English and social studies, inquiry is also highly valued. Children's learning in these disciplines is not characterized by memorization, for example, of a whole model essay or poems in order for them to imitate. Instead, they are required to investigate and analyze topics. For investigation in a history class, for example, children may dress up as historical figures in order to reenact an important event, or they may build a set and present a short scene about a historical movement. Children may also interview real people who lived through the Great Depression or World War II and then write a research report about what they found. My son in third grade engaged in his English project where he was asked to imagine himself as a plant. His task was to observe and record how he-as-the-plant grew, what support he needed, what enabled him to mature, and what maturity entailed. He went to his grandmother's vegetable garden behind their house and found a bitter squash sprout. He decided to be that sprout. He went out everyday and observed how the sprout grew. He also watered the plant. He took notes on all of his observations. Eventually, this plant bore many bitter squashes growing from small to large. He wrote an essay about the sprout's growth and its life stages. In this type of learning, inquiry as inspired by great scientists such as Darwin is still commonly promoted and prized in Western schools.

This exploratory and inquiring spirit is not limited just to school, but it also permeates the whole society, particularly children's TV programs and Web sites. As an example, in the United States, Public Broadcasting Services (PBS) presents preschool and school-aged children with many excellent daily shows that focus on engaging children in exploring and inquiring into the world, ranging from the jungle, the ocean, and space to the human world of cities, countryside, neighborhood, and home. There are also shows that teach children and teenagers how to design things and how to find out about things in the world. Among these shows, *Curious George, It's a Big, Big World, Kratt's Creatures*, and *Design Squad* are children's favorites. Similarly, many commercial TV programs also offer shows that encourage children to explore the world.

Finally, the Nobel Museum in Stockholm keeps the autobiographies of Nobel laureates. A perusal of recent Nobel Laureates in physics reveals clearly that all of these scientific icons, almost without exception, spent their childhood exploring, investigating, building things, and tasting the fruits of their own discoveries. Here is the testimony of George F. Smoot, who won the Nobel Prize in physics in 2006 for his co-discovery of the blackbody form and anisotropy of the cosmic microwave background radiation. As a child, he was curious about the moon:

> The first pivotal event I remember in my development as an inquiring scientist began with a visit to my cousins, as we took a night drive across the state of Alabama.... Excited from the visit with my cousins, I stayed awake, looking out the window rather than taking a nap. I noticed that the moon was following us mile after mile tagging along like my dog but with greater speed and persistence. I asked my parents, "How does the moon know to follow us?" They told me that the moon followed all the cars, not just ours. I was intrigued and wanted to know how the moon did this. Was it immensely superior to a dog? My parents patiently explained that the moon was very big and very far away and thus the angle did not change noticeably as we drove for miles. They gave examples of near and

far objects that we could see along the way, so I could realize this for myself. I was impressed by how big and far away the moon must be but even more impressed that one could understand what they saw in the world and that it was so beautifully simple and clear when visualized in the proper way. It was a startling revelation that the world could be understood by simple rational evaluation.[15]

Roy J. Glauber, the 2005 Nobel laureate in physics for his contribution to the quantum theory of optical coherence, also wrote about his childhood curiosity and exploration:

[W]hen I was four, we actually had a radio. It occupied a wooden cabinet about the size of a steamer trunk. I remember insisting there must be a man inside it. He had given his name as Maurice Chevalier. Discovering that the cabinet top was hinged, I opened it and can still feel my bafflement at discovering within it only a few glowing radio tubes. Electricity mystified me throughout childhood and I vividly remember once at age seven trying to see what it was all about. Plugging lamp cords into wall sockets must lead to the flow of something through those wires, but whatever it was, one never got to see it before it was swallowed up by the lamp. One morning I awoke early, determined to catch sight of it. I screwed the wires of a short length of lamp cord into a male plug and inserted it into a wall socket, leaving free the frayed wires at the other end. There was a bright blue flash at that end, accompanied by a muffled bang. That was followed by silence, till my parents awoke and began wondering why none of the light switches seemed to be working. The fuse was easily replaced, but I never overcame my surprise that what passed so silently through slender wires could behave so aggressively.[16]

Although these scientists received great encouragement and support from their parents or teachers, it is clear that their wonders about the world and their inquiring passion since their childhood have been the real drive for their later achievements.

Thinking and Critical Thinking
As discussed in Chapters 2 and 3, Western intellectual tradition places heavy emphasis on the mind, and one great power of the mind is to think. From my lexicon study on learning concepts, the following terms were rated as highly relevant to learning and sorted into the *thinking* category: *thinking, critical thinking, reasoning, derivation, deductive, inductive, infer, free thinking, absorbing, challenge, challenging assumptions, contemplating, pondering, enlighten, expanding, internalize, introspection, realize, recognition, self-reflection, discovery*, and *understand*. This array of thinking terms refers

to different aspects, processes, and functions of thinking. Profiles of ideal learners also contain many descriptions of all kinds of thinking processes.

There are three levels of thinking: (1) pure mental processes, (2) thinking geared toward understanding, and (3) critical thinking. With regard to pure mental processes, the Western learner engages in reasoning, which includes more specific steps such as breaking things down, separating things, using logic (deductive reasoning), inductive reasoning, comparing, contrasting, and constructing things, as well as more general processes such as imagining, making connections, and synthesizing. For example, when learning how a particular plant grows, the learner may try to think about what the plant needs in order to grow: water, sunlight, and nutrients. The learner can then explore if these things are supplied to the plant in a sequence or simultaneously. After these initial specific thinking processes, the learner can then compare and contrast this plant with a plant that requires a different amount of water and sunlight and a different kind of soil and nutrients, to generate fuller knowledge of the first plant.

For achieving understanding, the learner needs not only to engage in the specific processes of thinking to master the knowledge under study, but also to go beyond. As David Perkins at Harvard Project Zero has advocated, learners must be able to explain a given concept or a theory learned from a lesson/lecture to themselves and to others with telling examples. Being able to explain something to someone else is a common way to demonstrate understanding. But learners do not stop there; they further try to generate hypotheses in order to predict related phenomena. Finally, they continue to extend their knowledge to similar situations either to verify their knowledge or to generate new ways to think about the original topic under study.[17] For example, when an elementary school student has understood how fractions work, he or she should be able to explain the concept of fraction and demonstrate to others how fractions are related to decimals and how the two can convert into each other. Moreover, when given new problems of fractions, the student can solve them and even use fractions to compute real-life problems such as comparing unit prices for products at a grocery store.

Many European-American respondents in my ideal learner study also wrote about these thinking processes. For instance, in the words of a respondent who provided descriptions of his ideal learner, a great learner recognizes "situations where information theory is an appropriate method and where it is not; [he] ... performs calculations and knows why the specific steps of such theoretic calculations are as they are; [and he] understands how information theory can be applied to various issues."

The third level of thinking in which learners engage is critical thinking. As stated in Chapter 2, critical thinking is a highly valued learning process as well as outcome in the West. Many educational psychologists regard critical thinking as the cultivated personal disposition that marks the pivotal achievement of a learner. Although this educational goal has not been widely realized for all learners, it remains as a high ideal in the Western educational agenda, which continues to inspire Western parents, schools, and faculty in higher education in their effort to instill this ideal in their learners.[18]

Critical thinking is defined generally as "reasonable and reflective thinking that is focused on deciding what to believe or do."[19] More recent discussions point to the four key components that are of particular relevance to critical thinking for our purposes. The first is truth seeking, a process that leads the learner to seek the best knowledge in a given context. When engaged in this process, the learner casts doubts about existing knowledge and asks questions. Typical of Western learners is their much admired act of challenging authority. In the pursuit of truth and in exercising intellectual honesty and objectivity, the learner is encouraged to pose pointed questions and demand like responses. Similarly, the learners themselves also embrace, ideally, others' challenges to their own thoughts even when the results do not support their self-interests or preconceived ideas.

The second component is open-mindedness, which is the process that keeps the learner tolerant toward different views and propels the learner to examine his or her own possible bias. The third component is analytical process that engages the learner in examining rigorously available information that is obtained from seeking truth (e.g., gathering empirical data). A key step is using the skill and exercising the disposition of weighing the evidence against competing information and personal preferences. The learner must control his or her personal likes and dislikes and honor facts. This process is often linked to the process of problem solving, where the learner is sensitized to conceptual and practical pitfalls and to the need to revise his or her solution proposals. The fourth component is the same inquiring process as noted previously where the learner pursues personal curiosity, taking steps to explore the unknown and to find out the answers to his or her questions.[20]

These processes are frequently echoed in the descriptions of the ideal learners. For example, one respondent wrote that her ideal learner would "openly question society ... why things are the way they are," and another stated that his ideal learner learns by "thinking critically about *everything*" (emphasis in the original). The best examples, however, are again found in the Western icons of scientists. From the Nobel Museum, we read that Leland H. Hartwell, who won the Nobel Prize in physiology/medicine in 2001 for his co-discoveries of key regulators of the cell cycle, recalled his burgeoning skepticism in his childhood: "I was an avid collector of bugs, butterflies, lizards, snakes, and spiders. I remember on one of these adventures learning to be skeptical of everything one reads in books. I had read that lizards do not have teeth. I had grabbed a very big lizard and stared in disbelief as it turned its head, displayed a fine set of teeth and sank them into my thumb."[21]

Similarly, Craig C. Mello, another recent Nobel laureate in physiology/ medicine in 2006 for his co-discovery of RNA interference-gene silencing by double-stranded RNA, wrote on his critical thinking about a much larger topic:

> By the time I was in middle school, I had decided to reject religious dogma altogether. The "absolute knowledge" offered, was in my view, inadequate to explain the world around me. Furthermore, it seemed wrong to claim knowledge based on one's culture or upbringing. I saw the leap of faith involved in religion as smothering dialogue, closing the door on non-believers and walling them out of one's society. In contrast, the scientific method with its focus on asking questions and admitting no absolutes, was and continues to be refreshing to me. Science is grounded on, and values, dialogue. It is a human enterprise that breaks down walls and challenges its practitioners to admit ignorance and to question all ideas.[22]

It is important to point out that critical thinking in the West is not a value-neutral but a value-laden act. Unlike the more pure mental processes, critical thinking presumes a stance the person takes toward the world of knowledge and learning. This stance is also a direct manifestation of the Western notion of individual rights to question and to investigate anything, in any context. The only originating force is the questioner him- or herself having a desire to question. Critical thinking as learned and practiced in the West is only possible when such individual rights are granted and supported. As discussed in Chapter 2, Socrates, as a trying case, a pioneer in Western history, took as his life's purpose to question everything. During his own time, he was *not* celebrated by authority, although he amused many, particularly young people. His method of "eternal questioning,"[23] his great legacy, was retroactively admired and reified only by later generations. But because he was not guaranteed the right to do so by anyone, he was condemned to death for "poisoning youth" and for not believing in the gods of his city-state. Similarly, Western history is replete with persecutions of heretics (e.g., Bruno and Galileo) who dared to voice different interpretations and ideas of religious dogma.

Self-Expression and Communication

Self-expression and one's ability to communicate with others is another hallmark of the intellectual achievement of a learner in the West. All the active learning, exploration and inquiry, and critical thinking need to be expressed and communicated both as an integral part of the learning process and as the outcome of learning. The great emphasis in communication lies in the oral/verbal expression foremost, even more so than the written expression, although the latter is also of central importance.

There is a long tradition of oral eloquence that dates back to Greek antiquity through the Roman era and Christian tradition of delivering sermons to congregations (Chapter 8 is devoted to this topic). Modern democratic, academic, and business life all require the ability to speak publicly. Oral expressivity is not only taken as a sign of individual intelligence, but a skill that enables one to achieve just about any goal in life.[24] Accordingly, one needs to express one's thoughts and feelings in order to make friends, to date, to do well in school, to rise up the corporate ladder as a manager/leader, to articulate one's concerns in community living, to participate in democratic life, and to defend oneself in court or other official proceedings should one face such situations. Given the essential role of communication in the West, there is little wonder why learning how to self-express and to communicate is an essential task of any learner.

My lexicon study on European-American learning concepts yielded these terms of communication: *expression, communication, discussion, dialog, participation, interactive, listening, connection, engaging, collaborate, involving, illustrate, diagrams, essays, debate,* and *critique.* The descriptions of ideal learners images that I collected also showed that 70 percent of the respondents mentioned that these learners engaged in talking to others, discussion with professors and peers, and otherwise interacted with all kinds of people in all kinds of contexts (compared to only 30 percent of the Chinese respondents who referred to communication and discussion as a process of learning).

The socialization of self-expression begins early in Western learners' lives. Research on early mother–child communication indicates that European-American children, for example, talk more than their Chinese peers about their own qualities, thoughts, and feelings. European-American children's self-oriented talk is longer even when their total talk volume is less than that of Chinese children for the same controlled studies (in comparison, Chinese talk more about social relations and activities rather than themselves). When recounting past experiences, European-American mothers ask their children significantly more probing questions about how they lived through the experience, how they felt, what ideas they thought about, and how their individual selves were affected. As a result, as shown in research, these children express a great deal more of these aspects of their life experiences.[25] Within the family, a commonly documented opportunity to involve children in talking and discussion is dinnertime when family members sit together. Many children and parents attest that this is a very important social context in which parents and children engage in free exchange of their daily experiences. Children are encouraged to interrupt adults and to ask questions; children also chat with their siblings. Again, these repeated occasions serve to promote children's oral self-expressions.

Preschools in the West also make a great effort to develop children's speaking and expressive ability. Reggio Emilia schools as an exemplar, but Western preschools in general, very commonly encourage children to express themselves. When a child utters an idea, that idea will be recorded, listened and responded to, commented on, and followed up by a teacher in Reggio Emilia. Frequently a budding idea by the innocent child will evolve into a drawing, a sculpture, a poem, or a scientific project to engage the child.[26] This kind of attention to expressed ideas makes children value self-expression and motivate children to express more.

Across Western preschools, teachers frequently ask children how they feel, if they like a given activity, and what ideas and suggestions they have about a topic, which echoes home socialization as noted previously. The emphasis is on both the act of talking and on self-oriented talk. To achieve this goal, it is very common for teachers to tell children that there is no right or wrong answers and anything they say is fine. Since the notion of emotional intelligence was introduced in the 1990s,[27] Western preschools endeavor to help children articulate their emotions, particularly negative emotions, into words rather than acting on such emotions. For example, if a child feels angry about a toy that he or she cannot get from a peer, the child is encouraged to say what bothers him or her and how the situation makes him or her feel, instead of taking direct action such as fighting, grabbing, kicking, or punching the peer in order to achieve the goal of getting the toy. When a child has committed a transgression, the child is likely to be asked to apologize *verbally* to the teacher or peer. Similarly, when a child receives a nice act from another child or an adult, the child is also highly encouraged to *say* "thank you" to the other (rather than to return a kind *act* to the other such as giving the peer a toy or candy – the latter is a more common nonverbal expression of gratitude in Asian socialization).

In grade school, while continuing their learning in verbal self-expression, children begin learning how to express themselves in writing. As soon as they learn how to use words and make sentences, they are encouraged to write about their qualities, thoughts, relationships, and feelings. They are asked to write their own stories, describe their own families, and present their own ideas. When they advance into middle and high school, children are taught writing skills for argumentation. One important format for developing such skills is essay writing, where children are taught to come up with a thesis to support, gather evidence, present counterarguments, and substantiate the merit of their thesis.

In middle school, and even more in high school, children also learn how to debate. In class, one teaching method is to divide the class into groups, each of which takes a different side of the topic/issue being taught. After the groups have mustered counterarguments against the other group's position or issues, the class meets again to start an open debate. Not only do students enjoy this form of oral argumentation, but they also learn an essential skill. In all public and private schools, there are debate teams for children to join. Children are also taken to tour through the towns and states in order to experience different audiences. Local, state, and national competitions are held. The winners are much admired and celebrated.

In higher education, particularly in the liberal arts, students engage in formal training in public speaking. Every university offers such courses, with many as requirements for graduation. Where no such requirement exists, students stand in line to enroll, attesting to the unabating popularity of such training. Such courses provide students with the opportunity to analyze great orators in history, such as Martin Luther King, and to write their own speeches to deliver to the class. Teachers and classmates critique each speech to help students improve their craft of public speaking. Other than such formal courses, most liberal arts courses require that students give oral presentations of their projects in addition to writing papers. Finally, Western learners are also encouraged to use all visual forms such as diagrams, illustration, videos, and sound to enhance their presentational impact.

These four key components of the Western learning process are also resonated in the descriptions of the ideal learners in my study. Taking these elements together, European-American respondents almost unanimously (96 percent) made references to such mind-oriented learning processes. In comparison, only 68 percent of their Chinese peers did so.

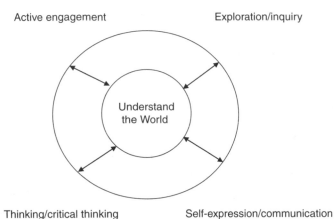

FIGURE 4.1. Diagram for mind-oriented learning processes in the West.

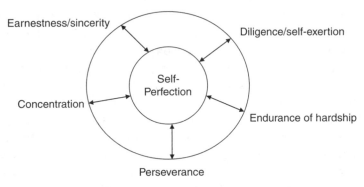

FIGURE 4.2. Diagram for virtue-oriented learning processes in China/East Asia.

Virtue-Oriented Learning Process in China/East Asia

In describing the virtue-oriented learning process in China/East Asia, I focus on the five key virtues of earnestness/sincerity, diligence/self-exertion, endurance of hardship, perseverance, and concentration (see Figure 4.2. Respect and humility are treated in Chapter 5).

Earnestness/Sincerity (認真/誠意)

As noted in Chapters 2 and 3, sincerity has been regarded as the first virtue in order to dedicate oneself to learning in the Chinese tradition. Sincerity was already clearly expressed in the *Analects* when Confucius discussed learning with his students. In *Mencius* and the writings by Xun Zi, sincerity was emphasized, but it was more centrally and clearly articulated as a required virtue for self-cultivation by the Neo-Confucians. Earnestness is the more modern term used to describe this initial commitment to learning that can also be applied to young children (sincerity as a term would be too abstract for them). Earnestness/sincerity means to take one's learning to heart and to be serious about learning. In other words, this virtue aims at making one instructable, teachable, receptive, and open to learning while putting one's ego out of the way.

How, then, do Chinese/East Asian learners demonstrate earnestness/ sincerity in their learning? My learning lexicon study[28] produced the following six terms/expressions from daily usage that give a first account of the process: *earnestness (認真), learn earnestly and make daily progress (好好學習, 天天向上), one shall not fear one's ability to learn; one shall fear one's lack of desire to learn (不怕學不會, 只怕不去學), a cause is perfected with diligence and neglected by frivolity (業精於勤, 荒於嬉), effort never lets down the resolute person (功夫不負有心人), and there is no difficulty on earth for the resolute person (世上無難事, 只怕有心人).* What these expressions have in common is their emphasis on earnest and sincere dedication as contrasted to lack of such (e.g., frivolity, neglect, and lack of resolution).

From observational research on Chinese/East Asian classrooms, it is clear that the learner, even a very young child in preschool, needs to cooperate with the teacher in the classroom. If asked to sit down, to listen, to look at the board, to take notes, to respond, and to do homework, the learner should do so without resisting such instructions. Learners need to give the instructions and learning activities their full attention. In this kind of cooperation, learners should not interrupt/disturb teaching and other children's learning, such as chatting with peers, laughing, moving out of a seat, or leaving the classroom while the teacher is teaching. Students' earnestness/ sincerity is needed not merely for their own learning, but also for respecting other children's learning.[29]

In such a setting, learning is taken not just seriously but also sacredly. It is not exaggerating to say that this seriousness is analogous to other children's "right to learn" and is imbued with all the moral meanings noted in Chapter 2. This "right" cannot be violated or taken away by anyone, even though there is no law to enforce this "right." But for the student inclined to disturb, it is his or her obligation to respect that right in others. Likewise, his or her own learning is also regarded as sacred and inviolable by other children. But because it is part of a strong cultural norm, there is no need to have written law for its protection. To use another analogy, this kind of commitment and seriousness in regard to learning is also similar to a

Western orchestra being conducted by the conductor who demands and actually receives the full cooperation and earnestness from the players. The mutually understood roles and responsibilities/obligations between the conductor and the players are guaranteed by everyone to such an extent that the whole orchestra would collapse if even one player no longer wanted to honor this cooperation. This resemblance probably made American education researcher Lynn Paine call Chinese classroom teachers virtuosos of performance. The kind of teaching described in her research was possible only when the learners exercised their virtue of earnestness/sincerity. Understood as such, there is no wonder why disturbing teaching and other children's learning by any student is regarded as a serious learning problem in East Asia.[30]

It is erroneous to assume that Chinese/Asian children must not enjoy such learning or that they must suffer from lack of freedom or creativity. Research indicates that they derive happiness and satisfaction and show enthusiasm even when they have to demonstrate their mistakes on the board and respond in chorus (a uniform learning activity instead of individualist activities).[31] Their joy and satisfaction are probably similar to the emotions of orchestra players when they produce a great performance under the direction of a conductor.

If homework is assigned and the student fails to do it for no legitimate reason, that behavior is regarded as lack of earnestness/sincerity. Further, even when the student does the homework but rushes through it, showing impatience (e.g., illegible handwriting) and carelessness, that behavior is also regarded as lack of earnestness/sincerity. Therefore, any learning behavior that is just going through the motions without the dedication of the heart, the affectively charged receptivity to learning, is interpreted as the learner not having earnestness/sincerity and consequently not being ready to learn.

An earnest/sincere learner does not stop at just following these basic expectations; he or she goes a step further. Ideally, he or she also takes initiative and seeks out ways to exceed such expectations. For example, such a learner may make a great effort to take good notes. To learn the material, he or she may visit a peer to ensure that his or her original notes are complete. He or she may seek out the teacher to clarify unclear concepts or resolve confusion. When learning that a peer may have deeper or clearer insights into the material, the learner may make an extra effort to learn from the peer. Whenever a learner endeavors to make sure that he or she acquires the skill or material in question and whenever the learner actually takes the various steps needed to achieve the goal, he or she is believed to show earnestness/sincerity in learning. As recounted in Chapter 2, the two students traveling from south to north across China to seek out Master Cheng's teaching and forced to stand in the snow during the Song time (程門立雪) were taken as a good example of displaying sincerity and dedication to learning (in addition to respect for the teacher). Thus, a great deal is expected of the learner in the ways of taking learning seriously as an initial engagement in learning anything from anyone.

Diligence/Self-Exertion (勤奮/發奮)

There are several terms in Chinese (努力/勤奮/用功) that are used very commonly and interchangeably to refer to the notion of hard work or effort (with the first term also commonly used in Japanese and Korean). Recall that the nearly 500 English learning terms I collected in my lexicon study did not contain either *hard work* or *effort*, but the Chinese lexicon contained 46 such terms that entered the core list (many more such terms were not included because of lower group ratings). The phenomenon of showing elaborations of a given conceptual domain in one culture but not in another was conceptualized as *hypercognition* versus *hypocognition* by Robert Levy who studied emotion terms in Tahiti.[32] Clearly, the conceptual domain of hard work/effort is hypercognized in Chinese culture (and other East Asian cultures) and hypocognized in the West (at least as captured and nominated in the learning terms of English). However, English *hard work/effort* hardly do justice to the many terms that refer to finely differentiated and detailed virtue-oriented learning processes of Chinese learners. To highlight this difference, I use the terms *diligence/self-exertion* instead of *hard work/effort* to discuss the various learning processes involving this virtue.

Upon careful inspection, the virtue of diligence/self-exertion describes at least three learning processes leading to three connected goals: (1) familiarizing oneself with the learning material (*shu*, 熟), (2) practicing (*lianxi*, 練習), and (3) achieving refined/perfected mastery (*jing*, 精). In the following subsections, I detail each of these processes.

Familiarizing Oneself (shu, 熟)

Familiarizing oneself is the first step to take whenever Chinese learners encounter new material, a new concept, or a new skill. Familiarizing oneself with the new material is necessary to ensure that the learner recognizes all the pieces, components, and details of a given task. For example, if a learner is introduced to a new song, a new poem, a new list of English words, or a new math proof, he or she usually begins to look at/read/sing each component. Next, the learner may begin chanting the poem, reading aloud each English word, or writing each math step to him- or herself, and he or she is likely to do so over and over again. Thus, we have the terms from my lexicon study: *one's mouth won't be fluent without chanting for three days; one's hand gets out of practice without writing for three days* (三天不念口生, 三天不寫手生), *well-versed in three hundred Tang poems, one will be able to chant if not compose poems* (熟讀唐詩三百首, 不會做詩也會吟), *familiarity leads to skillfulness* (熟能生巧). Familiarity *shu* is juxtaposed with its opposite state *sheng* (生/生疏), meaning rusted, unfamiliar, or out of practice.

The process of familiarizing oneself is believed to be the necessary first step of learning anything because it ensures fluency and first-level knowledge of the material. If one is to make any progress upon encountering the new material, the measure of it would be a step beyond unfamiliarity. Otherwise, one might as well not have encountered the new material at all. The idea of familiarity is not foreign to Western learners. It is the same idea as expressed in the common English phrase *having it at my fingertips*. The purpose is to make oneself familiar with all the "surface" details of a given learning task, not necessarily – or often even deliberately not – to aim for any deeper understanding of the material. The end result of familiarizing oneself is often a measurable achievement: memorization, or learning the material by heart.

Practicing (lianxi, 練習)

Practice is the absolutely central behavioral manifestation of the learning virtue of diligence/self-exertion in Chinese/East Asian learning. Based on what I can gather from available research, the notion of practice has four further processes aiming at four respective goals: (1) ensuring the length of time for practice that is perceived as necessary to accomplish the goal (e.g., the ten years in "ten years off the stage practice," 台下十年功), (2) reaching the desired cumulating achievement (e.g., the one minute in "one minute on stage performance," 台上一分鐘), (3) reviewing old material to gain new insight (*wengu zhixin*, 溫故知新), and (4) offsetting one's lack of talent and ability (*buzhuo*, 補拙).

Ensuring the required length of time for practice. After the learner has achieved some familiarity with the new material, he or she is likely to submit him- or herself to the rather prolonged and often arduous process of practice.[33] Again, my lexicon study revealed a glimpse into the nature of this part of practice: *lay down effort* (下功夫); *one minute on stage performance, but ten years off stage practice* (台上一分鐘, 台下十年功); *ten years of cold windows (studying)* (十年寒窗); *always have a book in one's hand* (手不釋卷); *never stop punching (practicing martial arts) and never stop singing (practicing opera)* (拳不離手, 曲不離口); *if you work at it hard enough, you can grind an iron rod into a needle* (只要功夫深, 鐵杵磨成針);

without accumulating small steps, one cannot reach a thousand miles/without gathering little streams, there cannot be rivers and seas (不積跬步無以致千裡, 不積小流無以成江海); *it takes more than one cold day for the river to freeze three feet deep* (冰凍三尺， 非一日之寒); *long-term diligence is the road to the mount of knowledge* (書山有路勤為經); *effort never lets down the resolute person* (有心人); *do one's utmost to self-study* (勤勉自學); *and Wang Xizhi practiced calligraphy (his clothes were damaged by his fingers practicing on them)* (王羲之練書法). All of these expressions highlight the key meaning of practice: The learner must recognize the importance of the long, dedicated process required for learning anything to which one has given earnestness/sincerity. Learning is not just a serious matter; it is a *long* endeavor. There are no shortcuts in learning.

Some of these expressions came from Chinese intellectuals such as Xun Zi and exemplary cultural icons of talent and learning such as Wang Xizhi. Most of these expressions reference ancient skill and artistic learning such as painting, calligraphy, martial art, dancing, and opera. Admittedly, such skill learning requires long-term practice regardless of time and space. A musician learning how to play the piano now would need to practice just as much as someone 200 years ago if he or she wants to achieve any level of mastery. There is also a shared view that any worthwhile knowledge/skill needs a solid foundation without which deep understanding is not likely to occur. Furthermore, such a foundation cannot be established overnight, but requires a long time. The most commonly recognized approach to such a foundation is long-term practice.[34] However, the impact of these expressions does not lie in actual skill or knowledge being learned, but a general adherence to diligence/self-exertion of practice as a *virtue*. As such, the learner needs to truly engage in the actual process of practice.

Keeping this long-term process in mind, Chinese learners work at each component, each key step repeatedly, over and over again, until they feel that they have achieved desired understanding or mastery. Then they move to the next component or step where they are likely to repeat the cycle of practice. Although there is much such recycled practice, it is not approached mindlessly, but carefully and attentively. Attentiveness and mindfulness are encouraged and admired.[35] With each practice, the learner needs to observe their own progress, although progress may be incremental depending on the actual skill or knowledge under study. Tolerance toward incremental progress is also important. A "great leap forward" in achievement without dedicated work is not believed real. Likewise, looking for tricks or shortcuts to circumvent this long practice is taken as a sign of lacking diligence/self-exertion. Moreover, the previously exercised earnestness/sincerity is not only expected to continue, but also to intensify. Because practice requires much more effort, earnestness/sincerity is assumed as an integral part of diligence/self-exertion.

Indeed, research on Chinese/East Asian learners in learning modern school subjects such as math and science documents that learners not only view the learning process as requiring effort over a long time, but they also engage in prolonged and repeated practice (with math and other science problems). For example, the well-researched topic of time spent on learning provides ample evidence that Asian learners spend much more time doing homework, reviewing covered material, and preparing for new material and assessment than their Western peers. They also spend much more time on practicing skills and materials outside class, that is, they practice above and beyond completion of assigned homework.[36]

Reaching the desired culminating achievement. All that practice is geared toward one goal: achieving understanding and mastery of the desired skill or knowledge under study. As the research by Dahlin and Watkins shows, Chinese learners, unlike their Western peers, do not believe that deep understanding or mastery comes from a sudden "ah-ha" moment,[37] although Chinese learners also experience such moments, as the term *suddenly see the light after being stuck* (茅塞頓開) indicates (which also entered my lexicon study). By looking at the terms in the preceding section, it seems that Chinese learners engage in long practice in order to get very deep and solid in their understanding and mastery. Consequently, one aims at reaching the condensed *one minute on stage* out of the *ten years of practice*, all accumulated knowledge from the *ten years of cold windows*, the *deeply frozen water* from many days, and the *thousand miles* from all the *small steps* as well as the *river/sea* from all the *streams of water*. Apparently, it is the breadth and depth of this result that they desire, not any small understanding or mastery. And breadth with depth is indeed a key goal for achievement in the Chinese learning conceptual map (see Figure 3.2).

But the question remains as to whether Chinese learners can really achieve this type of deep understanding and mastery. After all, the stated goals are rather vague; they seem more metaphorical and aesthetically worded than any real benchmark for achievement. If these goals are not obtainable, then why do Chinese learners still engage in this type of diligence/self-exertion? Two responses to this question can be given. First, it is quite possible that such learning goals can indeed be achieved, even though they may remain vague in the mind of the learner. Take the well-known case of practicing martial arts as an example. Even though one may not know for sure if one *will* achieve a high level of the skill, one still has a clear idea of what that end goal looks like, because the teacher embodies the skill. Moreover, one can see high levels of mastery in other highly accomplished martial artists. Thus, so long as the learner continues to practice, especially when he or she has been told that such practice was how the teacher and others achieved their mastery, that learner may indeed see that he or she can achieve the goal eventually. This is very similar to Western learners desiring to learn golf, gymnastics, figure skating, ballet, classical music, and instruments. Such learners exert effort not necessarily knowing that they *will* achieve a given goal. But they do know what to aim for because they know the accomplished musicians and athletes. They, too, are likely to engage in this kind of long, arduous practice if they are told that this kind of practice is needed for achieving anything in these domains. Learning other subjects such as math and science may also lead the learners to engage in long practice, because Chinese children are always given the causal link between long and hard practice and later achievement (whether such causality is true is beside the point). They receive this kind of deliberate socialization regardless of the discipline and regardless of how much talent a domain of work requires (see Chapter 7 for a focused discussion). Even great scientific discoveries are introduced to children as possible only when the scientists know the details of the topic and are deeply engrossed in their daily work.[38]

Second, in keeping with the Confucian learning ethos, the learner may not care much about the end goal because it is vague, and perhaps kept deliberately so (one wonders why Chinese have not made their learning goals measurably explicit for millennia). In all likelihood, learners may be quite clear that they *will not* achieve a high level of mastery just as they know that not all students will get an A in school. But as research shows, Chinese learners are still very willing and quite possibly happy to engage in diligent practice. For one thing, they know that they cannot get worse; they can only get better with practice. For the other – and most importantly – displaying learning virtues, as I have argued elsewhere, may be a highly motivating goal by itself regardless of whether the end goal of mastery will be reached. A learner's behavior is not judged retroactively positive or negative after his or her achievement has been determined, but as he or she engages in learning from the very beginning. Outcome cannot play a role because there is no outcome yet. Thus, showing earnestness/sincerity and diligence/self-exertion alone is inherent goodness and therefore reason for social reward and admiration. This indeed happens in Chinese schools. I personally witnessed the following scenario of honoring virtues despite low achievement:

In middle school, my class took a math test. I had one of the highest scores in my 60-student class. The teacher told the class that he wanted to honor a great student for this exam. I thought it was me whom he was going to honor. But instead, he asked a quiet girl sitting in a corner to stand up. Everyone knew that she was not the highest achieving student in class. But the teacher said "Class, let's give Yulin a round of applause for her great diligence for this exam. Although she did not do very well, her spirit is honorable. We all can learn from her."

The message from the teacher was very clear: It is not the outcome of one's achievement that calls for admiration, but one's diligence/self-exertion. The fact that one has given one's complete effort even without achieving stellar results in the process is cause for respect. In fact, high achievement or high intelligence without virtues is not admired very much. When asked to respond how their ideal learners would learn if they achieve highly or possess high intelligence, Chinese respondents wrote that they will continue to work hard to aim at even higher goals. High achievers would not feel full of themselves because their goal is to self-perfect for life.[39]

Ngai-Ying Wong provided a description of the Chinese approach to practice that further explains the point of practicing for Chinese learners. Accordingly, Chinese learners first try to "enter the way" (入法). For example, when learning calligraphy, a learner hopes to get a feel of the skill, that is, how to apply ink, force, attention, movement of one's arms, and so forth to produce similar work to that of the master that the learner admires (this is very similar to, say, Western golf learners trying to imitate a master). One will not stop one's practice until one can produce the desired result. However, this imitative perfection is only half of learning, not the end goal. Once satisfied with one's practice, one moves on to a higher level called "existing the way" (出法), retaining but transcending the imitative achievement.[40] A learner who has gone through both processes is said not only to have mastered the skill, but also to have developed a personal style. The latter is similar to Western classical painting. A novice painter, too, had to practice for a long time in order to imitate the master; it was only through rigorous practice that the painter could go beyond the original style to create something new. But this new style is also deeply grounded in the original master's techniques and skill. Thus, it seems that Chinese learners are quite methodical in their learning with the virtue of diligence/self-exertion.

Reviewing old material to gain new insight. Chinese learners inherit a strong principle, as taught by Confucius himself, that learning is a cumulative process. Anything one has learned in the past is actually not gone factually, but the learner may not benefit from that past learning experience if he/she does not reflect on it anymore. However, just thinking or reflecting on it may not lead to the best learning either because reflection is a pure mental exercise. Given that Confucian learning strongly emphasizes moral learning and practice, pure mental exercise is not regarded as the best learning; the learner needs to go a step further, reviewing the old to gain new insight. Thus, "reviewing the old as a means of realizing the new" as stated by Confucius is regarded as an important learning principle that virtually all Chinese children are taught to say and to use for their own learning.

This principle focuses on two related aspects. First is the review part. Accordingly, it is one's responsibility to ensure mastery and related further learning of whatever one has been taught or has learned. Review of learned material enhances familiarity, memory, understanding of the material itself, seeing the need to practice, and other related elements. By reviewing, one also engages in reflection, checking one's understanding, making connections, and synthesizing. The process of review necessarily leads to deepened understanding, hence the notion of "new insight." New insight as a concept cannot be anything else but deeper understanding. In fact, new insight is the real purpose of learning by review. Thus, from the very beginning, Chinese learning has been to aim at understanding and insight. The difference may lie in their focus. Unlike their Western counterparts who are likely to delve into mental understanding, Chinese learners focus on moral insight into self-perfection and other related learning. Confucius himself regarded this learning-by-review as such an important process that he considered those who could gain new insight by reviewing as those who could be or become teachers (溫故而知新, 可以為師矣).[41]

Review is thus a part of practice with the virtue of diligence/self-exertion. Furthermore, it should not be surprising that Chinese learners assume autonomy and personal agency in achieving this very high goal of learning. Teachers and parents openly emphasize review and provide opportunities for children to do so. In every Mainland Chinese school (and in most schools in other Chinese regions), there are scheduled self-study classes (自習課) every day, where students sit quietly in class, doing homework and reviewing what they have learned. Outside school, students also engage in review on their own. Research has consistently found that Asian students spend more time studying outside class and school than their Western counterparts. A recent study of Vietnamese and German students' learning activities also showed that Vietnamese students spent much more time reviewing material they learned in class than their German peers.[42]

Offsetting one's lack of talent and ability. In their informative research on why Asian students achieve better than American students, Stevenson and Stigler[43] found two key concepts. Whereas Western children believe in inborn ability, Asian children believe in effort. Research on Japanese education also indicates that they downplay inborn ability and emphasize effort.[44] The questions that I have heard people in the West ask often are: Do Asian people not know that individuals are actually born with different levels of intelligence? Or do they not care? If so, why not? These questions were indeed left unanswered in previous research.

As it turned out, Chinese learners are keenly aware of such individual differences, and they also know that these differences may give people advantages in learning. No one doubts that one needs talent to be a great athlete, artist, poet, writer, musician, or scientist. Few also deny that there are prodigies and wiz kids, and that some people have better memory, faster mental processing speed, more energy, ability to achieve higher work efficiency, and other superior abilities. It is also not the case that Chinese learners do not care about these important differences. They do care, particularly with regard to their need to know where they stand in their learning progress when they are grouped with high-talent individuals. However, they do not believe that just because they are not prodigies or lack apparent talent, they cannot learn much. In fact, they believe that they can learn very much if they apply diligence/self-exertion. They do not aim at becoming the next Einstein, but they can still achieve much scientific learning if they work hard. If, however, they do not work hard, then they can surely bear the consequence of not knowing much.[45]

In sum, Chinese learners are not oblivious to individual differences, and they actually care about these differences. They do not, however, care about them to the point where it has a debilitating effect on their process of learning. They do not lament their own lack of inborn ability, and they disagree that only talent can lead to great achievement. From childhood on, Chinese learners are exposed to many exemplars throughout history who have achieved great learning with personal virtues. Many of these exemplars had disabilities such as blindness, deafness, and other physical handicaps. These role models are contrasted with people who have "normal" intelligence, or even superior talent, but have not studied hard. What distinguishes the two kinds of people in their learning achievement is the level of exercising their learning virtues.[46]

Thus the fourth goal of practice is to offset one's perceived lack of talent or ability. There were two phrases in my studies that refer to this purpose of practice: *Diligence can offset one's clumsiness* (勤能補拙) and *the clumsy bird flies early* (笨鳥先飛). These phrases are told to children again and again, along with examples of real learners. If a person lacks talent or sufficient ability, that person will increase diligence. In my study on ideal learners, I asked the respondents to describe how their ideal learners would learn if they were not very bright naturally. Their descriptions indicated that their ideal learners would double or triple – and in some cases increase a hundredfold – their diligence (百倍努力). The respondents unambiguously expressed respect and admiration for those who perceived lacking ability or talent and decided to increase their diligence in order to achieve their learning goals.[47]

Achieving Refined/Perfected Mastery (jing, 精)

All that familiarizing and practice are not even the end goal. There is the ultimate goal toward which the first two processes are directed: refined and perfected mastery (*jing*, 精). Thus we have a set of Chinese expressions about this ultimate height of achievement that entered my lexicon core list. The first is *familiarity leads to skillfulness* (熟能生巧) *and skillfulness leads to eventual perfection* (巧能生精). While the first part has been written about quite a bit, the second part of the expression has not been discussed much. Refined/perfected mastery, *jing*, is a state that does not lend itself to clear definition or articulation because it is a state only the greatest masters can reach and display. This kind of virtuosity is found in every domain of human pursuit whether it is in Western, Asian, or any other culture. Other expressions show various aspects of this type of refined and perfected learning: *thorough understanding* (透徹理解); *refined understanding* (精通); *know something inside out* (滾瓜爛熟); *profundity* (精深); *striving for perfection* (精益求精); *superb achievement* (出神入化); and *reach the highest degree of refinement* (爐火純青). The goal is not just any understanding, but lucid and thorough understanding; not just mastery of the skill, but the refined/perfected skill; not just knowing something, but knowing it profoundly.[48]

However, the highest *jing* is knowing something inside out and using it *effortlessly* and at the same time perfectly. This way of working and performing has become the second nature of the person; it is the merging with the Way in both Confucian and Taoist persuasion. The best illustration is the story *Chef Ting Carves Bulls* (庖丁解牛) by Chung Tzu (369–286 BCE), Taoist philosopher and a contemporary of Mencius:

> King Hui of Wei had a chef named Ting. When Chef Ting was carving a bull for the king, every touch of the hand, every inclination of the shoulder, every step he trod, every pressure of the knee, while swiftly

and lightly he wielded his carving-knife, was as carefully timed as the movements of a dancer.... "Wonderful," said the king. "I could never have believed that the art of carving could reach such a point as this." "I am a lover of Tao," replied Ting, putting away his knife, "and have succeeded in applying it to the art of carving. When I first begin to carve I fixed my gaze on the animal in front of me. After three years I no longer saw it as a whole bull, but as a thing already divided into parts. Nowadays I no longer see it with the eye; I merely apprehend it with the soul. My sense-organs are in abeyance, but my soul still works. Unerringly my knife follows the natural markings, slips into the natural cleavages, finds its way into the natural cavities. And so by conforming my work to the structure with which I am dealing, I have arrived at a point at which my knife never touches even the smallest ligament or tendon, let alone the main gristle.

A good carver changes his knife once a year; by which time the blade is dented. An ordinary carver changes it once a month; by which time it is broken. I have used my present knife for nineteen years, and during that time have carved several thousand bulls. But the blade still looks as though it had just come out of the mould. Where part meets part there is always space, and a knife-blade has no thickness. Insert an instrument that has no thickness into a structure that is amply spaced, and surely it cannot fail to have plenty of room. That is why I can use a blade for nineteen years, and yet it still looks as though it were fresh from the forger's mould.

However, one has only to look at an ordinary carver to see what a difficult business he finds it. One sees how nervous he is while making his preparations, how long he looks, how slowly he moves. Then after some small, niggling strokes of the knife, when he has done no more than detach a few stray fragments from the whole, and even that by dint of continually twisting and turning like a worm burrowing through the earth, he stands back, with his knife in his hand, helplessly gazing this way and that, and after hovering for a long time finally curses a perfectly good knife."[49]

The phrase "the knife can surely find plenty of room" (游刃有余, i.e., accomplishing a task with ease), still used widely in daily Chinese, comes from this story. As can be seen, this level of knowing something and using it freely and effortlessly indeed requires much practice, much mindfulness, and much dedication. There is little chance that blind practice without engaging in careful study, attention to details, contemplation, and self-exertion would ever reach the level of *jing*. Moreover, chances are that this carver derived no less personal and intrinsic enjoyment and satisfaction, as well as admiration and acclaim, from his social world than did our contemporary masters such as Yo-yo Ma, Ben Kingsley, or Michael Jordan.

Having presented the intricate learning processes under the virtue of dil-igence/self-exertion, I wish to address the oft-condemned Asian rote learn-ing. When Westerners visit Chinese schools and observe how Chinese/ Asian children learn, they can clearly see the familiarizing and practicing process: Behaviorally, it is nothing more than repeating, reciting, and copy-ing things – that is, acts of committing the material to memory.[50] On the surface, such learning behaviors do not show any breakthrough in thinking and discovery. If the observer does not know that there is still a very long list of learning virtues and steps to follow, he or she is likely to conclude that Chinese learning is all rote learning. Together with the also observable teacher-dominated classroom and parent-dominated home learning envi-ronment, it is even easier to feel sad and indignant for Chinese/Asian chil-dren. There are no apparent freedom, creativity, exploration, inquiry, and self-expression – that is, forms that indicate personal agency in learning. Chinese/Asian learning appears indeed pathetic.

However, there are some major flaws in the reliance on such observa-tions (both empirical and passing impressions) alone. If what is observ-able is taken as mirroring what is going on inside the learner, then these observers commit the same error for which behaviorism has been crit-icized. Interpreting what is observed without checking with the learners' own experience, aspirations, and interpretations is a highly subjective act that is colored by one's own cultural and personal lens.[51] Here we have the perennial problem of substituting etic (outsider's) for emic (insid-er's) meanings. When I first encountered Western interpretations of Chinese/Asian learning, the prevalence of this problem was overwhelming. There was a complete disconnect between these observations and interpre-tations and my own experience of learning in China. Yet, such research has persisted to date.

The second fallacy in condemning Chinese learning is that researchers forget that much of valued Western learning is also similar to Chinese learn-ing, and such learning is foundational because it is necessary. As alluded to earlier, Western learners of piano (and other instruments), ballet, sports, phonics, many math problems for a given concept, introductory biology learning, and the notorious medical school beginner courses do just as much of this "blind" and "meaningless" rote learning and repetitive acts. There is likewise just as little freedom, exploration, inquiry, discovery, and creativity. And there just does not seem to be any way to avoid such learn-ing or to transform it into more creative and exploratory learning. Are we to claim that these learners are also stripped of their personal agency, or that they too must suffer from their teachers' authoritarianism? It is peculiar that once a genius arises, even after much of this type of foundational learning took place, the hard work of geniuses is usually edited out of the discourse of the accolades in the West (but not in East Asia). Sergei Bertensson, Jay Leyda, and Sophia Satina provide a telling biography on Rachmaninoff's early training for piano under Nicholai Zverev:

> Rachmaninoff and his peers, Leonid Maximov and Matvei Pressman, had to get up at 6 to practice piano for several hours. The schedule was not allowed to change even when a boy had gone to bed at 2:00 am the night before. These boys took turns facing the ordeal for the one piano in the house. When a note was mishit by any boy, the teacher would storm out shouting. And when he was out of town, his strict wife continued the drill.[52]

As illustrated by this story, hard practice is often a necessity at the beginning. The longer a given discipline such as philosophy, history, math, biology, or medicine has been in existence, the greater the accumulated body of knowledge that the discipline has, and, consequently, the more foundational learning is required. Learners eventually reach more sophisticated levels of mastery and excellence if they continue the so-called rote learning over time.

The third fallacy that such observers commit is to assume that what one observes does not change. When a Chinese learner is at the familiarizing stage, the learner is likely to show acts replete with repetition and memorization. Several days later, however, this learner may be able to explain what a given poem means and how the words and sounds are put together, which is a level of understanding and insight. In another few weeks, the same learner may have learned several different forms of poetry and may be able to compare and contrast the variations. Finally, after the whole semester, this learner may be able to compose his or her own poems. Whereas some early trials may resemble the masters' styles, later trials may be quite unique and creative. None of this later learning is the same as the first phrase of familiarizing and practice. Yet, the observer takes the one observed incidence in the beginning and falsely assumes that the learner is a perpetual repeater and memorization robot for the rest of his or her learning, not just for the given skill but for all learning throughout the learner's life.

The fourth fallacy that such observers commit is to assume that understanding must be immediate, either achieved immediately during the learning activity or displayed verbally or behaviorally, or both, by the learner. As stated earlier, understanding can have many stages and facets, some of which may even require cycles of thinking, reflection, practice, application, thinking again, revising the original understanding,[53] and so forth, which is the essence of reviewing as a means to gain new insight. Understanding depends on the nature of the knowledge, concept, or skill under study. I would argue that the understanding that is observable within a class or a given activity in a limited time (e.g., a class period of fifty minutes) is a low level of understanding that is quite possibly not very worth pursuing because it does not require deep thinking and dedication over time. The kind of understanding that Chef Ting displayed cannot be achieved and therefore observed within a short period of time. Rushing to label and condemn Chinese/Asian learners as lacking understanding during a stage when their teachers or they themselves do not even expect to achieve any worthy level of understanding is simply invalid.

Some researchers have tried to distinguish memorization for the sake of memorization from repetitive learning. Whereas the first kind is truly rote learning, the second type can be meaningful and can lead to understanding and skill refinement. These researchers further demonstrate that Chinese learners use memorization for creating a deep impression as their first step. Then they seek deeper understanding of the material. Ference Marton's team pioneered this line of research with phenomenological methods and collected learners' own thoughts and experiences. They found that Chinese learners indeed engaged in memorization, but memorization was not an end in itself, but rather the first step. With information committed to memory, they sought to understand the material. One student in Hong Kong attested to such a process: "[B]ecause each time I repeat, I would have some new idea of understanding, that is to say I can understand better."[54] Another recent study comparing Vietnamese and German students shows that repetitive learning is strongly correlated with deep learning strategies for Vietnamese students, but hardly so for German students. The researchers concluded that repetitive learning is not a mechanical and thoughtless activity for Asian students.[55]

It was a relief that researchers actually found evidence that Chinese/Asian learners were not just mindless learners, but actually were inclined to and did in fact understand what they studied. Of course, the need to find such evidence only came from the apparent paradox of the independent and repeated demonstration of Asian children's achievement in international assessments. In all of this effort, the worry that perhaps we would not find such deep learning that would vindicate the Chinese/Asian learners' methods also showed the power of the fallacious but unfortunately widely accepted condemnation that has been directed at Chinese/Asian learning for so long. The irony is that the learners themselves, teachers, and parents do not seem bothered by it. Why should they? After all, who would not admire Chef Ting in Chuang Tzu's story? And who would remain untouched by the young Rachmaninoff and his peers when they practiced piano in cold Russian winters with such discipline?

The virtue of diligence/self-exertion is the utmost learning process in Chinese learning that affords the learner a chance to be like Chef Ting and other masters. It is also clear that this process aims at a very long time-span for a very high level of understanding and mastery. Such a time-span and aim obviate passing observations of a class period or a child murmuring a poem. Practice understood as such may appear rote and boring, but to the learners it may be uplifting and gratifying.

Endurance of Hardship (刻苦)

The idea that learning is fun or should be a fun process can be difficult for Chinese/Asian learners to absorb.[56] Based on the research I have reviewed and done myself, very few Chinese talk about learning in this way, even after so many Western children's TV and online fun-orientated programs have been running in China for several decades (longer in Taiwan, Hong Kong, and Singapore). Chinese may accept some fun for young children's learning, but probably not for older children. Why would they not feel that learning should be fun? In my opinion, this stems from two related convictions. First, as discussed in the preceding chapters, learning is not just academic for Chinese/Asians; it is, more centrally, a personal moral obligation and commitment. It is a very serious endeavor. It would be odd to say that striving to be moral, to become a better person, or to take on the obligation for life is fun. Given this ultimate purpose, Chinese, in my view, rightfully regard learning not as a lighthearted process but as a weighty personal matter.

Second, this weighty matter has always been conceptualized and practiced as an ordeal that learners need to accept and to overcome, as expressed in the following quote from Mencius that a Taiwanese father gave to his college-attending daughter who wanted to quit her physics assignment: "When heaven is about to confer a great responsibility on one, it will first test one's resolution, subject one's sinews and bones to hard work, expose one's body to hunger, put one to poverty, and place obstacles in the path of one's deeds, so as to stimulate one's mind [and heart], strengthen one's nature, and improve wherever one is incompetent."[57]

However, this ordeal is not conceived of as a punitive, draconian measure, intended to harm the learner; rather, it is to guide the learner along the learning path. The ordeal is not supposed to deter the learner; it serves instead to summon and to test the learner's resolve and commitment. In stepping up to the ordeal, the learner forges personal strength and displays it to his or her family and community. This commitment also helps the learner accomplish the actual learning. Thus, Chinese learners are expected to engage in learning with the anticipation and readiness to face challenges.

Challenges, or any situation that makes learning difficult for the learner, are expressed in Chinese as hardship, *ku* (苦). In Chinese, this term also means bitterness. But bitterness is not something that overwhelms the person. Learning is the ultimate good, but the process is wrought with endless challenges. To achieve the ultimate good, one must face and overcome any challenge and hardship. The virtue that enables one to face up to and combat each challenge is endurance of hardship (刻苦).

To gain a sense of the kind of challenges that loom in the learning process, we can look at the expressions I collected from my lexicon study: *Endurance of hardship* (刻苦); *study assiduously* (刻苦學習); *study diligently and practice hard* (勤學苦練); *take great pains to study* (苦心攻讀); *endurance of hardship is the boat to the boundless sea of learning* (學海無涯苦作舟); *without bitter coldness, where does the fragrance of the plum flower come from?* (沒有一番寒刺骨，哪得今日梅花香); *the sharp blade of the sword comes from constant grinding, the fragrance of plum flowers comes only after bitter coldness* (寶劍鋒從磨礪出，梅花香自苦寒來); *there is no difficulty on earth for the resolute person* (世上無難事，只怕有心人); *a ten-year cold window (study ten years)* (十年寒窗); *Sun Jing hung his hair on a beam overhead (to keep himself awake for studying)* (頭懸梁); *Su Qin stung his thighs with an awl (to keep himself awake for studying)* (錐刺股); *digging a hole in the wall to borrow the neighbor's light (for studying at night)* (鑿壁偷光); *Zhu Maicheng studied while wood-cutting* (負薪讀書).

This set of expressions contains two kinds of hardship. The first one is the learning process itself, which has two further challenges. One is the length of time required to learn anything well, as discussed under diligence/self-exertion. The other challenge is the routine encounter of inherently difficult knowledge or skill that is worth pursuing. For example, learners face not understanding a concept or a math proof, or not being able to perform a specific artistic act. Giving up is not an option, so the learner has to accept the challenge. The learner will either spend more time on a given concept or performance, or seek out the teacher and peers for help. If such extra work will not lead to desired results, the learner will endure more hardship to double his or her effort. Each time the learner has to do that, he or she will take time away from leisure and likely experience such learning as overcoming hardship. In my interviews with Chinese college students about what hardship meant to them in school, one student shared a common scenario of enduring hardship: "I often force myself not to go to dance parties at weekends. I, too, want to have fun, and I, too, want to join my friends. But I have to let that go because I have to study. It's really hard, really hard (真的是苦, 真苦)!" But when asked if he felt regret, he said no; he was instead proud of himself for being able to endure such hardship.

As noted earlier, Chinese learners exert themselves also to offset their perceived lack of natural ability/talent. In my ideal learner study, lack of inherent ability was identified as another common form of hardship that such learners must face and overcome. Instead of giving up, one will spend more time, seek more help, and practice more. They believe that for a given amount of knowledge or skill, one can learn quickly if one is lucky enough to be born with superior intelligence/talent. But if one is not so bright, there is no use to lament over what one was not given at birth. Instead, one simply needs to increase the length of time and the amount of effort. One should focus on what one *can* do and try to use that to offset one's weaknesses. With this kind of attitude and work, it is believed, everyone will reach the finish line eventually.[58]

However, the most prevalent hardship throughout Chinese history has been poverty that learners had to endure. The subjects of the last four expressions on the aforementioned list are the cultural exemplars who endured great hardship of poverty in order to learn. There were numerous others who also belong to the pantheon of such cultural icons. But these four are representative. Every schoolchild knows these stories because they are in the textbook and are very popular readings for beginner schoolchildren, such as the household book *Three Character Classic* (三字经). These stories are taught to children in order for them to emulate the very virtue of endurance of hardship as embodied by these exemplars. The four expressions that entered my lexicon list are the condensed forms of the specific ways of overcoming poverty that these people showed. Here are the highly abridged four stories found in *Three Character Classic*[59]:

Su Qin Stung His Thighs with an Awl (錐刺股). Some time during the period of the Warring States (475–221 BCE), Su Qin was a very poor child. He had to do a lot of harsh labor to make a living. He had time only at night. But he kept falling asleep. One night he fell asleep at his desk but woke up by being accidentally scratched by an awl. He got this idea and used it to sting his leg whenever he got groggy. His family begged him not to do that again. But he said that he had to study. He studied all the books on politics and warfare and developed a new strategy for defense.

He persuaded six smaller states to form a union to defend themselves against the most powerful state, Qin. Su Qin became prime minister of the union that successfully deterred Qin's invasion for many years.

Digging a Hole in the Wall to Borrow the Neighbor's Light (鑿壁偷光). Kuang Heng, who lived some time during the Han Dynasty (202 BCE–220 CE), was also very poor. He learned the Chinese characters from a relative. During the day, he had to work in the fields. He studied only at night, but his family could not afford light. However, he was determined to learn. So he chiseled a hole in the wall to borrow the neighbor's light. This was how he read. Later he became prime minister of the Han Dynasty.

Zhu Maicheng Studied While Wood-Cutting (負薪讀書). Some time during the Han Dynasty, the poor boy Zhu Maicheng had to cut wood for a living, but never gave up on learning. Whenever he had a few minutes, he would study under a tree. Later, he put the book on top of his wood carrier and read while carrying wood on his shoulders. This was how he got his knowledge. Later he became a high official at the court.

Sun Jing Hung His Hair on a Beam Overhead (頭懸梁). Sun Jing, who lived some time during the Jin Dynasty (266–420 CE), had no time to study during the day because he had to do hard labor for a living. He could study only at night. He was afraid of falling asleep while reading his books at night, so he tied his hair with a string to the beam. When he dozed away, the string would pull his hair to awake him. This was how he gained his knowledge. Later Sun Jing became a famous Confucian scholar.

These learners were ingenious in inventing creative ways to study despite poverty, with some even using means not most conducive to their own well-being. Interestingly, historical records show that many family members could not bear this level of endurance of hardship and would rather that they not use such means. But these learners were determined and persisted. All of them had noted achievements in history. The message is clear that although poverty is very difficult to overcome, it is not a sufficient reason for giving up on learning. Additionally, endurance of hardship was indeed a strong theme in my ideal learner study. There was no reference to backing down because of poverty for any of the described ideal learners. The respondents showed much admiration and respect for these learners. This kind of admiration and respect is also extended to any such learners from any culture, for example, the young Abraham Lincoln reading by the candlelight and the courageous Frederick Douglass learning how to read as a slave boy.

Perseverance (恆心)

Perseverance and endurance of hardship are related virtues, but they have different emphases and therefore serve somewhat different psychological functions in the learning process, as noted in previous chapters. Endurance of hardship acknowledges the existence of hardship and the learner's need to overcome it. Perseverance emphasizes the completion of the whole learning process from the very beginning to the very end. This virtue is used to remove any challenge including, but not limited to, hardship, interruption (which may not be hardship, e.g., friends' invitation to have fun), disturbances, distractions, boredom, and setbacks. Perseverance is following through one's learning no matter what happens.

The expressions I collected for my lexicon study contain these items: *Perseverance (持之以恆); learning is like sailing against the current; it moves backward if not forward (學如逆水行舟，不進則退); utmost sincerity can break stone (精誠所致，金石為開); indefatigable (in learning) (孜孜不倦); study all night by the candlelight (秉燭天明); unremitting effort (不懈努力); and keep on carving unflaggingly, and metal and stone will be engraved (Xun Zi) (鍥而不舍，金石可鏤)*. These expressions point out that there are obstacles in learning, as captured in a metaphor, sailing against the current. One will not achieve much if small obstacles can deter one from continuing. No matter what happens, the learner shall keep on learning. With such persistence, one will achieve big things in the end, hence breaking stone. If, however, one aborts one's effort halfway, one will accomplish little in learning.

Long-term practice that was discussed in the practice section goes hand in hand with perseverance. Each time the learner is frustrated about not making sufficient progress, the voices from the self, teachers, parents, and peers remind one to keep learning and practicing. This process is identical to that of a marathon runner who may want to quit at moments but mentally pushes oneself to continue. The cheering crowds also give the runner encouragement and strength to continue. As a result, the runner finishes. Here is an example of such learning displayed by a Taiwanese student studying at one American university:

> Shirley was doing her physics homework one night. After having worked hard for several hours, she could not continue any longer. Her father called from Taiwan asking how she was doing. "Dad," said Shirley, "I have been working hard on my physics homework, but I can't figure out this problem, and I am tired. I am done for the day." Upon hearing that his daughter was going to quit, the father recited Mencius' above-quoted passage on how a person shall face challenges and persist if this

person is to assume great responsibilities in the future. Then the father asked Shirley to persist a bit longer. She did, until she solved her physics problem.

When discussing with me her family's support for her learning, Shirley expressed gratitude for her father's unflagging teaching of perseverance. Apparently, her father gave this kind of encouragement to her throughout the four years of Shirley's undergraduate education. Undoubtedly, Shirley understands what perseverance means.

One might ask what happens to children who quit. To be sure, learners quit all the time for all kinds of reasons. However, in school and at home, whenever a child shows signs of giving up, teachers, peers, and parents as well as the extended kin are mobilized to do what Shirley's father did: to reason with the child and to help the child improve. If the child does not have illness or another good reason, teachers and parents will show the child exemplary role models who persisted, overcame their inclinations to quit, and achieved their goals. Some of these models are historical figures, but others may be just peers in the same class. Chinese schools frequently hold a special meeting called "Exchange Study Methods" (交流學習方法), where peers share how they study and exercise various learning virtues. Children share obstacles they have encountered, particularly their own frustrations and difficulties, and specific strategies they used to deal with such problems. Hearing that one's peers also have these difficulties confirms that it is not unusual for one to experience similar problems. Children can learn from each other about how to improve one's perseverance (other virtues). When teachers see a given child make progress, there is often public praise for such improvement of virtue. Not only do such learning opportunities echo the importance of virtues, but they also provide specific ways to acquire and to exercise them in learning. These approaches in school help perpetuate learning virtues from generation to generation.

Concentration (專心)

The last, but of course not least, learning virtue is concentration. As noted in other chapters, concentration is particularly important in the actual learning process. If earnestness/sincerity is the overall virtue, diligence/self-exertion the temporal virtue, endurance of hardship is the hardship virtue, and perseverance the follow-through virtue, concentration is the virtue of each moment for each learning activity.

My lexicon study obtained these expressions: *Concentrate on learning* (專心學習); *devote oneself to studying* (潛心學習); *put one's heart into one's study* (用心讀書); *bury oneself in books* (埋頭書齋); *make great effort to study and research (努力鑽研); is engrossed in reading sacred books and oblivious to what happening in the world (兩耳不聞窗外事，一心只讀聖賢書); (so absorbed as to) forget food and sleep (廢寢忘食); and study with rapt attention (全神貫注地學習).* These expressions reveal a very high degree of concentration, attention, and wholehearted dedication to learning.

Chinese/East Asian cultures strongly emphasize contemplative learning – that is, the fact that the learner needs quiet time and space to study and to ponder. In classroom settings, children's undivided attention is demanded by the common learning topic at hand. Side talking with each other is not encouraged. Noisy environments with unrelated talking where the teacher is teaching and students studying are regarded as detrimental to learning. Talking aloud to oneself while studying is also believed not to be conducive to one's learning. In fact, the Neo-Confucians in the Song-Ming times borrowed from the Buddhist meditative practice to clear one's mind and promoted quiet sitting as a key method for concentration. Recent research by Kim[60] provides support that quiet learning is valued by Asian learners, and speaking while learning interferes with Asian learners' information processing (but it does not seem to interfere with that of European-American learners).

However, concentration is not an easy virtue to acquire. Chinese learners are keenly aware that much of anyone's struggle in learning is lack of concentration. This problem applies even to people who do not lack any motivation and conviction about learning. Today, neuroscience tells us that attention/concentration/focus is a manifestation of our executive functioning in the prefrontal lobe, which does not fully mature until late adolescence and early adulthood. Concentration is a clearly observable problem among young, normally developing children. And it is a tremendous challenge for children with the attention deficit and hyperactivity disorder (ADHD), a common neurological disorder affecting many children.

In order to help children, Chinese parents and teachers train children for concentration with a number of strategies. One of them is to create quiet space for children to sit down and to study without any disturbance. For example, teachers may ask a class of children to sit down and to count how long they can sit without fidgeting or moving away.[61] This training makes children sensitive not only to their own need for concentration, but also to how specifically they can monitor themselves. Another effective strategy is to have children practice skills that require slowing down and exhibiting fine motor control such as imitating Chinese calligraphy with exactitude (see Figure 4.3 for how a grandfather demonstrates rapt attention to his grandson in writing Chinese calligraphy), training for holding chopsticks,

FIGURE 4.3. A Chinese grandfather teaching his five-year-old grandson how to concentrate on writing Chinese characters with a brush. Courtesy of Heidi Fung.

and producing disciplined movements of martial arts, dance steps, and other athletic forms. A commonly observed classroom ritual is for the class monitor, a peer, to call the class to stand up as the teacher steps into the classroom. The class then greets the teacher in chorus: "Good day, Teacher!" The teacher returns the greeting "Good day, Students! Please sit down!" and "Let's begin class!" This ritual takes less than thirty seconds. Although short, it marks the end of the leisure time and the beginning of the serious and sacred class time to which all students' attention is directed and demanded.[62]

Parents also use various strategies to help improve their children's concentration. It is a common scenario in living compounds to hear parents instruct their children with the term concentration *zhuanxi* (專心) as "You need to be more *zhuanxi* in your studies" and "Are you not *zhuanxi* in school?" Our recent study with recorded mother–child conversations about learning in Taiwan indicates a much higher rate of exchanges about concentration than their European American mother–child pairs.[63] In spite of their very small living space, parents often clear off the dinner table after dinner and turn off the TV to ensure a quiet homework space and time for their children. When children are actually working, parents may stay nearby instead of leaving them to their own devices, engaging in a style of need-based intervention. When siblings distract each other, parents step in to remind them that they need to concentrate. This way, daily homework and review are done as expected because the time and space as well as the concentration are all ensured.[64] Some parents will even go a step further to help their children acquire and exercise the virtue of concentration. For example, when I was a child, our town had a semi-barter market system where farmers brought their produce and poultry to the market on a scheduled weekday to sell their goods and then to buy the goods they needed. When the day came, the whole town turned into a noisy, bustling market. My father used to put a stool on the street outside our courtyard and asked me to read a book without being disturbed by the market noise. I sat there and read my books until I was no longer distracted by the noise.

Those who demonstrate good concentration are not believed to have an inherent superior temperament or personality trait for concentration. Chinese learners believe strongly that anyone can acquire the virtue of concentration and everyone should. Students with good concentration are asked to share their learning experience and are admired. Other children are encouraged to emulate these models as well as finding ways to improve their own concentration.

The prominence of the Chinese virtue-oriented learning process received strong support from research conducted by others as well as myself. In my ideal learner study, for example, as many as 86 percent of the respondents mentioned one or more of these virtues. In comparison, only 38 percent of the European-American respondents wrote about virtue-oriented learning processes (but 96 percent mentioned mind-oriented learning processes). Another study on learning agency among current Chinese students from late elementary to high school also found that ordinary Chinese students in China endorse predominantly these learning virtues as underlying their daily learning processes.[65] Moreover, Chinese children as young as four start to internalize these learning virtues. The older children showed increasingly more such orientation.[66] Finally, the admiration that such displayed learning virtues engender in their teachers and peers is no less than the admiration expressed toward the exploratory, inquiring, critically thinking, and expressive spirit of Western learners.

NOTES

1. See DeCasper, A. J., & Spence, M. J. (1986). Prenatal maternal speech influences newborn's perceptions of speech sounds. *Infant Behavior and Development, 3*, 133–150 for a study on how fetal learning takes place. See also Brown, R. (1973). *A first language: The early stages.* Cambridge, MA: Harvard University Press for the documentation of lack of adult instructions for child language acquisition. See Rakoczy, H., Warneken, F., & Tomasello, M. (2008). The sources of normativity: Young children's awareness of the normative structure of games. *Developmental Psychology, 44*(3), 875–881 for research on young children's sense of social norms.

2. See Gardner, H. (1991). *The unschooled mind: How children think and how schools should teach.* New York: Basic Books for a review of research on how children learn before formal schooling. Human capacity to learn is most evident at birth. The fast mental growth in early infancy cannot be attributed to cultural influence because infants do not have enough time to acquire cultural knowledge. However, from the perspective of human evolutionary history, culture may have played an important role in its interaction with biology and thus may have jointly produced human learning capacity. See note 7 to Chapter 1 for more discussion on this process.

3. Smits, W., & Stromback, T. (2001). *The economics of the apprenticeship system.* Cheltenham: Elgar.

4. See Olson, D. R. (1994). *The world on paper: The conceptual and cognitive implications of writing and reading.* New York: Cambridge University Press for human literacy development. See Damerow, P. (1998). Prehistory and cognitive development. In J. Langer & M. Killen (Eds.), *Piaget, evolution, and development* (pp. 227–270). Mahwah, NJ: Erlbaum for earliest formal schooling in the Middle East; and Siu, M. K. (2004). Official curriculum in mathematics in ancient China: How did Candidates study for the examination? In L.-H. Fan, N.-Y. Wong, J.-F Cai, S.-Q. Li, & T.-Y. Tso (Eds.), *How Chinese learn mathematics: Perspectives from insiders* (pp. 157–185). Singapore: World Scientific for an account of early Chinese formal schooling. In the Chinese system, from the seventh century to 1905, all people in principle could participate in the Civil Service Examination. It is important to point out that only those who could afford education benefited from this system.

5. To be sure, ample research shows that just because compulsory education exists in the world does not mean that all children receive equal education. Large inequity exists between middle-class and low-income populations across the globe. The United States is a good example. Still, compulsory education is an important achievement in human history. See the first reference of note 1 to Chapter 3 for more discussions.

6. All of the terms/expressions in English and Chinese that I present in this chapter came from the study that is referenced in note 54 to Chapter 3.

7. The statistical analysis of the sorted lexicon placed the most frequently grouped items to the far left, the second most frequently grouped items next, and so forth. Thus, the order in which categories emerged indicates relative magnitude of group consensus of the category. The further left the cluster, the heavier the magnitude. See Figure 3.1 in Chapter 3.

8. Edwards, C., Gandini, L., & Forman, G. (Eds.). (1998). *The hundred languages of children: The Reggio Emilia approach – advanced reflections.* (2nd ed.). Westport, CT: Ablex.

9. Pintrich, P. R., Smith, D. A. F., Garcia, T., & McKeachie, W. J. (1993). Reliability and predictive validity of the motivated strategies for learning questionnaire (MSLQ). *Educational and Psychological Measurement, 53,* 801–813; and Purdie, N., & Hattie, J. (1996). Cultural differences in the use of strategies for self-regulated learning. *American Educational Research Journal, 33,* 845–871.

10. See Hidi, S., & Renninger, K. A. (2006). The four-phase model of interest development. *Educational Psychologist, 41*(2), 111–127 for research on interest and its development in learning.

11. See Cole, M., Cole, S. R., & Lightfoot, C. (2005). *The development of children.* (5th ed.). New York: Worth Publishers for basic knowledge on child development.

12. See the first reference in note 33 to Chapter 3. Gardner and Winner did not appreciate Chinese adults' interference with their son's exploration and concluded quite observantly that this Chinese adult behavior may reveal some fundamentally different beliefs about child development and learning.

13. See note 8 to this chapter.

14. Kuhn, D. (1991). *Education for thinking.* Cambridge, MA: Harvard University Press.

15. Nobel Museum (n.d.). Retrieved October 5, 2010 from http://nobelprize.org/nobel_prizes/physics/laureates/

16. See note 15 to this chapter. Also see Gardner, H., Csikszentmihalyi, M., & Damon, W. (2001). *Good work: When excellence and ethics meet.* New York: Basic Books for the testimonies of current scientists in the biomedical field and genetics on their "thrill of scientific inquiry" (p. 73).

17. Perkins, D. N. (1995). *Smart schools.* New York: Free Press; also see the second reference in note 16 to this chapter for the essential role of "quality of thinking" (p. 74) and "rational thinking" (p. 75) in scientific research.

18. See McBride, R. E., Xiang, P., Wittenburg, D., & Shen, J.-H. (2002). An analysis of preservice teachers' dispositions toward critical thinking: A cross-cultural perspective. *Asian-Pacific Journal of Teacher Education, 30*(2), 131–140 for a review of the importance of critical thinking in the West.

19. Ennis, R. (1987). A taxonomy of critical thinking dispositions and abilities. In J. Baron & R. Sternberg (Eds.), *Teaching thinking skills: Theory and practice* (pp. 9–26). New York: Freeman, p. 10.

20. Facione, P. (1990). *Critical thinking: A statement of expert consensus for purposes of educational assessment and instruction. Executive summary of "The Delphi Report."* Milbrae, CA: The California Academic Press.

21. Nobel Museum (n.d.). Retrieved October 5, 2010 from http://nobelprize.org/nobel_prizes/physics/laureates/

22. See note 21 to this chapter.

23. See note 18 to Chapter 2, p. 11.

24. A fuller account of this tradition will be presented in Chapter 8 in contrast to the reluctance to speak in East Asia. See Sternberg, R. J. (1985). Implicit theories of intelligence, creativity, and wisdom. *Journal of Personality and Social Psychology, 49,* 607–627 for his research on verbal ability as an important component of the Western conception of intelligence.

25. See Wang, Q. (2004). The emergence of cultural self-constructs: Autobiographical memory and self-description in European American and Chinese children. *Developmental Psychology, 40*(1), 3–15; and Wang, Q., & Leichtman, M. D. (2000). Same beginnings, different stories: A comparison of American and Chinese children's narratives. *Child Development, 71,* 1329–1346; and also the first reference in note 6 to Chapter 3 for differences in children's narratives.

26. See note 8 to this chapter.

27. Goleman, D. (1995). *Emotional intelligence: Why it can matter more than IQ.* New York: Bantam.

28. See note 54 to Chapter 3.

29. See notes 26 and 27 to Chapter 3 for detailed descriptions of Japanese preschool and elementary school classrooms. See Hsueh, Y. (1999). *A day at Little Stars Preschool, Beijing, China.* Unpublished video footage; Wang, T., & Murphy, J. (2004). An examination of coherence in a Chinese mathematics classroom. In L.-H. Fan, N.-Y. Wong, J.-F Cai, S.-Q. Li, & T.-Y. Tso (Eds.), *How Chinese learn mathematics: Perspectives from insiders* (pp. 107–123). Singapore: World Scientific; and Cortazzi, M., & Jin, L.-X. (2001). Large classes in China: "Good" teachers and interaction. In D. A. Watkins & J. B. Biggs (Eds.), *Teaching the Chinese learner: Psychological and pedagogical perspectives* (pp. 115–134). Hong Kong: Comparative Education Research Centre for documentation of how children show earnestness/sincerity in classroom learning.

30. Paine, L. W. (1990). The teacher as virtuoso: A Chinese model for teaching. *The Teachers College Record, 92*(1), 49–81.

31. See notes 21, 26, 27, and 50 to Chapter 3.

32. Levy, R. I. (1973). *Tahitians.* Chicago: University of Chicago Press.

33. See notes 43 and 44 to Chapter 3. Also see Marton, F., Dall'Alba, G., & Beaty, E. (1993). Conceptions of learning. *International Journal of Educational Research, 19,* 277–300 for their research on the role of memorization and understanding among Chinese learners.

34. Zhang, D.-Z., Li, S.-Q., & Tang, R.-F. (2004). The "two basics": Mathematics teaching and learning in Mainland China. In L.-H. Fan, N.-Y. Wong, J.-F Cai, S.-Q. Li, & T.-Y. Tso (Eds.), *How Chinese learn mathematics: Perspectives from insiders* (pp. 189–207). Singapore: World Scientific.

35. See the second reference in note 8 to Chapter 3. Also see two new books published recently: Colvin, G. (2008). *Talent is overrated: What really separates world-class performers from everybody else.* New York: Portfolio; and Coyle, D. (2009). *The talent code: Greatness isn't born. It's grown. Here's how.* New York: Bantam Dell for how great performances from the West also depend on this type of "deliberate" or "deep" practice.

36. Chen, C., & Stevenson, H. W. (1989). Homework: A cross-cultural examination. *Child Development, 60,* 551–561; Helmke, A., & Tuyet, V. T. A. (1999). Do Asian and Western students learn in a different way? An empirical study on motivation, study time, and learning strategies of German and Vietnamese university students. *Asian Pacific Journal of Education, 19*(2), 30–44; Peng, S. S., & Wright, D. (1994). Explanation of academic achievement of Asian American students. *Journal of Educational Research, 87*(6), 346–352; third reference in note 31 to this chapter; and Purdie, N., Hattie, J., & Douglas, G. (1996). Student conceptions of learning and their use of self-regulated learning strategies: A cross-cultural comparison. *Journal of Educational Psychology, 88,* 87–100.

37. See note 44 to Chapter 3.

38. Li, J. (1998). The power of embedding learning beliefs in everyday learning: Language arts texts as a vehicle for enculturation. Unpublished manuscript. I tallied all content in China's elementary school's language arts curriculum published in 1997. I found that 36% of all genres (e.g., stories, excerpts of novels, essays, songs, poems, letters, etc.) contained learning beliefs (e.g., moral self-perfection and contribution to society) and learning virtues (e.g., Madam Currie worked long hours in the lab).

39. See the first reference in note 61 to Chapter 3.
40. See second reference in note 8 to Chapter 3.
41. See in note 5 to Chapter 2, 2.11, p. 78.
42. See the second reference in note 36 to this chapter.
43. See note 21 to Chapter 3.
44. See notes 26 and 28 to Chapter 3.
45. See the first reference in note 61 to Chapter 3.
46. See the first reference in note 61 to Chapter 3. See Huang, H.-M. (2004). Effects of cram schools on children's mathematics learning. In L.-H. Fan, N.-Y. Wong, J.-F Cai, S.-Q. Li, & T.-Y. Tso (Eds.), *How Chinese learn mathematics: Perspectives from insiders* (pp. 282–306). Singapore: World Scientific for how, among other reasons, putting in more time and effort by attending the so-called cram schools in Taiwan is believed to compensate for children's lack of ability.
47. See the first reference in note 61 to Chapter 3.
48. See the third reference in note 4 to this chapter, and Li, J.-H. (2004). Thorough understanding of the textbook: A significant feature of [the] Chinese teacher manual. In L.-H. Fan, N.-Y. Wong, J.-F Cai, S.-Q. Li, & T.-Y. Tso (Eds.), *How Chinese learn mathematics: Perspectives from insiders* (pp. 262–281). Singapore: World Scientific.
49. Anderson, G. I. A. (Ed.). (1977). *Masterpieces of the Orient* (6th ed.). New York: Norton, pp. 421–422.
50. See references in note 75 to Chapter 2 and Kember, D. (2000). Misconceptions about the learning approaches, motivation, and study approaches of Asian students. *Higher Education, 40,* 99–121 for criticism of Chinese rote learning. Many Chinese educators themselves also join in this condemnation.
51. Geertz, C. (1973). *The interpretation of culture.* New York: Basic Books.
52. Bertensson, S., Leyda, J., & Satina, S. (2002). *Sergei Rachmaninoff: A lifetime in music.* Bloomington: Indiana University Press, pp. 10–11.
53. Marcovitch, S., & Zelazo, P. D. (2009). A hierarchical competing systems model of the emergence and early development of executive function. *Developmental Science, 12*(1), 1–18.
54. See note 44 to Chapter 3 and the second reference in note 33 to this chapter, p. 81.
55. See the second reference in note 36 to this chapter.
56. Chao, R. K. (1996). Chinese and European American mothers' views about the role of parenting in children's school success. *Journal of Cross-Cultural Psychology, 27,* 403–423.
57. See the second reference in note 71 to Chapter 3, p. 330. The original translation by D. C. Lau (note 50 to Chapter 2) was done with the English masculine pronouns *he, his,* and *him* for the Chinese term 人, which is not gendered. Although before the twentieth century, few women were ever educated and involved in political life, I maintain that the pronouns for ancient texts should be translated with the gender-neutral pronouns *one* and *one's.* This insistence is especially relevant given that the father quoted Mencius' passage to encourage his daughter.
58. This is probably why the Aesop's fable *Hare and Tortoise* (from its hundreds of fables) enjoys eternal popularity in Chinese/Asian cultures. The opportunity

to learn a skill over a very long period of time where these Chinese learning virtues are learned, applied, and preserved is likely to be a truer reason why so many Chinese/Asians parents enroll their children in learning how to play Western classical music instruments. This penchant of Asian parents stands in sharp contrast to Western classical music being viewed as "museum music" by pop musicians in the postmodern Era.

59. See note 77 to Chapter 2.
60. Kim, H. S. (2002). We talk, therefore we think? A Cultural analysis of the effect of talking on thinking. *Journal of Personality and Social Psychology, 83,* 828–842.
61. See note 26 to Chapter 3.
62. See the fifth reference in note 29 to this chapter and note 30 to this chapter.
63. Li, J., Fung, H., Liang, C.-H., Resch, J., Luo, L., & Lou, L. (2008, July). When my child doesn't learn well: European American and Taiwanese mothers talking to their children about their children's learning weaknesses. In J. Li & H. Fung (Chairs), *Diverse paths and forms of family socialization: Cultural and ethnic influences.* Symposium paper presented at a biannual conference of the International Society for the Study of Behavioral Development, Würzburg, Germany.
64. See the second reference in note 4 to Chapter 3.
65. Li, J. (2006). Self in learning: Chinese adolescents' goals and sense of agency. *Child Development, 77*(2), 482–501.
66. See the first reference in note 6 to Chapter 3.

5

Curiosity Begets Inquiry and Heart Begets Dedication

Affect is involved in learning as in other domains of human life. Affect is not just emotions but also feelings and attitudes, and it is part of our motivational system. Because of its larger scope, I use the term *affect* instead of *emotion*. Still, emotions make up the core of our affective life in general and are important in our learning. In this chapter, I first introduce the general concept of emotion followed by a description of research on the kinds of emotions and other affects that Western and Asian learners experience. Then I discuss how affects may function in these learners' respective learning.

EMOTION IN GENERAL

Emotions are part of our response system to the environment. They have physiological responses such as heartbeat, perspiration, body temperature (e.g., blushing), and involuntary facial expressions (e.g., crying for sadness and smiling for happiness); feelings and attitudes, however, may not have clear physiological responses. For example, we may feel strange in a place with which we are not familiar, or we may feel generally out of sorts, but such feelings are not necessarily accompanied by notable physiological responses. As for an attitude, we may feel that we are entitled to a higher pay than we actually receive, but have no bodily manifestations of this attitude.[1]

An emotion is regarded as both a discrete and an episodic phenomenon. It is discrete because when we experience a particular emotion, such as happiness, our happiness itself is not mixed with sadness or any other unrelated emotion, despite the fact that our happiness may be of a more or less subtle kind such as elation or relief. Sometimes we do realize that we have mixed emotions; for example, a warrior may win a great battle and feel triumphant and in the same second he may feel sadness for the loss of his comrades. However, this so-called mixed emotion does not mean that our discrete emotions of triumphant happiness and the sadness for the fallen are truly mixed. Quite the contrary, our happiness in this instance has an entirely different cause, namely winning. Our sadness has a different cause, namely our consideration for the dead and wounded. Therefore, we still experience our happiness first in the temporal sequence and our sadness later, no matter how closely the second emotion may follow the first one. The two emotions are thus still discrete.[2]

Emotions are also episodic because we experience our emotions temporally. Simply put, emotions come and go. Ross Buck notes that we tend to notice our emotions (and are often noticed by others around us) when they become relatively strong even though our emotional system is always turned on under normal circumstances.[3] Thus, any emotional episode can be seen as having three basic components that unfold in time: a cause or antecedence, a response/reaction, and coping afterward.[4] Nico Frijda advanced this basic understanding of emotions into a sequence of seven components, specifying how each phase happens: (1) *antecedent events* that generate emotions – for example, an event, a personal act (e.g., tasting good food), social interaction, or sometimes even a recollection or an image in our head can trigger an emotion in us; (2) *event coding* during which one characterizes the event in reference to event types as recognized by one's culture (e.g., a kind gesture versus an insult); (3) *appraisal* in which one evaluates the implications of the event to the self (e.g., "am I responsible?"); (4) *physiological reaction patterns* where a given emotion is linked to a set of autonomic reactions (e.g., shame leads to blushing and looking away); (5) *action readiness* where the person selects the next course of actions from a repertoire of possible actions (e.g., fear prompts the impulse to run away); (6) *emotional behavior* where one takes action (e.g., actual running away in fear); and finally (7) regulation where the person selects ways to deal with the emotion and the action taken (e.g., staying engaged with the event when feeling happy).[5]

Traditionally, affect is contrasted with cognition as two opposite ends in psychological research. However, recent research shows that affect and cognition are inseparable in human functioning. In order for us to experience any emotion, we use our mind to appraise the event to determine its relevance and importance to ourselves before our emotions are generated. In fact, Frijda's theory is called "appraisal theory" because it emphasizes how our mind perceives preceding causes, how we code such events and appraise them to determine to personal significance to ourselves before our emotions can be activated. Similarly, when we are engaged in mental work, our affective system is turned on to generate motivation for the task at hand if we are to sustain our engagement.[6]

Positive and Negative Affect in Learning

Affect in learning, like affect in general, has two valences: positive and negative. Because both affect and learning are temporal processes, it is helpful to discuss affect in learning as segmented in three phases that correspond to the three phases of emotion unfolding: prior to learning, during learning, and after learning. Each of these phases can have positive or negative affect.

We feel positive affect in learning when we are interested, curious, wondering about the world, and desiring to know/understand more. Prior to learning, we may feel hopeful, excited, and uplifted about the idea that we can learn new things.[7] Such positive affect motivates us to take action to engage in the actual learning, such as reading about the topic, seeking more information, and trying things. When we succeed in our effort, we may feel encouraged by, satisfied with, and proud of our learning. As a result, we are likely to seek such learning again.

On the other hand, we may experience negative affect if we are not interested and curious about the material, but rather are forced to learn by someone else. We may feel unmotivated and even anxious and dreadful about learning a particular piece of knowledge/skill. For example, if a person desires to learn how to swim but fails to learn the skill, that person's anticipatory excitement may diminish quickly, and he or she may feel lack of self-confidence. At this point, the person may either give up or attempt to try again. But if he or she is forced to learn swimming again against his or her will, the person may become fearful of it. Repeated failure may result in lower self-confidence, and depending on the importance of learning attached to the self, the person may develop the more global negative affect of low self-estimate or temporary frustration. Whenever we have such learning experiences, we are likely to have negative affect and consequently try to avoid such learning.

CULTURAL VARIATION IN LEARNING-RELATED AFFECT

Although there are common human affective responses to learning, culture, as it turns out, is a source of significant variations in the affect we experience in learning. Batjia Mesquita and Frijda maintain that culture is involved in all the seven phases of an emotion episode, because human emotional experience is a result of the combination of autonomic responses and regulated responses according to specific cultural models.[8] As discussed in Chapter 4, Robert Levy studied Tahitians and found that some emotions in that culture were elaborated and fully expressed whereas others were almost absent. Anger in Tahitian culture is the former and sadness is the latter, resulting from the norms concerning the function of these emotions in Tahitian social life. Levy proposed the terms *hypercognized* versus *hypocognized* emotions to capture culturally shaped emotional experiences.[9] Drawing on this framework, Mesquita argues that cultures can differ in the *frequency* of appraisals, action readiness, expression and behavior, and regulatory processes. Although humans across cultures may have similar physiological responses to a given emotion, such as smiling while happy, the high or low frequencies of the culturally framed processes indicate consistency or inconsistency with a given cultural model.[10] In other words, if pride in learning achievement is emphasized in a culture, the learners will likely feel pride, express it, and behave accordingly. If pride in learning is devalued in another culture, then we can expect to encounter a less frequent occurrence of pride in learning.

Learning-Related Affect in Western Learners

In order to proceed with learning-related affect in both Western and Asian learners, I follow the three distinct phases of prior to, during, and post-learning rather than Frijda's seven steps in the process of emotion activation. I do so because many affects in learning may not be clearly emotional in the strict sense, even though they overlap with emotions, as noted earlier. In addition, discussing the three-phase learning-related affect corresponds well with the process of our learning behavior and activities. However, it is also important to point out that any affect that is associated with a given phase of the learning process is not truly isolated, even though each emotion is discrete. Because learning (formal or informal) is an integral part of continuous human existence, a particular affective response at the moment may have been formed and strengthened with many repeated prior experiences. There is, thus, likely a loop of learning and feeling following each other and intertwined with each other. One's affective reaction to a particular outcome of learning may have everything to do with how that person may feel toward the next learning task. Therefore, the following discussions of prior to, during, and post-learning are not treated as separate phases per se but as a heuristic strategy to present research on learning-related affects.

Prior to Learning

Most research that deals with learning-related affect in Western learners is found in the large research body of achievement motivation. This research focuses on what motivates people for a particular achievement task, such as completing an anagram or a math problem in experimental situations. It is assumed that people's achievement motivation is a basic human need, and their beliefs about achievement are formed through their repeated life experiences with achievement outcomes. Accordingly, a person who faces any given achievement situation brings with him- or herself a set of prior beliefs and related evaluations that will influence the person's affective reactions to the task and outcome. In the 1960s, Western researchers discovered that people facing achievement tasks have two motives: the need to achieve success and the desire to avoid failure. Specific affects were involved in these expectations. For the need to achieve, the person expects to succeed and therefore to feel proud. This anticipated emotion motivates the person to take on the task. But if the person expects to fail, he/she is likely to anticipate shame, and the resultant action is to avoid the task (failure).[11]

At the core of achievement motivation research is the distinction of intrinsic versus extrinsic motivation. People experience intrinsic motivation when they desire activities and make efforts that are an end onto themselves rather than a means to some other goals. For example, we are intrinsically motivated when we enjoy reading a good book, but we are extrinsically motivated to go to a job that we would rather not do but we must do because we need the money. Needless to say, intrinsic motivation in learning is prized in the West and extrinsic motivation is shunned.

In general, researchers recognize three main areas that generate intrinsic motivation. The first is the affect of curiosity, and curiosity-based motivation is intrinsic by nature. Human beings are assumed to be naturally curious about novel events and activities that are incongruent with their expectations. As noted in Chapter 4, when learners are curious about a given topic, they tend to be motivated to seek such knowledge in order to satisfy their curiosity.[12] Again, curiosity is a highly valued trait in any learner in the West.

A related affect is interest. Based on research, interest could be similar to curiosity. For example, a student may be interested in black holes and would like to learn more about them. If the student's interest is in understanding black holes themselves rather than in the ability to impress people with his or her knowledge, then the student's interest is intrinsic. However, interest may be geared toward extrinsic purposes. For example, a person sitting in a doctor's waiting room happens to spot a magazine article about how a person can get an unconventional, high-paying job. Intrigued, this person picks up the magazine and reads the article, and afterward continues to seek additional information about this new job.[13] Although the person displays interest, this type of interest may not be intrinsic because it is serving another end (i.e., not the job itself, but the higher paycheck it offers). Thus, curiosity is a more pure form of intrinsic motivation, whereas interest by itself may not be exclusively intrinsic, depending on the end that a given interest serves.

The second form of intrinsic motivation comes from the observation that human beings have innate tendencies to seek opportunities to develop competence; therefore, they are intrinsically motivated to achieve. Achievement is testimony to our competence. Being competent, then, is not motivated by external rewards, although such rewards do frequently follow competent people. Even very young children display excitement about opportunities to develop and display their competence. For example, children often announce eagerly, "I want to kick the ball!" and proudly, "I can write my name!"

The best-known research on intrinsic versus extrinsic motivation emphasizes the notion that human beings have a natural need to feel autonomous and self-determining. Self-chosen tasks make people feel that they are in control of their own activities and work as directed by their own volition instead of by external rewards or avoidance of punishment. Research shows that when Western students can choose their own learning tasks – that is, when they have autonomy in learning – they feel motivated, happy, energetic, and excited in anticipation of success and enjoyment.[14]

An important part of research on achievement motivation is the notion of *self-efficacy* that has been studied extensively. Albert Bandura is the main researcher and theorist on this topic. The thrust of Bandura's theory is his focus on individuals' personal evaluation of their performance capabilities on a given task, not on their general sense of ability or their actual capability of succeeding. Bandura stresses that if a person lacks the skill, that person is motivated toward getting the skill.[15] Therefore, feeling efficacious moves people toward learning and mastery.

During Learning

Affect plays a key role in whether a person will continue learning once started. Several lines of research provide clues to how affect functions during learning. Carole Dweck's early research examined the notion of *learned helplessness* in learners. In her study, when children believed that they lacked the ability to succeed in a task, they gave up easily in the face of challenging tasks. Those who believed that they could increase their ability by learning persisted even when they failed. The former group of children exhibited low self-esteem and fear of failure, which was captured with the general notion of learned helplessness. But the latter group of children showed resilience and tenacity in the face of setbacks. These observations led Dweck to develop the theory of entity versus incremental intelligence. Accordingly, the entity-minded learners view intelligence as something that one either has or does not have. In contrast, the increment-oriented learners view intelligence as something that they can increase with learning and mastery.[16]

The decade-long research in this area shows that Western learners in general are particularly sensitive to the feedback on their ongoing learning and performance, which affects whether they will continue their effort. Two kinds of information are especially important. First, learners need the learning information that is relevant to the specific task because it is needed in order to understand the problem or issue at hand.[17] Second, they need feedback that informs them that they are doing well. However, if the feedback tells them that they are not doing well, they are likely to feel less motivated and ultimately may even give up.[18] This general pattern of Western learners' motivation in learning as a need to receive ongoing *positive* feedback corresponds to the general emphasis on self-esteem in the West and a deeper sense that the self is more or less fixed, and thus needs ongoing affirmation.[19] Learners, particularly young children, are believed to be in need of high self-esteem to facilitate learning. Parental and teacher praise is therefore widely used as a strategy to keep children motivated.[20]

The most significant research on affect during learning engagement was done by Mihaly Csikszentmihalyi and associates.[21] Their research began in the 1970s with an innovative empirical approach called "experience sampling method." The research participants were given a beeper and a booklet containing questions about where the person was, what the person was doing, what emotions they were feelings (both positive and negative), and if the person would rather be somewhere else or rather be doing something else. The beeper was programmed to beep randomly during the day and evenings. When the beeper beeped, the participant was asked to answer the questions in the booklet. Csikszentmihalyi's team collected a large body of such daily experiences from students, particularly adolescents.

They discovered a significant psychological phenomenon, which Csikszentmihalyi termed *flow*. Flow is a state of which any human being is capable. It is a state of human personal engagement in an activity, be it work, learning, performance, or just playing. Four key factors are at play, with two input factors and two resultant affective responses. The two input factors are one's skill and the task that one is tackling/performing. If one's skill exceeds that demanded by the task, such as a skilled violin virtuoso being asked to play a beginner piece, the person is likely to feel bored, which is one affective response. Although boredom is common in our daily lives, it is a state that most human beings would rather avoid. However, if the task's skill demand exceeds one's current skill level, such as a beginner violin learner being asked to perform a complicated piece of music, that person is likely to experience anxiety, which is the second affective response. Based on Csikszentmihalyi's extensive data, the best state is when one's skill matches that demanded by the task. In this situation, the person feels neither boredom nor anxiety. Instead, the person feels happy, lost in the task, enjoying it, frequently oblivious to time passage, and not self-conscious of his or her performance. This very state is the flow state.

What Csikszentmihalyi's research has revealed is intrinsic motivation at its best. Other related research on Western children in learning also supports the view that when learners can choose their own learning tasks and control their own learning directions and pace – that is, have a sense of autonomy – they enjoy the task more and do actually achieve better learning results.[22] Learners are thus likely to have stronger positive feelings about their learning and seek ways to engage in such learning further.

Post-Learning

Much research on achievement-related affect has been done to assess how people respond to their performance on tasks – that is, after learning has occurred. Following Atkinson's initial finding that affect is generated with regard to expectation of pride for success and fear of failure, researchers examined several related areas and provided more sophisticated views of the processes. Julian Rotter proposed a theory on people's *locus of control*, positing that individuals' expectations of success or failure depend on whether they perceive causes of success or failure to be internally or externally located.[23] Thus, if a person believes that his or her ability is the cause of his or her success, and given that ability is an internal attribute, that person will be more confident that he or she will succeed in the task. By contrast, if a person believes that luck will determine the outcome, then given that luck lies outside the person's ability to control, he or she will expect a low certainty of success. A person's sense of locus of control is therefore a key determinant to how he or she feels about an achievement outcome.

As it turned out, there was more to how Western students' expectation of success and failure operates. Bernard Weiner advanced Rotter's basic formulation into a new theory called *attribution theory*.[24] Weiner posited that human beings are naturally inclined to search for a causal understanding of events, thus making causal attributions, especially about events that are important to them (e.g., an academic performance). Such causal attributions in turn influence people's behavior and emotional reactions in later achievement situations. The theory specifies three factors and their interactions: *locus, stability,* and *control.* Locus here refers to where individuals believe the cause of their achievement outcome is located, again either the internal or the external being the two possible *sources.* Stability addresses the individual's belief in the *duration* of the cause, which is defined as either stable or unstable. Finally, control, originally within the concept of locus in Rotter's conception, now denotes only the *degree* of control the person perceives to have over the cause, which is postulated to be either controllable or uncontrollable. Using these factors, researchers can analyze important concepts in achievement motivation. For example, ability and effort, the two most frequently identified attributions, were now found to differ in their stability and controllability in addition to their common internal source. Whereas effort is usually perceived as controllable, it is often unstable from task to task. However, ability, viewed as a capacity, is generally perceived as a stable but relatively uncontrollable cause.

Weiner's theory has generated research that documents the specific affects associated with these three attributional factors. Accordingly, individuals reported feeling surprised when attributing their success or failure to luck, and guilty when attributing their failure to lack of effort. Gratitude is felt for receiving others' help. Pride and shame occur only in attribution to internal causes. Whereas individuals feel proud when ascribing their success to their ability and hard work, they feel shame when attributing their failure to lack of effort. Furthermore, pride is more likely to be experienced when success is believed to be a result of ability or hard work rather than of receiving help from others.[25]

Parallel to the attribution theory is another theory, the *self-worth* theory, that has important affective implications. Advanced by Covington and associates, this theory argues that human beings have the need to perceive competence as their self-worth – that is, the individual's appraisal of his or her own value. As a natural consequence, individuals are assumed to strive to protect their sense of self-worth when they feel it is threatened, for example by school failure.[26] Studies based on this theory concentrated on strategies individuals use to maintain their self-worth. In support of the attribution theory, research based on the self-worth theory also found that individuals took personal credit (usually attributing it to their ability) for their successes and attributed failures to external causes such as difficulty of task. Moreover, individuals will try to avoid negative implications of failure resulting from low ability by minimizing participation in performance activities.[27] Fearing revealing low ability, many students simply do not try, especially when faced with less challenging tasks (moderate difficulty), because failure with no effort could not be ascertained to result from lack of ability, thereby keeping their self-worth intact. Most striking is the analysis of effort likened to a "double-edged sword" by Covington and Omelich.[28] When they anticipate a threat of revealing their low ability associated with failure despite their high effort, students are unwilling to try, even if it means subjecting themselves to reprimand for not trying. Many more strategies for not trying have been identified, ranging from publicly downgrading the importance of studying, to using excuses for not trying, to choosing unattainable goals (guaranteed failure but no implication of low ability).

My own research on Western model learners indicated affects mentioned by a majority (62 percent) of the participants for being knowledgeable are happiness, joy, satisfaction, excitement, and fulfillment. Pride was the second most frequently mentioned emotion (53 percent). However, when not being knowledgeable, the set of affects most frequently mentioned by participants (47 percent) included frustration, discouragement, disappointment, and general unhappiness. Finally, 19 percent of these respondents mentioned feeling inferiority, low self-esteem, shame, embarrassment, humiliation, guilt, and low self-worth.[29]

The aforementioned research provides a consistent picture of a specific set of affects that Western learners experience in the learning process. Their curiosity and interest direct them to explore the world with personal initiative and autonomy. Such motivation is intrinsic by nature and generates excitement, enjoyment, and fun within the individual learner. For other tasks that are not necessarily self-generated and driven by curiosity/interest (e.g., typical school learning tasks that are more imposed by the social world), Western learners are likely to feel motivated if they expect a positive outcome of an upcoming achievement/learning task. The specific affect is pride as well as other related positive feelings such as happiness. During learning, learners are fine-tuned to the ongoing feedback of their own task performance. If they continue to do well, they are likely to be more motivated in the task engagement, continuing their effort. However, if the feedback is not positive, learners may become frustrated and discouraged, causing their effort to diminish, eventually causing them to give up. It appears that their afterthought – that is, determining the causes of their performance – may be a key factor in what kind of affect they feel vis-à-vis a given outcome. When attributing success to one's internal qualities such as high ability, the learner is likely to feel proud of him- or herself. When attributing failure to one's internal quality, the learner is likely to feel devastated (shame and low self-esteem) because it is a painful realization of a negative quality of the seemingly unalterable self. Although Western learners may also attribute their success to their effort, thereby feeling proud of themselves, they are likely to feel more proud and more self-worth with high ability. If an achievement situation is about protecting the self-worth, ability matters more than effort. Thus, Western learners' affects are part and parcel of their learning beliefs, and such affect-laden beliefs are formed in the loop of prior to, during, and post-learning over time.

Learning-Related Affect in Chinese/East Asian Learners

Unlike Western learning affect, Chinese/East Asian learning affect is largely based on personal conviction, not on personal curiosity about, interest in, or enjoyment of a particular subject of study or activity. It is conviction-based because of its moral and virtue focus as noted in previous chapters. However, just because it is conviction-based does not mean that Chinese/East Asian learners do not have very deep and powerful affects that propel their learning.

Prior to Learning

Because learning in Chinese/East Asian world is geared toward a life-long process of self-transformation, people's learning affect is also oriented toward this long-term goal rather than specific tasks that can change from situation to situation. As noted in Chapter 3, the Chinese cultural learning model indicates that dedication and commitment, rather than personal curiosity about, interest in, and fun with a specific subject, are the general affective focus. Because of this life-orientation, "prior to learning" as a concept and empirical strategy to segment the learning process does not quite apply to Chinese learners in the strict sense. Nevertheless, children must be brought on this learning path; therefore, there must be a beginning of the process, and there is one.

As found in my model learner study (see Chapter 3), the starting point for Chinese people's learning affect is the so-called establishing one's will (*lizhi*, 立志), a commitment to learning. Traditionally, when children entered the age of "understanding things" (*dongshi*, 懂事) around age six or seven, they were deemed cognitively and socially capable of engaging in dedicated studies.[30] To the extent that it could afford formal learning, a family usually found a private tutor in the local town, who taught Confucian texts to children, and held a ceremony to officially "acknowledge the teacher" (*baishi*, 拜師). Whether or not the child himself liked this parent-decided path and commitment was unimportant because every child (i.e., every male child throughout most of Chinese history, but now all children) has to learn to self-perfect in the Confucian learning tradition. Every effort was made to guide the child to understand this learning path, and backing out of this path was not an option. Some children never got very far on this path, but many did. Tutors and families continued to work with children so that the latter would embrace learning with their whole heart and mind. When the moment came, the child would "establish his will." There was no official rite for this moment of intellectual enlightenment, but it was still a personal coming to terms with learning for life. The child might share his will with family and friends, which served as a process of witnessing the commitment. The psychological function is very similar to a Western child who knew early on that he wanted to be, for example, a veterinarian and moved on to pursue that career for life. The difference lies in that the Western child's "will" or volition is purely based on his or her personal curiosity, interest, and sentiment; the family may have very little to do with what he might pursue for life. In the Chinese case, family was the key force for putting the child on the path in the first place.[31]

This long tradition of establishing one's will remains strong in the present-day Chinese societies. Families, schools, and society at large make a concerted effort to emphasize the importance of establishing one's will. State media and school discourse are replete with ongoing discussions about how children need to have a long-term purpose for learning so that they can contribute to society. There has been much research converging on the consistent finding that Chinese/East Asian parents monitor their children's learning much more intensively and enroll them in extra learning more frequently relative to other cultural groups.[32] This general research finding corresponds quite well with the very tradition that on the surface may have been jettisoned but deep down still operates strongly, albeit in modern forms (e.g., learning extracurricular artistic skills that require much dedication and commitment).

While the child is socialized toward establishing his/her will, parents and teachers on the one hand and the learner him- or herself on the other use this long-term goal as the motivator for each concrete learning activity. In my study on model learners, participants described how these learners felt uplifted, energized, empowered, and deeply grounded to pursue learning goals, regardless of how uninteresting a given subject was and regardless of how difficult the particular piece of knowledge a learner had to acquire. They used terms such as *love, passion,* and *thirst* to describe the general affect of learning motivation based on an established will.

My lexicon study also revealed a number of affect terms that indicate this type of orientation: *make a firm resolution to study (發奮讀書); if you don't learn when you are young, what will you do when you are old? (幼不學, 老何為?); devote oneself to studying (潛心學習); the best approach to learning is single-hearted devotion (學貴以專); desire to seek knowledge (求知欲); eager to learn (好學); and heart and mind for wanting to learn (好學心).*[33] These terms describe a general affective orientation toward learning in the long run rather than for specific learning tasks. In this regard, it is in sharp contrast to Western learners who may project success or failure on a particular achievement outcome and related affect. Chinese learners appear to orient themselves toward a longer and larger goal with commitment and devotion. As a result, the specific learning tasks and achievement outcomes may be less of the focus in their affect prior to learning any particular skill.

During Learning

Given their long-term goals, Chinese/East Asian learners may experience different affect during learning than their Western peers. My lexicon study yielded a number of terms that give some clues of their affect: *having studied, to then repeatedly apply what you have learned – is this not a source of plea-sure (Confucius)? (學而時習之, 不亦說乎?); put one's heart into one's study (用心讀書); study as if thirsting or hungering (如飢似渴地學習); and (so absorbed as to) forget food and sleep (廢寢忘食).* Pursuing life-long learning to morally transform oneself with a personal commitment was conceived of as a pleasure by Confucius; it should not be a dread. This phrase by Confucius is in fact the very first question recorded in the *Analects,* rhetorical in nature but inviting his students to think about the affect that such learning brings. Throughout Chinese history, learning/studying has been viewed as a serious personal endeavor, as discussed in previous chapters. Therefore, having a will established, it is only natural to study wholeheartedly (as a manifestation of sincerity). Then delving deeply into one's learning is likened to such a desire as feeling thirsty and hungry. The last phrase is reminiscent of Csikszentmihalyi's affective state of flow where the learner is so engrossed in study as to forget food and sleep (not even conscious of one's own physical needs). Indeed, many participants in my model learner study used these expressions to describe their model learners in the process of learning.

Empirical research on the actual affective experience during learning among East Asian learners is scant. But there are a few studies that shed some light on that experience. To begin with, a study completed most recently examined what types of goals motivated East Asian and European-American college students who were not interested in math. The researcher provided three types of goals: proximal (short-term, relevant to the learning task at hand), distal (long-term goals, not immediately relevant to the learning task at hand, e.g., career),[34] and self-discovered goals (regardless of proximal and distal reference). It was found that European-American students' motivation did not increase when they were told (therefore not self-chosen but externally provided) about the importance of a new math technique. In comparison, East Asian students worked harder and showed more interest in the new technique after being told that it could help them reach their distal goals. Moreover, when proximal and distal goals were examined side by side, it was found that European-American students were more motivated when told that learning the math technique could help them reach their proximal goals (e.g., tips for calculating math problems quickly). But East Asian students again showed higher interest and worked harder when they were told that the new technique could help them reach their distal goals in life.[35]

My own research on model learners also indicated that they did not focus on affect such as curiosity, interest, enjoyment, and fun – that is, the traditionally defined intrinsic motivation. Instead, they experienced personal striving, charging up to anticipated difficulties (enduring hardship), overcoming their natural tendency to relax, or to use their own term, "to be lazy" – in other words, challenging themselves. Two sets of open-ended responses were particularly revealing. The first contained responses to the question "How would your model learner learn if he/she has made great efforts but still couldn't learn?" Recall that research on Western learners shows that their continuous motivation is contingent on the ongoing feedback on how well they are doing. If the feedback is positive – that is, confirming the positive and able self – they are more likely to continue. In contrast, Japanese students persisted longer after being told that they did not do well.[36] Similar to Japanese responses, 50 percent of the Chinese participants in my study wrote "change study methods." Other statements were "persist" (32 percent) and "humbly ask others to teach oneself" (30 percent). The second set of responses was to the question "How would your model learner learn if he/she found a subject uninteresting or even boring?" Sixty percent of the participants wrote "force oneself to persist." The remaining expressions were "force oneself to persist if the knowledge is deemed important/useful" (28 percent) and "finding ways to make oneself interested" (24 percent).

Juxtaposing the two sets of responses of the two cultural groups, it seems that Chinese learners did indeed not focus on the negative emotions (no participants mentioned them regarding the first question, whereas 42 percent of European-American participants spontaneously did so). But half of the Chinese participants believed that the learner who could not learn despite great efforts will succeed with different methods. Only 13 percent indicated that the learner should give up (compared to 42 percent European-American respondents). Similarly, regarding the boredom question, the majority of Chinese participants wrote "forcing oneself to persist" (強迫自己學) as an antidote to combat boredom. Except one, no other European-American respondents used the language "force oneself to learn" to describe their model learners. Moreover, fewer Chinese participants offered study with less enthusiasm (17 percent) and not pursuing the subject anymore (17 percent) as solutions to the boredom problem (compared to 32 percent and 26 percent, respectively, by their European-American peers). European-American participants repeatedly expressed the belief that a learner cannot learn well without interest and should not have to spend time and energy learning things that he or she finds boring. Examples of actual responses are: "you have to follow your interest, and you can only learn well when the interest is there"; "he learns to enjoy"; and "the acquisition of knowledge must be an interesting and fulfilling process for him to want to pursue it." Such comments were far less frequent among Chinese participants.

To examine to what extent the ideal learner image is reflected in ordinary Chinese learners, I conducted another study on how Chinese adolescents viewed themselves in the learning process by asking them to complete ten identical sentences that began with "In learning, I ..."[37] A total of 259 adolescents (twelve to nineteen years of age) from two large regions of China gave open-ended responses. The most frequent self-descriptions were the various learning virtues. In comparison, there were few references to positive emotions such as enjoyment and excitement or negative emotions such as frustration and disappointment, as well as interest/disinterest, and confidence/lack of it. It seems clear that affect, either positive or negative, does not play a strong role in their views of themselves as learners.

In support of this basic finding on affective orientation of Chinese learner, Hsin Mei Huang provides a telling report on how children in Taiwan find the infamous "cram schools" actually motivating, beyond their parents' desire to continue their attendance.[38] For those who are unfamiliar with this unique Asian schooling phenomenon, "cram schools" are common in East

Asian countries like Taiwan, Japan, Korea, Hong Kong, China, Singapore, and Vietnam. They are private enterprises that offer additional academic and extracurricular enrichment programs to school-aged children for a fee, and according to popular belief, all are built to feed the academic pressure and hype in those countries (not surprisingly, such schools also exist in the American cities where large Asian populations reside[39]).

There are many critics of this Asian educational phenomenon, both within and outside Asia. They condemn these schools as a consequence of the idea of "examination hell" and point out that children go to regular school for the day and then have to attend extra school afterward. Their leisure and other meaningful, fun childhood activities are stolen, according to popular discourse.[40] As a response to such criticisms, Asian countries have issued policies to reduce a six-day school week to a five-day school week and to scale back homework assignments in order to allow children to have a childhood. Even the English term *cram school* for a rather neutral native term *Buxiban* (tutoring or supplementary classes, 補習班) in Chinese has been accepted as the official translation. The ease of Asian scholars' usage of the English term (without quotation marks) also shows the Asian acceptance of the disapproval and ridicule connoted in the term "cram." As such, it does not require a stretch of imagination to assume that Asian children should hate "cram schools." But research, surprisingly, indicates otherwise.

Despite mounting criticisms, "cram schools" continue to boom and flourish. Huang's research investigated reasons given by parents as well as children. In Taiwan, half of all school-aged children – a very high number – attend "cram schools." From parents' perspective, "cram schools" help prevent juvenile delinquency, enable children to put their precious time in young age to learning more, and provide a chance to make up for children's inadequacies in their formal schooling so as to increase their chances of getting into better schools. This is predicated on the belief that learning well in school is the most important task for children. It is not surprising that these are parents' reasons for sending their children to "cram school." What is counterintuitive is that the children themselves have positive things to say about their "cram schools." Children appear to accept the fact that there is widespread peer pressure to achieve better for everyone. High academic achievers are liked and accepted more by peers, and these children are not labeled as nerds as they may be in the United States and other Western societies. (see focused discussion on this topic in Chapter 6) By contrast, poor academic achievement can lead to peer rejection. Thus, even though children may not like the fact that they have to go to more school, they view such extra learning as important and necessary.

They therefore are motivated to continue "cram school" and try their best there.

Research on Japanese adolescents attending their "cram schools" (*Juku*, 塾) and extracurricular training schools (*Bukatsu*, 活部) shows the same pattern. Although youth did not have very positive emotions to report during these school hours, they nevertheless indicated that they wanted to go to *Juku* and to train hard at *Bukatsu*.[41] Such unique extracurricular activity reflects their culture's value of the concept *gambaru*, a value of the intrinsic benefits of persistence, which the Japanese culture desires in their children (as noted in Chapter 3).[42] Another related study also showed that Vietnamese students reported higher motivation for study than their German peers, despite their acknowledged higher pressure to study hard from home.

Taken together, the previously reviewed research indicates two important differences in affect during learning between the two cultural groups. First, it provides support for the idea that the East Asian learners' motivation may not be anchored in the curiosity about and interest in the specific learning task at hand – that is, in the self-based, task-specific affect. Neither do they seek enjoyment and fun as a *primary condition* under which to engage in learning. As noted previously, learning in Confucian heritage cultures is not conceptualized as a fun and purely enjoyable process, but one that is wrought with hardship that must be overcome. The Confucian conceptualization of moral self-perfection as a source of pleasure is not the kind learners may experience spontaneously, but one that comes only after a person has done much seeking and contemplation. It is a path that one walks willingly, knowing that it requires determination, commitment, and endurance of hardship, and with such personal dedication and enlightenment one may achieve a further goal: the transformation of the pain of self-exertion into a pleasure.

Thus, East Asian learning-related affect seems to be based more on the conviction and commitment to life-long goals. The specific learning tasks that may fluctuate from moment to moment may not impact (excite or frustrate) the East Asian learners as strongly as they sometimes do their Western peers. Instead, their self-striving and work toward longer-term goals may serve to tone down the excessively positive or negative emotions (which may well be perceived as disturbances and diversions from their ultimate goals).[43] Their attention is on how to master the current learning in order to move forward toward their longer-term goals. In other words, their overall emphasis on persistence may result in different affect than Western learners' experiences of curiosity, interest, fun, and intrinsic enjoyment in learning, as found by research.

Researchers' understanding of this tendency of East Asian learners received further confirmation in a recent study conducted by Hsiao d'Ailly, who used Western measures of autonomy and intrinsic motivation to study schoolchildren in Taiwan.[44] Although these measures were found to have validity and reliability, parental involvement and support of autonomy (encouraging their children to exercise autonomy) as well as teachers' modeling and instruction regarding autonomy (encouraging it or being more controlling toward children) did not make a difference in children's intrinsic motivation. Neither did children's level of autonomy impact how much effort they made in their studies. The most interesting finding in this research was that when children's own sense of control regarding their own ability and learning strategy was put aside, their so-called external motivation, surprisingly, had a positive effect on their achievement. The author thus concluded that

> for children in Taiwan, interest and fun ... may not be as strong a motivator for hard work as rules (external) and values [for learning]....
> Although ... children [may be] motivated by intrinsic interest in their learning, it is also logical to infer that students with a higher sense of autonomy, who study mainly for fun and interest and do not yield much to external pressures, are more likely to decide not to study when they cannot find fun and interest in their learning.

Another conclusion one may draw is that it may not matter to East Asian students where the source of their motivation stems from. In other words, the dichotomy of intrinsic versus extrinsic motivation may not be drawn as sharply among East Asian learners as among their Western peers. As noted in Chapter 3, research conducted by Iyengar and Lepper as well as by Xuehua Bao and Shui-fong Lam showed clearly that Asian-American children learned equally well and enjoyed their learning when their learning task was chosen by the trusted members of their social world (i.e., in good relationships), but European-American children learned better and enjoyed the learning when they themselves chose their tasks.[45] This is to say that the external world may give East Asian learners a stronger motivation and affect for learning than their Western peers. However, it may not be appropriate to assume that socially shaped motivation is the same as extrinsic motivation, as Maarten Vansteenkiste and associates have convincingly argued.[46] Children accepting parental and teacher's guidance on learning for their ultimate moral self-perfection, particularly after they themselves have established their will, is unlikely to be extrinsic because moral and virtue goals are ends in themselves.

Perhaps defining intrinsic motivation solely as interest and fun (which is sometimes couched as the best type of motivation there is in the whole human world) may need rethinking. Consider the case of the dedication and passion that deeply spiritual and religious people display in pursuing their goals. I would argue that this type of motivation is more intrinsic than the interest and fun-based intrinsic motivation because the latter is subject to situational, task, and mood changes, and therefore can be short-lived. A short-lived motivation, no matter how intrinsic, is not as desirable as a long-lasting and passionate intrinsic motivation for learning. For example, a child may find a particular book fun, but he or she may not find many other books fun, and hence may lose interest in reading these other books. But a person who is determined to read as many books as possible because he or she finds learning through books important and fulfilling for life has a passionate conviction about reading books for life. The kind of conviction and passion at which Confucian learning aims is the latter, not the former. And East Asian cultures believe that children have a better chance of developing long-term passionate motivation with the concerted social support from families, schools, and communities at large.

Respect – An Important Affect in East Asian Learners

Another important but hitherto not well-understood affect of East Asian learners is respect toward teachers. In Chapter 3, I discussed the basic idea of respect in Chinese learners. I focus here on the emotionality of respect that Asian learners may experience during learning. Elsewhere I have reviewed research on respect in the West and in East Asia and advanced the theoretical distinction between two kinds of respect – *ought-respect* and *affect-respect* – that may exist in both the West and in East Asia.[47] Ought-respect refers to the kind of respect everyone deserves based on political, moral, and legal considerations. As such, ought-respect is not generated in a specific social context or relationship because it is for everyone. This kind of respect does not vary based on temporal or contextual particularities that underlie the occurrences of emotions. Given that it is tied to a rights-based moral principle and mandated by law, and it is not person- or relationship-specific, ought-respect is unlikely to be a prototypical emotion, but a more reason-based social, moral, and attitudinal construct. Research indicates that ought-respect may be more prevalent in the West than in Asia.

Quite differently, affect-respect is mostly an emotion that is generated in a specific social context or relationship. This kind of respect occurs when an individual genuinely recognizes, acknowledges, and admires another for his or her merit, achievement, moral qualities, and/or status/position/role/power. Affect-respect necessarily rests on the awareness that the self is either of lesser quality than or shares a similar quality with the other. This self-awareness, particularly of the gap between oneself and the other, necessarily presupposes that the self values and desires the qualities of the other. The realization that one values/desires the quality, which the self should and can acquire but has not yet achieved, may be the very foundation of affect-respect.

Affect-respect may have important and positive implications for the self. First, it may be a key part of the process of finding role models. A role model is necessarily someone whom the self admires and desires to emulate, and it is one positive possible self.[48] When a person has identified a role model, that person has a clear, concrete, tangible, real human figure in mind to seek to emulate. The fact that a person is identified as a role model for the self indicates that the self has some understanding of the basic quality, merit, and achievement that the role model has. The identification of a role model also indicates at least some self-awareness of the *discrepancy* between the self and the role model and quite possibly also awareness of ways to narrow this discrepancy. Second, each time the self is made aware of the role model, the self may experience affect-respect, a highly positive emotion that also makes the self feel good about him- or herself, as discussed earlier. Finally, affect-respect may generate strong motivation for behavior that propels the self toward acquiring the qualities that the respected person possesses. In sum, feeling affect-respect for a person may make the self eventually become such a person. This may be called the "self-Pygmalion process" (named after the sculptor in Greek mythology whose sculpture came to life). Research shows that affect-respect may be more widely experienced by Asian people because their cultures emphasize learning from exemplary models.

Research on who receives affect-respect in the West found four categories of people: (1) those displaying moral and virtuous qualities (e.g., honest, trustworthy, just), (2) those who possess admirable talents/skills, (3) those who are sensitive toward others (e.g., considerate, accepting others, understanding, and empathic), and (4) members of a respect-worthy social category.[49] A study I conducted on Chinese conceptions of respect found two additional categories of people who receive affect-respect: (1) parents/elders/kin and (2) teachers/mentors/scholars.[50]

In terms of learning, the last category is of particular relevance to Chinese learners. Respect for teachers/mentors/scholars indicates that one has role models in the classroom to draw on. In addition, these role models are charged to teach the students. One needs to emulate the models and to self-improve continuously. At the same time, one needs to remain humble and receptive to teaching of these respected learning models. Hence, respect as an affect toward teachers is highly positive for Chinese learners because it may likely help them become like their teachers who, after all, are supposed to embody the Confucian image of self-perfection through learning.

Having clarified the meaning of Chinese learners' respect toward their teachers, I hope to say a few words on learners' affect under the influence of the Asian so-called authoritarian teachers. There is no doubt that how teachers conduct themselves in their instruction and interactions with students can directly impact children's affective experience. If Chinese teachers were truly authoritarian, then Chinese children should feel fear, instead of respect, for teachers.[51] Unfortunately, there is scarce research on students' affective responses to Asian authoritarian teachers. Nevertheless, available research may hint at unexpected affective experience when Chinese learners view their supposedly "authoritarian" teachers.

Hsueh and colleagues[52] asked European-American and Chinese elementary school and middle school children to indicate, from the following list, the reasons for which they might show respect toward teachers:

- Do what your teacher tells you to do (obedience)
- Work hard on your schoolwork (learning virtues)
- Help your teacher when she needs help (social approval)
- Don't cause trouble in class (avoidance of punishment)
- Treat your teacher like you would treat your parent (parent–teacher similarity).

These reasons were derived from interviews conducted with open-ended questions to which similarly aged children from both cultures responded. The research team found that similar numbers of children of the two groups – but in each instance representing the minority of children in their respective group – chose social approval, avoidance of punishment, and parent–teacher similarity. At the same time, obedience was chosen by significantly more European-American children (37 percent), whereas learning virtues were chosen by the smallest number of European-American children (8 percent). Chinese children showed the opposite pattern; significantly more of them (33.4 percent) chose learning virtues whereas the smallest number chose obedience (6 percent). These findings suggest that for Chinese children, showing respect for teachers is tied to how they themselves are motivated to learn with their learning virtues. For European-American children, on the other hand, respect for teachers is more about following the rules of authority, which is not closely tied to personal effort as applied to learning itself. These findings provide support that a significant number of East Asian learners' respect for teachers is primarily not a result of obedience, seeking teacher approval, and avoidance of punishment (fear), but of virtue-oriented learning.

Post-Learning

Because learning is a continuous process throughout life, Chinese learners may not put as much emphasis on the dichotomy of success versus failure of a particular learning task or activity. In other words, their affective responses may not zero in on the impact of success or failure in any given learning situation. This tendency of theirs may also stem from Asian Taoist worldview that there are no absolutes, fixed opposites, or true dichotomies in the world.[53] One state can change into the other, and the whole world is in constant flux. Human learning is no exception. If one does not learn well in one point of time on one task, it does not mean that that person will not learn well the next time. However, a learner cannot sit there, waiting for miracles to change his or her fate. Instead, the learner needs to understand what he or she did not know or did not do well and to find ways to change his or her learning approach. Likewise, if one learns well at one point in time and on one task, this does not mean that one will be guaranteed to do as well the next time. Again, one needs to continue one's effort and remain humble to seek further learning regardless of how well one learns at any given moment.

In fact, this is how many respondents of my model learner study responded to the question of how the learner would learn when facing failure or when achieving highly. As a result, their affective responses to this ongoing learning perspective may be less dramatically high for good learning and dramatically low for poor learning as discussed previously. The following are excerpts on failure (e.g., not getting a good grade on an exam or receiving unfavorable remarks from a teacher) that suggest the general response pattern:

> He would not be discouraged at all. On the contrary, he would be more invigorated and defeat difficulties eventually. He believes that failure is not to be feared. One needs only to learn from one's mistakes, and success is guaranteed.

> First, she would feel dejected for a short while. But then she would start looking for the cause of the failure by reflection. She does this because she thinks that nothing about falling down itself is a big deal; the key is that one can stand up where one has fallen down before.

> In the face of failure, he would think cool-headedly. Then he would know what to do next. He believes that only after reflection, one would not act on undue impulses. It's not necessary to be depressed about one failing exam.

For high achievement, these responses complement their expressions on failure:

> He would continue to study hard, aiming at the next success because he knows one-time success is only a mark on the road, but not the end of the whole course of learning.

> He would not be arrogant; instead he would have the right attitude. Achievement can only say something about one's past, and cannot indicate anything about one's future. If one is complacent about one-time success and stops making progress, one would fall backwards.

To obtain direct affective responses, I asked Chinese and European-American college students in the same study to describe how their model learners would feel emotionally about being knowledgeable as a general sense of learning achievement. Forty two percent of Chinese (and 62 percent European-American) respondents acknowledged that their model learners would feel generally happy and fulfilled (including other similar positive affects such as joyful, excited, satisfied, and pleased). However, only 22 percent of Chinese (but 53 percent of European-American, more than twice as many) respondents mentioned pride as the other distinct affect. In addition, 28 percent of Chinese (compared to only 9 percent of European-American – three times fewer than Chinese) respondents also expressed humility/calmness in the face of being knowledgeable and well-learned. Finally, 28 percent of Chinese (but only 2 percent of European-American) respondents stated that their model learners were not satisfied with their achievement and would be motivated to learn more.

When not being knowledgeable and not well-learned, 30 percent of Chinese (19 percent of European-American) respondents mentioned shame/guilt, but these Chinese respondents also included an expression of self-reproach. In comparison, no European-American respondents mentioned self-reproach. Instead, 47 percent of them (but no Chinese respondents) acknowledged frustration, discouragement, disappointment, and anger. However, 27 percent of them – a higher number than European-American respondents (19 percent) – wrote about these model learners feeling sadness and depression. Nevertheless, their sadness/depression did not appear to be related to a sense of inferiority and low self-esteem, because no one mentioned this kind of affect (but 19 percent of European-American respondents describe such feelings). Instead, 40 percent of them (but 28 percent of European-American respondents) wrote that these learners were motivated to learn more in order to make up for their inadequacies.

Lower Pride but Higher Humility

At this point, it is important to discuss two significant but related affects – pride and humility – that are experienced by East Asian learners. For East Asians, pride is a controversial emotion in empirical research, and humility as a virtue has been promoted in East Asia for millennia, although for some reason it has garnered little research attention. Because of the peculiar statuses of these two affects in research, I hope to discuss them together in order to shed some analytical light on these important affects in East Asian learners.

As noted in the section on Western learners, pride is a highly positive affect. Because the self is centrally implicated, pride is also regarded as a positive self-conscious emotion.[54] Pride arises when a person accomplishes a task of some difficulty or challenge. It could be any task or performance that requires a comparably significant level of ability/competence/skill/ knowledge, artistic or athletic talent or other physical prowess, quality of work, and standards of judgment or evaluation. For example, a dancer feels pride when she wins a competition, or simply is admired by others, or a child feels pride when he finally learns how to tie his or her own shoelaces. Even though individuals can self-impose any level of competence or standard of performance, their awareness of these levels and standards points to the sociocultural origin of such levels and standards, regardless of whether others are watching, or whether a particular level or standard is internalized. Thus, pride is unlikely to occur without some sort of social comparison – that is, an awareness of how one measures up to others in achievement and performance of similar tasks/skills. Because learning achievement, particularly in the formal setting, is directly evaluated based on social comparison, learners feel pride when they achieve well, in comparison with others.[55]

In the West, the opposite of pride is shame/embarrassment/inferiority/low self-esteem/low self-worth. Shame in the West is mostly a negative emotion, a disgrace that is believed to be harmful to people and is to be rid of. By contrast, in Confucian persuasion, feeling shame is regarded as a moral guide or inner voice that people need to exercise in order to examine their own wrongdoing as well as to summon their courage to admit wrong on the one hand and to desire to self-improve on the other. Shame therefore is one of the four cardinal Confucian moral sensibilities to be developed in people. These moral principles are carved on the Boston Chinatown Gate.[56] Michael Lewis's extensive research has demonstrated that pride and shame in the West are likely to be the opposite, particularly in individuals who feel globally low self-worth (that has presumably developed as a result of repeated failure). Such Western individuals show stronger pride when they succeed in a task, but they also show higher levels of shame when they fail a task.[57]

Pride in East Asian learners does not mean the same and is not experienced in the same way. First, there is no equivalent Chinese term into which the English term *pride* can be translated as a wholly positive term. Based on an empirical procedure I used to translate the English and Chinese terms, the closest term is *jiao-ao* (驕傲).[58] Accordingly, thirteen of fourteen (93 percent) fully bilingual and college-educated people (either born/raised or having spent at least ten years in the United States) translated the English *pride* or *feeling proud* into *jiao-ao*, with only one person translating it into the Chinese term *zihao* (自豪) (a related term that is probably better captured in the English term *honor* rather than *pride*). But 31 percent among these translators stated that *jiao-ao* also has a negative connotation of *arrogant* and *conceited*. Then another group of eighteen of twenty (90 percent) bilingual people from similar backgrounds translated the Chinese *jiao-ao* into English *pride/proud*. Out of these eighteen, two people translated *jiao-ao* as *stuck-up*, *overconfident*, *boastful*, *conceited*, and *arrogant*, and seven additional people (nine overall, or 45 percent of the entire group) mentioned that *jiao-ao* has a negative connotation indicating arrogance in general. They stated that which connotation to use depends on the context. These thirty-four bilingual people's translations led to the conclusion that *jiao-ao* and *pride* are the closest equivalent. It is also clear that *jiao-ao* and *pride* have very different meanings, even though they may share some core positive meaning.

Second, other empirical research documents that pride in Asian people is a paradoxical emotion.[59] This means that it is both positive and negative. For example, Chinese, compared to their European-American counterparts, were found less likely to judge pride as an emotion that they would like to experience.[60] By using a questionnaire method with college students, Deborah Stipek found that Chinese, unlike their European-American peers (who would feel and express pride for themselves), would feel pride more readily when their family members achieve well (e.g., getting into a prestigious university) than when they *themselves* achieve well.[61] Chinese respondents revealed that pride should only be experienced when the achievement benefits others – a research result that others have encountered as well. Other researchers used the experience sampling method to collect randomly sampled real emotional experiences for a week and found that Chinese and Taiwanese rated pride less desirable and appropriate than European-Americans and Australians. Moreover, although Asian

Americans and Japanese experienced pride as a positive emotion, they (but not European-Americans) also felt a host of unpleasant emotions (guilt, irritation, sadness, and worry) when they experienced pride. Statistical analysis shows that pride has both positive and negative valences (in factor loading).[62] Finally, my colleague and I conducted a study on how preschool children perceive their achieving peers. We found that Chinese children as young as five expressed what we called an "arrogance concern" about high achievers, believing that they might grow too proud of themselves to continue to self-improve. This tendency was significantly more prevalent among Chinese children than among their European-American peers.[63]

Further explication of the mixed nature of pride in East Asian learning is warranted. As my translation procedure and Stipek's research indicate, this double-valenced affect is context-specific. When an East Asian experiences good learning, for example, his or her initial response is likely to be positive – that is, similar to the pride of European-Americans. However, this first appraisal and related affective experience may be short-lived.[64] What ensues is the self-reflection with a preventive focus owing to the cultural orientation that influences how people regulate their own emotions.[65] The actual process may be something like the following: "I did it! I am happy that I worked hard at it and that I was able to succeed. But beware, don't be too full of yourself; there is more to achieve. If I express my happiness openly and publicly, people may think that I am arrogant. Besides, showing pride publicly will make others feel bad about not doing so well. So I should stay humble. It's good for me and for others." However, if the person feels pride as a result of a collective achievement, the negative feeling may not occur, even though Chinese people may still have preventive feelings to some extent.[66] For example, people may still say to each other: "Okay, our Olympic math team did well, but they need to work harder to achieve more."

It would be erroneous to assume that this negative valence of pride is debilitating and harmful to East Asian learners. Recent research documents that as a style of their self-regulation in life, East Asians tend to focus more on what has been termed as "prevention." Prevention focus serves to warn oneself against potential mistakes and wrongdoing in order to avoid such actions and consequences (instead of promotion focus on the positive gains and achievement).[67] Recent research shows that, compared to Westerners, Chinese people are more prevention-focused.[68] People with either focus can feel very positive about their style. Thus, the negative side of pride may serve Chinese learners well in their effort to strive to fulfill their moral and social duties. The duality of pride in East Asians compliments rather than contradicts.

The opposite of pride in Chinese people is humility, not shame as may be the case in the West. In general, humility is regarded as a disposition, an enduring quality of a person, as Tangney and others have theorized recently.[69] This dispositional view may be quite accurate. However, because in East Asia humility is the opposite of the clear self-conscious emotion that is pride, there may also be an affective component yet to be studied in humility. As an affect, individuals may experience humble feelings as they engage in learning (and other domains of life), particularly in their responses to learning outcomes.

Humility has been an integral part of Confucian teaching since ancient times. It appears to be more highly valued in Asia than in the West, although there is very little research on the subject. Humility is highly valued and actively promoted as a personal quality as well as an affective expression in East Asia. Recent research on Western notions of humility documents some positive views of humility in people who are religious or are involved in close relationships; however, it is evident that humility is not desirable in leaders and entertainers.[70] Contrary to the West, humility in the Confucian persuasion has never been conceived of as a personal weakness or lowly self-regard, but only as a strength one must have if one desires to self-cultivate.[71] In Chinese Taoist philosophy, the notion of fullness (滿) is also conceived of as a psychological dynamic in a person (or nature) that turns against oneself, impeding the self from achieving one's full humanity and greatness.[72] Both Confucian and Taoist schools of thought share the view that having a full sense of self (e.g., knowing all, being perfect, having all wealth, controlling all) is one true personal weakness (similar to the noted problems of narcissism in the West[73]). Therefore, self's fullness (自滿) is a serious impediment in learning.

The antidote against self's fullness is humility. This personal strength is not military force, wealth, dominant personality, or even persuasive power, but *inner* strength that interestingly results in a gentle, soft, and nonaggressive style.[74] Everyone is believed to possess this potential. Once developed, such strength is also believed to be inexhaustible and unbendable by any external force, enabling the person to seek self-improvement with tenacity and persistence. People with such inner strength can truly examine themselves, see their own inadequacies, and seek ways to self-improve. This kind of inner strength and agency has nothing to do with low self-regard, because the power in humility lies in the belief that the self has the capacity to grow and needs to grow. It generates hope, optimism, and motivation for reflective personal striving.

Humility in East Asia is especially desired and revered in the domain of learning. Most learning is accompanied by achievement; individuals who achieve well are believed particularly vulnerable to an inflated sense of self. Because learning in Confucian thought is not just academic but moral and social for life, humility is regarded as the single most important means to guard oneself against falling prey to arrogance and conceitedness after high achievement. This emphasis on humility has also been noted recently by Western scholars who attempt to address the neglected research on humility in the West. Accordingly, humility is characterized as:

- an ability to acknowledge one's mistakes, imperfections, gaps in knowledge, and limitations;
- keeping one's abilities and accomplishments – one's place in the world – in perspective;
- leaving oneself more open to learn from others.[75]

Research indeed shows this Asian tendency vis-à-vis one's own high achievement as well as others' attitude toward individuals of high achievement. In my model learner study, respondents were asked to describe how their model learners would respond to high achievement. Fifty four percent of them acknowledged humility (in comparison, 16 percent of European-American respondents did so). Only 5 percent acknowledged feeling proud. In fact, 22 percent (but no European-American respondent) specifically noted that their model learners would not feel proud (不驕傲/不自滿) despite their happy feelings. In addition, when asked how their model learners would act for not understanding learning materials, 62 percent of Chinese respondents wrote that they would seek others' teaching humbly (虛心請教); in comparison, only 10 percent of European-American respondents mentioned a similar behavior. More evidence comes from my study examining Chinese and European-American preschool children's perceptions of achieving peers. We found significantly more expressions among Chinese children about their need to emulate the learning models so that they can learn from the high achievers. By contrast, European-American children revealed significantly more social isolation and rejection toward high achievers.[76] Research in general psychology that has repeatedly found the so-called modesty bias among East Asians but self-enhancing bias among Western people[77] supports the idea that East Asians value and express more humility in learning (as well as across other domains of life).[78]

The aforementioned review of research on East Asian learners' affect also provides a general picture. Prior to learning, their affect may be less driven by curiosity about and personal interest in a given subject or topic, and more by a longer-term goal, a will to establish for life-long dedication. Affects such as commitment, dedication, and passion matter more than situationally generated affects such as enjoyment and excitement. During learning, they show less oscillation between high and low arousal of affect (i.e., neither highly excited nor strongly frustrated). Instead, their attention seems to be geared toward how to move along with their learning toward their longer-term goals. The predominant affects are those learning virtues of self-exertion, diligence, endurance of hardship, perseverance, and concentration. A significant affect among East Asians is that they experience affect-respect toward teachers who not only are regarded as authority for teaching, but also viewed as role models for students to emulate. East Asian learners' respect toward their teachers appears not to stem from fear of the commonly labeled teacher authoritarianism, but a sense of the shared common goal of learning by exercising their virtues. After good learning, East Asian learners feel happy, as their European-American peers do. After poor learning, they feel shame/guilt and self-reproach; they also feel sad/depressed (to a lesser extent than European-American learners). Nevertheless, they seem to gravitate toward a less extreme affective state for either learning outcome. Furthermore, unlike their European-American counterparts, they tend to feel little pride because pride is a sign of one's complacency, which their cultures discourage. Such fullness of the self is regarded as a hindrance to their continuous self-striving through learning. Pride is discouraged, whereas humility is valued and encouraged. Humility as both an inner personal strength and an affective response, particularly to high achievement, is believed to be important in guiding the learners in learning.

NOTES

1. See note 66 to Chapter 3.
2. See Davidson, N., Scherer, K., & Goldsmith, H. (Eds.) (2003). *Handbook of affective science*. New York: Oxford University Press for basic descriptions of human emotions.
3. See note 67 to Chapter 3.
4. Fischer, K. W., & Tangney, J. P. (1995). Self-conscious emotions and the affect revolution: Framework and overview. In J. P. Tangney & K. W. Fischer (Eds.), *Self-conscious emotions: The psychology of shame, guilt, embarrassment, and pride* (pp. 3–22). New York: Guilford.

5. Frijda, N. H. (1986). *The emotions.* Cambridge: Cambridge University Press.
6. See Damasio, A. (2005). *Descartes' error: Emotion, reason, and the human brain.* New York: Penguin; note 66 to Chapter 3; and note 4 to this chapter for research on the inseparability between cognition and affect.
7. See note 10 to Chapter 4.
8. Mesquita, B., & Frijda, N. H. (1992). Cultural variations in emotions: A review. *Psychological Bulletin, 112,* 179–204; and Mesquita, B. (2003). Emotions as dynamic cultural phenomena. In N. Davidson, K. Scherer, & H. Goldsmith (Eds.), *Handbook of affective science* (pp. 871–890). New York: Oxford University Press.
9. See note 32 to Chapter 4.
10. See the second reference in note 8 to this chapter.
11. Atkinson, J. W. (1964). *An introduction to motivation.* Princeton, NJ: Van Nostrand.
12. Berlyne, D. (1966). Curiosity and exploration. *Science, 153,* 25–33; and Litman, J. A, & Silvia, Paul J. (2006). The latent structure of trait curiosity: Evidence for interest and deprivation curiosity dimensions. *Journal of Personality Assessment, 86*(3), 318–328.
13. See note 10 to Chapter 4.
14. deCharms, R. (1984). Motivation enhancement in educational settings. In R. Ames & C. Ames (Eds.), *Research on motivation in education: Student motivation* (pp. 275–309). New York: Academic Press; and Ryan, R. M., & Deci, E. L. (2000). Self-determination theory and the facilitation of intrinsic motivation, social development, and well-being. *American Psychologist, 55*(1), 68–78.
15. Bandura, A. (1993). Perceived self-efficacy in cognitive development and functioning. *Educational Psychologist, 28*(2), 117–148.
16. Dweck, C. 1975. The role of expectations and attributions in the alleviation of learned helplessness. *Journal of Personality and Social Psychology, 31,* 674–685; and Dweck, C. S., & Leggett, E. (1988). A social-cognitive approach to motivation and personality. *Psychological Review, 95,* 256–273.
17. See Godes, O. (2009). *The effects of utility value on achievement behavior of two cultures.* Unpublished doctoral dissertation, University of Wisconsin, Madison for her research on the different motivational patterns of European-American and Asian students.
18. Heine, S. J., Kitayama, S., Lehman, D. R., Takata, T., Ide, E., Leung, C., et al. (2001). Divergent consequences of success and failure in Japan and North America: An investigation of self-improving motivations and malleable selves. *Journal of Personality and Social Psychology, 81,* 599–615.
19. Rothbaum, F., & Wang, Y. Z. (2011). Cultural and developmental pathways to acceptance of self and acceptance of the world. In L. A. Jensen (Ed.), *Bridging cultural and developmental approaches to psychology: New syntheses in theory, research, and policy* (pp. 187–211). New York: Oxford University Press.
20. Ng, F. F.-Y., Pomerantz, E., & Lam, S.-F. (2007). European American and Chinese parents' responses to children's success and failure: Implications for children's responses. *Developmental Psychology, 43*(5), 1239–1255; and Miller, P. J., Wang, S-. H., Sandel, T., & Cho, G. E. (2002). Self-esteem as folk theory: A comparison of European American and Taiwanese mothers' beliefs. *Parenting:*

Science and Practice, 2(3), 209–239. Also see Thomaes, S., Reijntjes, A., de Castro, B. O., & Bushman, B. J. (2009). Reality bites-or does it? Realistic self-views buffer negative mood following social threat. *Psychological Science, 3*(2), 1–2 for recent research showing that both inflated and deflated sense of self is maladaptive for people's coping with real negative social feedback. This means that a sense of self that is close to reality is more desirable.

21. Csikszentmihalyi, M. (1990). *Flow: The psychology of optimal experience.* New York: Harper & Row.

22. See note 50 to Chapter 3; and Grolnick, W. S., Ryan, R. M., & Deci, E. L. (1991). Inner sources for school achievement: Motivational mediators of children's perceptions of their parents. *Journal of Educational Psychology, 83*, 508–517.

23. Rotter, J. (1966). Generalized expectancies for internal versus external control of reinforcement. *Psychological Monographs, General & Applied, 80*(1), (Whole No. 609).

24. Weiner, B. (1986). *An attributional theory of motivation and emotion.* New York: Springer.

25. See note 24 to this chapter.

26. Covington, M. V., & Beery, R. (1976). *Self-worth and school learning.* New York: Holt, Rinehart & Winston.

27. See note 26 to this chapter.

28. Covington, M. V., & Omelich, C. L. (1979). Effort: The double-edged sword in school achievement. *Journal of Educational Psychology, 71*, 169–182.

29. See the first reference in note 61 to Chapter 3.

30. Wu, D. Y. H. (1996). Chinese childhood socialization. In M. Bond (Ed.), *The handbook of Chinese psychology* (pp. 143–154). Hong Kong: Oxford University Press.

31. Although the Western child may appear to have come up with the idea on his own, the inspiration is unlikely the child's own, but rather from the common discourse in Western culture about the value of treating animals with humanity. The child is the one who *endorses* and therefore internalizes an otherwise cultural idea as his own, which is the essence of the sociocultural origin of Vygotsky's developmental theory.

32. See the last reference in note 31 to Chapter 3; and the third reference in note 34 to Chapter 4.

33. See note 54 to Chapter 3.

34. See Bandura, A., & Schunk, D. (1981). Cultivating competence, self-efficacy, and intrinsic interest through proximal self-motivation. *Journal of Personality and Social Psychology, 41*, 586–598 for their concepts of proximal versus distal goals in learning.

35. See note 17 to this chapter.

36. See note 18 to this chapter.

37. Li, J. (2006). Self in learning: Chinese adolescents' goals and sense of agency. *Child Development, 77*(2), 482–501.

38. See the second reference in note 46 to Chapter 4.

39. See the last reference in note 9 to Chapter 3.

40. See Berliner, D. C., & Biddle, B. J. (1995). *The manufactured crisis.* Reading, MA: Addison-Wesley; and Hishino, H. J., & Larson, R. (2003). Japanese adolescents'

free time: *Juku, Bukatsu*, and government efforts to create more meaningful lei-sure. In S. Verma & R. Larson (Eds.). *Examining adolescent leisure time across cultures: developmental opportunities and risks* (New Directions for Child and Adolescent Development, No. 99). San Francisco: Jossey-Bass for examples of criticisms of Asian schooling.

41. See the second reference in note 40 to this chapter.

42. See the second reference in note 23 to Chapter 3.

43. See Tsai, J. L., Knutson, B., & Fung, H. H. (2006). Cultural variation in affect valuation. *Journal of Personality and Social Psychology, 90*(2), 288–307 for empirical evidence that Chinese prefer less high-arousal positive affect (excitement) but more low-arousal positive affect (calm) than European Americans.

44. d'Ailly, H. (2003). Children's autonomy and perceived control in learning: A model of motivation and achievement in Taiwan. *Journal of Educational Psychology, 95*(1), 84–96, p. 94.

45. See note 50 to Chapter 3.

46. Vansteenkiste, M., Zhou, M.-M., Lens, W., & Soenens, B. (2005). Experiences of autonomy and control among Chinese learners: Vitalizing or immobilizing? *Journal of Educational Psychology, 97*(3), 468–483.

47. See the reference in note 47 to Chapter 2.

48. Markus, H. R., & Nurius, P. (1986). Possible selves. *American Psychologist, 41*, 954–969.

49. Frei, J. R., & Shaver, P. R. (2002). Respect in close relationships: Prototype definition, self-report assessment, and initial correlates. *Personal Relationships, 9*, 121–139.

50. See note 47 to Chapter 2.

51. Additional discussion can be found in Chapter 3.

52. Hsueh, Y., Zhou, Z.-K., Cohen, R., Hundley, R. J., & Deptula, D. P. (2005). Knowing and showing respect: Chinese and U.S. children's understanding of respect and its association to their friendships. *Journal of Psychology in Chinese Societies, 6*(2), 89–120.

53. Peng, K.-P., & Nisbett, R. E. (1999). Culture, dialects, and reasoning about contradiction. *American Psychologist, 54*, 741–754.

54. Tracy, J. L., & Robins, R. W. (2007). The nature of pride. In J. L. Tracy, R. W. Robins, & J. P. Tangney (Eds.), *The self-conscious emotions: Theory and research* (pp. 263–282). New York: Guilford. Although the authors distinguish two kinds of pride in the West – authentic pride and hubristic pride – the everyday concept of pride is mostly the positive authentic type.

55. Lewis, M. (2007). Self-conscious emotional development. In J. L. Tracy, R. W. Robins, & J. P. Tangney (Eds.), *The self-conscious emotions: Theory and research* (pp. 134–152). New York: Guilford.

56. See the first reference in note 88 to Chapter 3.

57. Lewis, M., & Wolan-Sullivan, M. (2005). The development of self-conscious emotions. In A. Elliot & C. S. Dweck (Eds.), *Handbook of competence and motivation* (pp. 185–201). New York: Guilford.

58. Li, J., Fung, H., Liang, C.-H., Resch, J., & Luo, L. (2009). Is the glass half-empty or half-full? Emotional responses to children's learning among European American and Taiwanese parents. Manuscript under review.

59. Eid, M., & Diener, E. (2001). Norms for experiencing emotions in different cultures: Inter- and intranational differences. *Journal of Personality and Social Psychology, 81*(5), 869–885; Ross, M., Heine, S. J., Wilson, A. E., & Sugimori, S. (2005). Cross-cultural discrepancies in self-appraisals. *Personality and Social Psychology Bulletin, 31*(9), 1175–1188; and Scollon, C. N., Diener, E., Oishi, S., & Biswas-Diener, R. (2005). An experience sampling and cross-cultural investigation of the relation between pleasant and unpleasant affect. *Cognition and Emotion, 19*(1), 27–52.

60. Sommers, S. (1984). Adults evaluating their emotions: A cross-cultural perspective. In C. Z. Malatesta & C. E. Izard (Eds.), *Emotion in adult development* (pp. 319–338). Beverly Hills, CA: Sage.

61. See the second reference in note 84 to Chapter 3.

62. See the first and third references in note 59 to this chapter.

63. See the second reference in note 6 to Chapter 3.

64. See the first reference in note 61 to Chapter 3 for profiles of model learners who feel either a brief duration of happiness or do not make a big deal of high achievement. Instead, they warn themselves against arrogance and strive to focus on further learning.

65. Ayduk, O., May, D., Downey, G., & Higgins, E. T. (2003). Tactical differences in coping with rejection sensitivity: The role of prevention pride. *Personality and Social Psychology Bulletin, 29*(4), 435–448; and Grant, H., & Higgens, E. T. (2003). Optimism, promotion pride, and prevention pride as predictors of qualify of life. *Personality and Social Psychology Bulletin, 29*(12), 1521–1523.

66. See the first and third references in note 59 to this chapter.

67. See note 65 to this chapter.

68. Lee, A. Y., Aaker, J. L., & Gardner, W. L. (2000). The pleasures and pains of distinct self-construals: The role of interdependence in regulatory focus. *Journal of Personality and Social Psychology, 78*(6), 1122–1134.

69. Tangney, J. P. (2000). Humility: Theoretical perspectives, empirical findings and directions for future research. *Journal of Social and Clinical Psychology, 19*(1), 70–82; and Morris, J. A., Brotheridge, C. M., & Urbanski, J. C. (2005). Bringing humility to leadership: Antecedents and consequences of leader humility. *Human Relations, 58*(10), 1323–1350.

70. See the third reference in note 82 to Chapter 3.

71. See note 5 to Chapter 2.

72. See reference in note 74 to Chapter 2.

73. See the third reference in note 82 to Chapter 3.

74. In sharp contrast to the Western view, humility is strongly desirable in leaders at any level in any organization. For example, the Yellow Emperor (c. 2718–2597, legend has it; he lived 121 years), the acknowledged legendary chieftain of tribes who united China, is known not only for his achievement of uniting Chinese tribes, but also for his humble leadership style. He is said to have created an effective and innovative administrative system and many inventions of technology such as the lunar calendar, medicine, and twelve-tone music. But he also taught people how to sow and how to harvest by personally working in the fields (also clearly symbolizing the virtue of diligence and endurance of hardship). Throughout history, leaders who were admired by people were those

who displayed humility in spite of their great power and achievements. Current Asian political leaders that win support from people seem to show this quality as well. Chinese premier Wen Jiabao is a prime example. Similarly, Ma Ying-jeou, the president of Taiwan, along with other Asian leaders, also conveys an unequivocal sense of humility in his style.

75. See the second reference in note 82 to Chapter 3, pp. 73–74.

76. See the second reference in note 6 to Chapter 3, and Li, J. (2005). Mind or virtue: Western and Chinese beliefs about learning. *Current Directions in Psychological Science, 14*(4), 190–194.

77. Heine, S. J., Lehman, D. R., Markus, H. R., & Kitayama, S. (1999). Is there a universal need for positive self-regard? *Psychological Review, 106,* 766–794. June Tangney and others distinguish humility from modesty by pointing out that humility is a personal inner strength whereas modesty is more about external aspects such as clothing and gender-related behavior (e.g., female modesty, see the third reference in note 82 to Chapter 3). However, research on Asian modesty bias versus Western self-enhancing bias uses the two terms interchangeably.

78. Because so little attention has been paid to the construct of humility, research trying to measure low self-esteem in Asian learners needs to take the notion of humility into consideration, distinguishing true low self-esteem from humility as distinguished by Tangney and others. It has been a consistent finding that Asian learners rank low on self-esteem measures despite their high achievement. For example, in the 2006 PISA international education assessment, East Asian students had low self-esteem in both math and science (South Korea ranked thirty-second in mathematics and twenty-first in science; Japan ranked thirty-fourth and sixteenth, respectively; and Taiwan ranked thirtieth and eighteenth, respectively). In contrast, U.S. students scored highest on self-esteem for science and fourth in math. Yet, their achievement in TIMSS was nineteenth in math and eighteenth in science, and in 2006, PISA ranked them fourteenth in science, fifteenth in reading, and nineteenth in math (see the first reference in note 7 to Chapter 3 for a more detailed discussion on the data). In light of the important distinction between humility and true low self-esteem, I urge researchers to rethink their measures of self-esteem intended for East Asian students, which may have mistaken a strength for a weakness, thus producing these puzzling results about East Asian students.

6

Nerd's Hell and Nerd's Haven

Modern formal learning takes place with age-graded peers. Peers, therefore, are a significant social context for child development. When children depart early childhood and enter middle childhood (approximately between ages six and twelve), they become more oriented toward the social world beyond their family. However, in the modern world, the beginning of middle childhood coincides with the onset of schooling. Therefore, the major shift in children's social world is from home to school. Although they have less parental supervision, they continue to be supervised by schoolteachers and other school staff. What is dramatically changed is that children now spend much of their daily time with same-age peers.

Much developmental research documents the significant role peer context plays in child development.[1] Middle childhood is a period during which children's mental capacity increases (in addition to their increased physical capacity), particularly in the area of social cognition.[2] Whereas they are less able to appreciate how other people's minds work, they now are more sophisticated in their understanding. They now realize that what they know may not be known by others and what they see may not be seen by others; that is, other people have their own minds and do their own thinking. They become increasingly sophisticated in their ability to take new perspectives. They can anticipate, interpret, and explain others' desires, thoughts, and actions more accurately, independent of what they themselves desire, think, and do. Socially, they experience intensive peer interactions. They become interested in peer relationships, friendship, and their own social standing among peers, but at the same time, they care about their own quality, competence, and independence.[3]

Along with all of these developmental changes, children attend school and are under pressure to achieve. It is therefore important to understand how children's social experience with peers influences their learning and achievement in school. There is much more research on how Western children navigate and fare through these processes than how children in other cultures do so. Research involving Western children shows that when they have good peer relations and higher social standing, they tend to achieve higher.[4] This general finding is not surprising given the importance of children's social needs. It is not hard to see that a well-liked child feels safe and free of peer-related worry and can therefore focus on intellectual tasks in school. This positive social support from peers can also boost the child's self-esteem and self-confidence, which can generate higher learning motivation. But when a child is not well liked, is ignored, rejected, or even bullied, that child may fear school and may not be able to learn well.[5]

Despite all this informative research, there has been relatively less research on how peers regard each other as learners. In other words, how do children view each other as a result of the inevitable disparities in achievement? In this chapter, I thread pieces of research together in order to shed light on this neglected but important research topic. I make three claims. First, how children regard each other as learners/achievers has a significant impact on how they respond to, interact with, relate to, and treat each other. Second, the particular attitude children have toward their learning and achieving peers has serious consequences to children's further learning (in addition to their general social development and well-being). Third, children's attitudes toward their learning and achieving peers are profoundly shaped by the values of their respective cultures. Western and East Asian cultures offer an excellent contrastive perspective on these processes and outcomes.

THE WESTERN LEARNER IN THE EYE OF THE PEERS

In the West, if one is incredibly lucky, one's peer in middle school and high school may become one's friend.[6] More often, a peer in school is a competitor, a stressor, and – with surprising commonality – a harasser.[7] Desire to excel, or at least not to come below their peers, makes school a competitive setting.[8] A peer is a stressor because one frequently worries about how one is viewed by peers, and how one might run the risk of not being liked and consequently being excluded from peer groups.[9] A peer can become a harasser if one is singled out as a target to be picked on, ridiculed, or bullied.[10] Moreover, a peer can also be someone to ignore or to neglect, leaving peers in social isolation.[11] In Western school culture, peer harassment and victimization, based on extensive research, is quite prevalent.[12]

Nerd's Hell

Most striking and unbelievable (to me, who came from an entirely different culture) is the research finding that those who try to learn and to achieve are tormented with most peer harassment.[13] In fact, there are terms reserved for students in middle school and high school who are interested, motivated, and make an effort to pursue knowledge. They are infamously called "nerds," "geeks," "dorks," and a host of other derogatory names. This type of peer harassment occurs not only in the United States, but apparently in many Western cultures. In the English-speaking countries of Canada, Australia, and New Zealand, the terms popular in the United States also enjoy popularity. In Britain, the equivalent term for nerd is *swot*,[14] in Germany – *Schreber*, in France – *bouttoneux*,[15] in Holland – *stuud*,[16] and in Israel – *hnun*.[17]

What is a nerd? The term[18] is considered to be homegrown in the United States, perhaps with the initial invention by Dr. Seuss for his playful children's rhyme, "a Nerkle, a Nerd, and a Seersucker too," in his book *If I Ran the Zoo*.[19] Soon the term caught the attention of the popular media in the ensuing decades, as exemplified by the sitcom *Happy Days*. By 1960s and 1970s, the term was widespread across the United States and other Western cultures. It is typically used to label a student, more often a boy, during middle school or high school, who is socially and physically awkward. This alone does not earn the boy the title of a "nerd," however. The key defining attribute is that the boy is *intellectually* curious and makes an effort to pursue his interests (especially science, math, and technology, or else subjects that the rest of the peers find too complex and difficult to comprehend); above all, he is a high achiever in those subjects.[20] *American Heritage Dictionary of the English Language* now defines nerd as a "person who is single-minded or accomplished in scientific or technical pursuits but is felt to be socially inept."[21] It is this combination of characteristics that gives birth to labeling someone a nerd. Current research indicates that not only boys continue to be labeled as such; girls who show intellectual interest and achieve well are also subject to such labeling. Moreover, the term now extends to children from all ethnicities that fit the image of a nerd, whereas it was initial used exclusively for white boys.[22]

If this were just a game of labeling without any serious consequences, it would not be worth anyone's attention. But as Sheldon White[23] cogently argued, a newborn term in a culture signifies an important social reality, such as the term *adolescence* occurring in the Western culture in the late nineteenth century. The emergence of nerd and similar terms across Western cultures is no exception. As it turns out, labeling a peer as a nerd is a major daily form of peer harassment against those who actually do what schooling is intended for children to do by society, schools, teachers, parents, and children themselves. Unfortunately, any child, once stigmatized as a nerd, becomes the target of open ridicule, verbal taunts, social exclusion, and even physical attacks from peers.[24]

Research documents that such peer harassment is prevalent. In 1989, N. T. Feather[25] asked more than 500 high school students and 300 college students in Australia to respond to scenarios in which either a high achiever or an average achiever experienced failure, in addition to some general attitude toward these two kinds of achievers. He found that these respondents were more pleased to see a high achiever fail than to see an average achiever fail. He also found that high school students were happier with and friendlier toward a high achiever who fell to the average position than toward an average achiever who fell to the bottom. Feather used the apt metaphor of the "fall of the tall poppy" to capture the attitude students express toward high achievers. Moreover, Feather found that the high achiever was viewed as "less sociable and more of a loner than the average achiever."[26] In a follow-up study, Feather used his Tall Polly Scale with some 200 ordinary adults and found that those who had lower self-esteem and attached less importance to the value of achievement expressed more such negative attitudes.

John and Michael Bishop[27] recently conducted a large study on how such a peer norm functions in American students' school engagement and study effort. They interviewed tenth-graders from eight public schools located in predominantly white upper-middle-class suburban towns. This qualitative study enabled them to develop a comprehensive survey, which they administered to more than 110,000 middle-school and high-school students across 325 schools.

What they found was consistent with the studies by Feather and others but with more nuanced insights: students who are *average* in academic ability, pro-learning attitude, and achievement receive the least peer harassment (40–100 incidents per year). Students who fall either at the low end or the high end of the scale – that is, those out of the norm – receive the most peer harassment (120–220 incidents per year). At the lower end, peers harass two very different groups of students: those who are least motivated and are themselves disruptors and slackers (falling below the norm) and those who are perceived as low in ability but try to study hard to raise their achievement (striving to beat the odds, again attempting to go above the norm). The researchers used the phrase "try but not too hard"[28] to describe the peer norm that is strongly enforced in American public schools.

Against this cultural backdrop, students who want to do well in school are afraid of displaying their effort and their achievement. The researchers state: "Typically they are code switchers who affirm the 'try but not too hard' norm at school but hit their books when they get home.... Often high levels of effort are kept secret and academic accomplishments down played in order to fit in and to avoid jealousy."[29] The researchers further explain that getting good grades in and of itself is not the probable reason for inviting peer harassment; rather, it is one's intention, motivation, and behavior that accompany the good grades. If effort is seen by peers as "sucking up" or studying harder in order to get ahead, the effort is likely to be regarded as unfair and thus sanctioned. However,

> getting good grades because of a high IQ is not viewed as intentional and is seldom sanctioned. Indeed top grades achieved effortlessly signal high ability – something that peers and parents value a great deal.[30] Consequently, high GPA students often avoid peer harassment by claiming not to study, eschewing public displays of interest in academic learning and keeping their grades secret. Many high achieving students gain popularity by pursuing this strategy.[31]

Unless a student possesses an effortless, natural mental gift, he or she would be better off not to try hard. In a study comparing fourth-, sixth-, and eighth-grade students, researchers also found that eighth-graders (fourteen-year-olds), but not the younger children, were reluctant to disclose their diligence (amount of work they did) to their popular peers despite their willingness to disclose their effort to teachers. By eighth grade, children who were once regarded as popular as a result of high ability and hard work dropped lower in popularity. Those who did not work hard regardless of their ability enjoyed the highest peer popularity.[32] Another recent study comparing eighth- and ninth-graders in Canada, Germany, and Israel found that fear of peer rejection and ostracism takes a toll on students' motivation and achievement. The more students buy into this kind of peer culture, the greater the toll. Furthermore, the more prevalently such peer norms exist within the larger culture, the greater this negative impact.[33]

These studies compel us to draw the conclusion that in the West there exists a forceful peer culture (at least in public school) that pits academic excellence against peer acceptance; that is, high academic achievement comes at a high social cost. Given that social acceptance by peers is a matter of high concern for children, particularly adolescents, they are forced to choose between their need to learn well and their need for peer support. They cannot have both unless they possess inborn high intelligence and the ability to do well without trying. The effortful tall poppy is vehemently hacked down by peers initially but eventually by children's diminished motivation for learning. This force, as many researchers acknowledge, is the tyranny of mediocrity. It is quite amazing that this peer culture enjoys longevity and perpetuation even in the face of the concerted effort of parents and schools to motivate children for higher achievement. It is obvious that, as lamented by John and Michael Bishop,[34] these adult efforts are canceled out by peer culture to a large extent. This culture makes so much student effort and educational reform utterly futile, much like Sisyphus' pushing his rock up the hill only to watch it roll back down again (according to Greek mythology, Sisyphus was a king who was eternally punished for his mistakes by being made to push a large rock uphill only to watch it roll down again and again).

Sadly, most children do not possess top intelligence and cannot be schooled with "effortless perfection." The Lake Woebegone myth where all children achieve above average, as aptly told by the comedian Garrison Keillor, is just that – a myth. Teachers, parents, and children themselves are keenly aware of the reality. Many children also concur with their parents and teachers that they should learn well, and that the only way to achieve that is to make an effort. For such children, school is hell. Extensive research looking at schoolchildren under peer attack shows that they suffer, among other things, from anxiety, low self-esteem, and depression, not to mention low achievement.[35] Such psychological problems can have long-term negative impact on these children well into adulthood.[36] It may take years for these people to regain self-confidence. Some need to seek out clinical therapy to restore their mental health. Some may never heal. Parents also are fearful that such misfortune may befall their own children and feel hopeless if this indeed happens. To reduce the risk, parents encourage their children to engage in hobbies, extracurricular activities, and sports, which can increase their children's standing among peers.

My own son attended a public middle school with virtually no diversity in the student body. He happened to be somewhat shy, with below-average athletic prowess. But he was interested in and good at math and did well in school. His name was on the honor roll and adorned the school hallways. His experience was that of a typical nerd, and he was harassed by his peers on a daily basis. Not only did some of the peers verbally taunt and exclude him from peer groups and activities; one big boy once tried to throw him in a trash can. We managed to collect some twelve insulting terms addressed to him. Each day was an ordeal for both our son and us. If our son came back from school and reported no harassment, it was a day of blessing for him, and my husband and I would feel relief. But the problem became so severe that one day our son refused to go to school, demanding that we either home-school him or send him to a different school.

Unfortunately, this peer culture is fully present and well-functioning much earlier than middle school and high school. Available research indicates that children as young as kindergarteners and first-graders become aware of the double-edged sword of high achievement in the West. As alluded to in Chapter 3, my own research[37] using children's story completions shows that at as young as age five, European-American children are cognizant of the social cost of high academic achievement. They are fully aware that while the high-achieving child is very happy for him- or herself (and so are his or her parents and teachers), the peers are "unhappy," "sad," "mad," and "jealous" because the achieving child did better than the peers. Some children reported actual actions taken against high achievers, such as peers not wanting to play with them or saying hurtful words to them. Such peer isolation and rejection make the high achievers scared and worried.

Is It Human Nature to Harass Nerds?

When my husband and I went to see our son's principal and guidance counselor, we proposed to help the school launch a program called "respect for your peers." But our hope was shattered by the school leaders' attribution of such peer problems to human nature – that is, a universal claim that this type of nerd harassment is in the human genes. "Kids are just like that" was what they said. Their belief was that because it is human nature, the school could do nothing to change it.

We could not endure the situation any longer and enrolled our son in a private school where children suddenly were no longer "just like that," and the nature claim crumbled right there. Because his new school did not believe in the nature argument for nerd harassment, or perhaps because most children who enrolled in this new school were nerds themselves, no one was called or harassed as a nerd.[38] Luckily, our son made friends and experienced much better school life. The intellectual and the social were finally integrated for him.

For the longest time, psychologists, particularly developmental psychologists, treated this kind of peer culture and harassment as more or less a given. This universal argument found backing from research on animal hierarchy and the pan-cultural existence of social dominance and submission.[39]

The second support for the view of universality is actually a consequence of research relying on one cultural group, namely that of the West.[40] This is limitation mistaken as support. Research findings based on Western theories and people were believed to be applicable to people across all cultures, without actually studying these people or these cultures. However, in recent decades, researchers studying other cultural groups have produced evidence that peer culture in school differs from culture to culture,[41] as will be seen in the section on East Asian peer culture. The once held universal peer norm is just one norm of one particular type of culture (even within the West, this norm is not universal, as in the case of my son's new school, and as reportedly observable across the gymnasiums of Europe). It is therefore important to examine the norm of Western peer culture from the perspective of the West as a specific case rather than a universal human norm.

Inescapable Dooming of Nerds in the West

Why are motivated, interested, and serious learners so pejoratively regarded, and why do so many Western peers feel it legitimate to harass their peers for doing what they themselves also would like to do and to achieve? These questions become even more pressing when we consider the West as the culture that introduced and continues to uphold personal rights, human rights, equality, and democratic social order for all. It is a truism that everyone desires safety, respect, and a chance to receive a good education, yet Western school peer culture does not seem to grant it to everyone. In fact, it seems to do the opposite, to undermine these lofty human moral aspirations of the culture.

Based on my review of research and theoretical discussions, there are some plausible reasons for why this peer culture exists and functions the way it does. As discussed in previous chapters, the first and foremost reason has to do with how the individual and the self are defined. Extensive research in psychology shows quite convincingly[42] that Western people hold a *fixed* view of the self. Accordingly, the self is born with a unique set of characteristics such as temperamental differences that are present at birth and not shared with other individuals. Such unique characteristics are believed to be foundational to the person's eventual personality development. In the sphere of academic learning, many researchers have demonstrated and argued that Western people believe in the existence and validity of ability/intelligence, particularly the inborn nature of it, as well as related personal qualities such as talent, creativity, and style. The uniqueness of these individual qualities is the source of self-esteem and personal pride.[43]

Therefore, people feel positive about themselves when they achieve well in school because this confirms their sense of self-worth. However, when not achieving well, the self is inevitably implicated as lacking something inherent, usually intelligence, which is regarded as the underlying power for achievement. This realization can be devastating to the person's self-worth.[44] No one likes to face this personal devastation.

Yet, the schooling process serves to do nothing except to counter this very cultural ethos that celebrates each individual's uniqueness and self-worth. Schooling is a process that is heavily dependent on evaluation of individuals' learning outcomes. All schools, public or private, proceed with frequent assessment of pupils' learning process and achievement. This evaluation-dependent schooling process inevitably leads children to engage in increasing social comparison of who is smart, who is average, who is doing well, who is not, and above all where children themselves stand. Every time a teacher asks a question for children to answer, social comparison of this sort is occurring. The child who answers the question becomes the target for peers' self-other evaluation. And this takes place in addition to the teacher's formal and informal evaluation of children, which lies at the heart of schooling. When the evaluative outcome is favorable, the child is likely to feel good about him- or herself. But when the evaluative outcome is not favorable, the child may feel not only negative about the self, but also resentful toward the target child who is the very cause of the negative self-realization of the evaluating child.[45]

Hence, it is not exaggerating to say that the schooling process is one that breaks most children's sense of self as a unique and great person. The harsh reality is that only a handful of children in any school can ever be truly unique and great in this impersonal process of schooling and may emerge out of the process unscarred. Such children may truly be those who master academic learning with "effortless perfection." Schooling is intended to give most children needed competence, knowledge, and skills for a common life. As such, schooling makes children realize, unavoidably, that they are just ordinary. This is to say that as few children become the redefined unique and great individuals, the rest are likely to experience personal downgrading. In a culture that holds a fixed view of the self, it would be dubious if high achievers would be welcome by peers. Why would they be kind and respectful toward those who are seen as, and probably are, the very cause of their downgrading?

The second reason is that the West, particularly the United States, is an intensely competitive culture. Márta Fülöp, a Hungarian psychologist, studied U.S., Japanese, and Hungarian high school children's understanding of competition.[46] She found that all three groups of children acknowledged the prevalence of competition in their school life. However, American children found it most unpleasant and disliked it most. They viewed competition as a zero-sum game, meaning that if one child gets ahead and wins, the rest are necessarily behind and lose. The conceptual importance lies in the idea that competition cannot make both parties winners. Japanese children liked competition most, but they viewed it very differently from their U.S. counterparts. Instead of regarding it as a zero-sum game, Japanese children saw competition as a chance to catch up with their peers, and peers help each other so that all end up doing better in school. Children enjoy this type of competition because both parties are winners in the end. Hungarian children were in the middle, focusing on getting to the top ranks but not necessarily regarding competition as a zero-sum game. Based on her studies, Fülöp concludes that although competition is observed in nature and across the human world, it takes different forms, meanings, and processes depending on the culture and the goals of competition. Competition is thus a culturally constructed concept that guides human action.

Perhaps there is a connection between U.S. children's view of competition as a zero-sum game and the general fixed view of the self. Winning among competitors is the ultimate testimony of self-worth. So long as the individual's self-worth is prized above everyone else, such competition is likely to persist and flourish. These two processes function to feed off each other, making the dynamics reach new heights. Winning validates and solidifies the self that is likely to engage in competition to win. This process can continue as long as one is always the winner. But for those who experience more losing than winning, the assurance of self-worth cannot be sustained. Losing casts doubt on the self, weakens it, and discourages it from making an effort. In other domains of life, people could just abandon the activity at which they do not excel and move on to pursue other activities where they may shine. However, because compulsory education does not allow children to divert their learning time to other activities, they cannot escape academic learning and must face up to the challenges whether or not they personally like them. In academic learning, children become more vulnerable to the zero-sum style of competition and may become indifferent, give up, or, quite likely, turn to harass those who are seen as the cause of their loss.

The third reason is that Western culture seems to hold a talent assumption for intellectual achievement. Talent, as the term suggests, is something that one is born with. This view has deep roots dating back to antiquity.[47] Again, this idea is consistent with the fixed view of the self. However, this assumption is not easily refuted when we look at the fact that not all children are born with the same intelligence profile, with some apparently more talented than others in just about any domain of performance. The easily identifiable geniuses such as Mozart, Picasso, Einstein, and Marie Curie, as well as the existence of precocious children in math, science, reading, and writing, all lend support to the talent assumption.[48] Carol Dweck has studied this assumption for decades.[49] She uses the terms *entity theory* versus *incremental theory* of intelligence that children and adults hold about school learning. Accordingly, entity theorists believe that one's intelligence is fixed at birth, whereas incremental theorists believe that one's intelligence grows as one learns. Interestingly, Western kindergarteners think that smart people work hard and hardworking people are also smart. Unfortunately, as they reach middle childhood, they begin to realize that effort alone may not lead to great achievement; one also needs ability. Adolescents are clear that effort is actually an indication of one's low ability. Smart people do not *need* to work hard. Those who do must not be very smart.[50] Middle-school and high-school children have been widely documented to use all sorts of strategies to hide their effort (not just to fend off peer harassment) in order to avoid being viewed as low in ability (mostly likely by teachers).[51] Given the deep-seated nature of the talent assumption in the West, it is not hard to see how those who try to work hard to improve their achievement may be regarded as trying futilely to alter their "unalterable" lot. This is probably why the low-ability children were the first to take the brunt of their peers' harassment in Bishops' study. But it is also undeniable that the term *nerd*, along with its image, projects a pathetic air and consequent laughter in the listener. This is also likely the reason why those who manage to impress peers with "effortless perfection" are left alone.

I happen to know a boy who, in my view, offers an excellent illustration of how this talent assumption operates in school. In each of his high school English classes, his first essays would receive a B. His teachers were all highly qualified and caring and were always willing to help the boy. In ninth grade, this boy actually tried to do everything his teacher asked him to do such as writing an outline, drafting, and revising based on the teacher's suggestions. He still received a B. Being the inquisitive person he was, he began an experiment on himself. He deliberately did not submit his next essays on time, first just a few hours late, then one day late, and eventually several weeks late. When he did submit all of his work, he still received a B. In his sophomore and junior year, the same process repeated. This boy concluded that there was an unspoken ordinance at work here: once a student was labeled as a B-writer, there was no amount of good that he or she could do to change the teacher's view. The most bizarre finding of his self-experimentation was that there was also no amount of bad that the B-writer could do to reduce him/her to a C-writer either. He was held in his slot, so to speak! Of course, most readers would agree that his boy was foolish to experiment with his own academic performance. That aside, it behooves us to look at how deep-rooted the fixed view of talent is on school ground. Needless to say, this boy no longer enjoys writing, even though he writes, in my judgment, quite well, certainly much better than I began writing in English.

On the scholarly front, Heyman, Fu, and Lee[52] in a recent study explored European-American and Chinese late elementary school children's willingness or reluctance to disclose their achievement or failure to their peers. They found that European-American children disclosed their achievement only to peers who had similar achievement levels. They would not disclose their achievement to peers with higher or lower levels in fear that they would be regarded as bragging (if disclosed to lower achiever) or revealing their low ability (if disclosed to higher achiever, presumably fearing being viewed as stuck in their unalterably low slot).

Jeannie Oakes, a leading researcher on the American education system, conducted long and thorough investigations on the well-known high school tracking system. Her research provides the clear conclusion that high school education is not about improving children's learning but about confirming their exhibited ability. Oakes and Guiton write:

> What made these recommendations and initial judgments [from junior high school teachers for placing ninth grades] so powerful was the widespread belief that a student's educational prospects are virtually set by the time he or she gets to high school. Many considered motivation and intellectual ability to be fixed attributes over which educators have little control. We found little evidence that educators at any of the schools thought that high schools courses could (or should even try to) increase students' intellectual capacities or raise their expectations. This theme echoed in the words of many administrators, teachers, and counselors.... Some told us directly that they felt that it was "all over" by high school. For example, [a] principal ... said that he could tell by the end of kindergarten which children would be successful in high school.... One counselor reported that high school teachers generally believe that, once a student gets to high school, he or she is either intrinsically motivated or not and this cannot be changed.[53]

Given "the prevailing view that high school students' abilities are intractable,"[54] the purpose of curriculum and pedagogy is thus to accommodate what characteristics children already possess, but not to alter or improve them. Although the researchers studied high school teachers and administrators' beliefs that underlay the tracking philosophy and practice, the researchers' report suggests that this kind of view is not limited to high school; kindergarten teachers can also cast the same kind of judgment on much younger children's ability.

Finally, there seems to be an assumption of the intellectual-social divide. If a child is interested in intellectual pursuits, something must be amiss with that child. The missing and hence wrong part is that the child must lack social competence and may not ever acquire it, as Feather's tall poppies were viewed. Putting aside the serious moral problem of harassing someone who lacks some competence (this is similar to the moral problem of harassing a handicapped person), this assumption of the intellectual-social divide is flat out wrong. Developmental research as well as the fast-advancing field of neuroscience tells us that all human beings (even those who are born with congenital challenges) possess the capacity to develop all human competence to a very high, albeit varying, degree. Every human being, if given the opportunity and support, can flourish with just about any skill.[55] Not only are we not doomed at birth; we have potentials that are rarely fully realized. A child who lacks any competence initially – be it intellectual, social, or even athletic – can acquire them when put in the right nurturing environment. But if the fixed-self/fixed-ability view (contrary to what is scientifically known) reigns in the school yard, the so-called nerds are bound to be created, who are, sadly, doomed to suffer cruel peer harassment.

THE EAST ASIAN LEARNER IN THE EYE OF THE PEERS

The school peer culture is quite different in East Asia. In Chinese culture, the strongest influence came, undoubtedly, from the Confucian learning tradition. Japan and Korea may be similar to Chinese culture in this regard, owing to the same influence. To begin with, the very term "school peer" in Chinese is *tongxue* (同學), made of two characters. The first means "together" and the second "learning"; "peers" are thus literally "those who learn together." In Japanese, a more formal term 學友, also still used in Chinese written language, means "learning friends." *Douryou* (同僚) or *nakama* (仲間) are more everyday terms but also used for peers at workplace. 同 in 同僚 is the same character as the first one in the Chinese common term 同學, and 仲間 means people in the same group who do activities together. In Korean, the term peer is *kyo-woo* (校友), meaning "school friends." All of the terms in these three cultures have the shared characters, either "together" (同), "learn" (學), or "friend" (友).

The distinction between the Western concept of "peer" and East Asian terms is not trivial. According to Webster's English dictionary, a "peer" is "one that is of equal standing with another, one belonging to the same societal group especially based on age, grade, or status."[56] The key defining attribute is equal standing of age, grade, or status. Most highlighted is the idea of status in a group. The Chinese term *tongxue* is defined in the *New Dictionary of Modern Chinese Language* as "one that learns/studies with the same teacher and/or at the same school."[57] Status such as age, grade, and standing is not part of the definition. What is highlighted is learning/studying together at the same place from the same teacher(s), and the relationship is that of friends. For the Western peer, the key importance is placed on the status/standing in a group of school-aged children, whereas in the East Asian terms, it is friends learning from the same teacher(s) or at the same place.[58]

Significance of Learning Peers

How do Chinese tongxues (hereinafter the English term "peer" is used for convenience) regard and treat each other? From the very beginning, when Confucius first took his students, a peer is someone one studied with. Peers have the same goal of learning. As discussed in previous chapters, in Confucian persuasion, the goal is to follow a path to cultivate oneself morally. Despite a personal commitment to this process, the actual learning is not best achieved by oneself, contemplating and practicing self-cultivation alone. Peers are seen as essential in this learning process. Confucius' *Analects* opens with the first sentence: "Having studied, to then repeatedly apply what you have learned – is this not a source of pleasure?" The very next sentence, also cast in the same delightful question, is "To have [like-minded] friends come from distant quarters [to study with oneself] – is this not a source of enjoyment?"[59] Thus, learning with peers who are pursuing the same moral goals was conceived of by Confucius as an enjoyment.

One's peers are then not just strangers who happen to learn/study at the same time under the same mentor, but like-minded friends who pursue the same life goals. They are supporters of each other. The *Analects* records the following exchange between Confucius and Zigong, a pupil from a wealthy background who felt a need to show (off) his insight into human virtue when he no longer felt superior to the poor:

> ZIGONG SAID: "What do you think of the saying: 'Poor but not inferior; rich but not superior'?" The Master replied: "Not bad, but not as good as: 'Poor but enjoying the way (*dao*, 道), rich but loving ritual propriety (*li*, 禮)'"

ZIGONG SAID: "*The Book of Songs* states:
>Like bone carved and polished,
>Like jade cut and ground.
>Is this not what you have in mind?"

THE MASTER SAID: "Zigong, it is only with the likes of you then that I can discuss the *Songs*! On the basis of what has been said, you know what is yet to come."[60]

"Like bone carved and polished, like jade cut and ground" (*qiecuo zhuomo*, 切磋琢磨) is a verse of a poem in the *Book of Songs* [61] from which Confucius and his pupils drew wisdom and aesthetic guidance. This poetic verse through Confucius' teaching of Zigong has come to epitomize what learning peers do with each other in East Asia: studying, wondering, and discussing, helping, correcting, and above all, learning from and improving each other. There is no wonder why one's learning peers are the major part of one's life-long social circles beyond the family. One's shared learning is also one's shared living and shared growth, which is treasured dearly. Thus, the term *tongxue* in higher learning becomes *tongchuang*, shared study hall, and eventually may become *tongchuang haoyou*, good friends of a shared study hall. This basic regard of one's learning peers has lasted through millennia to the present (as will be seen in late sections on research from East Asia). "Friends" are part of the formal Japanese and Chinese term 學友 and the Korean term 校友. In this cultural ethos, calling a learning friend a derogatory name and harassing such a friend is, to put it bluntly, quite unthinkable.

Nerd's Haven

The reader may be wondering if there are no peer problems in this kind of cultural context. To be sure, there is also a term *bookworm* (書呆子) to describe someone who does nothing but study books. However, this term is not often used for and by schoolchildren, but rather for and by adults. There may be other terms in these cultures to refer to unusual behaviors and styles. Certainly, peer isolation and rejection also occur in East Asia. Recently, there have been reports about increasing peer bullying in East Asian schools.[62] But the important difference here is that peer unkindness has little to do with the target peer pursuing intellectual interests or being an excellent student. According to Xinyin Chen, an expert in Chinese children's social development, there are only two peer groups in Chinese school yard, at least within Mainland China: the good student group and the antisocial/delinquent group. Nerd as a type or a classification does not seem to exist (yet, there are many more peer groups in the West such as the jocks, geeks, brainies, goths, stoners, druggies, etc.).[63]

Quite the contrary, those who achieve highly are generally admired, popular, emulated, and sought after as friends regardless of whether these high achievers are "uncool" otherwise (e.g., appearance, athletic ability, and purely social prowess). Good learning alone is reason for peer respect and admiration. In my study on Chinese ideal learners, the respondents were asked to describe how the learners' peers would regard them; 87 percent wrote respect and admiration and 42 percent acknowledging them as role models and desiring their friendship.[64] Huang's research on why Taiwanese children are willing to attend the so-called cram schools also found that gaining peer respect was one of the top reasons.[65] The study my colleague and I conducted on kindergartners' perceptions of high-achieving peers also showed that Chinese children desired to be like the high achievers and to emulate them (but European-American children perceived more peer rejection and isolation toward the high achievers).[66] Most recent research[67] on how peer groups function in Chinese schools found that elementary school and middle-school children belonging to high-achieving groups become more socially competent two years later. On the other hand, high social competence alone did not have the reverse effect – that is, it did not make children achieve better academically during the same period of time – countering the theory and research on Western children's group functions.[68] Furthermore, even academically weaker students who belonged to high-achieving groups developed fewer social problems than children who belonged to low-achieving groups. Associating oneself with high-achieving peers in China has protective power against developing negative social behaviors. These studies confirm that in China, good learning does indeed bring peer respect and liking and other positive benefits. The otherwise persecuted "nerds" may flourish in such a protective haven.

In the domain of learning, the peer culture in China, unlike that in the West, is more or less in harmony with the culture of school, family, and society at large. In other words, although youth in East Asia also have their own music, fashion, group activities, and online sites, and generational gaps and clashes also exist, their culture seems to have less conflict between school and family when it comes to school learning. How does such a peer culture operate? There are at least three discernable levels that interact with each other to produce such a peer culture: school/community, family, and children themselves.

Peer Supported Learning in School and Community

Within school, students who achieve highly are often identified by the school as the leaders of their classes, and such leaders obtain this role not necessarily because of their marvelous personality traits (e.g., outgoing, gregarious, friendly, physically attractive), but serve the central role of modeling for the rest of children. That is, these students are held as model students for others to emulate. In China, for example, schools annually select the so-called Students with Three Excellences (三好生): in moral conduct, academic achievement, and artistic/athletic achievement. Teachers and peers nominate and vote for such students. The idea behind setting up model students is that everyone should learn and is capable of learning from the exemplars and achieving the same level as them. At the present time, schools adopt a more democratic process as a method to select student leaders. For example, nominees conduct campaigns where they engage in debates with their opponents and present their ideas for how they would like to work for their classes and grades. Peers then cast their votes, and the votes are announced and counted publicly. Regardless of the selecting methods, no student is likely to be chosen as a model student without academic excellence. Excellence in social relations and extracurricular achievements alone is not admired as much as academic excellence.[69]

Once chosen, it is regarded a high honor in school. To achieve a positive effect on the peers, schools may routinely organize workshops where high-achieving students share their personal challenges and strategies they used to overcome such difficulties. They offer tips on how to approach various school subjects, how they balance social and other extracurricular activities with learning tasks, and how they approach studying. Peers ask questions and exchange ideas. When such workshops are held, all children attend them. As discussed previously, high achievers do not necessarily feel uncomfortable in the spotlight because they are not believed to possess some inherent ability and special talent at birth, but rather skills that they have acquired. Likewise, those who do not achieve highly are not regarded as lacking inherent ability either. All children stand to benefit from learning how to achieve better from those model students. Indeed, different students may be put on the pedestal in different years.

Other than these kinds of workshops, higher-achieving students are openly "charged" by teachers to help their peers. For each subject, there is one subject representative (科代表). Teachers urge students to seek such subject representatives and other high-achieving students. Meanwhile, lower-achieving students are encouraged to seek help from their peers.

The helpers and help seekers work quite seamlessly in class. Teachers even pair high-achieving students with low-achieving students one on one in order to raise achievement for everyone (teachers have an incentive to do so given that their promotion depends, in part, on how their entire classes achieve). A teacher in Beijing gives a vivid illustration of how this kind or peer-supported learning takes place:

> An 8th grade student was very shy and quiet in class. Every time the teacher called on him to answer a question, he would not say anything, hanging his head and blushing. His classmates would mumble to the teacher to not bother him because "he didn't know." But the teacher soon discovered that the boy was very good at math. She told the class that whoever could make this boy talk would get extra credit for the course. Many peers approached the boy.... Now he is not afraid of talking in class, and he interacts well with his peers.[70]

It is quite clear that both the helpers and the help recipient have a mutual understanding that a student can improve, and nothing is shameful about getting help and nothing is inappropriate about offering help in this cultural context.

Recent research on how older elementary school children disclosed their achievement to peers provides a good glimpse into this process. As cited previously, Heyman and colleagues[71] found that European-American schoolchildren would only disclose their achievement to peers who have similar achievement levels, but they would not disclose their achievement to peers with higher or lower levels in fear that they would be regarded as bragging (if disclosed to lower achievers, likely fearing peer sanction for high achievement) or revealing their low ability (if disclosed to higher achievers). However, Chinese schoolchildren would disclose their own achievement to all peers regardless of their levels. If disclosed to a higher achiever, the disclosing peer is regarded as eliciting help from the higher achiever, and help is on the way. If it is disclosed to a lower achiever, the disclosing peer is regarded as offering help, and the lower achiever would be grateful for such help. These findings make good sense given how common peer-supported learning is in Chinese schools.

A more routine way to ensure such peer-supported learning is through the so-called small groups (小组). Chinese schools have large classes (forty for elementary school and sixty or more students per class for middle school and high school). However, each class is organized into small groups by seating arrangement. A sixty-student class may have six or fewer small groups. Often, small-group leaders are elected by group members, but many schools encourage students to take turns assuming the role of small-group leaders so that all children get a chance to develop leadership skills. Small-group leaders help teachers with their teaching such as distributing and collecting student work and quizzes, organizing group extracurricular activities, communicating on behalf of the class, and assigning cleaning jobs (Chinese children clean their own schools).

Other than these organizational tasks, small-group leaders ensure learning among group members. For example, they work together to complete their homework. Chinese and other East Asian children are assigned a much heavier load of homework each day than Western children.[72] Homework completion is required and checked by teachers carefully, with feedback. However, unlike in the West, homework is *not* graded as part of the student achievement record. Then why is homework assigned at all? And why so much? Homework is meant to serve the purpose of practicing, reviewing, and gaining new insight into the material taught during the day, not to demonstrate mastery per se, because mastery is believed to be acquired over time, as detailed in Chapter 4. Again, this design and use of homework is reflective of the Confucian principal of deeper learning through review and gaining new insight. Thus, homework is a learning process, not time and opportunity to show one's mastery.[73]

Frequently, the members of small groups may take turns to organize homework times at school or to invite peers to their homes. As a middle-school student, I brought in peers (not my personal friends) to my home. After dinner, my parents would clean the dinner table, and the children would do homework together. Group homework serves two significant learning goals: (1) ensuring that everyone completes homework and (2) helping each other digest what was taught during the day. Those who understood, say, a math concept would explain it to those who were struggling with it. At the end of the study group, all group members had something to gain. There are two important additional benefits of group homework: (3) reducing the otherwise impossible teaching load of the teachers and (4) fostering positive peer relationships. Finally, parents may not need to be highly knowledgeable of subject matter and intensively involved in the day-to-day learning and peer interactions of their children (as is the case in the West, where parents need to make play dates, drive children to different extracurricular programs, and help them do homework). Children are naturally involved with and for each other.

High-achieving students are not kept secret inside school but publicized across local communities through the media, as is done in the West. There are different levels of honor students – school, district, city, and provincial – with the three excellences. The higher the level, the greater the honor.[74] Communities take great pride in having highly achieving students. In 2005, I visited several cities and local towns in China and saw banners hanging across the roads and streets of towns, proudly announcing the top students in that year's college entrance examination. In the town's centers, businesses posted boards on the street, stating their donation levels to students for various ranks of college admissions. Apparently, this tradition continues abroad. In America, for example, Chinese-language newspapers also routinely print the profiles of winners of national, state, and local scholastic competitions.[75] It would be difficult, if not nearly impossible, to counter such a cultural ethos.

Peers as Role Models through Parents
Parents play a major role in further strengthening positive attitudes toward high-achieving peers. Parents in any culture are the key bearers of their cultural values because they socialize their children accordingly. Although parents are active promoters of their cultural values, they do so often without awareness of their own role. This interesting process is understood as *enculturation* by which people acquire the values of their cultures through participation in daily life. The power and success of enculturation lies, as anthropologists have long recognized, in the very mundane living in the culture, which does not require formal education. Chinese children's positive attitude toward their high-achieving peers has much to do with this kind of parenting process. Apparently, Chinese (and other East Asian) parents routinely engage in identifying model students for their own children and in ensuring that their children actually learn from them.

First, as noted in Chapter 4, Chinese culture has a long tradition of using models for teaching the young. All great scholars and learning models throughout Chinese history continue to live in oral tales, with many noted in the village records, the town's public monuments, as well as rendered in movies and dramas.[76] In school, children read these stories as part of learning the Chinese language. I examined the Chinese-language curriculum for China's nine-year compulsory education, which is still largely centralized in China, and found that 36 percent of the learning material contained these learner models.[77] Because the current students' parents learned these stories in their own childhood, these role models are equally alive for parents and students. To motivate their children, parents routinely cite these models (in concert with teachers' citations) and urge their children to emulate these models. Hence, children are familiar with and used to this style of parenting.

But parents do more than just rely on historical figures and distant high achievers. Parents are also active seekers of good students in the neighborhood. They frequently talk to their children's friends to find out who among their peers does better at school. These good students include relatives, children of their friends and coworkers, and otherwise acknowledged good students in the community. Once parents discover such models, they refer their own children to them often, in clear comparative terms, urging their children to emulate these models. My personal example is a case in point. When I received my doctoral degree from my university in the United States, my mother sent the photos of my robing ceremony to relatives in China. Unbeknownst to me, several of my relatives in China had the photos framed and hung them on their living rooms' walls. Their family pride aside, I became, apparently, a role model in their eyes. They used this model to motivate their own children to learn better. In our study on Chinese immigrant high school students, 77 percent of them reported that their parents used good students from their neighborhood as role models. Surprisingly, despite the fact that many found their parents' effort annoying, these Chinese immigrant adolescents acknowledged that their parents' citations of higher-achieving students made them motivated to work harder. The following excerpt from an interview with a student illustrates this parenting effort: "[M]y mother, she likes to brag about me for some reason, and then she ... sees someone else's report card for some reason ... and then she's like, look at this kid, she got all A's. And look at you, you got one B ... you're supposed to have more A's. And I'm like, isn't that enough? ... Well, I wouldn't say demoralize, I would say that it would motivate me a little bit more ... to work harder."[78] Whereas it is common among Chinese parents, this kind of model use as a motivational strategy for their children is rarely observed among European-American and other ethnic parents.

Children Seek Peer-Supported Learning on Their Own
Given the general attitude toward high-achieving peers, it is only natural for Chinese children to have similar attitudes toward such peers. In my study on model learners, I also asked college students to respond to the question "how would your model learner feel toward those who have a strong heart and mind for learning (好學心)?" The majority (77 percent) wrote that the model learner would respect, admire, revere, esteem, and appreciate those who have such love for learning. Forty-two percent stated that the model

learner would humbly learn from, be motivated to catch up with, take the model learner as his/her own example, and strive to improve themselves further. Forty-three percent acknowledged that model learners would find such people to be their soul mates, to share the same life goals, to desire to become like, or to be friends with.[79] Recent research on ordinary Chinese elementary school children, not ideal learners, by Heyman and associates and Chen and associates provide support for this very awareness of peer paragons.[80]

Thus, peers seek each other out even without the nudging from teachers and parents. In a study that my colleagues and I conducted, we found that Chinese immigrant high school students from low-income backgrounds continued to use this peer-supported learning to help each other in school. When we asked them who helps them with their homework, one-third said that they do homework with their friends either at school or at each other's places, because their parents had neither English proficiency nor American curricular knowledge to help them. These children had to depend on themselves, but they chose to use peer-supported learning rather than individual learning. For example, one peer might be better at math, and he would explain math concepts to the group. Another peer might have a better understanding of history, and she would look up the information online and help the group. Because of the advent of instant messaging technology, sometimes the group may not gather in one physical location but work online, doing homework together in real time. Such peer-supported learning was rarely mentioned by the other ethnic groups, including those from European-American background.

Deep Roots for Honoring High Achievers in East Asia

The preceding sections present a clear picture: Not only do high-achieving students suffer little peer harassment, but they are actually honored and upheld as role models in East Asia. What schools, communities, parents, and children themselves do to create a haven for learning in school is the first-order examination. However, the description of the reality and how it operates does not get to the question of why the culture is so different. In what follows, I attempt to outline, based on research, some underlying values and beliefs that are important for understanding the existence and continuation of such a peer culture for learning in East Asia.

First, as discussed previously, East Asian students inherit a cultural learning tradition that has been shaping children's lives and their education systems for millennia. Throughout history, there has been very little interruption of this tradition except for the ten years of Mainland Chinese official denunciation of learning from 1966 to 1976.[81] Ironically, even that unfortunate political downturn did not altogether eradicate Chinese people's desire for learning (although intellectuals were persecuted). What was truly denounced was particular knowledge, namely Confucian learning along with learning of science and other "bourgeois" material. Soon after the "catastrophe of ten years" (十年浩劫), learning of everything resumed with renewed energy and dedication. Except for China, other East Asian cultures have not experienced any notable discontinuity. Thus, it is not overstating that this tradition has been deeply entrenched in East Asia, with no sign of abating. Such a value system is not easily subject to any peer counterculture.

Second, a peer counterculture against high achieving has to have a clear cause. There is none, however, in my judgment. Why would children revolt against something that their parents and they themselves desire and regard as important? Besides, schools, communities, and families create conditions under which low- and average-achieving students have frequent interactions with high-achieving students to receive help and to self-improve. It makes little sense for peers to invent derogatory names to torment their helpers.

But a deeper reason for high achievers' haven is that East Asia does not hold the view that the self is fixed and likewise that one's ability is more or less determined at birth. Unlike in the West, the self in East Asia is regarded as malleable[82] through personal effort and social influence. As discussed before, personal commitment (along with the learning virtues) holds the key to personal development including the growth of one's ability and intelligence. Hence, if a person does well on a task, the self is not implicated as wholly positive; rather, the self is regarded as still changeable in any direction. Likewise, if the person fails, it does not implicate anything inherently negative in the person. Because life-long learning is taken as a fundamental life course for anyone, the self is expected and encouraged to improve regardless of how much one has achieved or failed. Of utmost importance is that the person is willing and actually makes an effort to self-improve.[83]

Belief in social influence is the second part of how the self may be subject to considerable change, which is an extension of the view that the self is malleable. Chinese culture strongly emphasizes the influence of the environment in child development.[84] Teachers, parents, and children use a common expression that epitomizes the general belief about one's potential to be influenced by others: "near cinnabar, one becomes red; near pitch, one becomes black" (近朱者赤,近墨者黑). The younger the child, the more changeable he or she is by the environment. Parents and teachers urge their children to be near good influence and stay away from not-so-good influence. That children are encouraged by teachers and parents to seek high-achieving students out for help is a direct reflection of this cultural belief. Upon discovery that their children have friends who display questionable behaviors such as not wanting to learn or delinquency, parents discourage their children from interactions with such peers. Given that good learning also signals good virtues and morals in Chinese culture, it is sensible for Chinese parents to promote their children's friendship with high achievers.[85]

Recent research on cultural variations between Western and East Asian people shows that East Asians perceive and think about objects very differently.[86] Whereas Western people focus on the object itself, East Asian people attend to a larger purview of the environment, the background. When given a group of the same objects, such as a number of identical red pencils and a single object that is different from the group, say, a green pencil, or a big fish in a group of small fish, Western people see the single object as standing out, unique, and so forth. But East Asians attend to the group of objects more. This tendency is taken by some researchers as indicative of their culturally influenced focus, awareness, and information processing. Most recent research[87] also documents that Asian children as young as three years of age are more likely to be influenced by adult consensus than their European-American peers. Although these lab experiments focus purportedly on cognitive differences between the two cultural groups, I would argue that East Asian people's attentiveness to the environment (i.e., factors other than oneself) provides support for their fundamental belief in "near cinnabar, one becomes red; near pitch, one becomes black," which underlies their effort to socialize their children toward desirable developmental outcomes.

A related explanation of the cultural differences in peer culture comes from Márta Fülöp's research on cultural difference in competition, as noted previously.[88] Fülöp started with the assumption that competition and cooperation are conceptualized in the West as the mutually exclusive dichotomy in people's behavior. According to this view, if a culture is high on competition, it is necessarily low on cooperation. The United States is a highly competitive culture, low on cooperation, because of its emphasis on individualism; by contrast, formerly socialist Hungary was a case of high cooperation but low competition (presumably because of their socialist rule). Yet, Japan poses challenges to this Western dichotomous view because Japan is both high in competition and cooperation. To find out how high competition and cooperation could coexist, Fülöp studied more than 700 high school students in these three cultures. She asked each student to describe how prevalent competition was in their school, how they viewed competition, and how they engaged in competition themselves.

She found that Japanese students reported the most competition in school, followed by the American students. Hungarian students reported the least competition. Examples students gave ranged from trying to get better grades, to win contests, to excel on entrance exams, to try to get into better colleges in academics, as well as to engage in extracurricular activities. However, despite the greatest prevalence of competition reported by Japanese students, they experienced competition most positively. American students had the lowest positive experience, with Hungarian students in the middle. More Japanese students regarded competition as a process of self-improvement, motivation, personal effort, achievement, exercising their willpower, self-evaluation, and joy. The category that American students acknowledged most was that competition enabled them to push themselves to be their best. Hungarian students mentioned ranking among students most frequently. On the negative side of competition, American students reported the highest levels of stress, losing, and feeling selfish. Both American and Hungarian students also experienced a higher level of conflict with peers than Japanese students. Fülöp concludes that Japanese students' experience with competition in school is most positive, American most negative, and Hungarian falling in the middle. Japanese students engage in competition to motivate each other and to help each other improve. Hungarian students seek to raise their rank among their peers, and American students try to be the best. For Japanese students, rivals are friends, and the degree of cooperation is high, which results in improved achievement for everyone. Their relationships are strengthened. For Hungarian students, rivals are enemies, and the degree of cooperation is low,[89] which results in winners versus losers and consequently deteriorated relationships. For American students, rivals are opponents to win against, and the degree of cooperation is also low, but relationships may not matter to begin with.

Most recently, Watkins and his graduate students adopted Fülöp's method to study high school students' perception and engagement in competition in Hong Kong (in both high-ability and low/average-ability schools as tracked in Hong Kong).[90] Similar to Fülöp's findings, the majority of the participants in both kinds of schools reported that their schools encouraged them to compete with other students (81 percent and 67 percent among the two respective groups of students). However, students felt more positive than negative or neutral about competition. Positive examples of student experience include:

1. Competition encourages me to improve myself; the feeling is quite good.
2. Competition motivates us to actively participate.
3. Through competition, our school encourages us to learn from each other.
4. I feel very happy because in competition all of us improve.

Some statements about negative experiences are:

1. Competition is hard work. I am unable to breathe and want to give up.
2. Very hard, very great pressure. I do not want to compete with others.
3. I feel nervous and I am desperate to win.

Furthermore, the researchers also asked students specifically whether they respected their opponents in study and sports. They found that the great majority (more than 90 percent) said yes, and the predominant reason was that their opponents were their "friends or classmates" and that the competitors should "respect everyone all the time."

These studies compel us to conclude that learning and achieving are for everyone. These findings cohere with the basic Confucian tenet that peers in learning are people for one to learn from, to work with, to respect, and, most important of all, to enhance each other. In such a culture, "nerd" harassment has, so to speak, no home.

Then how do we explain the common observation that those who emerge on the top are the "nails that will be hammered down," a common phenomenon in East Asia, much like the tall poppies?[91] I would argue that the observation is not wrong, but it is an observation blindly and inappropriately applied to all domains of life. In East Asian social life, particularly in the domains where socioeconomic resource distribution is at stake, those who claim more resources may be subject to the hammering-down destiny. But improving oneself in learning with the goal of cultivating one's virtuous and moral self is an entirely different thing. Self-striving to be virtuous and moral is not claiming more resources because virtuous and moral achievement is within reach of each person. And the more people in a society achieve the virtuous and moral goals, the better the society is as a whole. In this domain, the tall poppy is not only not a problem, but actually becomes a goal for everyone, especially when everyone is believed capable of becoming a tall poppy.

The final cultural value that explains the East Asian peer culture in learning, I would argue, has to do with the way social relationships are formed and maintained. Again, based on Confucianism, the most significant social relationships are formed at home. The family model serves as the lens through which the social world for the Chinese (and other East Asians) is conceptualized, classified, approached, and lived. Accordingly, children are taught at home to call their older siblings as either "older brother" (*gege*, 哥哥) or "older sister" (*jiejie*, 姐姐) and likewise to call their younger siblings "younger brother" (*didi*, 弟弟) and "younger sister" (*meimei*, 妹妹). Siblings are not usually called by their first names. All kin members have designated addresses by paternal or maternal (male/female) division, generation, and age. This model is also used to classify strangers, and children are taught this classification and approach social relations accordingly. For example, when meeting a neighborhood peer, the child needs to know if the peer is older or younger. If he is older, then the child will call him "older brother"; if the peer is younger, he will be called "younger brother." Similarly, when meeting an unfamiliar male adult, the child also needs to know if the adult is older or younger than his or her father. If he is older, then the child will call him "older uncle" (*bobo*, 伯伯), and if he is younger, then "younger uncle" (*shushu*, 叔叔), or if dealing with females (*ayi*, 阿姨).[92]

The most important purpose of this type of family extension to strangers is that all these roles by different addresses come with well-defined responsibilities/duties as well as care/privileges. For example, anyone that is addressed with "older" assumes a responsibility to care for, to instruct, to model, and to guide anyone addressed with "younger" by generation and by age. Even a slightly older sibling is asked by parents to show her younger sibling better behavior (e.g., yielding a candy to the younger), and this type of socialization can be observed by children from different families playing together, where the mother will reason with an older child by appealing to the age differential (e.g., "you are the older sister, and she is the younger sister, so please give your toy for her to play with"). Anyone addressed with "younger" also accepts the stance to respect/honor, to listen to, and to follow the "older" person's care, teaching, and guidance (e.g., a four-year-old child may be asked to look at what her six-year-old brother did in spelling and to emulate him). By the time they enter school, most Chinese children are familiar with this complex and finely differentiating system of address (at least for their immediate kin). Most children also have some sense of the responsibility/charge of those "older" people versus their own role as the "younger."[93]

Thus, children in Taiwan still address their peers with "learning older brother" (*xuezhang*, 學長), "learning younger brother" (*xuedi*, 學弟), "learning older sister" (*xuejie*, 學姐), and "learning younger sister" (*xuemei*, 學妹). When a younger peer comes to ask a question about a math problem, for example, the older learning peer will bear the responsibility to help the younger one. Likewise, when an older learning sister offers help or instructs the younger peer, the younger will accept this older peer's guidance. This cultural system lends itself to the teacher and parental requests for high-achieving students to assume more responsibility for helping the low- and average-achieving students. Likewise, it is the duty expected of the low- and average-achieving students to seek help from the high-achieving students. No shame and contempt are involved in this learning system. Those who seek help are regarded as displaying the virtue of humility, and those who offer help are regarded as displaying the virtue of generosity and responsibility, as discussed in previous chapters. This type of social relationship based on the family model makes it harder for peers to engage in "nerd" harassment.[94]

Asian-American Children as the "Nerd" Group

At least among Asian Americans, it has been widely known that their children have been called nerds and harassed routinely in school. This is not surprising given the cultural background they come from, the open emphasis on school learning, and the generally higher achievement associated with them. What makes matters worse is that Asian children have a smaller physique and are sometimes less impressive in the athletic prowess than their counterparts from other ethnic groups. Both physically and behaviorally they fit the image of a "nerd." Whereas other groups may have individual children suffering from the nerd-calling peer culture, Asian-American children as a whole are America's default "nerd" group.

As such, they bear the brunt of peer harassment from all sides. My son's experience is a case in point. On the national scene, the current lawsuit in Philadelphia filed by the Asian American Legal Defense and Education Fund against the school district for not protecting Asian-American students attests to the new height of peer harassment against the Asian "nerds." According to NBC news, twenty-six students were attacked by their non-Asian peers (beaten up, with thirteen students sent to the hospital, one with a broken nose).[95]

The best-documented peer harassment against Asian-American students came from the research done by Niobe Way and associates at New York University. In 2004, Susan Rosenbloom and Niobe Way[96] conducted an in-depth qualitative study over a two-year period. They interviewed Chinese immigrant youth attending diverse public schools in New York City. They also conducted school observations. They found widespread peer discrimination and peer victimization as experienced by Chinese adolescents from their non-Asian peers (twenty-six incidents of physical and verbal attacks against Chinese, but only one and three against African-American and Latino peers, respectively, during the same period). The following excerpts from their report provide details of such peer attacks:

> A Chinese girl reported "The people in the school, they call me chino, stupid, or geek, or anything like that because I'm Chinese."
>
> Participant observation and the interviews revealed numerous incidences of physical harassment of the Asian American students by the non-Asian American students in school. Students reported random "slappings" by male and female peers as they walked through the hallways. Slappings are quick, pop shots often to the head or body as students passed one another in the hall or anywhere else. Asian American students described them as unnerving, randomly occurring, and humiliating violations that are particularly harrowing for the boys when girls slap them.
>
> Along with slappings, Asian American students were observed and reported being pushed, punched, teased, and mocked by their non-Asian American peers. The racial slur "chino" or "geek" was often heard as Asian American students passed by. The physical and verbal harassment of the Asian American students occurred when adults were present and when they were not.
>
> Kit Wah told the interviewer that a male Asian American friend was held up with a knife in the gym locker room by a student in his class. His friend was robbed of several items.
>
> Incidents such as these that included having money, jewelry, and jackets stolen are typical events that Asian American students described when discussing how they were victimized for being Asian American in school.... Asian American students appeared to be more frequently targeted for robbery. These events seemed to be a part of the normalized landscape of behaviors that Asian American students endured in this school.

Niobe Way[97] in a subsequent paper states that such peer harassment against Asian-American children by non-Asian peers is not limited to New York City, but is a common problem across the United States.

In a recent study, Desirée Qin, Niobe Way, and Preetika Mukherjee[98] interviewed Chinese immigrant youth aged from nine to fourteen in both New York City and Boston. They reported a similar finding but also clear reasons for such peer discrimination from non-Asian peers: the perception that Chinese children were high achievers and that teachers give Asian-American students preferential treatment.

Finally, Deborah Rivas-Drake, Diane Hughes, and Niobe Way used standard measures of peer discrimination to study how that predicts early adolescents' psychological well-being. They found that compared to African Americans, Chinese-American students reported nearly twice as many peer harassment incidents, higher depressive symptoms, and lower self-esteem. All of these differences were statistically significant. The researchers concluded that "Chinese American early adolescents ... reported feeling that they are treated badly, unfairly, teased, harassed, and called names by peers, who are individuals whom they encounter on a regular basis."[99]

Asian-American children who try to do what they are supposed to do in American school – that is, learning and achieving well – face very harsh peer problems regularly. I hope this chapter has provided some insights into the cultural roots of this harassment. But regardless of the root causes, this reality is truly hell for many Asian-American children.

NOTES

1. See note 11 to Chapter 4.
2. See Perner, J., Leekam, S. R., & Wimmer, H. (1987). Three year olds difficulty with false belief: The case for a conceptual deficit. *British Journal of Developmental Psychology, 5*(2), 125–137; Astington, J. W. (1993). *The child's discovery of the mind.* Cambridge, MA: Harvard University Press; and Wellman, H. M., Cross, D., & Watson, J. (2001). Meta-analysis of theory of mind development: The truth about false beliefs. *Child Development, 72*, 655–684 for research on children's social cognitive development.
3. See note 11 to Chapter 4.
4. Wentzel, K. R., & Caldwell, K. (1997). Friendships, peer acceptance, and group membership: Relations to academic achievement in middle school. *Child Development, 68*, 1198–1209; Wentzel, K. R., & Wigfield, A. (1998). Academic and social motivational influence on students' academic performance. *Educational Psychology Review, 10*(2), 155–175; Uguroglu, M. E., & Walberg, H. J. (1986). Predicting achievement and motivation. *Journal of Research and Development in Education, 19*, 1–12; and Kindermann, T. (1993). Natural peer groups as contexts for individual development: The case of children's motivation in school. *Developmental Psychology, 29*, 970–977.
5. Wentzel, K. R., & Asher, S. R. (1995). The academic lives of neglected, rejected, popular, and controversial children. *Child Development, 66*, 754–763.

6. Ladd, G. W., & Troop-Gordon, W. (2003). The role of chronic peer difficulties in the development of children's psychological adjustment problems. *Child Development, 74*(5), 1344–1367.

7. Feather, N. T. (1989). Attitudes towards the high achiever: The fall of the tall poppy. *Australian Journal of Psychology, 41*(3), 239–267; Boehnke, K. (2008). Peer pressure: a cause of scholastic underachievement? A cross-cultural study of mathematical achievement among German, Canadian, and Israeli middle-school students. *Social Psychology of Education, 11*(2), 149–160; and Bishop, J. H., & Bishop, M. M. (2008). An economic theory of academic engagement norms: The struggle for popularity and normative hegemony in secondary schools. Unpublished manuscript.

8. Fülöp, M. (1999). Students' perception of the role of competition in their respective countries: Hungary, Japan, and the USA. In A. Ross, *Young citizens in Europe* (pp. 195–219). London: University of North London.

9. Asher, S. R., & Coie, J. D. (Eds.) (1990). *Peer rejection in childhood*. New York: Cambridge University Press.

10. Pellegrini, A. D., & Long, J. D. (2003). A longitudinal study of bullying, dominance, and victimization during the transition from primary through secondary school. *British Journal of Developmental Psychology, 20*, 259–280.

11. See note 5 to this chapter.

12. See note 11 to Chapter 4, and Nishina, A., & Juvonen, J. (2005). Daily reports of witnessing and experiencing peer harassment in middle school. *Child Development, 76*(2), 435–450.

13. See the third reference in note 7 to this chapter.

14. See Elliott, J. G., Hufton, N. R., Illushin, L., & Willis, W. (2005). *Motivation, engagement, and educational performance: International perspectives on the contexts of learning*. New York: Palgrave Macmillan for discussion of *swot* (pp. 122–123); see the second reference in note 7 to this chapter for German *Schreber* and Hebrew *hnun*.

15. Personal communication with Marie Suizzo for French *bouttoneux*.

16. Personal communication with Marieke van Egmond for Dutch *stuud*.

17. See note 14 to this chapter.

18. For convenience, I use *nerd* or *nerds* instead of naming all other similar terms to discuss this phenomenon.

19. Seuss, G. T. (1950). *If I ran the zoo*. New York: Random House.

20. Nugent, B. (2007, July 29). Who's a nerd, anyway? *New York Times Magazine*. Retrieved July 28, 2007 from http://www.nytimes.com/2007/07/29/magazine/29wwln-idealab-t.html?_r=1&ref=magazine&oref=slogin

21. *American heritage dictionary of the English language* (3rd ed.). (1992). New York: Houghton Mifflin, p. 1212.

22. See Fordham, S., & Ogbu, J. U. (1986). Black students' school success: Coping with the "Burden of 'Acting White.'" *The Urban Review, 18*, 176–206 for similar problems with African-American schoolchildren.

23. White, S. H. (1998). What do we have to do to create a better social design for adolescence? Paper read in honor of Theodore Sizer at Brown University.

24. See the third reference in note 7 to this chapter; and Juvonen, J., & Gross, E. F. (2005). The rejected and the bullied: Lessons about social misfits from

developmental psychology. In W. D. Kipling, J. P. Forgas, & W. von Hippel (Eds.), *The social outcast: Ostracism, social exclusion, rejection, and bullying* (pp. 155–170). New York: Psychology Press.

25. See the first reference in note 7 to this chapter.
26. See the first reference in note 7 to this chapter, p. 256.
27. See the third reference in note 7 to this chapter.
28. See the third reference in note 7 to this chapter, p. 22.
29. See the third reference in note 7 to this chapter, p. 12.
30. See Nicholls, J. G. (1978). The development of the concepts of effort and ability, perception of academic attainment, and the understanding that difficult tasks require more ability. *Child Development, 49*, 800–814 for research on how New Zealand children's view of ability and effort changes from kindergarten to adolescence. Also see the second reference in note 16 to Chapter 5 for Dweck and Leggett's review of research on this topic.
31. See the third reference in note 7 to this chapter, pp. 14–15.
32. Juvonen, J., & Murdock, T. B. (1995). Grade-level differences in the social value of effort: Implications for self-presentation tactics of early adolescents. *Child Development, 66*(6), 1694–1705.
33. See the second reference in note 7 to this chapter.
34. See the third reference in note 7 to this chapter.
35. Fisher, C. B., Wallace, S. A., & Fenton, R. E. (2000). Discrimination distress during adolescence. *Journal of Youth & Adolescence, 29*, 679–695; Greene, M. L., Way, N., & Pahl, K. (2006). Trajectories of perceived adult and peer discrimination among Black, Latino, and Asian American adolescents: Patterns and psychological correlates. *Developmental Psychology, 42*(2), 218–238; La Greca, A. M., & Harrison, H. M. (2005). Adolescent peer relations, friendships, and romantic relationships: Do they predict social anxiety and depression? *Journal of Clinical Child & Adolescent Psychology, 34*, 49–61; Storch, E. A., & Masia-Warner, C. (2004). The relationship of peer victimization to social anxiety and loneliness in adolescent females. *Journal of Adolescence, 27*, 351–362; and Rivas-Drake, D., Hughes, D., & Way, N. (2008). A closer look at peer discrimination, ethnic identity, and psychological well-being among urban Chinese American sixth graders. *Journal of Youth and Adolescence, 37*, 12–21.
36. See note 11 to Chapter 4.
37. See the second reference in note 6 to Chapter 3.
38. Indeed, his new school, the Wheeler School in Providence in Rhode Island, was attended mostly by children who were motivated, serious learners. High achievement was expected and celebrated and was a school pride. Both our son and we are grateful to the school for promoting the right values and for creating a safe learning environment for children.
39. Strayer, F. F. (1991). The development of agonistic and affiliative structures in preschool play groups. In J. Silverberg & P. Gray (Eds.), *To fight or not to fight: Violence and peacefulness in humans and other primates*. Oxford: Oxford University Press; and Fiske, A. P., & Haslam, N. (2005). The four basic social bonds: Structures for coordinating interaction. In M. W. Baldwin (Ed.), *Interpersonal cognition* (pp. 267–298). New York: Guilford.

40. See Arnett, J. J. (2008). The neglected 95%: Why American psychology needs to become less American. *American Psychologist, 63*(7), 602–614 for discussion of this problem.

41. See Chen, X.-Y., & French, D. C. (2008). Children's social competence in cultural context. *Annual Review of Psychology, 59*, 591–616 for a review of cross-cultural research.

42. See note 81 to Chapter 3 and note 19 to Chapter 5.

43. See Fischer, H. A., Manstead, A. S. R., & Rodriguez Mosquera, P. M. (1999). The role of honor-related vs. individualist values in conceptualizing pride, shame, and anger: Spanish and Dutch cultural prototypes. *Cognition & Emotion, 13*(2), 149–179 for an example.

44. See notes 26 and 28 to Chapter 5.

45. Tesser, A., Campbell, J., & Smith, M. (1984). Friendship choice and performance: Self-evaluation maintenance in children. *Journal of Personality and Social Psychology, 46*(3), 561–574; and Ruble, D. N., Frey, K. S., & Greulich, F. (1995). Meeting goals and confronting conflicts: Children's changing perceptions of social comparison. *Child Development, 66*, 723–738.

46. See note 8 to this chapter.

47. See the classic Galton, F. (1869/2006). *Hereditary genius: An inquiry into its laws and consequences.* Amherst, NY: Prometheus and its recent reincarnation; Hernstein, R. J., & Murray, C. (1994). *The bell curve.* Chicago: Free Press.

48. See Steenbergen-Hu, S.-Y., & Moon, S. M. (2011). The effects of acceleration on high-ability learners: A meta-analysis. *Gifted Child Quarterly, 55*(1), 39–53 for an example of research on this topic. The fact that the West has the term *gifted children* and a whole journal devoted to research on such children indicates the importance of the concept "talent" and born intellectual "gift" in children. Also see Winner, E. (1996). *Gifted children: Myths and realities.* New York: Basic Books for more discussions.

49. See the second reference in note 16 to Chapter 5; and Dweck, C. S. (1999). *Self-theories.* Philadelphia: Psychology Press.

50. See the first reference in note 30 to this chapter and note 32 to this chapter.

51. See Covington, M. V. (2000). Goal theory, motivation, and school achievement: An integrative review. *Annual Review of Psychology, 51*, 171–200 for a comprehensive review.

52. Heyman, G. D., Fu, G.-Y., & Lee, K. (2008). Reasoning about the disclosure of success and failure to friends among children in the United States and China. *Developmental Psychology, 44*(4), 908–918.

53. Oakes, J., & Guiton, G. (1995). Matchmaking: The dynamics of high school tracking decisions. *American Educational Research Journal, 32*(1), 3–33, pp. 10–11.

54. See note 53 to this chapter, p. 12.

55. Doidge, N. (2007). *The brain that changes itself: Stories of personal triumph from the frontiers of brain science.* New York: Penguin.

56. *Webster's new collegiate dictionary.* (1973). Springfield, MA: Merriam, p. 845.

57. Wang, Y.-T. (Ed.). (1992). 新現代漢語詞典 [A new dictionary of modern Chinese language]. Hainan: Hainan Publishing House, p. 1636.

58. It is important to point out that when scholars use the English term *peer* to describe Chinese, Japanese, and Korean *tongxue, douryou,* and *kyo-woo,* important cultural meanings are lost.

59. See note 5 to Chapter 2, p. 71.

60. See note 5 to Chapter 2, p. 75.

61. Legge, J. (Trans.). (1960). *The Chinese Classics, 5 volumes.* Hong Kong: University of Hong Kong. Songs 55, vol. IV.

62. See Child Welfare League Foundation (n.d.). *Report on school bullying.* Retrieved March 15, 2010 from http://www.children.org.tw/database_report. php?typeid=34 for increased bullying in Taiwanese schools as an example.

63. Chen, X.-Y. (2008, October) at the conference, *Bridging developmental and cultural psychology: New syntheses in theory, research, and policy,* Worcester, MA, Clark University. Although I am aware of no research on "nerds" in East Asian schools, all my personal inquiries with scholars across East Asian confirms that nerd harassment is virtually nonexistent in Hong Kong, China, Singapore, Japan, and Korea.

64. See the first reference in note 61 to Chapter 3.

65. See the second reference in note 46 to Chapter 4.

66. See the second reference in note 6 to Chapter 3.

67. Chen, X.-Y, Lei, C., Liu, H.-Y., & He, Y.-F. (2008). Effects of the peer group on the development of social functioning and academic achievement: A longitudinal study in Chinese children. *Child Development, 79*(2), 235–251.

68. See note 4 to this chapter.

69. Private communication with Yongmei Wang (March 14, 2010), a former lead teacher at Beijing 4th Secondary School for ten years. According to her, students at her school who did not achieve 85 out of 100 for all subjects including music, athletics, and art are automatically disqualified as nominees (as well as those who have too many absences). Anyone who qualifies can put him-/herself forward as a candidate for peers to vote for.

70. Private communication with Xiaoling Wang (March 14, 2010), a middle-school teacher in Beijing.

71. See note 52 to this chapter.

72. See the first reference in note 36 to Chapter 4 for an example. However, homework overload has been a controversial issue in East Asian education. A decade ago, China's Education Ministry even passed regulations to set limits on how many hours of homework are permitted per day and to forbid schools and teachers to push children to take afterschool and weekend academic classes. However, this kind of policy did not meet with great success because parents still hire tutors and enroll their children in "cram" schools in order to help their children achieve even better.

73. Honor students at different levels receive different extra scores for entering more competitive middle schools, high schools, and colleges.

74. Periodical quizzes, midterms, and final exams are the means to determine student mastery. Homework in Russia is used for the same purposes. See Hufton, N., & Elloitt, J. (2000). Motivation to learn: The pedagogical nexus in the Russian school: Some implications for transnational research and policy borrowing. *Educational Studies, 26,* 115–122.

75. See the third reference in note 9 to Chapter 3.

76. Wilson, R. (1980). Conformity and deviance regarding moral rules in Chinese society: A socialization perspective. In A. Kleinman & T. Lin (Eds.), *Moral and abnormal behavior in Chinese culture* (pp. 117–136). Dordrecht: D. Reidel.
77. See note 38 to Chapter 4.
78. See the second reference in note 4 to Chapter 3, p. 19.
79. See the first reference in note 61 to Chapter 3.
80. See notes 52 and 67 to this chapter.
81. See note 3 to Chapter 1.
82. See note 16 to Chapter 5.
83. As discussed in Chapter 3, my lexicon study on learning terms showed that ability is placed as a consequence of learning on the Chinese conceptual map, but intelligence and ability for European Americans are placed as an internal learner characteristic that enables learning.
84. See the first reference in note 26 to Chapter 3.
85. See research findings on the susceptibility of Western adolescents to peer influence despite their stronger belief in the fixed self: Gardner, M., & Steinberg, L. (2005). Peer influence on risk taking, risk preference, and risky decision making in adolescence and adulthood: an experimental study. *Developmental Psychology, 41*(4), 625–635.
86. See the first reference in note 29 to Chapter 2.
87. Corriveau, K. H., & Harris, P. L. (2010). Preschoolers (sometimes) defer to the majority in making simple perceptual judgments. *Developmental Psychology, 46*(2), 437–445. Also see Hess, R. D., Azuma, H., Kashiwagi, K., Holloway, S. D., & Wenegrat, A. (1987). Cultural variations in socialization for school achievement: Contrasts between Japan and the United States. *Journal of Applied Developmental Psychology, 8*, 421–440; and Hess, R. D., Kashiwagi, K., Azuma, H., Price, G. G., & Dickson, W. P. (1980). Maternal expectations for mastery of developmental tasks in Japan and the United States. *International Journal of Psychology, 15*, 259–271 for Japanese mothers' greater expectation of their children's mastery of social courtesy, self-control, and compliance with authority, and how such maternal socialization predicts school achievement but is associated with negative outcomes among European-American children.
88. See note 8 to this chapter.
89. Presumably because Hungary is now a democracy and market economy. Fülöp's findings might have tapped increasing competition and decreasing cooperation in Hungary.
90. Watkins, D. A. (2009). Motivation and competition in Hong Kong secondary schools: The students' perspective. In C. Chan & N. Rao (Eds.), *Revisiting the Chinese learner: Psychological and pedagogical perspectives* (pp. 71–88). Hong Kong: Comparative Education Research Centre (CERC), University of Hong Kong and Springer Press, pp. 82–84.
91. Kwan, V. S. Y., Bond, M. H., Boucher, H. C., Maslach, C., & Gan, Y. Q. (2002). The construct of individuation: More complex in collectivist than in individualist cultures. *Personality and Social Psychology Bulletin, 28*, 300–310.
92. Please note that for older or younger female adults (than their mothers), children just call them ayi, which is still a deferential address, despite the fact that ayi is undifferentiated by age as their male counterparts.

93. See Liang, C.-H. (2007). Shame and pride: Age, kinship terms and socialization practice in a middle-class Taiwanese preschool. Poster presented at the Biannual Meetings of Society for Research in Child Development, Boston, MA; and Fung, H., & Liang, C. H. (2008). 越南媽媽,台灣囝仔: 台灣跨國婚姻家庭幼兒社會化之初探 [Vietnamese mothers, Taiwanese children: Socializing practices with young children in Sino-Vietnamese cross-border marriage families in Taipei, Taiwan]. 台灣人類學刊 [*Taiwan Journal of Anthropology*], 6, 47–88 for research on this topic. It is important to point out that cultural misunderstanding is common when Asian immigrant children attend host countries' schools. One of the Chinese first-graders in our current study lived in a suburban town with predominantly middle-class European-American residents. One day, this boy told his European-American peers that he had a sister. Surprised, the teacher called his mother and learned that this so-called sister was the boy's cousin and lived in China. Not knowing the significance of the Chinese family system and social relationships, this teacher proceeded to "correct" the boy by asking him to stand up and tell his class that he had no sister. Needless to say, this boy burst into tears because he was treated as an idiot and a liar. This is a sad but telling example of cultural insensitivity and misunderstanding (and poor teaching).

94. There is evidence that peer bullying is also on the rise in East Asia (see note 62 to this chapter). Some researchers report the Internet being a conduit that permits peer harassment without consequences. In Japan, social isolation and rejection have been reported; see, for example, Mishima, K. (1996). Bullying amongst close friends in elementary school. *Japanese Journal of Social Psychology,* 19(1), 41–50; and Masataka, N. (1999). Nihonteki ijime no seiritsu to ikuji [The formation of Japanese bullying and child-rearing]. *Japanese Journal of Addiction and Family,* 16(4), 438–444. As mentioned before, peer unkindness also exists in East Asia, and those who are perceived as lacking effort or being antisocial may face peer sanction. Research does need to pay attention to such peer problems. However, it is rare that high-achieving students suffer from peer harassment.

95. Johnson, D. (2009, Dec 7). Attacked Asian students afraid to go to school: 26 Asian students were attacked last week. Retrieved from November 20, 2010 from http://www.nbcphiladelphia.com/news/local-beat/Attacked-Asian-Students-Fear-Returning-to-Class-78652997.html

96. Rosenbloom, S. R., & Way, N. (2004). Experiences of discrimination among African American, Asian American, and Latino adolescents in an urban high school. *Youth & Society,* 35(4), 420–451, pp. 433–343.

97. Way, N. (2005). Seeking engagement: Reflections from a qualitative researcher. *Journal of Adolescent Research,* 20, 531–537.

98. Qin, D. B., Way, N., & Mukherjee, P. (2008). The other side of the model minority story the familial and peer challenges faced by Chinese American adolescents. *Youth & Society,* 39(4), 480–506.

99. See the last reference in note 35 to this chapter, pp. 18–19.

7

Socratic and Confucian Tutors at Home

Where do children's learning beliefs come from? Do they come from their inborn capacity, or from their social and cultural environment? This seemingly prosaic question is actually far from being so as it lies at the heart of the persistent debate about nature and nurture. This very question is also at the center of the never-ending debate on parenting styles and child outcomes. We know that children are born with capacity to learn.[1] But we also know that no child is born with set learning beliefs (or any beliefs, for that matter). Their learning beliefs develop as they grow older. Because children acquire different learning beliefs that reflect their cultural learning models,[2] I focus on the sociocultural contribution to their developing learning beliefs. In this chapter, I hope to show that European-American homes are full of Socratic tutors whereas Chinese homes host plenty of Confucian tutors. These tutors are the *parents* who use culturally informed strategies to foster learning beliefs in their children.

MOST WILLING AND EFFECTIVE EXECUTORS
OF CULTURAL PRESCRIPTIONS

It is a truism that home is where children are nourished and loved, which is undoubtedly the foundation for human survival and well-being. But home, as anthropologists have long discovered, also does for humans something extraordinary, yet largely unnoticeable: It serves as the most fertile ground for the transmission, maintenance, and renewal of culture, any culture.[3] Richard Shweder, a leader in cultural psychology, wrote recently that the task of cultural psychologists is to describe and understand cultural prescriptions and how such prescriptions are carried out in child development.[4] By "prescriptions" Shweder meant the values and preferences held by culture that inform childrearing practices.

As it turns out, the most willing and effective executors of cultural pre-scriptions are parents and other caregivers in the home. They are tireless in their effort to bring up children, purposefully but more often unintention-ally, according to the values they hold dear. People acquire values via the process of experiencing, appropriating, internalizing, or even reconfiguring various events and norms of their daily lives. However, regardless of how they enter individual people's minds, these values are inevitably those of their own culture (or more than one culture if a given child is raised in vary-ing cultural settings, such as immigrant children). Although individual par-ents have their idiosyncrasies in their childrearing practices, they also share related cultural values with other parents. Consequently, what appears to be a mundane routine of parents' work is not mundane at all, but a testimo-nial to the immense power of culture. That power lies in the very fact that individual parents' diligence in raising their children is repeated many a time and all the time, resulting in the certain achievement of enduring cul-tural values. Yet, astonishingly, despite being the most willing and effective executors of cultural prescriptions, parents often are not even aware of the essential role they play. There is little wonder why developmental research-ers turn their attention to their work in the home. Home is a gold mine for understanding the nurture part of the nature-nurture equation.

The work parents do to raise their children is generally understood as the process of *socialization* in child development. Socialization refers to the process by which the social world tries to guide, encourage, instill, instruct, model, correct, and discipline children toward the acquisition of desired beliefs and behaviors according to cultural values and norms. Clearly, socialization is not limited to parents, but parents do most of the work, par-ticularly in the formative years of children's lives.[5] To describe how children develop their learning beliefs, we must look not only at what children know at what age independent of their social world, but what parents do and how they do it to socialize their children.

In this chapter, I present research findings – mostly my own research with Heidi Fung from Academia Sinica, Taiwan, as my collaborator – on how European-American and Taiwanese parents socialize their children in developing their learning beliefs. We focus on the daily communications between parents and children. The research findings seem to encourage the view that parents from both cultures are not only highly motivated in their parenting effort, but also are skilled tutors of their children. Despite some common socialization processes, there are indeed large cultural dif-ferences in the kind of habit of thought they forge, as well as the kind of affect they promote. In particular, European-American parents resemble the age-honored Socratic tutoring style in the West. Likewise, Taiwanese parents tutor their children similar to the Confucian style. Each serves to reproduce generations of learners desired by their culture.

CAPTURE THE FLOW OF SOCIALIZATION

In spite of the recognized importance, research on socialization of children's learning beliefs is surprisingly limited, although socialization of other areas such as cognition, the self, gender roles, and emotion has been well studied. Scarce research on the socialization of learning beliefs owes in part to the fact that learning beliefs have only been studied recently (although achievement motivation has been studied extensively). Another impediment, as far as I see, lies in the inherent difficulty of conducting research on the process of socialization. Socialization is not a static state but a process, and is ongoing. It is notoriously hard, if not altogether impossible, to try to capture something that is by nature changing constantly, like the flowing water in a river. The empirical difficulties become even more pronounced when researchers attempt to consider different cultural patterns. Even if capturing the enigmatic nature of flowing socialization could be done, researchers would still face the perennial problem of limited resources and time. Such limitations prevent them from the ideal research of immersing themselves in the cultural settings to observe naturally occurring events.

Thanks to advancements in empirical methodology, there are ways to conduct such research within the confines of limited resources without compromising the validity of the flowing socializing process. I find particularly useful the empirical method of collecting a simulated conversation between a parent and his or her child about a given topic. Parent–child talk is a core component of the flow of their daily interactions. Much socialization is achieved via such communication at home. Although socialization is ongoing, researchers can still take a specimen for a manageable duration to examine. Or to continue the river metaphor, we can scoop the flowing water for a short time and then analyze what is inside the water. In such samples of daily communication, we are likely to see a spectrum of culturally encoded concepts, beliefs, and affects that are expressed, exchanged, and responded to. What is valued or not valued, approved or disapproved, and accepted or rejected are displayed. We are also likely to see negotiations, disagreements, and resolutions between parents and children. Of course, the specimen is not the full picture, but it nevertheless represents a reasonable degree of real parent–child interaction because the specimen is collected in real time in which the parent is trying to socialize the child. This method has been used successfully by researchers on children's memory development. Their work has revealed important findings about the content, structure, and style of maternal talking that affect children's autobiographical memory and emotional development.[6] Cultural similarities and variations have also been well documented with this method.[7]

My colleague Dr. Heidi Fung and I adopted this method and conducted a study where we recorded 209 mother–child conversations, half from European-American and half from Taiwanese families.[8] Because both cultural groups were middle-class families, they were comparable in their socioeconomic background. We targeted early elementary school children because these children had sufficient experience of schooling where deliberate teaching and learning are the daily routine. To collect data from our simulated mother–child conversations (MCC), we asked each mother to converse with her child about two learning incidents. The first is an incident where the child showed, in the mother's judgment, good learning attitude and behavior, and the second is an incident the mother noted her child's poor learning attitude and behavior. For convenience, we use the term "good learning" for the former and the term "poor learning" for the latter. Both incidents were worded identically except that one was for good learning and the other for poor learning, as follows:

> Recall an actual incident where your child showed, in your judgment, good [not good] attitudes/behavior in learning. It could be in school or outside school. The incident does not need to be something that you personally witnessed. But you should know about it in some detail to talk about it with your child. You have unlimited time to talk about this incident, and the conversation can go in any direction.

We collected a rich set of data, and it took several years of laborious effort to analyze. As for any rich data, doing full justice to them requires more time and further effort. But from what we have done, we provide a summary of the findings from three kinds of analysis: structural, sequential, and discourse. Each deals with different aspects of the data and therefore provides different insights into the socialization process. Together they enrich our understanding more than any single type of analysis. We discuss each in the following subsections.

Structural Analysis: Elements of Mother–Child Talk

The first set of analyses we performed concerns the so-called structural elements of human discourse.[9] The elements provide a global contour of the communication under inspection. Whereas there are many structural elements to examine, the basic ones involve turns that mothers and children took in their MCCs, the lengths such conversations lasted, and the amount of exchange that took place in MCCs. The averages of these elements for both topics were similar between the two cultural groups. Therefore, we conclude that any observed differences in the further sequential and discourse analyses were not because of the structural elements but cultural patterns of socialization.[10]

Sequential Analysis: How Mother–Child Talk Unfolds in Real Time

Whereas they indicate the common contour of MCCs, structural elements analyzed previously do not show how MCCs proceed with real content of conversations. It would be informative if we could peek inside the MCCs as if they were taking place right in front of us. It is true that one could just replay and listen to all 209 MCC recordings. But such listening may not help us gain greater understanding of the general patterns. A more effective approach to analyze MCCs is the so-called sequential analysis.[11] This approach, equipped with software used to conduct the analysis, allows tracing of steps of all 209 MCCs to be aggregated, resulting in discernable patterns by cultural group.[12]

Sequential analysis requires that naturally occurring conversations between people be coded into mutually exclusive codes. Although there are different ways to code MCCs, we chose to code our data by event.[13] An event in an MCC is defined as a theme or a topic about which the mother and the child are talking. For example, the mother asks what learning activities the child did on a given school day. Then the child recounts the activities. Talking about learning activities here is an event. If the mother moves on to talk about how the child felt about his or her accomplishment, and the child responds with "I felt O.K. about that," then talking about achievement-related feelings is another event. Event coding tracks who said what and what the response was; these are then aggregated over all MCCs by good-versus-poor learning and by culture. This way of coding basically converts expressed ideas, themes, and topics into frequencies of occurrence in their original sequence. Such sequenced frequencies are then submitted to computation for significance. If, say, a sequence of A→B→C→D (where A, B, C, and D represent four different events) is found to occur beyond chance for Group 1 but not for Group 2, then this sequence is a research finding indicating a difference between the two groups. If, however, a sequence of

TABLE 7.1. *Eight sets of collapsed codes for sequential data on mother–child conversations about learning*

Code	Meaning	Examples
mP	Mother probes child positive affect	Happy, liking, pride, interested, eager, and fun
cP	Child refers to own positive affect	
mN	Mother probes child negative affect	Frustrated, disliking, sad, anger, bored, and unmotivated
cN	Child refers to own negative affect	
mV	Mother probes/instructs learning virtue	Effort, work hard, diligence, practice, persistence, dedicated, concentration, and humility
cV	Child refers to learning virtue	
mM	Mother probes learning process/ mental functions	Reading, homework, research, making projects, thinking, smart, and intelligence
cM	Child refers to learning process/ mental functions	

C→A→C→D is found for Group 2 but not for Group 1, then this sequence shows another difference between the two groups.

After we coded our data,[14] we found that about 80 percent of codes from the two teams were highly similar in meaning. This indicates that mothers from both cultures talked to their children about similar concepts of learning attitudes and behaviors. Despite this shared conceptual space about learning, the *amount* of talking as assigned to these codes and related *sequences*, as will be seen later, differed markedly.

It is important to note that mothers in both cultural groups were not rigid in their talking regarding good-versus-poor learning. Whereas many mothers generally focused on the *positive* aspects of good learning and negative aspects of poor learning based on the topic card they drew randomly, many also moved back and forth between positive and negative aspects for both topics. We therefore were compelled to use the same codes,[15] which contained both positive and negative thoughts and feelings, to code our data on both good and poor learning conversations.[16]

Sequential analysis required a much larger amount of data if we were to compute for more codes and longer turns. Thus, we regrouped our larger-number themes/topics into eight sets (see Table 7.1 for these themes/ topics),[17] with four for mothers and four for children as they took turns in

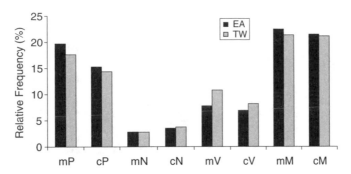

FIGURE 7.1. Eight codes for GOOD learning. mP = mother positive affect, cP = child positive affect, mN = mother negative affect, cN = child negative affect, mV = mother talks about learning virtues, cV = child talks about learning virtues, mM = mother talks about mental processes and learning activities, and cM = child talks about mental processes and learning activities.

their conversations. As can be seen, the first set of codes refers to mother and child positive affect and the second set to their respective negative affect. The third set indicates mother and child talk about learning virtues, and the fourth set deals with learning activities/mental functions (for convenience, I refer to learning activities/mental functions as simply *mental*). Finally, our data volume permitted analysis of only four turns. Thus, the sequences we computed for significance followed the pattern of mother→child→mother→child for any given theme/topic.

Before presenting the findings of sequential analysis, it would be informative to look at the general patterns of each culture's MCCs. Figures 7.1 and 7.2 show the distributions of the volume of conversations held by these two cultural groups for good and poor learning, respectively. The dark bars are European-American MCCs and gray bars are Taiwanese MCCs. Apparently, the two cultures' MCCs for good learning in Figure 7.1 did not differ much. Generally, mothers talked about mental the most, followed by positive affect and virtue, with negative affect being last. It makes sense that mothers would focus on positive rather than negative affect given that they recalled with their children a *good* learning attitude/behavior. In addition, because the mothers took the lead in their MCCs, as requested by us, they naturally talked more than their children, but their children also responded, albeit, as expected, less voluminously than their mothers. Nevertheless, it is noticeable that Taiwanese mothers and children talked more about virtue than their European-American counterparts.

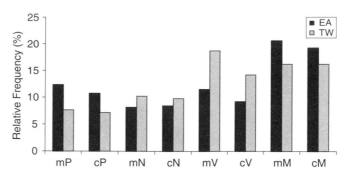

FIGURE 7.2. Eight codes for POOR learning. The abbreviations are the same as in Figure 7.1.

These trends were tested for an index called odds ratio, taking into consideration the relative amount of talk of the mothers and children within each of the two cultural groups.[18] Whereas for good learning there were no statistically significant differences in the four pairs of codes between the two groups of children, there were two significant differences between the two groups of mothers. European-American mothers talked more about positive affect and Taiwanese mothers more about virtue. Specifically, European-American mothers were 20 percent more likely to talk about positive affect for good learning than Taiwanese mothers. Conversely, Taiwanese mothers were nearly 50 percent more likely to talk about virtue than their European-American mothers.

For poor learning, the distribution of MCCs in Figure 7.2 is quite different. There are significant cultural differences for every set of variables. First, European-American mothers and children still talked most about mental followed by positive affect, then virtue, and negative affect last. Taiwanse mothers talked most about virtue, and next about mental, negative affect, and positive affect last. It seems that European-American mothers stressed mental and positive affects over learning virtue. Negative affect was to be avoided. By contrast, Taiwanese mothers focused on virtue and then on mental. Unlike their European-American peers, Taiwanese mothers elaborated more on negative affect with their children. Positive affect in comparison was the least emphasized.

Tests for odds ratio further confirmed that overall, European-American mothers talked more than twice as much about positive affect and nearly 70 percent more about mental than Taiwanese mothers. European-American children were similar to their mothers (nearly 50 percent and 80 percent more about these topics, respectively, than their Taiwanee counterparts). More pronounced than the previous pattern, Taiwanese mothers and children talked more about virtue (almost twice as much as than their European-American peers); Taiwanese children also did so nearly 70 percent more than European-American children.

In what follows, I discuss the sequential analysis that traces the turns of MCC in these two groups. To do so, I present four sets of graphs, with each comparing the European American (EA) with the Taiwanese (TW) sequences. The first four graphs show what happens when *mothers* start to talk about a given topic, how that topic is followed by their children, how mothers respond, and finally how children follow up again, with a total of four turns. The next four graphs show the same four turns with *children* as starters of the conversation.[19]

The statistical index is again odds ratios. Take the mother leading with positive affect as an example. We computed the odds of EA children following their mothers' talk on the same topic versus the times children did not follow their mothers but talked about something else. Then we computed the EA odds against the TW odds, resulting in an odds ratio for positive affect. Because any topic could be followed with any of the four codes, we computed odd ratios for all of them for four turns. These odds ratios enabled us to construct statistically significant turns on the graphs. Any significant sequence indicates that a group, either EA or TW, is more likely to follow a given sequence and is marked with a solid, thicker arrow in Figures 7.3–7.10. Any sequence that shows no difference between the EA and TW groups is marked with a broken line and a check mark (it is important to note that broken lines do not mean that mothers and children did *not* talk about a given topic. They could have, in fact, talked a lot – see Figures 7.1 and 7.2 for relative distributions of these topics, although the two cultural groups did not *differ* in the frequency of their follow-ups). Finally, T1, T2, T3, and T4 simply indicate the four turns.

Figures 7.3 and 7.4 show the sequences in which mothers are starters and their children's good learning is the topic. In Figure 7.3, when EA mothers begin talking about mental, their children are more likely to follow up with positive affect, not the same topic. Interestingly, as mothers begin with positive affect, their children follow up with mental as if these two topics followed each other. However, when mothers start with negative affect and virtue, their children were less likely than their TW peers to follow up with these topics. Moving to Figure 7.4, the sequences for TW differ somewhat. When mothers begin with mental, their children

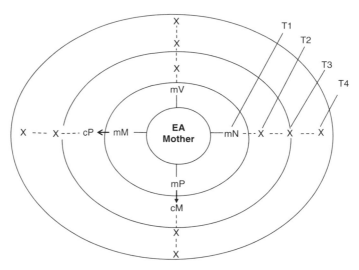

FIGURE 7.3. When European-American mothers start talking about their children's good learning. The abbreviations are the same as in Figure 7.1.

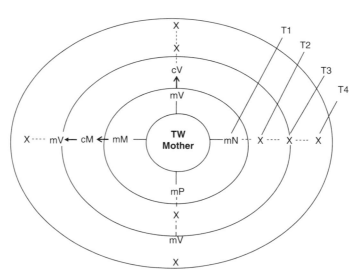

FIGURE 7.4. When Taiwanese mothers start talking about their children's good learning. The abbreviations are the same as in Figure 7.1.

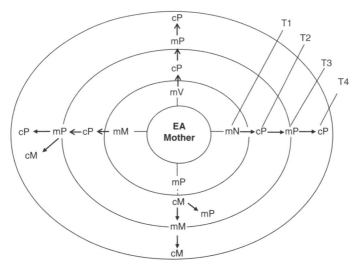

FIGURE 7.5. When European-American mothers start talking about their children's poor learning. The abbreviations are the same as in Figure 7.1.

are more likely than EA children to follow up with mental, with mothers following up further with virtue. Moreover, when mothers start with positive affect, the follow-up did not differ between the two groups' children, but in the third turn, TW mothers bring up virtue again. For mothers' starting with virtue and negative affect, TW sequences were similar to those of EA without differences.

Figures 7.5 and 7.6 show the sequences in which mothers are starters, and their children's poor learning is the topic. These sequences display the same but much more accentuated trends than the ones for good learning. When EA mothers' talk about mental, children follow up with positive affect as before, but their mothers continue to talk more about positive affect in the third turn, which is followed by children also talking more about both positive affect and mental. A similar pattern also emerges for maternal talk that opens up with positive affect. The conversational partners alternate between positive affect and mental in their turns. More striking is the fact that when mothers begin with virtue and negative affect, their children still steer the conversation into positive affect more, which is followed up by the two partners to the end again, with less likelihood of discussing mental than the TW group.

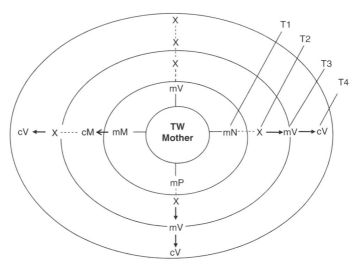

FIGURE 7.6. When Taiwanese mothers start talking about their children's poor learning. The abbreviations are the same as in Figure 7.1.

The TW graph also shows their previous trend with more emphasis. Maternal mental talk is followed with child mental talk, and then continued with maternal virtue talk. The same pattern can be seen for maternal positive affect as well as negative affect. The follow-ups of maternal virtue talk did not differ between the two cultural groups.

By now, there is less need for me to innumerate each remaining graph. Figures 7.7 and 7.8 show sequences in which children, rather than their mothers, are starters, and good learning is the topic, whereas Figures 7.9 and 7.10 show the same but with poor learning as the topic. The patterns are as expected.

Taken together, the sequential analyses compel us to conclude that mothers and children in both cultural groups talk about all four topics. Whereas the follow-ups on the topic of learning virtues itself do not differ that much between the two cultural groups, the follow-ups on the *other* three topics are quite revealing in their differences. EA mother–child conversations about learning center on positive affect and learning activities/ mental functions, regardless of what topic the mother or the child brings up first. In contrast, TW conversations are mostly followed up with learning virtues, also irrespective of what topics the conversational partners begin with.

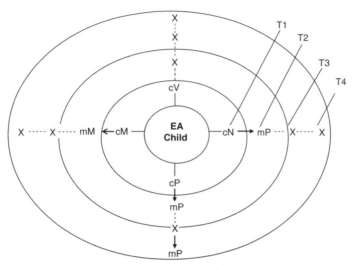

FIGURE 7.7. When European-American children start talking about their good learning. The abbreviations are the same as in Figure 7.1.

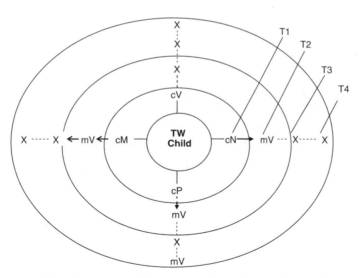

FIGURE 7.8. When Taiwanese children start talking about their good learning. The abbreviations are the same as in Figure 7.1.

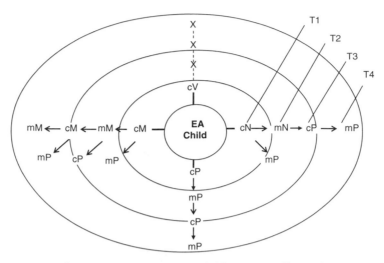

FIGURE 7.9. When European-American children start talking about their poor learning. The abbreviations are the same as in Figure 7.1.

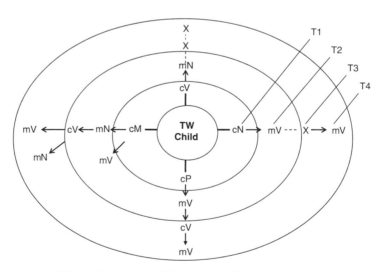

FIGURE 7.10. When Taiwanese children start talking about their poor learning. The abbreviations are the same as in Figure 7.1.

Discourse Analysis: What Mothers Do with Their Talking

Discourse analysis is a well-established approach to analyzing person-to-person or group communicative processes across social settings. This approach was originally developed in sociolinguistics. Today, many education researchers and some developmental researchers prefer this approach not only to quantitative analysis, but also to some forms of *qualitative* analysis, such as behavioral observations, interviews, or traditional ethnography. Whereas traditional forms of qualitative analysis accomplish the goal of addressing the complexity of a research topic in depth, it is discourse analysis that aims primarily at understanding the speech-based communicative interactions between people.[20] The unique – therefore indispensable – nature of discourse analysis lies in the simple fact that many human interactions, including socialization of children, proceed via verbal communication (in conjunction with nonverbal communication). To exclude this aspect of human interaction is to miss the core of human lives and child development.

There are many types of discourse analysis that address different aspects of human speech. As a whole, however, discourse analysis pays attention to the moment-to-moment exchange between people and to the overtly expressed, but also to the subtext of the unsaid. Discourse analysis also zeroes in on what action and goal a speaker intends to achieve and how such speech acts are responded to and further shaped by participants.[21]

Both the structural and sequential analyses of the MCC data provide the basic contours and proceedings of the communication between each culture's mothers and children on the subject of good-versus-poor learning. However, because of the limitations of each type of analysis, much rich *content* of the conversations is not captured in these two types of analysis. By employing discourse analysis, we can glimpse the intricate communicative exchanges. However, because it seeks to zero in on the moment-to-moment exchange, the in-depth look of the processes, discourse analysis, unlike quantitative analysis, precludes analysis of a large number of mother–child dyads. In addition, as shown in the distribution of the eight sets of codes as part of our sequential analysis, maternal talks for good-versus-poor learning do differ in the amount of talk they engage in with their children across these codes. Still, it is more sensible to use examples from conversations in both cultural groups for discourse analysis, considering this type of analysis utilizes very detailed exchange rather than larger patterns. Thus, I present only twenty-two such exchanges from each culture in order to illustrate the key points, recognizing the trade-off but also compensating for the different types of analysis.

There is little doubt that our near-naturalistic mother–child conversations about learning lend themselves to many kinds and layers of discourse analysis. For example, even merely looking at stylistic elements, one could examine how the two cultures' mothers preface their MCCs with their children, how they initiate a conversation about the good-versus-poor learning incidence that actually took place, how they respond to their children's replies, disagreements, and negotiations, and how they close the conversations. Sociolinguists delve deeply into each of these and many other aspects of communicative exchanges.[22] For my purposes here, rather than trying to present exhaustive discourse analysis, it is more productive to focus on some key content of MCCs. Thus, it is beneficial to take an initial look at *what* mothers talked about, with what intentions, and how they went about achieving their goals.[23]

Although my analytical focus is on cultural variations, I begin by discussing common features of the mother–child discourse that are shared by both groups. Next, I present what I see as large variations, highlighting different maternal attempts to socialize their children in learning. Hence, I focus on two topics: cognitive socialization and affective socialization.

Cognitive Socialization

Cognitive socialization here concerns the mothers' efforts to provide maternal *mental* frames used to draw their children into a given topic. Such mental frames include, but are not limited to, how to perceive/characterize/recount the learning event/behavior to be discussed, how to explain/attribute/interpret the cause of the event/behavior, and finally how to think about future attitude/behavior. The primary theoretical guide for my analysis of cognitive socialization in these MCCs is the cognitive scaffolding or coaching as conceptualized by the Vygotskian school of thought.[24] Accordingly, children do not acquire skills in a vacuum and by themselves, but through the ongoing guidance from their social world. The caregivers at home are their primary guides for learning culturally valued cognitive skills. Research from this school of thought has documented clearly that a child who receives such support is likely to achieve greater cognitive development and cultural competence than a child who receives minimal social support.[25]

Common cognitive socialization: Maternal mental frame for the child to enter. Both groups of mothers routinely set up mental frames for the events/

behaviors. Such mental frames serve to bring their children into the parental thinking mode in order to achieve mothers' purposes. The following example comes from an EA mother and her nine-year-old son Neil.[26] In second grade, which was a year prior to the interview, Neil received a grade P from his teacher, standing for "progressing." Despite the positive sound of the term, P in this case shows the opposite, specifically, Neil's lack of taking responsibility for his own learning. His mother decides to talk to Neil about receiving a P and the associated impact on him given that he was, in her words, a "perfectionist ... doesn't like to do things wrong."

EA Example (1)[27]:

1. Mother (M): How did you feel when you brought home a P?
2. Child (C): Bad (whispering, but joking).
3. M: Did you expect that Mrs. Wood was gonna give you ...?
4. C: No (whispering).
5. M: Do you think that you deserved it?
6. C: Yes (whispering).
7. M: So what did you do to make – what did you do to ...?
8. C: Worked on it.

To open the MCC, the mother does not attempt to establish the fact that Neil received a P, but rather asks a direct question about how getting a P made him feel. Apparently, the mother assumes the shared knowledge and related issues of getting a P between herself and her son. This assumption holds true, because Neil answers "bad" (T2)[28] without any hesitation. But the observed nonverbal behavior also indicates a degree of lightheartedness about this seemingly serious topic. Next, the mother makes sure that her child is not still in a mindset to blame the teacher or someone else for getting a P. So she asks another straightforward question about whether Neil thought he deserved a P. This time he answers, albeit still whispering but no more joking – a certain "yes." The mother then moves to remind the child how he responded to a P, and Neil replies very crisply again that he "worked on it" (T8).

Although this exchange is very short, the mother succeeds in setting the mental frame effectively. Four related meanings for her son to know and to confirm are discernable: (1) she regards her son's P as a negative outcome in school; (2) this negative judgment by the teacher ought to have a negative emotional impact on the child's sense of self; (3) her son was personally responsible for getting a P; and (4) her son responded correctly to this negative outcome by trying to rectify his poor learning.

Similarly, a segment between a TW mother and her nine-year-old boy Wei on the topic of poor learning also shows the mother's attempt to set up a mental frame into which to usher her son:

TW Example (2)[29]:

1. M: Do you remember that mom told you ... to review your schoolwork before you come home from school? You should look at your schoolwork to make sure that you know it well, right? Sometimes, you don't review it. What happens when your teacher gives a test?
2. C: Pretty bad.
3. M: Pretty bad, right?
4. C: Uh-huh.
5. M: Does mom scold you?
   . . . .
6. C: No.
7. M: What does mom say to you then?
8. C: I need to work harder.
9. M: You need to review the material, don't you?
10. C: Yeh!

Like the EA mother, the TW mother also brings out a negative learning outcome. Unlike the EA mother, who opens the MCC by asking a direct question on negative emotional impact of poor learning on the child, the TW mother points out the *cause* of her son's poor learning: He does not review the material taught in school (T1). Similar to the EA mother, the TW mother tries to ensure that Wei knows first the negative consequence of his failure to review schoolwork (T1). But knowing the negative consequence does not necessarily mean knowing the *cause* of poor learning because the two lie at the opposite ends of the process. This is why she attempts again with "what does mom say to you then?" (T7). When her son gives an appropriate but generic answer, "I need to work harder" (T8), the mother elaborates on a specific learning behavior: "You need to *review* the material, don't you?" (T9). In this opening short exchange, this mother, too, succeeds in making her child understand her firm belief that failure to review material taught in school leads to poor achievement.

Common cognitive socialization: Child's quibble. None of the sequences in either group have mothers expressing desires and expectations and demanding children's obedience and acceptance unilaterally, but both groups reveal much disagreement and negotiation within each dyad. In other words, the child's quibble is a rule rather than an exception. An EA example between a mother and her seven-year-old daughter Kate illustrates this inherent nature:

EA Example (3):

....

1. M:.... So do you think when you get home from school ... is it because you want to relax and maybe have a snack or play a game or something, and you don't want to come and do some more reading, because I notice that later in the evening you get tired, so that's not really a good time to learn something new, is it?
2. C: Well, maybe if you let me have some time to like play, a little, just like for 5 or 2, 5 or 6 minutes, and let me like get used to being home for a little while, maybe I'd read like five books.
3. M: Well, we can certainly try that, that's a great idea. I didn't realize that you were feeling that way, so what we can do is try maybe having a snack and playing for a few minutes, but then what that means is...
4. C: Is you need to –
5. M: When I ask you, say it's time to do your reading homework or it's time to –
6. C: And you can't, you can't say, "Oh mom, I'll do it later, I'm in the middle of a game right now!"

....

In the prior exchange in this dyad (not shown in the excerpt), the mother first praises Kate for liking to read and then moves to point out how important it is for Kate to read not just simple books but more challenging and different kinds of books, because reading is a life-long process. After this introduction into the maternal frame, the mother hints that Kate does not like to read more. Nevertheless, the mother is also careful not to scold Kate for her lack of enthusiasm, but instead to reason with her about an external problem: timing – "in the evening you get tired" (T1), and so it is "not a good time to learn something new" (T1).

Despite her mother's diplomatic style, Kate picks up on her mother's critical tone and snaps back: "maybe if you let me have some time to ... play" (T2) for a few minutes and "let me ... get used to being home for a little while, maybe I'd read like five books" (T2). Her request does not seem unreasonable, either, given that she offers something back, namely reading five books – an outcome supposedly desired by her mother. Indeed, her mother finds her complaint reasonable, and in fact is surprised that her daughter feels deprived of relaxation time before being asked to read again

(T3). Hence, her mother agrees to try the suggestion made by Kate. But then, being skillful in maternal negotiation and never losing her parenting goal, the mother also bargains for a commitment to read from her daughter if she is to give her a break to play first. The dyad succeeds in this negotiation by the two of them jointly reaching the agreement, with the mother saying "but then ... when I ... say it's time to do your reading homework ..." (Ts 3 and 4), and then, after the child seamlessly completes the intended maternal request, closing with "you can't say, 'Oh mom, I'll do it later, I'm in the middle of a game right now!'" (T6).

Whereas it is quite common for EA authoritative parenting to engage in disagreement and negotiation with their children,[30] Asian parenting style has been said to be more one-sided toward parents. As such, parents are characterized as authoritarian, asserting, pressuring, and demanding without giving their children room for discussion.[31] Our data, surprisingly, show quite the opposite. Child's quibbles are just as prevalent for TW mother–child dyads as for EA mother–child dyads.

The next excerpt comes from a TW mother with her seven-year-old daughter Ruli, also showing disagreement between the mother and the child. After sharing with the interviewer that she can hardly find anything to complain about her daughter's learning attitude/behavior, the mother says that the only thing she wishes that Ruli could improve upon is her impatience for writing words. No sooner does the mother open her mouth than she meets Ruli's resistance:

TW Example (4):

1. M: When you write, you need to write slowly.
2. C: Only you are talking; I haven't talked [referring to her mother's prior complaining about her writing to the interviewer]!
3. M: Oh OK, it's your turn to talk now. Please tell me then what you think you don't do well.
4. C:.... [silence for 4 sec.] Not much, none, rarely any.
. . . .
5. M: But you're not very serious [認真, give your 100 percent] in writing words.
6. C: I can write "I love you" though [writes].
7. M: Oh, good.
8. C: [Continues to write].
9. M: [Mother directs] then write this one, good, keep writing good.
10. C: I did it!
. . . .

11. M: Keep writing good.
12. C: My writing is beautiful.
13. M: You think that your writing is beautiful, but you need to write seriously.
14. C: Yes, I know.

In this example, the child is not happy that her mother chats with the interviewer about her not being serious in writing; therefore, she lets her mother know that she dislikes her mother's criticism and the fact that she is not given a chance to rebut: "Only you are talking; I haven't talked!" (T2). Her mother immediately yields to Ruli's charge and invites her to talk, but she also does not let go of her parenting responsibility; hence she redirects Ruli to address her weaknesses, but this time by herself: "Please tell me then what you think you don't do well?" (T3). After some silent mulling, instead of backing off, Ruli denies that there is anything she does not do well in learning. Then, the mother reasserts her complaint "But you're not very serious in writing words" (T5). At this point, Ruli changes her strategy: she circumvents very cleverly the verbal standoff by showing her mother that she can write not only seriously and beautifully but also lovingly (T6). After successfully refuting her mother in action and obtaining her mother's acknowledgment of her beautiful writing, she declares that she knows what "writing seriously" means ("Yes, I know" T14) when her mother presses the point in the end.

Common cognitive socialization: Maternal persuasion and child alignment. Despite the prevalence of disagreement and negotiation between mothers and children, the effect of maternal socialization is clearly observable during the MCCs from both groups. It is true that not all dyads succeed equally, but most mothers tend to influence their children by persuasion and reasoning. Here I provide an example where an EA mother tries to get her eight-year-old daughter Sue to realize that not understanding math but not asking the teacher for help out of fear of embarrassment is trouble for learning.

EA Example (5):

....

1. M: So if there's something in, like, you don't really have trouble except in math so far right?
2. C: So far I don't have trouble.
3. M: Well, there were some things that you didn't understand in math.
4. C: Yeah, but the teacher made things too hard for me.

5. M: OK, so what about if something – it gets hard … and it doesn't come easy like the rest of the stuff … what do you think *we* [emphasis added] should do about it?

6. C: We should …

7. M: How would anyone know?

8. C: Liz would know.

9. M: Well, but Liz wouldn't be in your class. Liz is your tutor this summer, a friend of the family. So you'd need to tell somebody.

10. C: Teacher?

11. M: The teacher? That would be a great person to tell.

12. C: Mmm.

13. M: What if you didn't feel real comfortable telling the teacher, who would you tell?

14. C: You?

15. M: And how could we, so you don't want to be embarrassed by telling the whole class that you don't know something?

. . . .

16. C: We could talk about it privately?

17. M: How? Maybe go to school early?

18. C: OK!

19. M: And talk to the teacher?

20. C: Mm-Hmm.

. . . .

At the beginning, Sue denies that she has any trouble in school, including math (T2). When her mother makes it clear that she does not understand some math concepts, Sue claims that it is the teacher's fault for making math too hard for her (T4). Her mother, realizing that Sue at least admits her challenge in math (even though she blames the teacher, not herself), seizes the opportunity to engage Sue in thinking about how to learn better instead of continuing to look for someone else to blame. So "what if something … gets hard … and it doesn't come easy … what do you think *we* should do about it?" (T5). Notice that the mother uses "we" here, hinting to the child that overcoming this learning difficulty is not solely her task, but that of the caring and able mother as well. When Sue is at a loss in coming up with a workable idea, the mother highlights the heart of Sue's trouble: unwillingness to ask anyone for help. But instead of pushing Sue to actually ask for help, the mother skillfully switches the perspective from the receiving end of Sue's trouble: "How would anyone know?" (T7). Sue then suggests Liz, a familiar person, family friend, and Sue's tutor. But that is not where the mother wants to guide Sue to learn. She probes now about Sue's need to tell: "So you'd need to tell somebody" (T9). Sue then comes up with what the mother desires all along – her teacher (T10). The mother is elated and welcomes Sue's willingness to ask the teacher for help (T11). But she does not stop there. Knowing that her daughter fears embarrassment stemming from telling the teacher in front the class about her difficulty with math, the mother then adeptly addresses the problem of Sue's discomfort in class (T13 and T15). In this fine attunement, Sue realizes that her mother would be a perfect intermediary between her and the teacher (T14). At this moment, the mother suggests that the best way to achieve this goal is for them to go to school early when there are no peers (T17). Then, privately, she, along with her mother, can ask for help from the teacher (T19).

This example illustrates the step-by-step guiding process in which the mother is able to change her daughter's mind from not willing to admit her shortcoming in math, to blaming the teacher, to her willingness to let others know her learning challenge, and to finding a viable solution to the problem. This mother uses careful persuasion to open her child's mind and to enable her to learn something very important in learning: It is not the actual math concept one fails to understand that matters (e.g., how to tell time on a clock, which they do discuss later in the MCC), but one's willingness to *tell* the helper what one does not know. But such willingness does not have to cost the child's self-esteem; one can find a good solution to the problem with the mother's help.

The following is an MCC between a TW mother and her eight-year-old daughter Lanyi for a similar process:

TW Example (6):

....

1. M: Your mind runs fast, and relatively speaking, this makes mom very happy, but there is one thing about you that makes me stressed out.
2. C: Uh, I write words wrong.
3. M: Oh, you already know that! Then, what do you think we should do? Would you like to make a plan? Hmm, I think that this is something you and I should negotiate.
4. C: Uh-huh.

....

5. M:.... Mom really has a headache over this thing. You give good explanations, but on your test, it's like half of the page is filled with wrong words! How'd you feel?

6. C: Where? I also have tests that are all right ... no mistakes!

7. M: If you were mom, and I were Lanyi, would you feel happy about this?

8. C: Uhh ...

9. M: If I were your kid, would you scold me?

10. C: No, I wouldn't.

11. M: Then what would you do? Encourage me, Mmm?

12. C: Yes, encourage you.

13. M: Really? Keep doing wrong, like saying "it's great that you got things wrong, how wonderful that you got wrong words?" Would a mom think like that? That would be a strange mom! I don't want to be a strange mom like that.

. . . .

14. C: Oh, oh.

15. M: Let's have a resolve to correct this thing, can we?

16. C: Alright!

. . . .

When the mother brings up poor achievement (T1), luckily, Lanyi acknowledges it (T2). However, when the mother probes, "what do you think we should do?" (T3), she (similar to her EA peer) also uses "we" to show that she as a parent has a joint stake in her daughter's learning. The mother offers to make a plan in order to address the problem (T3). When she tells Lanyi that she is stressed out and wants to know how Lanyi feels about such poor achievement (T5), her daughter resists her mother and counter-argues for her good achievement (T6). Then the mother uses a strategy to switch roles with her daughter: "If you were mom, and I were Lanyi, would you feel happy about this?" (T7), which leads to the absurd conclusion that a mother should encourage her child to continue to do poorly in school (T13). Therefore, in order to fulfill her parental duty, she must instruct her child to change. This apparently persuades Lanyi to agree that it is time to have a resolve (T16) (and subsequently a plan for how to practice writing in order to prevent wrong words again in the MCC later: writing words on the wall so that both of them can see Lanyi's progress).

These six examples show clearly that it is common for both cultures' mothers to attempt to set mental frames into which to appropriate their children. But it is also common for cognitive socialization by parents to be replete with resistance and quibbles from their children. Yet, both groups of mothers succeed in aligning their children's thinking with theirs gradually by reasoning and persuasion.

Despite these commonalities, there are marked differences in cognitive socialization between the two cultures' mothers. As noted before, the difference does not lie in whether one group's mothers set up more or fewer mental frames, but rather in the fact that their mental frames for their children are very *different*, and these frames reflect cultural orientations and priorities. Based on reiterative and cyclical reading of the MCC transcriptions, a recurrent pattern for maternal mental framing emerged with two related foci: *source* of learning and *causality* for learning. "Source" here indicates two ideas. First is the perspective that informs the mother as to how to conceptualize learning with her child. Second, "source" is also power or fund from which the mother draws legitimacy of reasoning, justification to guide, to move along, and eventually to influence the child's beliefs about learning.[32] In other words, the mother is not alone in struggling to make sense of her child's learning. Behind her, there is conceptual wealth for her to rely on. This conceptual wealth is her cultural backing that provides her with both cognitive sources and resources.

Different cognitive socialization: EA maternal focus on child's mental source. More typical than not, EA mothers draw on the mental source to talk with their children about their learning, both good and poor. This tendency is more noticeable when mothers talk about their children's good learning. The following example comes from an EA mother with her seven-year-old son Ed regarding his liking to talk to his friend Bob about books in his free time, even before the teacher discusses them with class.

EA Example (7):

. . . .

1. M: You really liked Harriet Tubman's [book] too, huh?
2. C: Mm-hmm.
3. M: And you would talk about that in your free time, too?
4. C: Sort of. Sometimes, we ... sometimes maybe.
5. M: Do you know that that's what smart people do, smart grown-ups, when they ...
6. C: Talk about books.
7. M: Yeah.
8. C: But guess what, last time when we were talking about Bunnicula [children's book series], we spent *all* [emphasis added] of recess.
9. M: You're kidding?!
10. C: Really!
11. M: That's great! So that's a pretty smart thing to do, to talk about a book.

. . . .

12. C: We read it, and ... looked up what might happen in later chapters, so that we could get a better explanation ... in our reading journals.

13. M: Oh, so you like to peek ahead sometimes when you read?
14. C: Mm-hmm.

. . . .

15. M: [Laughing] well ... you and Bob are pretty smart readers for your age.
16. C: Mm-hmm. And we actually wanted to be ... the greatest scientists in the world!

. . . .

This example shows clearly that the mother has in mind to steer her son into thinking that not just reading but *talking* about books is a behavior that marks very smart children and adults (T5). The mother is delighted that her son would spend his free time to talk with his friend about books (T11). This very reaction reveals that what her son and Bob do in their free time is quite unusual among children of their age, thus the exclamation "You're kidding?!" (T9) and the admiring "you and Bob are pretty smart readers for your age" (T15). Such learning attitude and behavior are naturally deserving of praise and admiration because they are, in the mother's view, very intelligent child behavior that bodes well for eventual adult life.

This kind of maternal guide results in the matching type of cognition on the part of the child. Notice how Ed's response changes as a function of his mother's steering him into smart learning behavior. When his mother initially probes about Ed's talking about books in his free time (T3), his response is somewhat hesitant: "Sort of. Sometimes, we ... sometimes maybe" (T4). But after his mother makes it clear that talking about books is what very smart people do (T5), Ed becomes very energized and shares that his talking about books with his friend happens not just "sometimes" or "maybe" but at times takes up "*all* of recess" (T8). As his mother further affirms his good learning behavior, Ed elaborates on even more exceptional behavior, namely that he and Bob would read ahead into the chapters in order to prepare themselves with better explanations for their reading journals (T12). After the mother confirms this very impressively intelligent behavior, Ed expresses his life aspiration: "... we actually wanted to be ... the greatest scientists in the world!" (T16).

The next MCC takes place between an EA mother and her eight-year-old son Kevin, also about good learning:

EA Example (8):

. . . .

1. C: ... someone said air and I said oxygen. So I basically was ... naming all of the categories but using a scientifical [*sic.*] name for them.

2. M: Where did you learn those scientific names?

3. C: Reading different dinosaur books can tell you many things because, not only does [*sic.*] they interact with dinosaurs but ... it can actually mean the same thing with animals.

4. M: So ... reading on your favorite subject which was dinosaurs ... when you were able to use that in class and share it with your class.

5. C: But using the dinosaur names ... they also work the same for different species of things.

6. M: Mm-hmm ... so not just for dinosaurs. They work for other kinds of animals, too?

7. C: Mm-hmm.

8. M: So you were able to just use those labels for, for a bigger group of animals ... not just the dinosaurs?

9. C: Mm-hmm.

10. M: Yeah. OK ... What did Mr. West think of you being able to get the ...

11. C: He thought it was really nice. And as all the teachers had always said about me ... I had a photographical memory.

12. M: Of what?

13. C: Of many different things. It's basically ... what it basically means is one thing pops in your head ... Boom! It's not going out. Just won't leave. It's stuck in.

14. M: Uh-huh.

15. C: It's like when you take a photograph. You just can't rip the colored picture out of the frame....

16. M: Yeah. It's just stuck there. So if you ever read or heard about it, you remember it?

....

17. C: It's like a bee buzzing around in your head. You can't get it away unless you make it go away.

....

The mother helps Kevin recall a specific learning activity in class where children are learning animal names and habits. Apparently, Kevin shares his knowledge about animals he obtained from reading outside school. Kevin uses scientific terms instead of everyday words such as oxygen for air (T1). His mother then asks him, quite typically among EA mothers, where he got these scientific names (T2), given that his peers do not seem to know them. Kevin gives a very elaborate and sophisticated answer about how his interest in different dinosaur books benefits his knowledge base in many ways, including his general understanding of animals: "it can actually mean the same thing with animals" (T3). However, his mother responds to his reading in general, and sharing his knowledge with class in particular, without commenting on his last and important point (T4).

Kevin knows that his mother does not quite get this point (in fact it is not clear what he means by "the same thing with animals," which is probably why his mother fails to appreciate that idea). Thus, in T5, he states much more clearly "But using the dinosaur names . . . they also work the same for different species of things." It is upon hearing this point that his mother realizes how her son's mind is able to take dinosaurs as one incidence and apply similar naming to other species. As such, her son has the very impressive ability to use one phenomenon to derive a generative scientific insight into other phenomena. After confirming her understanding (T6 and T7), the mother clarifies and formulates her son's existing cognitive feat into a clearer mental principle: "So you were able to just use those labels for, for a bigger group of animals . . . not just the dinosaurs?" (T8).

To signal the significance of her son's mental achievement, she probes how his teacher reacts to Kevin's feat (T9). Unsurprisingly, her son says that all teachers appreciate his special mental ability, one which is likened to photographic memory (T10). The remaining lines serve to establish attribution that Kevin possesses this higher ability to keep things in his head when encountering them only once. It is clear that both his mother and Kevin agree that he has an unusual mental gift for learning.

Despite different learning events, these two EA examples show mothers' effort to shape their children's thinking toward the mental aspects of learning. Particular attention is paid to intelligence, the mind, its functions, and mental processes. These, as discussed in the forgoing chapters, are the hallmarks of Western learning conceptions.

Different cognitive socialization: TW maternal focus on child's virtue source. Unlike their EA counterparts, most TW mothers rely on the virtue source to provide cognitive socialization. The following segment between a mother and her seven-year-old son Ren exemplifies this tendency:

TW Example (9):

   . . . .

   1. M: Oh, why does your teacher think that you behave well? . . .
   2. C: It's that I concentrate well [上課很專心] in class.
   3. M: Is your good concentration the concentration to talk to your peer at the next desk?
   4. C: I listen to teachers.

5. M: Oh, is it so only for Mr. Chang's class or is it for all classes?

6. C: Almost all classes like that.

7. M: Oh, why do you want to be serious [認真] in class?

8. C: Oh, yes.

9. M: You could sleep while attending classes, why do you want to be serious in class?

10. C: … if I can't answer the teacher's questions, misbehaving little friends [common term used to refer to young schoolchildren] will lose points.…

11. M: Uh-ah! So you want to behave well because you want to get an … honor award. Is that so?

12. C: Yes.

13. M: Or is it also that you yourself want to behave better?

14. C: Yes, I also want to behave better myself.

15. M: Oh, why do you want to behave better yourself?

16. C: Because my tests are pretty bad.

17. M: Okay, hmm, your tests are pretty bad?

18. C: Yeah.

    ....

The mother first tells Ren that she has heard his teacher say that he behaves well in school. She then asks Ren to share with her why the teacher said that (T1). Without any hesitation, Ren responds, "It's that I concentrate well in class" (T2). Because Ren gives a crisp claim of his virtuous behavior, which, to the mother, may seem a bit self-congratulatory, showing a less culturally valued self-portrayal, the mother asks a half-humorous question: "Is your good concentration the concentration to talk to your peer next desk?" (T3). Ren remains cool and answers firmly that he listens to teachers, dispelling his mother's lurking doubt (T4). But his mother still does not seem fully convinced and probes if Ren listens only to the teacher who reported Ren's good behavior (T5). Now Ren gives an answer that seems to ring truer for his learning virtue because he does not claim concentration in *all* classes but only in "*almost* all classes" (T6).

At this point, his mother seems to believe what he is saying. She now turns to probe why Ren displays such learning virtue and comes up with a seemingly child-friendly but actually quite prickly question, "You could sleep while attending classes, why do you want to be serious in class?" (T9). She offers her son a way, albeit somewhat facetiously, to contemplate what it means to concentrate in class with seriousness. Ren then reports that he does not want to lose his honor award (T10). However, getting an external reward for learning virtues is not what the mother hopes, because learning virtues are moral in nature and are ends in themselves. The mother then asks if Ren also recognizes that there is a greater purpose of having concentration and seriousness in its own right beyond the extrinsic incentive: "Or is it also that you yourself want to behave better?" (T13). The child concurs (or more likely is compelled to concur) that this is also his goal (T14). Finally, the mother wants to ensure that Ren does not just agree with her superficially but sincerely by asking him to explain why he cares about making himself better (T15). Ren admits honestly his inadequacy in learning: "Because my tests are pretty bad" (T16).

This mother does not focus her socialization of her son's intelligence, ability, or mind and mental processes. In fact, throughout the segment, she never touches on this topic. Instead, she stresses the learning virtues of concentration, sincerity, and seriousness. She takes the opportunity of teacher's praise of her son to steer him toward further self-improvement. Note that this mother is talking about good learning, yet the MCC turns into probing her son's inadequacies. It would be erroneous to assume that this mother is being harsh; her son does not regard her as such. Quite the contrary, her son knows the importance of these learning virtues and cooperates with his mother. The mother's cognitive socialization lies in making her son see the point of possessing these learning virtues not for external rewards, but for his own personal growth. Later in this MCC, the mother tells her son that he is very cute because he now knows why he needs to be serious in class. Like her EA peers, she draws on the cognitive sources and resources of her culture that regards learning virtues as fundamental for learning.

In the next TW example involving good learning, the mother talks to her 9-year old daughter Jia about how to be more diligent, making further effort to self-improve in writing composition.

TW Example (10):

1. M: … what's more, you still need to make extra effort; your composition writing needs to be strengthened. Tell me … you go deep in reading texts, hmm, your understanding of the gist of texts is great now, and you don't even need me to teach you anymore, right?
2. C: . . . .
3. M: A bit louder! Do you still need me to teach you or not?
4. C: No more.
5. M: No more. Now you can do it yourself; you are even better than me.… All of this comes from your own effort, right? Can you tell me how you've gotten better at writing? How do you think you improved?

    . . . .

6. C: I looked at how other people write.

7. M: Looking at how others write it. Did you not think for your own writing? How come you looked at others' writing?

8. C: I looked at what is it that they write better.

....

9. M: Oh, it's good that you know how to look at other's better writing … that's very good. Well, then you just keep working on it, alright? But I think you also need to persist in other areas, do you know?

10. C: Alright!

11. M: How about reading? You should read more books, and this will help you write compositions later. Your teacher called. He said that you should learn more Chinese set expressions and write more.

....

In this MCC, the mother acknowledges her daughter's merit in going deep in reading texts and understanding the gist (T1) because it is about good learning. The mother is delighted that Jia has learned the skills so well that she no longer needs the mother to teach her. The mother even points out that Jia is better than herself (T5), which is significant praise in Chinese culture. However, two important cognitive goals accompany her delight. The first is making Jia understand that her writing needs further improvement, which the mother mentions before she even starts to recognize Jia's positive side (T1). This urging continues in T9: "… But I think you also need to persist in other areas, do you know?" This expression urges Jia to read more and learn more Chinese set expressions because all of this extra effort will, as recommended by the teacher, help Jia improve her writing (T11). The second goal is to lead Jia to retrieve and recount how specifically her effort enabled her to improve writing thus far: "Can you tell me how you've gotten better at writing? How do you think you improved?" (T5). Jia's response about how she looked at others' writing initially does not meet her mother's approval (probably because she suspects Jia of copying others' work) (T7). But when Jia explains that her looking at others' work is for figuring out how others write better (T8), her mother appreciates Jia's own effort (T9) to learn from others. The mother ends that point by nudging Jia to keep working on this way of learning.

This TW segment shows common Asian parental socialization for children to understand the value of diligence, extra effort, and continuous striving no matter how much the child has already achieved. Even when parents are delighted with their children's strengths and merit, they still urge them to self-improve further by exercising these virtues. Undoubtedly, these tendencies reflect Confucian learning orientation and values.

The aforementioned four examples, two from each cultural group, illustrate how mothers set up mental frames for their children by drawing on their cultural source, which is the first focus that emerged from my discourse analysis. The second maternal focus is causality for learning. Causality here is understanding the mother's *explanation* or *attribution* of what causes learning to happen, including what learning activity, attitude, behavior, or event causes what outcomes. Causality also includes reasoning about how good learning achievement comes about and how poor learning can be changed. The difference between source and causality is that the former may not offer any explanation and attribution of learning events and outcomes. But the maternal discussion still proceeds within the realm of a given source, namely cultural orientation and values.

To be sure, maternal explanations of causality in learning are not to be evaluated against traditional philosophical demarcations of logic or scientific definitions of causality. In fact, very little of what these mothers do qualify them as philosophical or scientific logicians. In actuality, parents are unlikely to care about whether their logic meets philosophical and scientific definitions when they engage in cognitive socialization of their children. Thus, I would argue that formal – and for that matter, any stringent – logic is unimportant in childrearing, if not wholly irrelevant. Nevertheless, parental logic has its own chain of reasoning, hence coherence and integrity. In parents' ways of conceptualizing the learning world, they are what might be called folk logicians. It is therefore important to analyze their own logic because it is prevalent in daily socialization, and it is undeniably efficacious and influential in child development.

Different cognitive socialization: EA maternal causality of mind potency. A common way for EA mothers to help their children understand the cause for good learning is to lead them to think about how to use their minds to achieve greatness. The following two examples demonstrate this pattern. The first features a mother and her seven-year-old son Tim.

EA Example (11):

1. M:.... I wanted to talk to you about ... that time when you had that one math paper that "Oh my goodness!" like mostly everything was wrong and you never bring home papers like that. Remember that one?
2. C: Mm-hmm.
3. M: And it has ...
4. C: I just had a clumsy day.

5. M: You had a clumsy day. You sure did, but there was, when we finally figured out what it was that you were doing wrong, you were pretty happy about it.... And you were very happy to know the right way to do it, and then you were very happy to practice it. Right?

6. C:....

7. M: ... cause at first remember I looked at it and I couldn't figure out why you were coming out with the answer ... and you were having a tough time explaining it to me. Right? Yea, and once we figured it out you were pretty happy that I figured it out. And then ... I gave you a whole big paper with lots and lots of problems on it just so you could practice, and so I could make sure you really understood it. And you did the whole thing lickety split; you got everything right, and you did it with a smile on your face ... you were very happy about it. Why do you think that was?

8. C: I don't know, because I was frustrated, and then you sat down and went over it with me, and I figured it out right with no distraction, and then I got it right.

9. M: So it made you feel good to do well?

10. C: Uh-huh.

11. M: And it's OK to get some wrong sometimes, right? Cause ...

12. C: And I, I never got that again, didn't I?

....

Note that this MCC is about good learning. However, the learning experience that the mother brings up first is a negative one (T1). But very quickly, she turns the negative to the positive: "but ... when we finally figured out what it was that you were doing wrong, you were pretty happy about it.... And you were very happy to know the right way to do it" (T5). In T7, the mother elaborates on the process of discovering Tim's problems with math because he had "a tough time explaining" to her. Subsequently, she used her mind to figure out what it was that Tim did wrong and made sure that he understood it. Once she found the "cause" of Tim's difficulties, Tim's problem was solved, which made him happy and motivated to do "lots and lots of [math] problems" that were created by the mother for him to practice on. In the same turn, the question at the very end, "Why do you think that was?" serves to highlight the maternal explanation of causality for turning Tim's negative learning experience into a positive one. Tim recounts the chain of events (T8). The mother generalizes this learning experience into a normative expectation: "And it's OK to get some wrong sometimes, right?" (T11). Tim offers a happy closure to this exchange (T12).

The reasoning train for causality can be written in the following steps:

1. Tim is initially frustrated about not knowing how to do his math problems.
2. Mother discovers this problem.
3. Mother sits down with him and uses her mind to figure out what he fails to understand.
4. Mother makes sure that he understands it.
5. Mother creates practice problems for him to do.
6. He does all of them right.
7. He feels happy.
8. He never did math wrong again.

Whereas all of these steps are regarded as causal for the mother and the child, the most essential causal link is (3), where the mother uses her mind to figure things out and to show her son and to make him understand. Without (3), Tim would not have understood the math and would not have regained his motivation. Thus, the maternal belief about causality for good learning is built on the potency of the mind to figure things out and to understand.

The next example, a segment between a mother and her eight-year-old daughter Nina, also highlights the mental as the key causality for learning:

EA Example (12):

1. M: ... but I like that you ... do the research part and do it correctly, and you read the books you're supposed to read, so that you know ... what you're doing. And you get ideas about how you want your project to shape up. And ... that's really important to the planning part. It's important ... because if you just rush ahead and do the project without the information, it's not gonna come out very well as it....
2. C: And you'll be lying, pretty much.
3. M: Well ... you'd have to make up the facts if you didn't really do the research, right?
4. C: Uh-uh.
5. M: But, when you do the research, you're armed with the knowledge that you need ...
6. C: Especially if you take notes.
7. M: You take notes to make sure you can verify your facts, right?
8. C: 'Cause if you don't take notes, you'll forget. And then, you'll end up making up stuff again.

The mother first mentions to the interviewer that Nina has high enthusiasm about schoolwork. She jumps in full of excitement, but quickly loses her motivation. However, the mother finds Nina's approach to doing her research to be very good. In T1, the mother lays out her reasoning for causality for Nina's good research work. She emphasizes that doing all the research is "really important," because without obtaining the information, Nina's project will not "come out very well." Knowing the implications of her mother's reasoning, Nina fleshes out an even graver consequence that is not mental but moral in nature: "And you'll be lying" (T2). The mother's follow-up explanation brings Nina back to a more mental causality: "Well ... you'd have to make up the facts if you didn't really do the research, right?" (T3). In T5, the mother offers the causal antidote for combating the problem of not having the needed knowledge: doing your research. Nina, being in harmony with her mother's reasoning, comes up with the specific activity of taking notes for research (T6). Her mother further reiterates her main point of verifying facts in order to avoid the situation of having to make up facts (T7). Her daughter, now completely aligned with her mother's reasoning, reaffirms the ultimate benefit of doing research, taking notes, and getting information in order not to "end up making up stuff again" (T8).

Here again, the mother's causal explanation of doing research right is to prevent her daughter from having to make up facts. When her daughter hints at the moral consequence of lying, the mother skillfully steers her back to the mental, because not doing research right may not be a moral transgression but the mind's failure. What may cause Nina to have to fabricate facts is her waned motivation and rush through research, not moral failure. What the mother needs to do is to reason with her daughter about a mental process for how to do her research right. This segment demonstrates again the weight of mind and mental processes in maternal causal thinking about children's learning.

Different cognitive socialization: TW maternal causality of: virtue potency. TW mothers use a different causality to explain and to attribute their children's learning. Their focus is on the power of learning virtues. The following example takes place between a mother and her eight-year-old son Ming.

TW Example (13):

1. M: My boy, I'd like to talk about your swimming because I think that you are great at swimming. Am I right?
2. C: Uh-uh.
3. M: Yes, you are very good at swimming, but why did you say you were scared, afraid of touching water? How come you were not afraid of water anymore later?

4. C: I don't know.

5. M: ... Uh? Now there is another kid who is also afraid of water, how'd you help him, uh? If he is also afraid of water, but he also really wants to swim, how'd you help him, uh? ...

6. C: I think ... I'd first teach him how to hold breath ...

....

7. M: ... I think that you are great at swimming, how did you overcome that ...?

8. C: It was the coach ... who taught me how to hold breath ...

9. M: But initially you didn't want to get into water ... how come you wanted to learn then?

10. C: Because ... it's fun in the water ...

....

11. M: That was why you make an effort to learn! But how about your fear of water, how'd you overcome that?

....

12. C: That I don't really know.

13. M: Were you afraid at the beginning?

14. C: At the beginning ... I was very afraid.

15. M: How did you become less and less afraid?

16. C: Because ... I learned how to hold my breath.

17. M: Uh-ah! Someone taught you, right? You knew how to do it, you used it, then you weren't afraid anymore, right? Then you practiced and practiced, and then you got better and better, right?

18. C: That's right!

19. M: OK, did you feel like too hard [辛苦 exhausted] to practice holding breath at the beginning?

20. C: Not really.

21. M: How can that not be hard [exhausting]?! Then, is it hard [exhausting] to learn other things?

22. C: Yes, how can it not be hard?

23. M: So, can you be lazy?

24. C: No ... no!

25. M: Then other things ... don't you think that you need to make more effort, not be so lazy ... would you?

26. C: OK, OK ...

....

This somewhat lengthy segment shows how a TW mother accomplishes reasoning with her son that learning virtues are the real cause for good learning. Not only do they help the child overcome challenges such as fear, lack of motivation, unwillingness to practice, and falling into laziness, but they also are the general principles for learning anything.

The mother begins by affirming Ming's swimming skills (T1). But instead of just praising him, the mother wants him to know the underlying cause of his achievement. So she immediately asks him to think about how he changed from fearing water to not fearing water anymore (T3). When Ming says he does not know (T4), the mother sets up a concrete scenario of a peer who fears water but also wants to swim (just like Ming at the beginning) for Ming to tap the real cause of his learning (T5). Instead of getting into learning virtues, however, Ming mentions a technical skill, "holding breath" (T6). Apparently, his mother is not satisfied with his response and probes further (T7), but Ming gives an even more technical recount of learning the technique from the coach (T8). Seeing that her son is not going where she wants him to go, the mother asks about his motivation for why he wanted to learn (T9). Ming, being a typical child, mentions fun as his initial motivation (T10). Because Ming is drifting further from learning virtues, the mother simply connects Ming's desire for fun to the necessity of making a great effort to learn: "That was why you make an effort to learn!" (T11). Right after this causal link, the mother probes again how effort was responsible for helping Ming overcome his fear of water in the same turn. But Ming does not seem to quite get his mother's idea any further. After a few back-and-forth turns, his mother seizes Ming's idea that the coach successfully taught him and elaborates a series of reasoning steps in T17: "Uh-ah! Someone taught you, right? You knew how to do it, you used it, then you weren't afraid anymore, right? Then you practiced and practiced, and then you got better and better, right?" She finally makes Ming see her point "That's right!" (T18).

It would not be worthy of such a discussion if what Ming did just applies to swimming. The mother wants Ming to know how learning virtues are the real cause and guarantee for everything worthy of learning beyond swimming. Therefore, she acknowledges that working hard is hard/exhausting (T19). But Ming does not think learning how to hold breath is that hard (T20). The mother then categorically denies Ming's dismissal of the necessary price learning entails (T21) and moves on to ask him to think about learning in general in the same turn: "Then, is it hard [exhausting] to learn other things?" Now, Ming has completely entered his mother's causal frame and concurs with her: "Yes, how can it not be hard?" (T22). Finally, his mother returns to the issue that she mentions to the interviewer prior to the MCC, namely that Ming does not make enough effort in learning despite being very bright – "So, can you be lazy?" (T23) – followed by Ming's agreement (T24). The mother ends her probing by extending more effort (i.e., not be lazy) into a general virtue for any learning (T25).

The reasoning chain of this TW mother can also be written in the following steps:

1. Ming is initially afraid of water, but he wants to have fun.
2. He is willing to learn how to swim.
3. Someone teaches Ming some techniques.
4. He masters them, which helps him overcome his fear.
5. But mastery is only possible with much practice.
6. The more he practices, the better he gets.
7. Hard work is necessary to learn how to swim.
8. Ming cannot be lazy in learning how to swim.
9. Hard work is required for any learning.
10. Ming cannot be lazy in learning anything.

Similar to the reasoning steps EA mothers take to socialize their children, all of these steps are regarded as causal by the mother. But the most important ones are (5), (6), and (9) because they are the true purpose of this TW mother's socialization effort.

The next MCC segment, featuring another TW mother with her nine-year-old son Wei, follows these essential causal reasoning steps, albeit in shorter and simpler forms.

TW Example (14):

....

1. M: I thought that the best thing to do was for you take initiative ... to hurry to learn how to play [Beethoven's] "Für Elisa!"
2. C: Mm-hmm.
3. M: Then you made a great effort to practice it, right?
4. C: Uh-uh.
5. M: Well, Ms. Jin didn't want to teach you anymore because she said that your hands were too small, not big enough to play, right? But you insisted on practicing yourself, one segment at a time. In the end it got really hard; then you told Ms. Jin that you had already practiced everything well, but the last segment you couldn't do. Then Ms. Jin agreed to teach you, which made you really happy, didn't it?
6. C: Yes.
7. M: Then you came home, and you practiced and practiced, with lots of energy. Mom didn't even need to urge you anymore. You did it on your own, didn't you?
8. C: Yeah.

9. M: Then you entered a competition with this piece, right?
10. C: Yes.
11. M: Last week you got the No. 1 prize, did you not?
12. C: Yes, I did.
13. M: Therefore ... therefore mom keeps telling you "as thou sow ..."
14. C: So you shall reap.
15. M: You shall reap, right?
16. C: Right.

The mother recounts most of Wei's learning virtues while he confirms his mother's reasoning. To her mind, the only causality of Wei's winning the No. 1 prize was his self-initiated, persistent, undaunted tenacity in practice. Because the mother admires and is so moved by Wei's learning virtues, he does not need to say much. But when his mother endeavors to distill a general learning virtue out of Wei's good learning with "as thou sow," Wei joins her in completing the coda: "So you shall reap." This is as if they were singing a duet, with the mother singing the main tune and Wei complementing it. Together they present the song of learning virtues.

In sum, these four MCC examples, two from each culture, demonstrate clearly from where each group of mothers draw their understanding of causality of good learning. They use this understanding and conviction to socialize their children. More often than not, children move closer to the intended influence of their mothers. The potency of each culture's learning orientation is revealed.

Affective Socialization
Affective socialization concerns parental efforts to guide their children in their affective responses to learning. They do so based on their beliefs for how their children should feel about their own learning. Intuitively, one might think that emotion/affect in general is something that simply happens to us spontaneously and may not be subject to human volitional control. Indeed, some very basic human emotions may be quite automated and universally experienced; for example, a sudden and loud boom is likely to startle most human beings, regardless of their cultural origin. However, as discussed in Chapter 5, even such a basic emotion requires appraisal, that is, cognitive assessment before our body can respond to the stimulus, even if such appraisal may happen in a split second. Most other, particularly socially generated, emotions are likely to require more and longer appraisal. The more socially complex a given emotion is, the more complex cognition is likely required for appraisal.

As noted in Chapter 5, the appraisal process involved in human emotional response is judgment that our minds make to determine the significance of the event. As Frijda's[33] theory describes, we first register, code, and appraise the given event in order for us to know if it is positive or negative, benign or adverse, and so forth. Only after such appraisal is done can our body respond emotionally to the event.

Because appraisal is evaluative, it is bound to be sociocultural in nature. We cannot judge and evaluate the significance of an event neutrally. To appraise an event is to appraise it according to our culturally defined meanings and significance. This is why we observe that a given event may be appraised as an insult in one culture but as a friendship overture in another. For this reason, much of *how we feel* in fact comes about by our cultures socializing us *how to feel* during the long developmental process of our lives.[34] To borrow Kenneth Gergen's[35] insight, our physiological capacity to emote is likely only an instrument for achieving our culturally organized ends.

From this standpoint, how children feel in learning is also, to a significant degree, subject to and indeed under parental socialization. As such, children's affective responses to learning are far from spontaneous and "natural," but are colored by their parents' ethnotheories[36] about how best to feel – that is, their culturally informed beliefs. Indeed, John Gottman and colleague proposed parental emotion socialization as guided by their "meta-emotion philosophy" that shapes parental awareness, acceptance, and coaching of their children's emotion.[37] Similar to this new conceptualization, Nancy Eisenberg and colleagues define socialization of emotion as

> behaviors enacted by socializers that (a) influence the child's learning … regarding the experience, expression, and regulation of emotion and emotion-related behavior, and (b) are expected to affect the child's emotional experience, learning of content, and emotion-related behavior in a manner consistent with socializers' beliefs, values, and goals about emotion and its relation to individual functioning and adaptation in society.[38]

Subsequent research has documented that parental emotion socialization indeed influences children's physical health, socioemotional competence, learning motivation, academic achievement, and peer relations among infants/toddlers, preschool children, and elementary schoolchildren.[39]

Surely, in the MCCs, mothers commonly discuss affective responses in learning with their early elementary school children. They talk about how a given learning activity or experience makes their children feel or how children's affects influence their learning engagement and outcome. But more importantly, mothers stress how a learning activity *ought* to make their children feel and how children's affect *ought* to shape their learning. If children seem not to align initially with their mothers, it is usually the case that the mothers will make the children align.

Common affective socialization. Undoubtedly, there are commonalities between the two cultural groups in the maternal effort to socialize their children's learning-related affect. The following segments, one from each culture, provide examples, with the first from an EA mother and her eight-year-old son Tom on the subject of good learning:

EA Example (15):

....

1. M: And did you enjoy that part of it?
2. C: Yeah, and Mom, we also got some extra details.
3. M: We did, we got extra details, yep.... So ... when you came home and showed daddy, what did he say, do you remember?
4. C: No.
5. M: He said [in a goofy voice], "how come you didn't get me involved in this, cause I'm the scientist!" Remember? He was jealous, wasn't he?....
6. C: [Giggles] I did it just to get through with my homework.
7. M: But ... so what do you enjoy about science?
8. C: Hmm ... [silence, 3 sec.]
9. M: You enjoy knowing how things work, right?
10. C: Yeah.

....

Before this segment, the mother helps the child recall a good learning incidence where Tom made, with his mother's assistance, a nice wind sock to hang on the tree as his science homework. They searched on the Internet for information. Then, at the beginning of the preceding segment, the mother changes the factual recollection to emotional probing (T1). The particular affect that the mother wants her son to savor is enjoyment. However, that does not seem to catch Tom's attention initially, so he still talks about the details from the Internet (T2). His mother responds a bit more (T3) but turns back to the affective impact of Tom's work on his dad (T3), showing how Tom's good learning made both his parents happy. But Tom does not remember that (T4). At this juncture, his mother uses dramatic reenactment to elaborate on the positive affect involving his dad (T5). This makes Tom giggle, but he does not seem to join his mother's excitement fully and returns to the fact that he just tried to get through his homework (T6). His mother is unaffected by Tom's apparent lesser excitement and continues to ask him what he enjoys about science (T7). When Tom seems to be at a loss for words, his mother supplies a response with a rhetorical question at the end: "You enjoy knowing how things work, right?" Finally, Tom concurs with his mother, helping end the segment.

This segment shows clearly how the mother intends to link her son's science homework to his enjoyment. Clearly, her son is initially quite neutral about this link. Even when his mother becomes very excited herself and later brings up his father's enthusiasm with dramatic reenactment, Tom remains somewhat slow in catching up with his mother's effort to socialize him in feeling enjoyment about his homework. However, his mother does not give up and continues to probe him until he becomes more aligned with her purpose.

The next segment is between a TW mother and her eight-year-old son Sheng, also involving good learning:

TW Example (16):

....

1. M: You got your new belt, didn't you?
2. C: Hm-hmm.
3. M: Uh-huh, so would that make you think that I will ... try to get that victorious feeling back and apply it to other times ... you can also ... achieve the same thing, right?
4. C: Yeah ...

....

5. M: I thought that you were a little afraid when you just began ...
6. C: Mm-hmm.
7. M: I remember that in the morning right before the test, you were a little afraid, right? Then what did mom tell you how you should feel?
8. C: Courageous!
9. M: Yes, yes, then what should you try to show?
10. C: My power!
11. M: Power, yeah, did you show it?
12. C: Yes, I did ...

....

The mother talks to Sheng about achieving his new belt for taekwondo by overcoming his initial fear. Apparently, his mother coached him for better affect, which the mother believed to be the condition for his success.

After helping Sheng recall this event (T1), the mother asks Sheng if he has thought about applying his victorious feeling to other taekwondo competitions (T3). Sheng says yes. Having obtained Sheng's agreement, the mother now goes back to Sheng's initial fear (T6). With his admission, the mother then asks him directly what she said to him about how he *should feel* (T7). Unequivocally, Sheng responds "courageous!" (T8). She probes further for how Sheng should manifest his courage. He supplies "my power!" (T10) and tells his mother that he showed it in action (T12).

In this segment, the affect that the mother hopes to socialize her son in feeling is courage to overcome fear and to generate power to display in his competition. Once successful, her son should hold on to the sense of victory and apply it to later competitions. Evidently, the mother has in mind how her son should feel when he feels fear and when he achieves success. Like her EA peer, this TW mother is also skillful at linking obstacles and outcomes of learning to the affects that she believes are important for her son to feel.

As for cognitive socialization, there are large differences in affective socialization between these two groups. My analysis yielded two distinct foci in maternal affective socialization: affect involved in the learning *process* and affect about *achievement*. These two cultures' mothers talk about different affects for both. In what follows, I present two examples for affect in learning process and one example for achievement for each group.

Different affective socialization: EA maternal focus on interest and fun. Consistent with discussions in previous chapters, particularly in Chapter 5, EA mothers focus much more on how to cultivate and acknowledge their children's interest, curiosity, and fun in their learning process and how such learning enables the child to learn better. The following example takes place between a mother and her seven-year-old son Evan.

EA Example (17):

....

1. M: Do you think it's interesting to learn about math?
2. C: No, not really.
3. M: What if math was like, you know, instead of what's 7 plus 5, what if it was like, there were 7 frogs, and 5 frogs hopped over to visit them, how many frogs were there all together? Would that be more interesting?
4. C: Well yeah, I'd be more interested, but ... I still wouldn't really like it.

> 5. M: Would you rather ... see a problem that said 7 plus 5, or would you rather see a little story saying there were 7 frogs, and 5 frogs hopped over, which would be more interesting to you?
> 6. C: The frog, like the 5 frogs and some hopped over, that one.
>
> ....

This segment follows much discussion on the fact that Evan likes to learn about frogs and tadpoles because he is fascinated by them (not shown). Apparently, the mother wants to bring her son to a different realm of learning, that of math, which she knows her son does not like (T1). She adeptly takes Evan's original interest in frogs to explore his interest in math (T2). But Evan only inches a bit in the maternal direction; he still rejects liking math (T3). Then, the mother comes up with a different and very clever suggestion about hearing a story about frogs hopping and visiting others rather than the dry abstract addition with numbers (T5). She successfully moves Evan to liking this way of learning math (T6).

The next segment shows how a mother probes her eight-year-old daughter Shelley about her fun in doing her project.

EA Example (18):

> ....
>
> 1. M: You were learning things but it was fun, wasn't it?
> 2. C: Yeah.
> 3. M: ... do you think it's better when you're doing things ... that like having a play or something, do you think that's better to learn than sitting there and reading a book? Do you think it's more fun, or do you think you learn more, you just think it's just more fun?
> 4. C: I think it's better to learn ...
> 5. M: You think it was easier to learn, when you're ... speaking your lines, going over the lines every day.
> 6. C: Yeah.
> 7. M: Cause I'm sure, you going over those lines every day, doing the play, I betcha you would remember more than just reading it in the book once or doing a little essay about it.... Don't you think?
> 8. C: Yeah.

Like Evan's mother, Shelley's mother wants her daughter to think about what role fun plays in her learning – why she separates learning from fun for Shelley (T1). However, Shelley's simple response ("Yeah," [T2]) does not quite get at what her mother has in mind. So she juxtaposes the more fun way of learning and just "sitting there and reading a book" and then contrasts "just more fun" versus "learn more?" (T3). Shelley understands her mother's sophisticated probing and acknowledges "it's better to learn" (T4). The mother further points out how fun helps make learning specific things easier (T5) and helps Shelley remember more things than without fun (T7). Shelley fully concurs.

Different affective socialization: TW maternal focus on pain but persever-ance. TW mothers sometimes also talk to their children about their inter-est, liking, and fun. More often, however, their focus is on their belief that there are difficulties, hardship (bitterness, 苦), and therefore pain in learn-ing anything well. Therefore, they coach their children on how to overcome such inherent challenges. They rely heavily on unequivocal learning vir-tues. The following example, involving a TW mother and her nine-year-old daughter Hua, is on unavoidable pain in learning:

TW Example (19):

....

1. M: Hmm, would you like to become a natural scientist later on?
2. C: No.
3. M: Why? Didn't you say you like that?
4. C: Yeah, but I feel that would be so much hard work [很辛苦].
5. M: Not so, you will learn a lot.
6. C: I don't want it.
7. M: Uh, there is delight in hard work! [辛苦中有快樂啊!].
8. C: I don't like it.

....

Before this segment, the mother talks to Hua about her liking and interest in her class about nature. But Hua says that there is one thing she does not like about that class – the teacher is too strict. The mother then changes that topic to the possibility of Hua becoming a natural scientist because she really likes nature (T1). But Hua does not share her mother's career aspira-tion (T2). The mother takes Hua's own interest in nature and questions her denial (T3). Hua confirms that she does indeed like nature but does not like so much hard work in science (T4). Her mother uses a typical East Asian reasoning that hard work yields much learning (T5). Hua goes back to her not wanting to work hard. The mother then appeals with "delight in hard work" (T7), a set phrase in Chinese frequently cited in daily communica-tion. Unfortunately, Hua would not budge (T8).

Although Hua ultimately is not convinced by her mother's affective socialization (amid cognitive socialization), this fact does not deter her mother from attempting and persisting. She acknowledges hard work as inherent reality in science learning and presses Hua to adopt the view that there is delight in hard work. Similarly, recall TW Example 13, where Ming's mother also brings up the notion of pain (exhaustion in practicing swimming) during T21–T24. When Ming denies hard work, his mother pleads "How can that not be hard?!" (T23).

The following segment between a TW mother and her seven-year-old daughter Wenyi addresses how pain in learning can be combated:

TW Example (20):

....

1. M: ... why did you feel it hard to spell words, but now you feel easy? Before you were afraid of Chinese, and you didn't like it, but why did you change to liking it now?
2. C: ... because I did well on my tests, and I understand the teacher in class, so I like it now.
3. M: That's why mom urges you to hold on to persistence toward things ... the attitude, you need to have seriousness toward learning anything, not afraid of difficulties, don't I?
4. C: Yes.
5. M: Like you were afraid of the standard sound of Chinese ... right?
6. C: Mm-hmm.
7. M: Mm-hmm, when you began learning the spelling, you understood your teacher sometimes but not other times. But after a while, you got it; then you weren't afraid of it anymore. This is for sure an achievement.
8. C: Mm-hmm.

....

This segment shows how the mother links Wenyi's success in learning standard Chinese spelling to her persistence. Actually, from T2, it is not clear whether Wenyi really persisted. In fact, it seems that she just got lucky on her tests despite her lack of understanding the teacher well. What is clear is that Wenyi did well on her tests, and then she began to understand the teacher, which made her like learning Chinese. But ascertaining the facts is not the point her mother wants her to understand in this segment. Instead, she wants to attribute (or to be more accurate, fit) Wenyi's success to her holding on to persistence, which, in her mother's conviction, enabled her not only to learn Chinese spelling but more broadly to face any difficulty in learning (T3). A specific persisting behavior the mother demonstrates next is to hang in there, being patient and serious for enough time, until Wenyi tastes some success. The mother highlights this moment by connecting it to no more "afraid of it," which she unambiguously declares as a sure achievement (T7). Wenyi, like her EA peer, concurs with her mother.

Different affective socialization: EA pride for achievement. The second focus of maternal affective socialization is response to achievement. EA mothers in general emphasize pride more than any other emotion (the importance of pride in the West is discussed at length in Chapter 5). Here is an example of a sequence taking place between an EA mother and her eight-year-old son Ian regarding good learning.

EA Example (21):

1. M: Oh cause it was something you really liked ... because everyone was impressed ...

. . . .

2. C: Mrs. Bernard looked at you when I was finished ...
3. M: Oh cause she looked at me. . . . So you wanted us to be proud.
4. C: Hmm-hmm.
5. M: Or you wanted to be proud of yourself?
6. C: Yeah.

Ian likes Shakespeare's *Romeo and Juliet* (part of the sequence not shown in the excerpt). When students were assigned to give a presentation on this story, Ian showed high enthusiasm. He asked his dad to help him gather information and did an "excellent job" with it and gave a great presentation. This segment is about what happened after Ian did all of that. The mother recounts that "everyone was impressed" (T1), and Ian tells his mother that the teacher looked at his mother when he was done with his presentation (T2). All of this is interpreted by the mother as a moment for parental pride (T3). But parental pride is only one part of the affective response to Ian's achievement; the child himself also *should* be proud of *himself* (T5), with which Ian agrees (T6).

Different affective socialization: TW more perseverance for future achievement. TW mothers talk much less about their children's pride and their own pride in response to their children's achievement. Instead, they tend to socialize their children in an outlook toward the future with more perseverance. The following segment between a mother and her nine-year-old son Yun exemplifies this tendency.

TW Example (22):

. . . .

1. M: Mom was very moved that time.
2. C: Mm-hmm.

3. M: Knowing that you weren't willing to give up, fighting to the very end in the chess competition, persisting, persisting, did you ...?

4. C: Mm-hmm.

5. M: Wow, you turned from losing to winning, was it not true? That's why ... mom was very relieved that time. So mom really hopes that you will use the same normal speed in your future chess play. But not willing to give up, not accept losing so quickly, and giving your 100% can be applied to doing anything.

6. C: Giving my 100% to anything I do.

7. M: Oh, yes, that's great.

The mother helps Yun recall his dramatic achievement in one chess competition where Yun was losing at first, but did not give up and instead persisted with the same effort. He ended up winning. His mother was very moved by her son's virtue (T1 and T3). But she does not express pride, although surely a sense of relief (T5). In the same turn, she offers a general principle of applying all of these good virtues to anything that Yun does. Without any quibble, Yun recites this principle (T6), which meets his mother's full approbation in the end (T7).

I attempted to show twenty-two examples of MCC, half from each culture. It is, however, important to point out that this set of discourse analysis barely scratches the surface of the very rich data we collected. Earlier in the chapter, I acknowledged that there are many more topics, layers, and perspectives that discourse analysis can enlighten. Nonetheless, the current set of analyses yields important insight into the role culture may play in parental socialization of children's learning beliefs. The unique contribution of discourse analysis is displaying an otherwise enigmatic process of child development in real time but in slow motion.

PREVALENT AND EFFECTIVE SOCRATIC AND CONFUCIAN TUTORS AT HOME

Both sequential and discourse analysis suggest that there are ample Socratic tutors in the EA homes and ample Confucian tutors in Chinese-heritage homes. Although we only collected mother–child conversations, there is no reason to believe that EA fathers would be any different. Given that many Confucian heritage families have grandparents and even other relatives living together, there is also no reason to believe that Chinese extended kin would be any different either. In fact, our research[40] on immigrant Chinese adolescents' homes shows that this Confucian tutoring style is offered not only by the parents, but also grandparents and other relatives even when they reside on different continents. For low-income families, when parents are not able to offer such help, the more capable of the extended kin step in.

Taken together, EA socialization in learning centers on the core beliefs about the child's mind and positive affect. Particularly emphasized are the distinct qualities of the self with two sides. First is the child's mind with heightened attention to how his or her mind works and how the child is to use it to explore the world, to gain understanding, and to achieve ingenuity, creativity, and productivity. Second, the child's intrinsic motivation such as interest, curiosity, excitement, fun, and enjoyment in the learning process is of utmost importance. The affect for achievement is pride in oneself. The task of molding their children into honoring these beliefs and behaving and feeling accordingly is carried out by parents, which is crucial during the preschool and early elementary school age. Our data show that mothers are highly skillful tutors. The best model of Western mind socialization is the age-honored Socratic tutoring style that is still widely admired and promoted in today's Western education. Comparing the two, the way mothers engage the less-than-fully qualified members of the culture – their children – is not very different from the master Socrates himself when he demonstrated his tutoring of the slave boy in geometry and succeeded in opening a nascent but capable mind. Unsurprisingly, the Socratic tutoring style finds tireless and effective replication in the EA homes. Such socialization aims at helping the child discover the greatness of the self as a learner.

Socialization of Confucian learning values also takes the form of parental tutoring of children at home. Like their EA counterparts, mothers are equally adept at carrying out this task. The difference lies in *what* they tutor their children about and *how* they go about doing that. The core beliefs are the Confucian learning virtues that are held to have causal power for the learning process and outcomes. The tutoring style also resembles the Confucian way of talking: the mother's guiding authority is assumed by herself and her child; not guiding their children in learning is a parental moral failure in Chinese culture. She attributes good learning to application of good virtues and poor learning to lack thereof. Positive and negative affects are also pivot around the learning virtues. Attributing learning to virtues clarifies for the child what is inherently in the child: capacity to be virtuous, and therefore the inherent, inexhaustible ability to learn well. But the realization of such morally endowed potential requires continuous effort on the part of the child. For this reason, mothers are compelled to instruct more rather than to leave learning to be a matter of children's choice, driven by their interest and fun. Also for this reason, maternal focus is always on the child's continuous betterment in learning rather than on securing pride and self-greatness in the child, regardless of good or poor outcomes.

NOTES

1. See note 11 to Chapter 4.
2. See note 6 to Chapter 3.
3. See note 15 to Chapter 1; Chamberlain, P., & Patterson, G. R. (1995). Discipline and child compliance in parenting. In M. Bornstein (Ed.), *Handbook of parenting, Vol. 4* (pp. 205–225). Hillsdale, NJ: Erlbaum; Edwards, C. P. (1989). The transition from infancy to early childhood: A difficult transition and a difficult theory. In V. R. Briker & G. H. Gossen (Eds.), *Ethnographic encounters in Southern Mesoamerica: Essays in honor of Evon Z. Vogt, Jr.* (pp. 167–175). Austin: University of Texas Press; and Eisenberg, N., Cumberland, A., & Spinrad, T. L. (1998). Maternal socialization of emotion. *Psychological Inquiry, 9,* 241–273 for general reading on this topic.
4. Shweder, R. A. (2011). Commentary: Ontogenetic cultural psychology. In L. A. Jensen (Ed.), *Bridging cultural and developmental psychology: New syntheses in theory, research and policy* (pp. 303–310). New York: Oxford University Press.
5. See note 3 to this chapter.
6. Fivush, R., & Nelson, K. (2006). Parent–child reminiscing locates the self in the past. *British Journal of Developmental Psychology, 24*(1), 235–251; and Van Abbema, D. L., & Bauer, P. J. (2008). Autobiographical memory in middle childhood: Recollections of the recent and distant past. *Memory, 13*(8), 829–845.
7. Miller, P. J., Sandel, T. L., Liang, C.-H., & Fung, H. (2001). Narrating transgressions in Longwood: The discourses, meanings, and paradoxes of an American socializing practice. *Ethos, 29*(2), 159–186; Wang, Q. (2001). "Did you have fun?" American and Chinese mother–child conversations about shared emotional experiences. *Cognitive Development, 16,* 693–715; and see the first reference in note 25 to Chapter 4. Researchers also collect observational data and videotape mother–child interactions, also a real-time socialization process.
8. See note 63 to Chapter 4; and Li, J., Fung, H., Liang, C.-H., Resch, J., & Luo, L. (2008, July). Guiding for self-discovery or self-betterment: European American and Taiwanese mothers talking to their children about learning. In A. Bernardo (Chair), *Achievement motivation and achievement attribution among Asian students: Insights from qualitative data.* Invited paper symposium by the International Congress of Psychology, Berlin, Germany.
9. Atkinson, J. M., & Heritage, J. (Eds.). (1984). *Structures of social action: Studies in the conversation analysis.* Cambridge: Cambridge University Press.
10. See note 8 to this chapter.
11. Bakeman, R., & Gottman, J. M. (1986). *Observing interaction: An introduction to sequential analysis.* Cambridge: Cambridge University Press; and Bakeman, R., & Quera, V. (1995). *Analyzing interaction: Sequential analysis with SDIS and GSEQ.* New York: Cambridge University Press.
12. See note 11 to this chapter for technical details.
13. See note 11 to this chapter.

14. See the second reference in note 8 to this chapter and the first reference in note 61 to Chapter 3 for technical details of how we quantified our qualitative data in general. For the current sequential analysis, we first took a random 20% of our MCCs (about forty-two) in order to code our data. Two coders from each culture, unaware of our hypotheses, looked at the MCCs from their respective culture. A list of possible codes was generated by each coding group. Then the two teams met to integrate their codes into a single list. These procedures led to the establishment of fifty-nine sets of codes, one for mothers and one for children, given that each MCC followed the mother→child→mother→child sequence.

15. See the second reference in note 8 to this chapter and the first reference in note 61 to Chapter 3 for achieving reliability in such coding as a convention in the field. Two steps were taken for coding: (1) reliability coding, where two coders from each culture, unaware of the study's hypotheses, followed a procedure to code another random sample of 20% of our data. Their task was to apply independently the fifty-nine sets of codes accurately and reliably to code the data. After coding a few MCCs, they discussed their agreements and disagreements and continued their coding/discussion until they completed the whole 20%. While keeping track of agreements, the coders also listed two kinds of disagreements: (1) an event noted by one coder as present but by another as absent and (2) an event noted by one coder as belonging to one code but by another coder as belonging to another code. The second step was for either coder of each cultural team to use the fifty-nine sets of codes to code their respective MCCs after reliability was achieved.

16. See the first reference in note 11 to this chapter. Both disagreements and agreements were computed for Cohen's *kappa*, an index for reliability coding. For European-American MCCs, Cohen's *kappas* were .83 for good and .91 for poor learning, and Taiwanese MCCs, Cohen's *kappas* were .85 for good and .94 for poor learning. These were excellent according to established conventions in the field.

17. Because our data came from only 209 mother–child pairs, we needed to reduce our codes in order to accommodate the amount of data we collected. Thus, we collapsed the coded data based on our fifty-nine sets of codes into eight sets. This regrouping of coded data necessarily moved the conceptually more concrete themes/topics to more abstract ones.

18. All odds ratios were computed at 95% confidence interval, and all presented differences were significant at $p < .05$. I am tremendously grateful to Roger Bakeman for his step-by-step guidance on sequential analysis we conducted here. I am also grateful to Wanchun Wei who helped code the Taiwanese data with another coder and subsequently ran these analyses with different versions of Bakeman's GSEQ software.

19. As an advantage of sequential analysis, any time the mother starts is tallied for four turns, and the same applies to the child as a starter. Of course, each MCC began with the mother as the lead as structured by our interview. However, as the MCC unfolded, the two took turns to converse. Therefore, either the mother or the child could lead a given sequence. Because MCC was done with the two topics of good-versus-poor learning, I present two graphs that juxtapose EA and TW on good and two on poor learning.

20. Schiffrin, D. (1994). *Approaches to discourse: Language as social interaction*. Malden, MA: Blackwell; and Gumperz, J. J., Drew, P., Goodwin, M. H., & Schiffrin, D. (1982). *Discourse strategies*. New York: Cambridge University Press.

21. See the section titled "Western Classroom Discourse and Socialization" in Chapter 8 for several examples of discourse analysis in both European-American and Chinese-heritage language classrooms, which shed important light on the effects of teacher talk on students' learning and self-understanding.

22. See notes 9 and 20 to this chapter.

23. To be sure, in order to do full justice to our data, we are continuing our analysis beyond this initial step and awaiting different insights from this ongoing endeavor.

24. Vygotsky, L. S. (1978). *Mind in society: The development of higher psychological processes*. Cambridge, MA: Harvard University Press; Cole, M. (1998). *Cultural Psychology: A once and future discipline*. Cambridge, MA: Harvard University Press; Bruner, J. (1987). *Actual minds, possible worlds*. Cambridge, MA: Harvard University Press; Rogoff, B. (1990). *Apprenticeship in thinking: Cognitive development in social context*. New York: Oxford University Press; and Wertsch, J. V. (1996). A sociocultural approach to socially shared cognition. In P. Baltes & U. Staudinger (Eds.), *Interactive minds* (pp. 85–100). New York: Cambridge University Press.

25. See Gottfried, A. E., Fleming, J. S., & Gottfried, A. W. (1998). Role of cognitive stimulating home environment in children's academic intrinsic motivation: A longitudinal study. *Child Development, 69*, 1448–1460; and Bradly, R. H., & Corwyn, R. F. (2005). Caring for children around the world: A view from HOME. *International Journal of Behavioral Development, 29*(6), 468–478 for examples.

26. All names are pseudonyms.

27. The first column of numbers indicates turns taken by the mother and her child.

28. T1, T2, and so forth are abbreviations of turns corresponding to the numbering in note 26 to this chapter.

29. Jin Li translated all Taiwanese MCCs.

30. Baumrind, D. (1980). New directions in socialization research. *American Psychologist, 35*, 639–652.

31. See Steinberg, L., Dornbusch, S., & Brown, B. (1992). Ethnic differences in adolescent achievement: An ecological perspective. *American Psychologist, 47*, 723–729; and Eaton, M. J., & Dembo, M. H. (1997). Differences in the motivational beliefs for Asian-American and Non-Asian students. *Journal of Educational Psychology, 89*(3), 433–440 for examples of such characterization.

32. See the fourth reference in note 24 to this chapter; and Moll, L. C. (1995). *Vygotsky and education: Instructional implications and applications of sociohistorical psychology*. New York: Cambridge University Press.

33. See note 5 to Chapter 5.

34. See Tsai, J. L., Louie, J. Y., Chen, E. E., & Uchida, Y. (2007). Learning what feelings to desire: Socialization of ideal affect through children's storybooks.

Personality and Social Psychology Bulletin, 33(1), 17–30 for research on how we feel originating from how our cultures socialize us to feel.

35. Gergen, K. J. (2010). The acculturated brain. *Theory & Psychology, 20*(6), 795–816.

36. Harkness, S., & Super, C. M. (Eds.) (1996). *Parents' cultural belief systems: Their origins, expressions, and consequences*. New York: Guilford.

37. Gottman, J. M., Katz, L. F., & Hooven, C. (1996). Parental meta-emotion philosophy and the emotional life of families: Theoretical models and preliminary data. *Journal of Family Psychology, 10*(3), 243–268; and Gottman, J. M. (1996). *The heart of parenting: How to raise an emotionally intelligent child*. New York: Simon & Shuster.

38. Eisenberg, N., Spinrad, T. L., & Cumberland, A. (1998). The socialization of emotion: Reply to commentaries. *Psychological Inquiry, 9*(4), 317–333, p. 317.

39. See the first reference in note 37 to this chapter; Ramsden, S. R., & Hubbard, J. A. (2002). Family expressiveness and parental emotion coaching: Their role in children's emotion regulation and aggression. *Journal of Abnormal Child Psychology, 30*(6), 657–667; Spinrad, T. L., Eisenberg, N., Gaertner, B., Popp, T., Smith, C. L., Kupfer, A. et al. (2007). Relations of maternal socialization and toddlers' effortful control to children's adjustment and social competence. *Developmental Psychology, 43*(5), 1170–1186; and Brophy-Herb, H. E., Schiffman, R. F., Bocknek, E. L., Dupuis, S. B., Fitzgerald, H. E. et al. (2011). Toddlers' social-emotional competence in the contexts of maternal emotion socialization and contingent responsiveness in a low-income sample. *Social Development, 20*(1), 73–92 for such research findings.

40. See the second reference in note 4 to Chapter 3.

8

The Devil's Advocate and the Reluctant Speaker

Speaking – this biologically endowed capacity – is the hallmark of human intelligence. Although humans with various impairments can still fare well with soundless communication, thanks to the advent of the human invention of written symbols, text, and sign languages, speaking with sound from the vocal cord undeniably represents a remarkable achievement of human evolution.

Despite this unique human capacity, speaking is far from being a mere biological phenomenon. When looked at from the perspective of brain science, speaking is an outer manifestation of our inner brain connectivity. When looked at from a psychological perspective, speaking is a function of our immense mental world. When looked at from the perspective of a social function, speaking is a human communicative act. When looked at from political, legal, and other systems, speaking is the means to achieve our greater ambitions. As complex and vast as it is, for most people, the sound of speaking is, without exaggeration, the sound of life.

Relevant to this chapter is speaking's role in learning and education. Speaking obviously has much to do with human learning and education. From learning how to utter words, to how to count, to ask and answer questions in class, and all the way to how to express thoughts and advance positions in public, speaking is generally involved in all aspects of learning. To the extent that education is delivered face to face (or even in today's online style) to students in school, speaking in teaching and learning is the primary means to achieve educational ends.

However, available observations and research indicate that the role of speaking differs considerably from individual learner to individual learner.[1] And individual variation, as it turns out, is not solely explained by the differences in individual learners' temperaments (or associated later personality traits), a factor thought of as more genetically determined. There is evidence that the cultural values and norms of learners matter more crucially.[2]

The West and East Asia offer a telling case in point. Surely, we observe that East Asian learners are quiet and reluctant to speak in class, whereas Western learners are more talkative and eager to express themselves,[3] frequently even turning into devil's advocates. It is unquestionable that there are expressive and even pugnacious learners in East Asia, and likewise, quiet and timid learners in the West. Therefore, any attempt to take the observation of the quiet Asian learner or the expressive Western learner to fit any random individual learner in any place is doomed and cause for intellectual obscurity. Nevertheless, the preponderance of research evidence shows that there are more quiet East Asian learners than Western learners. Moreover, this oft-noted characteristic transcends time and space; that is, it is seen regardless of when the observations were made, and either in Asia or among the East Asian diaspora across the world.[4] With this research evidence in mind, I argue that it is not very helpful to be stuck on the irritation caused by the stereotypical view of the quiet Asian learner. A more productive effort is to try to understand *why* East Asian learners tend to be reluctant to speak in class and why Western students are characteristically eager to self-express. To my mind, it is even more beneficial to analyze how speaking – or, for that matter, not speaking – serves learners from different cultural backgrounds. In what follows, I intend to review Western and East Asian traditions regarding speaking and not speaking, and speaking styles; I then discuss Western and East Asian learners.

LONG WESTERN TRADITION OF VERBAL ELOQUENCE

Speaking in the West is a highly regarded skill. This high regard for speaking dates back to the long political, religious, and intellectual tradition of the West. Four emphases are particularly noteworthy: speaking as distinct personal quality, as a right, as a leadership trait, and as art.

Speaking as Distinct Personal Quality

Speaking in the West is regarded as a personal quality, an expression of self.[5] It signals a person's individuality and distinctness (as well as well-being[6]). Throughout history, many individuals achieved fame or notoriety because of their speaking ability. Verbal performance is a marker of one's intelligence and cognitive brilliance,[7] which are believed to underlie much of what humans do and accomplish in life.

It seems that the high regard for verbal fluency in the West projects a halo effect on how people perceive and evaluate each other. Research shows that verbally fluent and articulate people are viewed as more intelligent, more creative, and wiser than shy, quiet, and less talkative people.[8] However, measured objectively, these two groups of people do not show any difference. Even more surprising is the research finding that this basic perception of speaking being associated with higher intelligence is not only endorsed by people who evaluate others, but also by those evaluated. In other words, those who are quiet, shy, and inarticulate concede to the view that they *themselves* are not as intelligent as those who are expressive, talkative, and articulate. These very intriguing research findings point to another possible fundamental psychological error of attributing a characteristic to a person when in fact that person should not be ascribed this characteristic. Apparently, the shaping power of Western culture in people's perceptions of others and self cannot be underestimated.

Speaking in the West is also an act by which the authorship and ownership of ideas is ascertained and admired in communication.[9] When speaking in public or in organized social settings such as a classroom or a meeting at the workplace, people's ideas, suggestions, or strategies are taken as important contributions to the group goal, as in most other cultures. In the West, however, more emphasis is placed on the identification and acknowledgment of the *individual*'s ownership and authorship of expressed ideas and suggestions (see more discussion in the section on classroom discourse in this chapter). For example, the chair of the meeting or teacher of the class is often inclined to comment as part of the flow of communication that "Person A proposed a change of X, but person B disagrees with person A." Here persons A and B are named and highlighted; thereby, the ownership/authorship, not just the contrastive ideas, is acknowledged. A chair or teacher in a similar Chinese setting is likely to contrast the ideas without naming the speakers such as "what do you all think about idea X and idea Y?" As Agnes He's insightful analysis of American Chinese-heritage language classrooms shows,[10] this distinction between the West and Chinese is nontrivial.

Speaking is further testimony of personal character and moral strength. Those who speak up about an issue or speak up to challenge questionable authority are respected and admired by others for having personal courage and integrity. Many well-known whistle blowers in the West are treated as heroes, such as Bethany McLean who revealed (in writing but also speaking)[11] the wrongdoing of the Enron Corporation, a Texas-based energy company that was brought down by fraudulent accounting. "Speaking one's mind" is the phrase used in English to refer to someone who is upright, honest, not willing to compromise principles of morality and ethics. Such a person will express his or her true opinions without regard to intimidation by authority, concern for personal gains, or even fear for personal safety.

Finally, speaking well manifests personal charisma in leadership more than any other behavior. Personal charisma is found not only among people who hold leadership positions, but also among people in simple, daily social life. Those who speak well emerge as natural leaders who attract followers. Charisma as a psychological perception of individuals is defined in the dictionary[12] as "a personal magic of leadership arousing special popular loyalty or enthusiasm for a public figure" or "a special magnetic charm or appeal" of a person. The terms "magic" or "magnetic charm" are not very precise for scientific research. Yet, most people recognize charisma in others when they see it. In the West, speaking well in front of an audience or in a social setting is probably the most identifiable feature of charisma. It would be unthinkable for a person to be viewed as charismatic if that person is an indiscriminately quiet, shy, timid, and inarticulate (e.g., stammering or stuttering in speech).

Speaking as a Right

Among the great legacies that Greek antiquity left to the Western civilization is the due process of trial by jury that was, purportedly, introduced by the goddess Athena, the patron of Athens. According to mythology and dramatization in Aeschylus' trilogy *Oresteia*,[13] Athena declared that a trial was necessary in Orestes' case (for killing his mother Clytemnestra, who in turn had killed her husband Agamemnon for sacrificing their daughter Iphigenia for the success in the Trojan War). The Furies (deities of vengeance and supernatural personifications of anger or death) were pursuing and condemning Orestes, but it was Athena who stepped in to give each party equal voice. Apollo argued Orestes' case against the Furies in front of the jurors, who then cast a tie vote. Athena's own vote broke the tie and acquitted Orestes in the end.

Undoubtedly, the greatness of this Greek democratic invention for judging disputes between the parties lies in establishing a process that ensures the fairness owed to each party involved.[14] Because of the fairness inherent in this due process, the outcome of judgment is usually regarded as fair and acceptable to both parties. The jurors act on the principle of impartiality, listening and considering each side's argument. To proceed, this very process encourages reason and demands evidence rather than rage and suspicion.

As a result, all sides resort to what is the best mental power available to humans: rational thinking.

Although other cultures may not have invented such as a reason-dependent system, fairness is nevertheless the central and common criterion for judging and ending disputes as well.[15] Some cultures rely on tribal elders for such judgment because they are known to be fair and wise by the community. Other cultures may depend on the judge in the court to hear both sides and cast his or her vote without a jury. For example, the well-known court case as presented in the variety play *Chalk Circle* (灰闌記) by Chinese playwright Li Xingdao (李行道, during Yuan Dynasty 1206–1368),[16] portrayed two women who claimed to be the birthmother of the same child. Judge Bao (999–1062) drew a chalk circle on the floor and ordered the child to be place in the middle. The two women were asked to use their strength to pull the child to their sides. Whoever succeeded in pulling the child to her side would be declared the birthmother. Of course, the one who loved the child could not bring herself to hurt the child and let him go. Judge Bao declared this mother to be the real mother. The dramatized court case still captures readers' interest in the judge because he, like his Western predecessor King Solomon, employed the humanistic ruling in addition to fairness (pulling the child from equal distance).

What sets the Greek system apart from these other systems is that the former required verbal argumentation from both sides as it unfolded in real time. The parties had to speak in order to present and argue for or against their case in front of the jury and the judge. In Classical Athens, there were no legal experts – that is, prosecution and defense attorneys – as we have today. Instead, the litigants had to deliver their own speeches in court.[17] The essential role of speech was apparent. Thus, it was not just reason, but *verbalized* reason, that mattered in the Athenian system. In contrast, the revered Chinese Judge Bao did not depend on verbalized argument to rule. Instead, he acted out his argument by drawing the circle and by having the two women act as well. In fact, no reference was given to whether the judge even explained his reasoning and his humanistic act to anyone at the court. It is quite conceivable that the attendants of the case, including the plaintiff and the defendant, were kept mystified each step of the way until the judge delivered his verdict at the very end. The entire process unfolded without much need to speak. When the final judgment was made, everyone understood it. But it was not possible for the Athenian court to proceed without the verbal give and take, presentation, refuting, challenging, and conclusion.

The Athenian trial court laid the foundation for the subsequent Western legal system. The direct lineage of present-day Western trial system to the Athenian trial court is clear. All Western courts since Greek time have been accusing and defending via oral argumentation, presentation, cross-examination, and building and challenging each other's credibility to persuade the jury and the judge for a fair ruling.

But what is more significant in the West is that speaking is not only a granted legal right, but, more importantly, a political right that all people enjoy. In the U.S. Constitution as in every other Western nation' constitution, freedom of speech is a right that is guaranteed to every citizen. Speaking – that is, voicing one's political, social, and personal views – has become part and parcel of Western democracy and much of daily work, education, and social life. The right to speak is a right that cannot be challenged and denied by anyone, any organization, or any institution. As such, the public demands and is encouraged to participate in debates, by radio, TV, town hall meetings, and calling their political representatives and leaders about any issue that concerns the nation, the state/providence, the local community, and the person himself or herself. Any attempt by anyone to silence people is shunned and cause for legal action.

Speaking as Leadership

The role of speaking has also been an important shining beam that penetrated across the temporality and complexity of the history of Western civilization. The power of speaking is, unequivocally, linked to the power of leadership. In Greek antiquity, delivering speeches was a primary means to achieve legal and political goals. Like all litigants, politicians had to rely on oration to persuade each other and the people of their intentions and ambitions. Oration was thus essential to propose ideas, to form political factions and alliances, to mobilize the military, to attack one's political enemies, and to clear one's name. Those who emerged on top were revered as master orators and sought after as teachers for youth. The "Ten Attic Orators" were upheld on the pedestal, not only during the classical era (500–400 BCE), but remained influential in subsequent millennia.[18] One of these orators, Demosthenes (384–322 BCE), has come down through the ages as the greatest orator. His oratory achievement enabled him to become an accomplished statesman who defended Athens' liberty against the encroaching power of Macedon.[19] Likewise, during the Roman time, Cicero (106–43 CE), among many other eloquent men, was regarded as the second greatest orator after

Demosthenes. As a statesman, philosopher, political theorist, and lawyer, Cicero, too, used his oratory prowess to achieve his political goals.[20]

These masters of oration from the ancient times have served as inspiration for later generations of leaders. Delivering speeches has been an integral part of public life in the West. From Robespierre and Danton's zeal of the French Revolution to Hitler's ability to arouse people's support, from Churchill to Roosevelt during World War II, from Kennedy to Clinton to Blair in recent decades, and from Martin Luther King of the American civil rights movement to the history-changing Obama, the West has a long and impressive list of political leaders who distinguished themselves as eloquent speakers. A triumphant example is the British King George VI who overcame a great personal challenge, his stammer, and succeeded in delivering a key speech to his people at the dawn of World War II. He was revered and followed then and is still celebrated today.

In democratic societies, such oratorical skill is of utmost importance for running campaigns, directing movements, and managing crises in order to galvanize voters' support. Within the legislature of the government, oral debates are the primary means to deliberate on any legislative issue and process. And the entire process is watched, analyzed, and responded to, via media commentaries, publicly. Senators and members of Congress engage routinely in oral argumentation for or against a given bill. In light of the fundamental role of speech, it is simply unthinkable how Western-style democracy could possibly proceed and function without verbal procedure and performance.

Beyond the political scene, Western religious leaders are the backbone of holding communities together for spiritual and moral guidance. Christianity with its many denominations as well as Judaism are practiced with sermons and exhortations, with the priest, minister, reverend, and the rabbi delivering a speech to arouse or enlighten the congregation. Anyone who aspires to become a religious leader in a community needs to master the skill of delivering speeches that resonate with profundity and elegance. This very skill may hold the key to whether the church can retain the congregation. Indeed, for many people, the decision to continue or not to continue to attend a given church in a particular town hinges on whether one likes the quality of the sermons.

In the secular life aside from politics, such as industry, business, or school, the speaking ability of a leader is equally important. Leaders have frequent need to address the whole organization or teams to report the organization's operations, performance, and plans. Leaders' speaking skill matters even more when the organization faces uncertainties, challenges, and crises. Almost without exception, those leaders who can convey the organization's vision and articulate the important issues to its people effectively are likely to succeed in leading their organization.

Speaking as Art

In the West, speaking is not only a distinct personal quality, a right, and a leadership trait, but also an art. This very conception also dates back again to Greek antiquity. Significantly, oratory, the art of speaking, was not purely thought of as a personal talent or intelligence,[21] unlike our current understanding, but a skill that one can learn, practice, and perfect. An inspirational model is Demosthenes' self-training with pebbles in his mouth to control his stuttering and practicing against the roaring sea to improve his articulation.

The earliest experts who made oratory a profession were the sophists in ancient Greece. Sophists were the itinerant intellectuals who taught youth rhetoric and oratory – that is, how to use language well in order to persuade or convince others (given that Greek litigants had to give personal speeches to present and argue their cases in court). Socrates was thought by some of his contemporaries a sophist because he, too, parsed words and posed many questions in order to force his interlocutors to examine their own thoughts and beliefs. He, too, taught youth and had many followers. However, there was a large difference between Socrates and the sophists: Socrates offered free teaching whereas sophists charged a fee for teaching oratory and rhetoric. It was said that sophists' teaching was a lucrative profession. Despite the criticisms levied against sophism (they might have comprised moral principles by manipulating language for personal gain), sophists attracted many students and followers.[22] Sophists took on this specialized intellectual terrain and made a craft out of language and speaking itself, rather than exercising mental prowess per se as exemplified by Socrates. They left a uniquely Western legacy that has not only lasted millennia, but is also more flourishing now and highly likely to continue to blossom owing to the importance of media in our present world.

There have been many notable figures who contributed to this Western legacy, but three stand out for advancing the theory, standard, and education of oratory in the West: Aristotle, Cicero, and Quintilian. Aristotle proposed in his *the Art of Rhetoric*[23] the three core components of any persuasive speech: ethos, pathos, and logos.[24] Ethos is the moral character that the speaker needs to convey in order to have credibility before the audience. From our current time, moral character and credibility can be established by drawing on authority of knowledge such as scientific evidence, the position the speaker holds that is publicly honored, such as a court judge or a CEO of a reputable company, or proven accuracy of information such as a journalist's investigation. Pathos is the use of emotional appeal to influence the audience's perception and judgment. Speakers can use all contents and forms such as stories, anecdotes, tragedies, comedies, jokes, and metaphors, to arouse the audience's emotion in order to win over their support for the speech.

Logos is the employment of reasoning, which, as stated in other chapters, is a central concept in the Western intellectual tradition. Speakers can establish objectivity by presenting information in an unbiased fashion, such as stating the facts without personal commentaries and judgment. Speakers can also give evenhanded treatment of a given topic or issue and let the audience draw its own conclusion. Inductive and deductive reasoning are key strategies. Using examples to support an argument is an effective strategy of inductive reasoning. Using proofs – that is, logical steps without the interference from unrelated and extraneous information – is deductive reasoning. Take an example from our current public issues, the speaker can present a commonly known fact as a starting point, such as "every day, X number of animal species are extinguished, and the cause of such a pace of extinction is human destruction of animal habitats." Cutting down trees is an incidence of such human destruction. Therefore, preserving trees is necessary, and everyone should do so.

Cicero's influence on oratory is through his book *On the Orator*,[25] in addition to his own well-known speeches. Cicero considered oratory the "divine art" in the voice of one of the debating characters in his book. In this book, he treated a great many topics of oratory, ranging from the education of the orator and the responsibility of the orator to the scope of oration and the technical elements of oratory. Cicero emphasized the importance of all forms of appeal such as emotion, humor, irony, digression, and pure reasoning. He also outlined the method of oratory into five sequential parts called the "fundamentals of rhetoric."

Invention (*inventio*) is the process that leads the orator to the development and refinement of an argument. After the argument is formed, the orator uses arrangement (*dispositio*) to determine how it should be structured effectively, usually in a logical order by importance. With the speech content developed and structure laid out, the orator focuses next on style (*elocutio*) and presentation (*pronuntiatio*). The orator then retains all these elements in memory (*memoria*) by recalling each of the elements during the speech. Finally, the orator delivers (*actio*) to the audience the speech with grace, dignity, gesture, and modulation of voice and face.

But the most significant argument that Cicero made was that an orator needed a broad education, studying not just the techniques of giving a speech, but addressing the general and broader questions. For example, if a person was wrongfully accused of treachery, the orator should not just speak about the specifics of the accusation, but also on the significant harm done to the culture, society, and citizenry as a whole. Thus, an orator needed to study law, politics, history, literature, ethics, warfare, medicine, and mathematics. In fact, only after the person had studied these and other subjects sufficiently could he become a good orator. He introduced the idea of the "ideal orator" who is well versed and well rounded in all branches of human learning. This very idea of a well-educated person being able to use his or her broad knowledge to express thoughts and opinions is the essence of what is known today as Western liberal arts education. Owing its origin to Cicero, this very Western core of higher education has enjoyed the testing of time and now embraced by other cultures.

Building on Cicero's ideas and works of other influential orators before him, Quintilian (35–100 CE) wrote his treatise, *The Orator's Education*, on the education of the "perfect" orator from birth to old age.[26] He detailed the whole process of how to select a nurse for the orator in the beginning, how to train in reading, writing, grammar, and literary criticism, how to exercise oratory composition, and how to craft full legal and political speeches in the end. Like Cicero, Quintilian emphasized the usage of many materials such as fables, narratives, humor, and comparisons. His training curriculum became the standard component of education for subsequent centuries.

Of the Western traditions, Judaism places a very high, if not the highest, value on education. Most fundamentally, the practice of traditional Judaism has a high barrier to entry: Any serious Jew must be able to read and understand biblical Hebrew, for that is the language of the liturgy and the sacred texts. Beyond the basic texts, the most frequently studied and most important of the Jewish law codes are written in Aramaic, which requires assiduous, dedicated studies (if one page is studied each day, it takes seven and a half years to study the entire Talmud). Anyone who has completed the project is held in extremely high regard. Furthermore, according to some rabbis, it is required that scholars study in a *chavruta*, or pair (it is highly discouraged to study Talmud and Torah on one's own). A chavruta is considered to have major spiritual and social significance, as it is written, "When two scholars of the Torah listen to one another, God hears their voices" (Talmud Shabbat 63a). Also as an integral part of the tradition, scholars are encouraged to debate and disagree about the text at hand, for the Talmud itself is not a listing of laws, but a record of conversations and debates between the ancient rabbis themselves. Jewish children celebrate bar mitzvah (for the boys) and bat mitzvah (for the girls) as a rite of passage into adulthood at age thirteen and twelve, respectively, at which point they are considered competent to pass the Jewish tradition on to the next generation. A key part of this celebration is the required chanting of a portion from the Torah and delivering a commentary on the Torah portion of the week in front of the entire congregation. The child spends much time studying with a teacher and preparing for the ceremony for the day.[27]

To date, throughout Western university campuses, the basic art of public speaking and training methods are taught commonly to students. Such courses enjoy enduring popularity[28]; often students have to be put on long waiting lists to get a place in such a course. While in the course, students study many speeches as models, such as Martin Luther King's famous speech *I Have a Dream* as a video or audio recording. Students then draft their own speeches on a topic of their interest. They work with the professor to perfect their speeches and then deliver them to their fellow students as an audience. Frequently, the audience peers critique each other's speeches according to the models, formats, and standards they study. As a result, students improved their speaking skills and become informed consumers or even connoisseurs of the verbal art of public speaking. As mentioned previously, Western students are encouraged to master the skill of debating, from middle school onward. They participate in both intra-school and inter-school competitions, and the winners arise to the city, state, and national levels. Those who won recognition are highly sought after for college admissions by selective universities.

In present-day universities, communication and modern media studies are common majors for undergraduate students and specialized graduate programs. In addition, every high school and university teaches drama on stage. Students receive training on how to project their voice, how to act with words, and how to deliver their ideas and emotions effectively on stage. These opportunities undoubtedly indicate the importance of such skills on the one hand and provide students with actual skill development on the other. Finally, professional speechwriters are also in high demand by political, business, and other organizational leaders. Those who master the art of public speaking and those who can help leaders deliver successful speeches are respected, admired, and sought after.

Given the importance speaking assumes in the West, it seems that the default mode of Western communication is to speak whenever one is faced with a choice of speaking or not speaking. The West thus privileges speaking and speakership. By doing so, it devalues, or values much less than other cultures, not speaking, silence, and listenership.

WESTERN SPEAKING STYLE

Thus far, I have discussed the overarching importance of speaking throughout Western history. In this section, I turn to the topic of speaking style as it pertains to communication both in organized settings and in daily life.

In the 1970s, the philosopher H. P. Grice proposed his well-known conversational rules that govern how people talk to each other in daily communication.[29] His four maxims of "cooperative principles" have become the guidepost for understanding what in human communication underlies the content of people's speech. As will be seen, these conversational rules, or talking grammar, initially conceived of as universal human conversational patterns, may not be that universal after all. Nevertheless, they are more commonly observed and therefore more particular to Western people's speech than in other cultures.

The Maxim of Quantity: Speak No More and No Less

Grice noticed that when speaking, people in general are quite conscious of the notion of quantity – that is, the *amount* of speech as required in a conversational context. For example, when asked by a friend "where are you going?" on a campus street, the reply is usually "the gym." Few people would take the trouble to utter the full sentence, "I am going to the gym." The first part is unnecessary in the context because it is well understood by the first party. If instead the speaker said the full sentence, it would likely lead the interlocutor to form a number of undesirable impressions about the speaker, such as: (1) the speaker is not attentive; (2) the speaker is inappropriate or quirky because he/she would take the trouble to say something unnecessary; (3) the speaker is joking or being sarcastic, but for no apparent cause; (4) something may be bothering this speaker so as to make him/her behave strangely.

Although speaking is highly valued, sheer verbosity and jabber without providing the requested information is regarded as a waste of time even in this kind of mundane communication between people. Put in another way, the idea of "necessity" in speech quantity reflects quite clearly the concern of *economy* or *efficiency*, a sensitivity to quantity in life that is an integral part of the West since Greek time (which is the foundation for scientific thinking).[30] Speaking in this manner confirms and continues how the West parses and construes the world in the domain of human verbal interaction.

It is important to point out that maintaining the efficiency of speaking is not just a task for isolated speakers to attend, but a joint, cooperative process for everyone as mandated by the culture. As such, interlocutors share this understanding and talk accordingly. As will be seen in the section on the Chinese speaking style, this type of speech driven by a concern and calculation of necessity, economy, and efficiency may be a speech faux pas that is likely to lead to the breakdown of the conversation rather than cooperation and continuation of the conversation.

The Maxim of Quality: Speak Truth and Avoid Falsehood

This Gricean maxim is of high importance in speaking. In general, it is unlikely that people in any culture intentionally speak falsehood without any reason. Grice is correct in his analysis about this universal human tendency. However, the extreme premium placed on speaking truth is, I would argue, characteristically Western. This tendency reflects Western emphasis on the moral standard of *honesty* that weighs heavily in judging each other's character and moral integrity. Those who are perceived as less straightforward in their speaking are suspected of dishonesty and consequently distrusted by others. Research indeed shows that Western people express aversion toward circumlocution – that is, indirect and beat-around-the-bush kind of talking. People who are identified as speaking circumlocution are viewed as manipulative because they have something to hide. Truth telling is preferred regardless of circumstances, even when truth may hurt.[31] Even though hurtful truth may be hard to swallow, its tellers are often seen as courageous and heroic and therefore are extended greater admiration and trust in a workplace and even in intimate relationships. It was not an accident that Al Gore's celebrated documentary film on human responsibility for our deteriorating planet, which won him the Nobel Peace Prize, is called "An Inconvenient Truth."

Whereas other cultures may differentiate certain areas of life, or some areas to a greater degree, as off limit or improper for truth telling (out of concern for the listener's well-being, emotional distress, or social awkwardness), the West may insist on fewer such areas, or a narrower range of areas. For example, if a parent is terminally ill, the adult child and even a younger child may be viewed as entitled to the truth about the parent's condition, even though telling this truth may be very distressful and hurtful. But in Chinese culture, family members may conceal the information about a terminally ill parent from a daughter who lives afar and without any means to travel to pay a visit to her parent. The daughter may not be told about the parent's death until the parent has been buried and the bereavement ceremony over, at a time when the family ascertains the daughter's better ability to travel. Telling the truth to the daughter beforehand may be regarded as an inhumane act on the part of the family, knowing that the daughter would be grieving alone without any family support. Thus, speaking such truth may indeed be curtailed, and not speaking such truth may be regarded as more appropriate.[32]

Consistent with the Gricean maxim, it is common to hear Western people preempt their speech relaying accuracy of the information or accountability of the opinion as follows:

This is just my opinion . . .; this is my two cents . . .;

I am not an expert, but I . . .;

As I recall . . .; it appears to be . . .; it seems to be . . .; I may be . . .; it might have been . . .;

I don't suppose we . . .; I assume that this . . .;

But it is rare to hear Western people preempt their speech with "from my *stupid* opinion, I would say . . .," "in my *humble* view, I think . . .," and "apologizing for my ignorance, I . . ." – a style quite commonly observed among Asian speakers. The Western style of preempting speech is anchored on truth or assumed truth in question or fending off any potential charge against the speaker's untrue statement – that is, the quality of the information about to be presented. The Asian style, on the other hand, is not about the quality of information, but about humility – that is, a virtuous quality of the speaker him- or herself.

The Maxim of Relevance: Speak to the Point

Grice's maxim of relevance is related to his notion of quantity. This maxim requires sensitivity to logic and privileges its use as a guide in communication. The idea of "to the point" or "make a point," so commonly encountered in Western people's speaking, emphasizes the *precision* and *conciseness* of information or opinion expressed. Those judged as sharp usually are those able to identify the relevant and the essential from the irrelevant and unessential and speak with precision about the matters. Much of the speaker's persuasive power lies in this maxim.

If speaking has a clear goal such as political, social, religious, commercial, and work-related, Western speakers show a heightened sense of the message and message delivery in their speech. This message orientation is described as sender-centered,[33] which is reflective of the great Western oratorical and rhetorical tradition. The speaker's focus is mainly on how to formulate the best message to convey to the audience. Topics that concern the speaker are how to frame the issue, how to set the tone, how to improve the source of credibility, and how to increase the significance of the message. As a matter of cultural cooperation, Western audience also expects a "significant message" from the speaker.[34]

Convoluted speaking – the opposite of relevant speaking – long-windedness, or inability to speak to the point is regarded as a sign of lack of intelligence and a disappointment. Listeners lose interest and patience with people who mumble on without any point to make.[35] At meetings in the workplace, we frequently hear Western people say "we've already talked about that, can we move on?" "can you clarify the relevance of X?" or "you talked about X, but what is the issue you came to talk about?" These questions are not taken as anything offensive to the speaker, but as a signal that the audience has no more patience or need to listen to the speaker and that the speaker should either speak to the relevant point, or the conversation needs to turn to another topic.

But even when speaking does not have a clear goal as previously discussed, speakers in daily conversations are also cognizant of the elements of relevance. At dinner table, if a husband asks his wife to share how her day was, she is also attentive to the relevance of the information she is providing. Her husband, likewise, may remind her that she may have taken too long to finish her story or even tell her to "cut to the chase." When friends see each other, they share their life stories. But such sharing also needs to be carried out in a manner consistent with the maxim of relevance under discussion or sharing.

As will be discussed in the Asian section, this type of to-the-point talking can often be offensive to people, and not uncommonly even lead to a breakdown of relationships. Frequently, speaking with precision is regarded as inappropriate in hierarchical relationships either at home, work, or in class, and as flat-out rude, impatient, and disrespectful in a variety of Asian contexts.

The Maxim of Clarity: Speak Directly

This maxim first concerns the need for clarity when speaking in any context. The idea is to avoid obscurity, making clear what one intends to convey without the risk of the listener misconstruing the speaker's information. Again, the burden is on the speaker to make his or her message unambiguous so as to ease the reception of the message. Any kind of unclear speech ranging from utterances to articulation and arguments should be avoided. Prime examples of speech successes and failures are found in political campaigns. Without exemption, political consultants, analysts, and news commentators focus on the clarity or lack of clarity of important political speeches whenever they provide any post-speech analysis. Interestingly, by characterizing the level of clarity of a speech, these professionals, in a way, either help increase or reduce the effect of a given message.

In daily communication, family members, friends, and school peers also share the view that if one wants other people to know what one wants, one needs to speak up and make one's desire clear. The idiom "the squeaky wheel gets the grease" is actually not just about the loudness of speaking, but loudness of speaking one's desire *clearly* and *unambiguously* so that others will hear the squeaky sound but not some other sound and be likely to respond to one's expressed need. Similarly, a husband may say to his wife, "Please do not ask me to read your mind; please tell me what you want." Romantic partners succeed more when they are able to express their desires and needs clearly and appropriately to each other. Undoubtedly, friendship making also depends on involved parties having the social competence to express their desires, likes, dislikes, shared interests, and issues clearly to each other. Waiting for the other to construe one's needs and preferences is likely to lead one to be friendless.[36]

The maxim of clarity does not concern only clarity in daily conversation, but also a large cultural mandate of speaking *directly* and *unambiguously*.[37] As noted previously, speaking directly rests first on the moral standard of honesty and transparency in personal conduct. Accordingly, one should speak one's mind without withholding information. Then one strives to present, explain, or argue clearly so that the audience will understand one's information, reasoning, and position. Muddying the water, obscuring an otherwise clear issue, or making confusing statements is considered less desirable or even unethical if the speaker is known to purposely create obscurity and confusion.

WESTERN CLASSROOM DISCOURSE AND SOCIALIZATION

With little doubt, children are not born possessing a particular speaking style. Their style is a result of socialization and personal development. Because speaking in the West is not just a private activity but a desired skill for citizens, social participants, and contributors at work and school, much of the training and socialization of speaking in the way previously described takes place in school. The large research literature that focuses on speaking in school concerns classroom discourse. Although this section of the chapter cannot do full justice to this research literature, it is still helpful to highlight some key aspects of classroom discourse in the West.

Classroom discourse in the West covers the whole scope of verbal interaction between teachers and students. It ranges from teacher talk, student talk, teacher–student talk, and student–student talk to how each of these talks unfolds, how each step functions in these talks, and what goal is achieved by each kind and each process. For example, by looking at teacher–student talk, researchers examine how much time each talk takes (time allocation), how each talk functions (e.g., presents/offers information, asks closed-ended versus open-ended questions), whether the talk aims at learning tasks or non-learning tasks (e.g., classroom logistics), how different kinds of talk facilitate or impede learning, and what kinds of discourse lead to better student achievement.[38] Research has found, to the disappointment of many, that teacher talk remains predominant, despite much avowed belief in change and much teacher training to the contrary.[39]

As researchers acknowledge, classroom discourse in the West has undergone much change, from traditional training of oratory in the distant past, to the emphasis on the aesthetics of oral performance in the nineteenth and early twentieth century ("echo the voice of high culture"),[40] to the current authenticity of popular oracy, the expressive forms of talking, as lived experiences that children bring to school. Nevertheless, the classroom, where formal schooling is compulsory, still strongly adheres to the commitment to speaking as a cognitive, intellectual activity and skill to be mastered by schoolchildren. Starting from preschool, children are taught to verbalize their thoughts and feelings. "Use your words," "tell me in your own words," or "I can't tell what you want to do if you don't say it" are common instructions preschool teachers give to young children to urge them to verbalize their desires, intentions, and actions.[41] For older children, although lived oracy is recognized and sometimes even embraced as an entry point for children to ground their talk training in school, their end goal is not to stay in their familiar community speech, but to reach a higher level of culture of the educated.[42] Such classroom teaching still aims at helping children achieve communicative competence that stresses conveying information concisely, clearly, and fluently. Children still need to learn how to present a thesis backed with evidence, how to argue, and how to persuade the audience through the manipulation of language. Hewitt and Inghilleri[43] observed British classroom activities where children were taught how to deliver speeches to their class and how to engage in the ensuing discussion afterward. The researchers' analysis indicated that children learned how to disagree and how to argue despite the fact that they use much more coop-eration-dominated speech outside of school.

A key characteristic in Western classroom discourse, as pointed out by Mary O'Connor and Sarah Michaels, is to help each student take him- or herself seriously as a learner.[44] The significance of this teaching anchors in the notion that each student is the *author/owner* of his or her own ideas. Intellectual socialization is thus thought to lead students into the realm of their own ideas vis-à-vis others' ideas and the take-on of each other's ideas through verbal interaction.

O'Connor and Michaels drew on two related sociolinguistic theories as a lens to show how this type of teaching takes place in an American middle school. The first theory, as advanced by Goodwin,[45] addresses the speaking rights and responsibilities by students as structured in a classroom discourse. For example, when a student (A) asks another (B), "May I have that crayon?" another student, not participating in the dialogue (C), may interject, "No, he is giving it to me." The bystander (C) then denies the right of the student to whom the question was addressed (B) to answer Student A's question. But Student A can also say, "Wait a minute, I was the first to ask for the crayon!" As such, classroom discourse affords students oppor-tunities to recognize, take, and negotiate their rights and responsibilities. The second theory, by Goffman, delineates the roles of the "animator" and "author" in human communication.[46] By the puppeteering metaphor, an animator is one who produces an utterance – that is, animating oneself or the other through talk. But an author is one from whom beliefs and senti-ments originate, and the author's beliefs and sentiments can be uttered by him- or herself or any animator. In classroom discourse, students and the teacher take on these roles in their academic learning.

As O'Connor and Michaels' observational research shows, the finely attuned teacher plays a unique role because he or she becomes the anima-tor that does two essential things for students: (1) highlights the ownership/authorship of students' ideas and (2) links students' own ideas to the greater sphere of their culture. The researchers call this strategy "revoicing." With regard to (1), they give an example of a routine verbal interaction between the teacher and the students where one student suggested a solution to a science task that was different from another student's idea. The masterful teacher then interjected by saying: "So then, you don't agree with Sarita that ..."[47] By doing so, as O'Connor and Michaels explain, the teacher refor-mulated the original utterance as a disagreement, which is an intellectually more demanding level. Second, the teacher signaled the student to use her speaking right to "validate her inference, and, thus, take on a position herself." Thirdly, the teacher deliberately placed two students in opposition and primed them to evaluate the merits of their own and each other's proposals. The teacher effectively led the students to the very notion that they were the authors/owners of their ideas and that they have the right to take a position to validate, defend, challenge, or affirm other people's interpretations of their ideas. By doing so, the teacher alerts the students to the significance of their intellectual contributions in the classroom.

Regarding the second way of "revoicing," O'Connor and Michaels presented an example where the teacher elicited multiple suggestions from students for deciding what were the most popular mass transit trips people make. After students gave their ideas, the teacher asked how they made their personal guesses, prompting students to find evidence for their claims. One by one, students gave their reasons. One student said that she liked the way a terminal looked. The teacher then revoiced the student's reason as "So you chose ... based on your *own personal experience*." Another student confirmed that he, too, named the first student's choice because "a lot of people like to ride on the train for a long time ... some might just ride ... just for the heck of it." The teacher then recast the utterance "So you made your guess based on what *you know about human behavior?*"[48] Both students concurred. Clearly, these student initial ideas were cruder, weaker, and less well formed. But the skillful teacher elevated their ideas to more standard knowledge and a larger intellectual scope without qualitatively altering the students' original ideas. By doing so, the teacher provided a chance for students to claim full credit for the intellectual merit of their own, albeit elevated, ideas, thus recognizing their individual potential, growth, and greatness.

GROWING UP A DEVIL'S ADVOCATE

While school plays an essential role in socializing children into the desired roles of speakers in the West, home also plays a compatible role. In fact, there is strong evidence that Western children are more encouraged to speak from an early age. When babies are born, Western mothers (as other caregivers) talk to them more than Asian mothers (and other Asian caregivers) do to their infants. As soon as babies can vocalize, their caregivers engage them in talking as if they were real conversational partners. When caregivers hear their babies' babbling, cooing, and jargoning, they respond with more talking and excitement. Compared to the rest of the world's cultures, Western caregivers talk most to their infants and toddlers.[49]

When children reach preschool age and beyond, parents engage them in more talking. Research shows that Western parents prefer a particular style called elaboration. Shirley Brice Heath's landmark research on the differences among European-American middle-class and working-class as well as African-American parents in home language socialization in the early 1980s[50] shows how similarly European-American middle-class parents talk to their children at home as in school. Children were asked questions to which parents already knew the answers. Children were encouraged to recount and reflect on events in the past when they had been guided to intellectualize their lived experiences. This kind of talking style was followed up with more extensive research in the areas of children's autobiographical memory development, which is a core component of the self and self-making.[51] Accordingly, when reminiscing about a past experience, the mother will probe the child for what happened, how the event happened, and why it happened that way. This elaborative style provides the child with the opportunity to *account for* and to *explain/interpret* the past experience, or, if the talk is about a future event, about what will happen next. Here the child is afforded the opportunity to *predict* future events based on the information at hand. Verbally accounting, explaining/interpreting, and predicting events in the world as children experience them emphasize the authorship and ownership of the child's autobiography on the one hand and the analytical and narrative skill on the other. Undoubtedly, such a talking style prepares children for school where further training for speaking takes place.

As an important part of this early training for speaking, Western caregivers offer much modeling and room for children to elaborate on their feelings and emotions about the event, particularly when the experience and feelings are positive.[52] For example, a mother may say to her four-year-old daughter, "How did it make you feel when your friend Suzie invited you to swim together?" If the child just says "good," the mother may probe further, "What's good about that?" or "Did that not make you feel that Suzie likes you?" This emphasis enables the child to develop verbalization about his or her inner world, attitude, opinions, and emotional responses to her own experiences.

Noteworthy is a particular kind of speaking socialization that many well-educated Western parents offer to their children: the practice of the devil's advocate. Devil's advocate – originally from the canonization process of the Roman Catholic Church – has come to refer to someone who takes a position with which he or she does not necessarily agree simply for the sake of argument. The purpose of the devil's advocate is to expose flaws and weaknesses of the argument. As a result, the original argument becomes stronger. For example, if one argues that bottled water is a waste of money because it is no cleaner than tap water, as research shows, the interlocutor can say, "Just to be a devil's advocate, people may still buy bottled water because it makes them feel safer." As a result, the first person can include this perspective in the argument by saying, "Although people may feel they are doing something to protect their health by buying bottled water, it does not give them any health benefits. In fact, they are just throwing money away." The revised argument is better because it juxtaposes the flawed psychological reason next to scientific evidence for people's purchase of bottled water. In a similar vein, parents also model for children by using phrases such as "in fairness, I can see ...," "taking the other side's perspective, I can sympathize with ... although I disagree with them." Indeed, socializing children in practicing the devil's advocate can foster children's argumentation skill that is treasured in their culture.

DISTRUST IN SPEAKING IN EAST ASIA

Unlike the high value attached to verbal eloquence in the West, East Asia has an absence of such a value. We could easily name a long list of great speakers in the West, but we could name *none* in East Asia, not even after an ardent search through the triumphant democracies of Japan, Korea, and Taiwan where eloquence of public speaking is supposed to matter. Even the great Gandhi was not known for his words but for his nonviolent deeds: sitting, marching, and fighting *quietly* despite his unprecedented, monumental moral and political achievement. As it turns out, it is not an accident, or mere failure, or regrettable incompetence that East Asia does not have such a tradition. The reason is that it actually devalues – or more appropriately put, distrusts – verbal eloquence as a means to achieve worthy ends.

To begin with, none of the three major spiritual traditions – Taoism, Buddhism, and Confucianism – emphasizes speaking. Taoism regards as infinite wisdom human harmony with nature, fitting into the seamless unity without the need to speak, as expressed in the well-known phrase by Lao Tzu: "[T]hose who understand are not talkers; talkers don't understand."[53] Buddhism pursues meditation as a means to quiet down the mind and to be rid of worldly desires in order to achieve personal enlightenment. Furthermore, East Asia never had a comparable (to the Greek) political or legal system that promoted public speaking. Undoubtedly, these important historical forces played a role in the lack of an oratory tradition. However, the East Asian attitude toward speaking was not formed by chance but by a serious intellectual, moral, political, and social discourse that took place at the time when their cultural foundation was laid down.[54] Subsequent development further solidified this foundation into a long-lasting tradition.

The most influential discourse was, undoubtedly, led by the Confucians. Because the core of his teaching emphasized learning to become fully humane – that is, to follow the path of moral self-cultivation throughout life – Confucius saw the ultimate measure of this personal development as lying in what a person *does*, not what a person *says*. From the very beginning, Confucius recognized that the greatest challenge of such a personal moral project is anchored in the discrepancy between what a person can desire, will, and even resolve and what the person actually does and practices. Thus, Confucius, to use a modern term, problematized this personal life path as the constant struggle between one's words and one's deeds. Consistency between these two sides is the gauge of and feedback of one's own moral self-cultivation. Therefore, a person's speaking cannot be divorced from his or her moral character. Speaking is not just one's cognition and knowledge or any spontaneous, freestanding utterance, but a reflection of one's moral quality. For one to make real progress on this path, one needs to work at one's deeds rather than one's words. Those who pursue moral self-perfection must be cautious about their words. Clearly, the Confucian discussion about speaking is framed not to explore the cognitive and linguistic nature of human communication, but to compare what one chooses to talk about to what goals one tries to achieve.[55]

Inspection of the *Analects* reveals a rich discourse on the relationship between one's speaking and moral/virtuous development. As far as I can discern, Confucius discussed mainly three kinds of problems with verbal craftiness, all of which are potential impediments to one's moral self-cultivation: (1) a glib tongue divorces the mind from heart, (2) flattering speech undermines sincerity, and (3) boastful speech lacks humility.

Out of all kinds of problematic speaking, Confucius admitted himself that he regarded a glib tongue most difficult to accept. A glib tongue (巧言 or 佞人), sometimes translated as "sharp tongue" or "clever talk," is the kind that deceives, manipulates, and pretends, operating with ill intention, hypocrisy, and falsehood. Confucius commented "it is a rare thing for glib speech and an insinuating appearance to accompany authoritative conduct (*ren* 仁),"[56] and "glib words corrupt virtue,"[57] and glib talkers are seldom trustworthy. As noted in previous chapters, *ren* is the ultimate humane quality that a person can achieve through life-long learning and practice of self-perfection. Confucius saw people who engage in glib talk as misusing the power of words that are put together by the able mind but apart from the feeling and caring heart. Such talkers give themselves permission to indulge in ends justifying means at any cost: "[W]hat the exemplary person (*junzi* 君子) hates most is having to declare in favor of something that he has already rejected, and then to have to come up with some excuse for doing so."[58] Having witnessed the devastating chaos during the Warring States of his time, Confucius was also wary of the dangers of the glib tongue in causing states to fall apart: "glib people are dangerous" and "I detest the fact that glib-tongued talkers bring down states and families"[59] because such people can distort and manipulate events and "confuse moral standards"[60] so as to lead the kings and princes to take wrong actions.

Flattering speech, the second despised kind, undermines the speaker's sincerity. When one engages in flattery of others without believing in what one is saying, one moves away from sincerity. As noted previously, sincerity occupies a central place in the *ren* conduct by Confucians throughout Chinese history. Ingratiating speech is usually directed toward someone who holds power or has access to resources that the speaker desires for him- or herself. Because the motive is self-serving by pleasing the other, like the ministers in *The Emperor Has No Clothes* by Hans Christian Andersen, ingratiating speech also leads the recipient of flattery to sink further into vanity. Both the speaker and the recipient are denied the opportunity to connect to the virtue of sincerity, thereby losing the opportunity for moral growth. This is why Confucius cautioned against association with "friends who ingratiate and feign compliance" in addition to glib talking.[61] Confucius also regarded excessive, extravagant, and beautiful speech without substance as suffering from the same problem, related to the slyness of ingratiation.

Whereas flattering speech harms the other (as well as the self), boastful speech reveals the speaker's *own* character flaw. Boastful speech reflects the self as being in need of artificial boosting, inflating the sense of self. This kind of speaking lacks humility, which is another important quality in the *ren* conduct, particularly regarding learning. As discussed in Chapter 5, humility is conceived of by Confucians as a fundamental need and attitude for anyone in learning. When a person engages in self-boasting through speech, that person is not in touch with this very need. The projected positive image is achieved through empty and often aggressive language, but it is not based on real knowledge, wisdom, and moral growth of the person. Boastful speech is therefore more harmful to the self than to the audience because most of the time the audience can detect the overstatement and the weakness of the speaker's character. In a vivid conversation where Confucius asked four of his students to express their ambitions, one, Zilu, "hastily replied, 'give me a state of thousand charots[62] to govern, set me in among powerful neighbors, harass me with foreign armies, and add to that widespread famine, and at the end of three years, I will have imbued the people with courage, and moreover, provided them with a secure direction."[63] Confucius smiled at Zilu. When another student later inquired why he did so, Confucius responded, "[I]n governing a state you need to observe ritual propriety, and yet in what he said there was no deference at all."[64] Apparently, Confucius was unimpressed by Zilu's boastful and aggressive speech because it lacked humility irrespective of its eloquence (these words were quite eloquent in Chinese).

All three kinds of speech have in common the discrepancy between what is outwardly verbalized and what the internal state of the speaker is. Moreover, Confucius' concerns focused on the lost opportunity for the speaker to grow further toward the *ren* conduct.

While addressing these three problems of speech, the *Analects* also presents three virtues to counter the three flawed ways of talking: (1) heaven (*tian*, 天) is the speechless, but most virtuous, to be emulated; (2) deeds shall exceed words; and (3) attunement to social context and relationships is necessary for talking.

Confucius and his later followers, but also virtually all schools of thought during his era, revered Heaven, conceived of as an all-encompassing spiritual entity that is intimately involved in human affairs. Great sages and ancestral spirits ascend to *tian* to join an ultimate power that cares, nurtures, watches, regulates, and judges (impartially) how humans operate on their own and with each other. According to Ames and Rosemont,[65] the Chinese *tian* is not the other world or the Creator as conceptualized in Judeo-Christian tradition, but the world as known to humans. *Tian* is thus the perfection that humans can see, feel, contemplate, emulate, and integrate with. *Tian* is the inspiration for humans as stated in *The Book of Change*: "*Tian* cycles by itself emitting unending strength; the authoritative person shall likewise strive unremittingly (天行健, 君子以自强不息)."[66]

A significant quality of *tian*, as pointed out by Confucius, is *not speaking* (*wuyan*, 無言), yet it nurtures the natural and human world, provides moral ordinances, and extols great human achievements as seen in the sages. In a conversation with his student Zigong, Confucius said that he would leave off speaking. Zigong pursued him further: "'If you do not speak, how will we your followers find the proper way?' The Master responded 'Does *tian* speak? And yet the four seasons turn and the myriad things are born and grow within it.'"[67] This passage has come down to represent the articulation of "the highest ideal of virtuous behavior"[68] for which humans are to strive: doing and showing one's good deeds without the need to speak.

The *Analects* unequivocally articulates the second way to counter our urge to speak: Deeds shall precede and exceed words. By ordering action before and exceeding speech, Confucius highlights the "worth of action."[69] Confucius said that "the exemplary persons accomplish what they are going to say, and only then say it"; they want "to be slow to speak yet quick to act"; and "the ancients were loath to speak because they would be ashamed if they personally did not live up to what they said."[70] These expressions emphasize the "desire for a speech true to the life and character of the speaker.... The lived character of the [speaker] is more important than his speech." Instead of delineating a "rhetorical silence" as commonly used in the West (e.g., pause for a greater effect on the audience or recusal from speaking to ensure impartiality), the Confucian order of deeds and words "repudiates glibness and puts an emphasis on ... action. Human character is revealed in our worldly acts, not in the articulation of ideas and plans, not in senseless shouting, pontificating, or manipulating of others."[71] Not speaking before one's action or not in accordance to one's action thus serves to "foreground" full ethical significance of action in contrast to the insignificant, even irrelevant, role of speech.

As part of Confucian discourse on speaking, there is also an emphasis on attunement to social context and relationships, the third virtue for speaking. As noted in Chapter 2, Confucian thought separates neither the moral nor the individual from the social. The individual learns to cultivate self (修身), to regulate family (齊家), to order the state (治國), and ultimately to bring peace to the world (平天下). One's moral self-perfection is grounded in one's most primary social realm: the family. Learning how to relate to people in the cosmos of family is learning to understand the world at large. In fact, successful learning in the home is requisite for greater social responsibility for the community. Therefore, learning to speak well is no doubt learning how to speak with attunement to the social contexts and relationships.

Confucius saw as essential the understanding of ritual propriety, *li* (禮) in helping people achieve the goal of speaking appropriately. As discussed in Chapter 2, *li* covers social interactions at all levels ranging from the intimate relationship between friends to ceremonial performance in the larger society. But the key to *li* is to attend to people's feelings, emotions, and each other's senses and sensibilities – in other words, attending to humanity. One speaks when the appropriate context calls for it and does not speak or speaks in a particular way so as to promote relationships rather than embarrass or cause distress in the other. Having articulated what *li* is and how it regulates human relationships and interactions, Confucius made many remarks about speaking with social attunement. When his student Yan Hui inquired about how to practice *li* in order to achieve *ren* in daily life, Confucius replied that not speaking about anything that violates the observance of *li* is one important way.[72] Confucius remarked further that "by taking care in choice of language and mode of expression, exemplary persons keep vulgarity and impropriety at a distance," and "speaking before the time to speak is called being rash; not speaking when it is time to speak is called holding back, and speaking without observing the person's countenance is called being behind." Confucius himself set a good example for such attunement when he was observed in his home village to speak "deferentially, as though at a loss of words, and yet in the ancestral temple and at court, he spoke articulately, though with deliberation."[73] This basic outline of speaking with social attunement has had a strong influence on Chinese and other East Asians in their daily social interactions.

Clearly, the virtues of speaking lean toward *silence*. However, silence in Chinese and East Asian cultures is not regarded as the absence or opposite of speaking, but a virtue in its own right. As Arabella Lyon points out, silence in the West may be equated with "disengagement and disregard"[74] or inaction, which is a personal weakness. But Chinese/East Asians respect "chosen silence" as having a significant role to play in human affairs and relationship. For them, "it is a constitutive part of interactions, communication, and even making of fulfillment, knowledge, choice, and commitment. Silence can indicate questions, promises, denial, warning, threats, insult, request, command, deference, and intimacy."[75] The *Analects* is a text that offers a full discourse on how silence needs to be understood, valued, and practiced in service of one's moral and virtuous development.

SPEAKER'S BURDEN

Unlike some other specific cultural practices in the past (e.g., foot-binding or low social status of women) that have been jettisoned in modern time, the tradition of distrust in speaking for anyone in East Asia does not seem to abate. This tenacious persistence can be observed in Japan and Korea despite a well-functioning democracy running for decades and in Hong Kong despite a century-long British colonial rule.[76] Even though freedom of speech in those democracies is a constitutional right (as well as the right to defend oneself legally) for all, this political and legal right is not to be confused with the *cultural norm* of speaking. The source of this cultural persistence, I suspect, lies in the Confucian persuasion for personal moral development. Even when eloquent speakers emerge as they do, people may not admire and trust them as much as they do in the West, resulting in less power granted to such speakers. Consequently, political, social, business, and education leaders may not be eager to develop or to display oratory skills either. None of the current Asian political leaders are distinguished speakers. Instead, they project an image of speaking cautiously, slowly, softly, and hesitantly, as exemplified by the UN Secretary-General Ban Ki-moon.

Against this millennia-long cultural background, I would argue that present-day Chinese/East Asian speakers continue to carry three concerns/burdens in weighing their choice of speaking or not speaking as well as how they speak: (1) moral, (2) social, and (3) personal. These sensitivities may dissuade them from speaking more, and more forcefully.

Moral Concern

The notion of speaking versus action as an epistemological consideration weighs heavily on anyone before deciding to speak or not to speak, regardless of the social context and personal risks. Whenever a person is confronted with and contemplates the choice of speaking, he or she is likely to think about whether or not the idea about to be expressed, particularly criticisms and suggestions, can be backed up in action by the person him- or herself. To put this reasoning more simply, speaking in Chinese/East Asian cultures is regarded more as speaking up to voice a concern, to change the status quo, or to offer a promise. The standard of knowing (hence the source of expression), namely epistemology, is not merely cognitive but the *practice* of what one knows.[77] Thus, words are not finished when merely spoken, and the message alone is not enough until the words turn into practice. In East Asia, speaking commits the speaker to action and delivery of deeds. If one is unsure about this action-commitment and delivery, one would be better served to remain silent. Such chosen silence is understood, respected, and valued.

Research indeed shows this tendency of present-day Chinese. Kwan and colleagues[78] used a common instrument for measuring individuation in the West and found that Hong Kong Chinese regarded this measure as consisting of two factors: (1) attention seeking for oneself and (2) taking the lead for the group. Whereas attention seeking for oneself is a negative characteristic, taking the lead on behalf of the group is a positive behavior. Statements indicating attention seeking include "raise your hand to ask a question in a meeting or lecture," "publicly challenge a speaker whose position clashes with your own," "give an informal talk in front of a small group of classmates," "speak up about your ideas even though you are uncertain of whether you are correct," and "give your opinion on a controversial issue, even though no one has asked for it." In contrast, taking the lead include "give a lecture to a large audience," "volunteer to head a committee for a group of people you do not know very well," "accept a nomination to be a leader of a group," and "perform on a stage before a large audience." As can be seen, the statements on attention seeking all involve public speaking. Given the moral burden for holding the speaker personally accountable for his or her opinions, it is not surprising that Chinese regard such public speaking as more negative. However, European-American people in the study did not distinguish the two factors and viewed them as a single factor indicating a positive personal quality.

Relatedly, boastfulness is a sign of personal weakness and violates the cautious norm of speaking in East Asia. Learning in Confucian persuasion is geared to counter such personal flaws. Boastfulness is also thought of as narcissistic in Western psychology, in spite of the strong cultural encouragement for self-enhancing speech. Asian-American students have been found less narcissistic and more modest than their European-American peers.[79] Similarly, college students in Hong Kong are reluctant to ask their professors questions and seek ways to modify the knowledge until they have studied the material and applied it to real life (after practice).[80] My most recent research also shows that a greater percentage of Chinese words referring to speaking are rated as negative (3.5 times more than positive words) by Chinese college students than English speaking terms referring to speaking are rated as such (1.5 times more) by European-American students.[81] Moreover, we contrasted speaking versus doing and asked Chinese and European-American adults to rate which kind of persons they liked more. Results show that Chinese liked the most a person who talks little but does more (but European-Americans liked the most a person who talks a lot but also does a lot).

Social Concern

Chinese/East Asians carry what might be called a social burden whenever they face speaking in a social setting. Clearly, there are many rules about such speaking in East Asia. In any culture, speaking in social context is a highly delicate social act. But for East Asians, the delicacy lies not in whether to speak, but in how to speak *appropriately* as it is one central teaching of Confucius. Therefore, Chinese/East Asians pay a great deal of attention to it. Such attention and care serve to reduce the amount of thoughtless and random speaking among Asians. Speaking appropriately is a life-long learning task that starts from childhood and continues through old age. It enables people to achieve their goals, but it can also destroy relationships and cause grave consequences.[82] Appropriateness hinges on the following two discernable sensitivities: (1) to the particular relationship as part of the social context and (2) to conflict.

Chinese/East Asians are socialized to attend to the specific social role and status of the listener. A set of guidelines for speaking or not speaking is enacted depending on whether the listener/interactant is an authority figure, a family member, a friend, or a stranger. There is no such thing as a general audience, well-educated or not, or an average person on the street as one's listener. Every social interaction is a particular relationship that demands a judgment of how one needs to respond in speaking.[83]

In general, there are three types of relationships to which one is highly attuned. The first type, as discussed in Chapters 2 and 5, includes the authority figures such as leaders, professors, teachers, parents, and elders toward whom East Asians show dereference and respect.[84] Again, it is erroneous to assume that Asian deference toward authority figures is equal to loss of personal agency to think independently and to challenge them. The issue here is speaking in a way that is appropriate to a given social relationship as required by the culture. One can challenge authority figures without being rude and abrasive. In Asian cultures, speaking appropriately may help one achieve one's goals much better than making a lot of speaking blunders. Accordingly, one usually listens attentively to authority figures, remains humble in posture and countenance, speaks – and especially interrupts – little, but answers questions earnestly. In such relationships, one takes in information and tries to digest well what was said.[85] When one is asked to offer opinions and suggestions, one is expected to do so readily. Thus, one cannot be unthinking or remain indifferent in such settings. Instead, there is a high demand for one's attentiveness and quick response on the spot. When speaking to a professor, a teacher, or someone who has noted accomplishments, the student or person at a lower level normally use a self-effacing and other-enhancing style such as "in my humble opinion" but "in your wise opinion …" and "in my unworthy work …" when preempting one's speech.[86]

In the 1980s, In-Mao Liu[87] predicted that because Chinese children must learn rules for respect toward authority figures, they are likely to under-develop self-assertiveness and unlearn it even when they somehow learn it early on, because self-assertiveness clashes with respect. There is a large body of research that verifies this Asian tendency.[88] For example, Douglas Smith observed that elders in Taiwan spoke much more at the dinner table than children, while the latter remained attentive.[89] In an experiment examining assertiveness, Chinese-American students showed a much lower score for the item "asking a professor to clarify a lecture" and ranked it much more difficult than their European-American peers.[90] The interviews by Kenneth Lieberman showed that many East Asian students attending American universities thought American students disrespectful toward their professors.[91] Finally, my most recent study compared Chinese and European-American college students' responses to the appropriateness of challenging a professor in class.[92] The study found that although they approved of such inquisitiveness of students in class, Chinese students questioned the *appropriateness* of students challenging the professor directly in class. They quarreled with the style but not with students' need to ask questions. They suggested a more acceptable style: seeking the professor out after class to discuss questions and issues face to face rather than making a public scene in class. In contrast, European-American students did not display such distinctions in speaking.

On the other hand, the relationship with the second type of people – peers and people of the same status (e.g., position, age, generation, even coethnicity) – is one that calls for mutuality in communication. In this kind of relationship, after familiarity has been achieved, one is encouraged to speak more freely, openly, and directly.[93] Exchange and display of emotions and true feelings are treasured. In fact, Chinese people would find it strange not to engage in such verbal expression with same-status and familiar peers such as relatives, friends, and schoolmates. My own recent research shows that Chinese college students disapprove of peers and siblings who are non-talkative with each other, because there is "no reason for caution and reservation."[94]

A related attunement for communication is to the context. The most important distinction is inside-versus-outside context, often referred to as in-group versus out-group.[95] Chinese people's speaking is differentiated along the line of these two contexts. The speaker needs to know which of the two contexts he or she faces. Within the inside context that includes one's family, close friends, and social circles, one speaks more openly, freely, and assertively, except toward older generations. The older they are, the more respect is extended toward them. Thus, to a grandmother, children must be deferential in speech (as well as in nonverbal interactions). For example, children need to use the honorific to address her in the second-person pronoun *nin* (您) instead of *ni* (你). Usually, children also address their parents and elders in their parents' generation (uncles and aunts) with the same honorific, which is audible when the dialect differentiates the sounds (e.g., northern dialects. However, many Chinese dialects do not distinguish the sounds, but such deference is evident in children's writing). Despite this generational deference, one still talks more openly and assertively and expresses emotions more freely within the inside context including family elders. This is so because Chinese stress life-long ties with these inside people, called "one's own people" (自己人).[96] One builds a lifelong, dependable, and mutual support system with these people.[97] Speaking openly with and giving advice (frequently down-to-earth, even hurtful truth) to each other is a sign of the strength of this relationship. Avoidance of such speaking signals weakened ties.[98] Finally, because coethnics among immigrants are considered an inside context, Paulhus and colleagues found that Asian-heritage college students in Canada are not shy with other Asian-heritage peers (but are more shy when interacting with European-heritage peers, an outside group).[99]

With strangers, the third type of people, also in the outside context, Chinese/East Asians tend to be cautious, avoidant, and reserved, not easily displaying emotions and inner thoughts.[100] East Asians tend to be polite, agreeable, and respectful toward strangers but keep them at a distance. Hence, Chinese/East Asian people find it hard to believe that a stranger whom one just met at a bus stop or only after a brief meeting would call one "my friend" or even "my best friend." Disclosure of personal information such as one's marital status and relationships with parents to strangers is not done among Chinese. Such sharing of personal life only takes place among trusted people. While strangers are part of the outside context, this context includes many types of people who may not necessarily be strangers, such as coworkers and neighbors. To people one does not consider as one's own (外人), one weighs carefully whether to speak or not to speak. Whenever possible, East Asians tend to lean toward silence if they do not have to speak. If they do, they are likely to choose their words with great care, speak more tentatively, less assertively, and even ambiguously on purpose. The key concern is not to make mistakes that can come back to haunt oneself, or to get oneself into a situation that can make oneself vulnerable.[101]

Beyond the concern for social relationships and contexts, East Asians are especially sensitive toward conflict in communication. For a significant part, their social life is about avoiding conflict. Conflict is a high stress producer because it violates the basic life-orientation of harmony. Conflict leads to embarrassment of the other and self and lingering distress.[102] Speaking up to challenge the other in public, particularly the one in authority and status (e.g., challenging the teacher or professor in class), may be considered deliberate sabotage of the other's face and can result in serious interpersonal consequences. Yet the Chinese social system functions in such a way that makes it difficult, if at all possible, for one to abandon family ties and other important relationships such as the teacher–student relationship. Therefore, direct confrontation is discouraged and avoided at all costs. When faced with a need to speak, the person is even more attuned to the notion of appropriateness in conflict-laden situations.[103] For example, when a subordinate disagrees with the supervisor at work, instead of saying something to the effect of "I disagree with you," "I am uncomfortable with you," or even "I respectfully disagree with you," a Chinese/East Asian person is likely to say "I will try my best to see if a slightly different way might work better," "I heard from XX that this way might …," or "It was my fault not to explain this well to you [even when it is apparent to both the boss and the speaker that the boss is at fault]." Display of strong negative emotions in conflict situations is also discouraged. This is probably why East Asians tend to show no emotion on their face when they are found in conflict.[104] These strategies are common and effective and enable people to achieve their goals and at the same time avoid direct confrontation.

Personal Concern

In light of the preceding discussions of the sensitivities, it is logical that speaking in organized and public settings is also likely to result in greater personal concerns for East Asians. To be blunt, when forced to speak before they are ready, East Asians may experience psychological distress that can take a toll on their socioemotional as well as cognitive functioning.

Several studies have zeroed in on this very topic and have yielded important findings. As noted previously, Chinese-American college students ranked the assertiveness-prone situation of "asking a professor to clarify a lecture" much more difficult than their European-American peers.[105] East Asian Canadian college students were found to feel significantly more anxious and guilty following assertive responding (e.g., telling a friend who calls frequently about her relationship issues not to call so often because one is too busy) than European Canadians. This Asian tendency is especially relevant to acquaintances but not to strangers.[106] In another study, significantly more recent East Asian immigrant Canadians reported to feel shy in class (91 percent) than European Canadians (51 percent). And the most frequent reason for their shyness was "fear of being wrong" for Asian Canadians (30 percent), compared to 5 percent for European Canadians.[107] Finally, Heejung Kim studied how East Asians and East Asian Americans view speaking as a cognitive function in comparison with European-American college students.[108] She found that whereas European-American students believed that speaking enhances thinking, East Asians believed the opposite effect of speaking. Her experiments examining performing cognitive tasks in silence versus talking aloud demonstrated that whereas speaking did not interfere with and even enhanced European-American students' performance, it did interfere with Asian students' performance. Her further study shows that having to speak while trying to solve problems not only reduced Asian students' performance (more recent immigrants), but also caused higher stress in them as measured in cortisol levels (but verbalization benefitted European-American students performance and relaxed instead of stressing them).

These research findings compel us to conclude that there are indeed very large differences in speaking between the two cultures. The three important concerns that East Asians carry with them may serve to reduce the amount of speaking among East Asians and to shape how they speak in social settings and in learning.

EAST ASIAN SPEAKING STYLE

The preceding sections discussed the Chinese/East Asian cultural tradition of speaking and concerns people may have when faced with the need to speak. In what follows, I discuss the speaking style of Chinese/East Asians. Similar to the four Gricean maxims governing Western people's speaking style, there seem to be four different maxims guiding Chinese/East Asians when they do speak.

The Maxim of Paucity: Speak Little

As previously discussed, the default for the Chinese/East Asian mode is not to speak if there is no need. Volunteering to speak without a need may be regarded as inappropriate or insensitive to a setting, not to mention making unnecessary promises when one is not prepared to back them up with action. Speaking little is very different from the Western maxim, "Speak no more and no less," which stresses the need for the speaker to calculate the *right amount* of speaking as required by the conversation. This maxim still presumes a speaking mode. It is just that the speaker needs to adhere to the right quantity. Unlike this Western maxim, paucity in speaking is a virtue, preferred and valued, for Chinese/East Asians as noted before.

Paucity in speaking may even be a sign of intelligence in Asia. Research conducted by Shih-Ying Yang and Robert Sternberg found that Taiwanese people regarded an intelligent person as one who knows "when to assert him/herself and when to draw back" beyond other common attributes of intelligence such as having a quick mind.[109] However, verbal fluency was one of the primary definitional attributes of intelligence in the West. Certainly, knowing when *not* to speak was not part of the definition.[110] In Japan, talkativeness is considered superficial and unintelligent.[111] This is probably why Judge Bao in court did not speak much either. Given the positive image of the reluctance to speak, there is little wonder why East Asians have been observed across time and space as more reserved in speaking.

When they do decide to speak, Chinese/East Asians do so more likely in two ways. The first way is to speak slowly, cautiously, hesitantly, and self-effacingly.[112] Such a style signals to the listener that the speaker is well aware of the liabilities of speaking, is willing to revise what he or she has spoken about, and is not ready to commit him- or herself to the expected action. The second way is to speak with assurance and certainty but still with reservation and less assertiveness. This style indicates that the speaker has a responsibility for and command over the topic or the issue and is ready to back up the spoken ideas with action. Because such speech conveys assurance, the listener is likely to take the speaker up on the ideas and suggestions.

In learning, the student is also guided by these two ways of speaking. Because the student is supposed to seek the teacher's guidance with a humble attitude and receptivity, the student may have a greater need to be hesitant, cautious, and self-effacing. In East Asian cultures, such a speaking style, coupled with the need to show respect to teachers, makes Asian learners appear docile and passive to the non-Asian eye. The following example illustrates the case in point well: several years ago, a European-American colleague and I went to a rural area in China to collect data on children's conceptions of teaching and learning. Although these children had never seen a real European-American, they did interact with my colleague one on one, as requested and encouraged by us and their teachers. One by one, these children followed our instructions and completed the research tasks. But my colleague observed that these children did not initiate any contact with him, particularly did not verbalize much in front of him; they stood straight and just did what they were told. However, when they worked with each other, they whispered and gestured to each other rather than speaking audibly. After being puzzled about these children for four weeks, my colleague finally asked me why Chinese children were not talking and appeared not even very lively to him. I pointed out that the same speechless and "unlively" children would become loud and rambunctious in their own yards. Indeed, my colleague saw the difference of behavior and made an insightful comment about his discovery: "[T]hen this is a sign of intelligence because these very young children are able to differentiate and conduct themselves according to different social contexts!"

The Maxim of Ambiguity: Speak Indeterminately

East Asians are known for speaking with circumlocution and vagueness. Ambiguity in communication is common.[113] This stands in sharp contrast to the Western maxim of speaking clarity. Western people may find this style difficult to deal with, but East Asians may find the Western style equally hard to adjust to. As Agnes He points out, the Asian style of ambiguity is not semantic or logical failure, but a preference.[114] Hui-Ching Chang in her studies of Chinese daily communication also came to the same conclusion, namely that Chinese thrive on the style that fits their need to maintain the social system with clearly defined roles, but at the same time that fits their need to keep a space for communicative indeterminacy.[115] This flexible space between their fixed roles (e.g., parental or child role) and the vagaries of daily life allows them to be creative in achieving their goals. Mastery of this style may generate high regard from people and surely requires much learning and understanding.

This particular style may owe its origin to Taoism as a philosophy of dialectics. Taoism claims that the universe consists of two fundamental forces: yin and yang, the feminine for the former and the masculine for the latter. However, yin and yang complement each other and coexist at all times. Moreover, these two forces are never fixed and stable, but always in flux. Their changing nature is the principle according to which the universe operates. As illustrated in the yin-yang symbol, the universe is oneness with infinite dynamics for change (Figure 8.1). The visual depiction of this dynamic oneness is diagrammed as a perfect circle divided into a white fish next to the identically shaped but opposite-positioned black fish. The tail of the white fish is adjacent to the head of the black fish. Both the body contours and the lines of the two fish are fluid, indicating their potentiality of morphing into each other. Thus, the seeming opposite of the most basic forces of the universe, visualized as white and black, is not opposite at all. Each pole of existence in this philosophy is the beginning dynamic of the other. When the dynamic reaches the other pole, it becomes the other and at the same time begins to return to the original state. Life recycles ceaselessly in yin and yang.

Such is the world in which East Asians have been living for millennia. This way of viewing and living the world is so natural to them that their

FIGURE 8.1. The yin-yang symbol.

food, music, dance, arts, sports, medicine, even science (e.g., agriculture and hydraulic engineering), and personal creativity are all influenced by this worldview. Because the world is believed to always change, there is no point of seeing any one thing as fixed eternally. Kaiping Peng and Richard Nisbett have investigated this topic in East Asian and Western thinking and have found large, consistent differences in their beliefs.[116] Western people view the world by following three laws of logic: (1) identity (e.g., the statement "a teacher is a teacher" is true because of the identical names of both sides), (2) noncontradiction (i.e., if something is A, it cannot be not-A), and (3) the excluded middle (i.e., if A is true, it cannot be false; there is no middle term to which these contradictions belong). But Taoism holds three different principles: (1) constant changes (e.g., A is A only now, but A can become X and thus no longer be A), (2) contradiction (e.g., A can be not-A depending on the context and perspective of the viewer), and (3) holism or interconnectivity of all things (i.e., A, B, ... *n* are all connected so that A can be part of B ... *n* and vice versa). All three principles are clearly illustrated in the yin-yang diagram. These researchers have done many studies showing that East Asian and Western people perceive differently even the most basic objects such as a triangle made of wood or clay, as well as basic relationship such as a larger fish among smaller fish or a green pencil in a group of red pencils. Whereas Western people view things in sharp distinctions, East Asians see more background as part of any single object or see all elements more relationally.

Living with such a perspective of life enables East Asians to be tolerant toward, comfortable with, expectant of, and even embracing change, contradiction, and interconnectivity of things in life. In other words, to them, ambiguity is but a norm in life. Speaking ambiguously is thus natural. Because speaking and listening require each other as cultural cooperation, East Asians are equally adept at listening to ambiguity. Speaking too clearly and sharply may bewilder them and generate discomfort. It is not an exaggeration to say that figuring out ambiguity in communication is not merely socially necessary, but also intellectually challenging, highly motivating, even fun at times.

East Asians use ambiguity in speech to accomplish many goals. I highlight two common ones here. As many scholars have pointed out, East Asians' speaking leaves much greater room for interpretation in order to achieve their goals.[117] For example, in class, a teacher sees a student talk to a peer, not paying attention to her instruction. Instead of calling out the student's name, which would embarrass the student, the teacher may say, "There are people seeking others out to talk" (有人找別人講話). In fact, in Chinese, the quantity in the phrase "there are people" (有人) is not linguistically marked (owing to lack of morphology for quantity in Chinese). For the whole class, it is not clear whom the teacher is referring to – a particular peer, oneself, or everyone. Hearing this teacher comment, all children become more attentive to the class. The child who actually sought out another to chat is likely to stop. As observed by Agnes He in Chinese language classes, this strategy of speaking is commonly used by teachers to achieve disciplinary results.[118] It is worth noting that no student would demand clarity in such a situation. Ambiguous speech is appropriately delivered by the teacher and accepted cooperatively by students.

When one is not sure about one's response or if one's response might usher in unwanted consequences, one may use ambiguous speech to manage the situation. For example, the chair of school department is asked when a decision will be made regarding the hiring of a new teacher. Instead of giving some reference to a time (e.g., a week or as soon as possible, which is a more typical response in the West), the chair can say, "We will let you know when we get to that point." This kind of responding serves to create indeterminacy. It signals to the listener that the chair is working on the issue, no definite answer is available, and pressing the chair for a definite answer at this point may be inappropriate. An East Asian questioner is less likely to demand a definite answer again. Such a strategy is also used in the West and other cultures, but in East Asia it represents a routine way of speaking.

The Maxim of Indirectness: Speak Amicably

This maxim rests on the very high value of *harmony* in East Asian cultures. As discussed earlier, East Asians do not like confrontation and conflict,

particularly regarding interpersonal relationships.[119] Their interactive principles are regulated by the role each person occupies. An authority role
requires respect that comes with specific speech and behavior. A subordinate or a person at a younger age or in a younger generation also needs to
speak within the acceptable *li* (ritual propriety). Harmony happens when
the speaker and the listener uphold the same principles and honor each
other's roles. Speaking out of one's role and relationship is something that
East Asians would like to avoid.[120]

However, disagreement and conflict are unavoidable in life. When they
happen, East Asians become highly sensitive to a principle to which they
adhere: "give others face."[121] This basic style is to watch out not to cause
embarrassment or, worse, shame in the other. Speaking that manages to
avoid embarrassment and to honor the other is considered an important
interpersonal skill. Insensitive and malicious speaking that causes people
to lose face is a serious offense. Lost face or "broken face" (撕破脸) often
results in termination of a relationship (e.g., friends turning into enemies),
family feud, and even physical violence.

Thus, when speaking, Chinese/East Asians prefer an unassertive style.
They use indirect speech to achieve many goals. For example, a student is
not sure how her professor thinks of her, but she would like to ask for a rec-
ommendation letter. So, instead of saying directly to the professor, "Would
you be willing to write a letter on my behalf?" she would say, "I wonder
how professors write recommendations letters for students." In the East
Asian context, a professor is probably alerted to an upcoming request from
the student. In reply, the professor can say, "Well, usually professors write
letters for students who show good learning attitude, work hard, and do
well." The student then can say, "I guess I need to improve myself in these
regards." If the professor thinks well of the student, he might offer, "I think
you were a good student in my class." By speaking indirectly, the student
avoided a potentially embarrassing situation for both her and the professor
if the latter did not think well of her. But with her indirect approach, she
obtained the desired information and is likely to succeed in getting a rec-
ommendation letter.

Chang studied how people in Taiwan use indirect speech to create space
in their defined roles for negotiating their relational status.[122] She observed
a mother-in-law who wanted her son to drive her and her husband to a
department store. But she was not sure that she would succeed, given the
difficult relationship with her daughter-in-law. The mother-in-law said:
"We are going to the department store. We'd better take the bus and take
our time getting there." Upon hearing this nondemanding expression, the
daughter-in-law, in trying to fulfill her filial duty, replied "Mom, why do

you need to take a bus? We'll take you there." The mother-in-law is masterful in using indirect speech and managed to give the daughter-in-law a
chance to be kind and at the same time to achieve her goal of being taken
to the store.

On the negative side, I observed a bilingual research assistant who was
caught between the two cultures' communication styles. This assistant is of
Chinese heritage but grew up in the United States. She is a straight-A student
and a caring person. By Western standard, she is very sharp, speaks clearly,
and gets her message across efficiently. Her task was to interview Chinese
immigrant parents who were born and raised outside the United States.
Therefore, she spoke Chinese to these parents. One of the areas that Chinese/
East Asian people consider to be private is their marital status. Typically,
when experienced interviewers ask such a question about a mother's marital
status, they speak cautiously, interjecting many fillers such as "hm, hm...,
uh, uh..., I apologize, I regrettably request for ..." as if they were stuttering
and stammering. These fillers serve to soften the tone and show hesitation,
making something direct sound indirect. They convey to the listener that
the speaker is kind, caring, feels bad to have to ask such a question, in order
to ensure smooth communication. Sharpness and directness are the wrong
style, to be avoided at all costs. Because the assistant was interviewing these
parents on the phone for the first time, she was a stranger to them (which
demands even more indirect speech for such a private topic). Unfortunately,
she asked the question sharply, directly, and efficiently (as written on the
questionnaire). Quite a number of mothers were offended by the manner in
which she asked her questions. They questioned if she was with the police
and told her that they were very uncomfortable with her way of speaking,
despite the fact that she spoke linguistically perfect Chinese. Some even
wanted to quit their participation in the research on the spot.

As these examples illustrate, indirect verbal interaction is of key importance in Chinese/East Asian lives. Direct speech stands to hurt and worsen
relationships, but skillfully expressed indirect speech can help build and
strengthen relationships as well as heal and repair strained ones.

The Maxim of Listenership: Listening before Speaking

In their insightful analysis of the Taiwanese parent–child narratives, Heidi
Fung and Peggy Miller showed how listening is not passive but *active* in
parent–child communications.[123] Unlike their European-American peers,
Taiwanese children listen attentively; they do not use the typically Western
style of argument to interact with their caregivers. Only after they listen

carefully do Taiwanese children interject responses and even voice challenges to adults' instructions and actions. Although other scholars have identified the East Asian style as listener-centered as opposed to speaker-centered,[124] it was Fung and Miller who articulated the active nature of listening for East Asians and backed the observation with empirical data. Based on their and others' research, it is clear that East Asia *privileges* listening (emphasizing listenership) whereas the West *privileges* speaking (emphasizing speakership) because it is a matter of choice and preference. Viewing the East Asian style as some kind of deficiency or a problem is not conducive to our understanding.

East Asians' need to listen well is a natural component of the other three maxims of speaking as discussed previously. Because the style of speaking emphasizes little talk, silence, ambiguity, and indirectness, the interlocutor has to do a lot more work in listening in order to decipher the full meaning of what is spoken about. From available analysis, it seems that Chinese/East Asian listeners make three kinds of effort when following the maxim of listenership: (1) figure out "fine and hidden" meanings, (2) extend, if deeming desirable, the unexpressed but intended by the speaker, and (3) interject speaking at the right moment in the right context.

Gao observes that in communication, Chinese people need to figure out "fine and hidden meanings"[125] from the speaker before they can respond. At least in Chinese, there are many sayings acknowledging the need and demand on the listener: for example, "not saying all that is felt" (言外之意), "more is meant than meets the ear" (只可會意, 不可言傳), "meaning lies beyond words" (意在言外), and "meaning lies in the unspoken" (意在不言之中). It is expected that the listener will be sensitive to and endeavor to decipher the intended but unexpressed meanings. I would add that it is also the Chinese artistic and aesthetic philosophy to create art works (e.g., poems, paintings, architecture, and other visual forms) according to the same suggestive but not exhaustively expressive style. Aphorisms such as "words have ended, but meaning is infinite" (言已盡, 而意無窮) and "at this moment, it's better to have silence than sound" (此處無聲勝有聲) convey this principle.[126]

Thus, the listener needs to "examine a person's words and observe his/her countenance" (察言觀色)[127] by drawing meanings from linking "what is said to personal experiences (體會) and "to contemplate/ponder" (琢磨).[128] Such work on listening is likely to lead the person to recover the fuller meaning of the spoken words and to respond more appropriately.

When the listener has gained a fuller understanding of the spoken words, he/she may engage in the second kind of effort: extending the unexpressed but intended meaning by the speaker, if such an extension is deemed desirable and appropriate. This kind of extension is well illustrated by the student Zigon's conversation with Confucius (quoted already in Chapter 6 but repeated here for ease of reference):

> ZIGONG SAID: "What do you think of the saying: 'Poor but not inferior; rich but not superior'?" The Master replied: "Not bad, but not as good as: "Poor but enjoying the way (*dao*, 道), rich but loving ritual propriety (*li*, 禮)"
> ZIGONG SAID: "*The Book of Songs* states:
> Like bone carved and polished,
> Like jade cut and ground.
> Is this not what you have in mind?"
> THE MASTER SAID: "Zigong, it is only with the likes of you then that I can discuss the *Songs*! On the basis of what has been said, you know what is yet to come."[129]

Here, what impressed Confucius was that Zigong not only understood the teacher's alerting him to be humble and urging him to strive further in his self-cultivation, but also *extended* the meaning implied by Confucius: Students need to bounce off each other's ideas and understanding like bone being carved and polished, like jade being cut and ground. Only this way can students go deeper in their learning. Zigong's connecting what his teacher said to the highly cherished *Book of Songs* adds further testimony of him being a very attentive listener and dedicated learner, thus earning Confucius' praise.

The third effort of the listener is to interject speaking at the right moment in the right context. Learning how to time one's interjection is key. Interjection in this manner includes comments, questioning, disagreements, even challenges. Here, Fung, Miller, and Lin provide a telling example[130]: Angu, a four-year-old Taiwanese girl, was being reprimanded by her aunt, the caregiver, for her misdeeds of spilling food, misbehaving at the table, and dashing into and kicking dishes (breaking them and endangering herself). As a common socializing effort, Taiwanese parents routinely recount these daily mishaps to the child and other family members. In the process, the child is cast as the focal actor but also the listener of the story about herself (along with other listeners), with the misdeeds highlighted. The child's role is first to listen attentively and then to respond when questioned and taught for better future behavior. For the unfamiliar eye, East Asian parents are just authoritarian and disciplinarian, not allowing the child a chance to defend herself. Fung and colleagues' data show a much more dynamic and nuanced picture. Angu listened to her aunt's harangue for more than ten minutes, patiently waiting for her aunt to calm down. Then she began her challenge by saying "I am asking you a question." Angu asked why her aunt was unreasonable with her (yelling). When her aunt pressed her why she did not know how to walk carefully around the dishes, Angu replied, "because I fell." Angu then threw the question at her aunt: "Why did you not reason with me nicely?" She went on to question her aunt if the latter made any mistakes when she herself was a child. When the aunt tried to fend off Angu by saying that she was a well-behaved child and never spilled food, Angu called her grandmother to verify her aunt's claim of herself being a perfect child.

This example illustrates vividly how listening is not just an end in and of itself, but a requirement for further verbal (or nonverbal) social interaction. East Asian children indeed are expected to listen more than to speak in a situation where adults clearly have more authority (correcting the child's transgressions). However, children also learn that they can interject at the right moment in the right context in order to express their own ideas, even to challenge the authority; they do so without engaging in the immediate verbal argument, but by listening fully first.

EAST ASIAN CLASSROOM DISCOURSE AND SOCIALIZATION

All the sensitivities to and the four maxims of speaking are taught and practiced in the classroom as the major socialization context outside of home. First, as Agnes He noted in her informative analysis, neither ideas – as in the case of correct answers and thoughtful comments by students – nor their wrong answers and less impressive expressions are attributed to children as owners/authors by Chinese teachers.[131] Instead, teachers focus on the *content* of what needs to be learned. She gave several examples where the teacher elicited children's responses on how to write Chinese characters or their opinions about a story. There was plenty of ambiguity regarding who made a better or weaker suggestion, who deserved the credit for an idea, who disagreed with whom, and so on to be cleared by the teacher. However, the teacher did not even attempt to do so, nor did the children request/demand such clarification. Instead, they discussed what the correct writing of Chinese characters was and then moved on to the next learning task. In the case of discussing responses to a story, the teacher collected the various responses from students but without singling out any individual student. The same pattern has been found by many researchers in their observations of classrooms in China and Hong Kong.[132]

Another vivid example was captured by Yeh Hsueh in his video study on a day at the Chinese preschool in Beijing.[133] In the video, there is a scene where the teacher holds, as a daily routine, a reading session with every child looking at a book. Children's reading is guided by the teacher's questions. When she asked, "What is the elephant doing?" many hands went up. She picked a child, who stood up and answered the question correctly. The teacher then asked her to sit down without a single word of affirmation or praise and moved on to the next question.

Such focus on the learning content rather than on the ownership/authorship of individuals' ideas practically eliminates the potentially adverse effect of students' social comparison on each other. This style may underlie the common practice of calling students to display their misunderstanding or weak skills publicly (on the blackboard or just sharing with the class verbally). According to recorded proceedings of classroom teaching, children do not show discomfort with this display of their errors.[134] As noted in Chapter 3, when the self is regarded as malleable and improvable through learning, children know that a mistake does not indicate an inherent flaw in themselves, but rather an opportunity to self-improve. This kind of classroom teaching is based on the belief that asserting the self verbally is unimportant in the process of learning. What is important is the focus on the improvable nature of oneself. Since ascertaining the moment-to-moment quality of the self is not ever the focus, authoring oneself through speech becomes trivial, if not discouraged altogether.

The preceding discussion may give the impression that Chinese classrooms are passive, which has been the indictment against East Asian education.[135] However, the indictment may operate on the assumption that active engagement in learning has only one manifestation: verbalization. Not verbalizing then is passive learning. This may be a strong Western assumption and practice, but it may not hold true for East Asian learners.

Closer examination reveals that speaking little does not mean that Chinese/East Asians are uninvolved. Quite the contrary, East Asians' little speaking/silence is evidence that they are highly sensitive and attentive to the situation. As alluded to previously, in settings where one finds oneself in need of speaking little or remaining silent, one pays more, not less, attention to the speaker. For example, it is repeatedly observed that in East Asian classrooms, children show rapt attention even when the teacher does not seem, to the outside eye, that engaging.[136] Pupils often respond to the teacher's question by responding in unison if the answer is definite or elicited by a rhetorical question such as "how much is 5×6?" For open-ended questions, pupils are called on to respond. Being ready to respond and respond well is taken as a sign of student engagement and a good learning attitude. Lack of such readiness is cause for concern for parents and teachers. Apparently,

Chinese/East Asian children's rapt attention and participation are not conditioned by their need to speak very much.[137]

Research on Japanese classrooms shows a very high level of participation and active thinking. Despite little verbalization, students' journals and other written work were full of questions, puzzlements, even disputes with their peers who did speak. Such a form, common in Asian schools, is even dubbed as "silent participation" by Inagaki, Hatano, and Morita.[138] The same pattern is also found in Chinese classrooms. Cortazzi and Jin give two responses by Chinese students, one from an elementary school child and the other from a Chinese student at a British university:

> I may be listening but I am not passive. I am learning in my head. I learn from my teacher. I also learn from what my friends do. If they make a mistake, I learn from that too.

> We are active in our minds. We are thinking all the time. Our minds follow the lecturer with questions and challenges. We are just not used to speaking out. But all of us know very well what is going on and we know the answers to the questions those lecturers asked or other students raised.[139]

These testimonies from students themselves, as well as independent observations, confirm this active nature of learning, which does not depend on momentary verbalization, but rather on attentive listening. Such listening is likely to generate more thoughtful verbal responses at a later time. This focus on listening in Chinese classrooms led Cortazzi and Jin to dub the style as "listening-oriented learning."[140]

GROWING UP A RELUCTANT SPEAKER

As already alluded to in the previous section, home is the fertile nursery for cultural transmission of values and norms pertaining to speaking (along with other values). Values that parents uphold may be spoken about, enacted, and modeled frequently and forcefully. Ideas and behaviors that are not valued or even rejected by parents are handled with aversion, vagueness, or ignored altogether. In general, research finds that early on, Japanese mothers are less verbal with their infants, and their children produce significantly fewer utterances per turn than their European-American counterparts.[141] Likewise, Chinese babies vocalize less than European-American babies to respond to laboratory tasks, and this trend continues in adulthood.[142] On a more ethnographic account, Douglas Smith observed Taiwanese children speaking little but listening very attentively to adults talking at a dinner table.[143]

To peek into the actual process of socialization for reluctant speaking, I provide two examples of my own research: My colleague and I asked rural Chinese mothers to teach their children a new household chore. A mother said very little but gestured to her preschool child (usually surrounded by a group of curious neighborhood children) to indicate a task such as peeling vegetables. First, the mother demonstrated how to peel the vegetable in slow motion. Then, she handed a half-peeled vegetable to the child for her to continue. After some hand-holding and a few gentle corrections, the child succeeded in learning the skill. When successful, the child smiled and the mother made some sound, indicating that the child could go out to play. There was no praise at all. Children seemed to carry out their daily routines without expectation of parental praise for anything they did. But we observed a boy who, after learning a similar skill, uttered, "Oh, that was too easy!" showing off his achievement. Upon hearing this reaction to his success, the mother broke her nonverbal mode: "You are so full of yourself!" and "Are you also like that in school?" Without any reply, but turning away, the boy ran out to play with other children.

Notice who talked and who did not in this exchange. The one who was motivated to call attention to his achievement in front of the other children – the boy and the learner – spoke first. By contrast, the one who actually had a skill to teach – the mother – spoke little. Instead, she acted her teaching out by demonstrating, simplifying, and correcting with gestures, much like Judge Bao in his court. When the mother chided her child for showing off his achievement (our post-teaching interview revealed that the mother regarded this learning too trivial for her boy to display such pride in public), the initially proud child became silent, exiting the scene quickly. Nonverbal teaching and learning proceeded smoothly and successfully until there was a need to speak. Unfortunately, the boy's need to speak did not fit the cultural norm for humility when facing one's own achievement (particularly trivial for household chores). This lack of virtue as cherished in Chinese culture was surely cause for the mother to speak to the child. By remaining silent and exiting the scene, the child showed receptivity to his mother's teaching. By speaking as her parenting duty required, the mother achieved her goal of teaching humility. What is more interesting was that other children also stood there silently in this whole episode, with rapt attention. They also learned by watching this adult–child teaching and learning interaction attentively. They knew that it was not their place to speak either, as it was likely to be a repeated experience for them with their own parents at home.

Nevertheless, the four-year-old Taiwanese girl who listened carefully and patiently and then seized the right moment to challenge her aunt is also responded to by adults with due respect. Her aunt did not shut her up – in fact, she did not even criticize her for speaking up. Instead, she became a defendant by claiming to be a good young child herself. These examples illustrate that Chinese/East Asians' choice and preference to speak or not to speak are a matter of great sensitivity, sensibility, and skill to be cultivated in their culture. Unfortunately, in cross-cultural contexts of learning, the Chinese/East Asian reluctance to speak is often taken as lack of thought, disengagement, verbal ineptness, worse yet, inscrutableness, character flaw, or point-blank dishonesty. Not only does this view miss the point, but it breeds mistrust and causes harm to children and students from East Asian cultural backgrounds.

NOTES

1. See note 11 to Chapter 4.
2. See note 61 to Chapter 3.
3. Paulhus, D. L., Duncan, J. H., & Yik, M. S. M. (2002). Patterns of shyness in East-Asian and European-heritage students. *Journal of Research in Personality, 36,* 442–462.
4. See, for example, note 3 to this chapter; Fukuyama, M. A., & Greenfield, T. K. (1983). Dimensions of aggressiveness in an Asian-American student population. *Journal of Counseling Psychology, 30,* 429–432; Johnson, F. A., & Marsella, A. J. (1978). Different attitudes toward verbal behavior in students of Japanese and European ancestry. *Genetic Psychology Monographs, 97,* 43–76; and Klopf, D. W., & Cambra, R. E. (1979). Communication apprehension among college students in American, Australia, Japan, and Korea. *Journal of Counseling Psychology, 102,* 27–31.
5. Katriel, T., & Philipsen, G. (1981). "What we need is communication:" "Communication" as a cultural category in some American speech. *Communication Monographs, 48,* 301–317.
6. The whole psychotherapy as a healing process is predicated on the assumption that verbalizing one's memories, experiences, thoughts, and emotions is a process from mental illness to mental health. See Petrie, K. J., Booth, R. J., Pennebaker, J. W., & Davison, K. P. (1995). Disclosure of trauma and immune response to a hepatitis B vaccination program. *Journal of Counseling and Clinical Psychology, 63,* 787–792; and Frattaroli, J. (2006). Experimental disclosure and its moderators: A metaanalysis. *Psychological Bulletin, 132,* 823–865 for research and review of this topic.
7. See note 24 to Chapter 4.
8. Paulhus, D. L., & Morgan, K. L. (1997). Perceptions of intelligence in leaderless groups: Dynamic effects of shyness and acquaintance. *Journal of Personality*

and Social Psychology, 72, 581–591; Cheek, J. M., & Buss, A. H. (1981). Shyness and sociability. *Journal of Personality and Social Psychology, 41,* 330–339; Jones, W. H., & Carpenter, B. N. (1986). Shyness, social behavior and relations. In W. H. Jones, J. M. Cheek, & S. R. Briggs (Eds.), *Shyness: Perspectives on research and treatment* (pp. 227–238). New York: Plenum; and Traub, G. S. (1983). Correlations of shyness with depression, anxiety, and academic performance. *Psychological Reports, 52,* 849–850.

9. Goffman, E. (1981). *Frames of talk.* Philadelphia: University of Pennsylvania Press.

10. He, A. W. (2010). The language of ambiguity: Practices in Chinese heritage language classes. *Discourse Studies, 3,* 75–96.

11. McLean, B., & Elkind, P. (2004). *The smartest guys in the room: The amazing rise and scandalous fall of Enron.* New York: Portfolio Trade.

12. See note 56 to Chapter 6, p. 188.

13. Aeschylus (1996). *The Oresteia trilogy: Agamemnon, the Libation-Bearers and the Furies.* Mineola, NY: Dover.

14. Cooper, C. (2004). *Sights and sounds of the Athenian Court.* New York: Routledge.

15. Gluckman, M. (2006). *Politics, law and ritual in tribal society.* Piscataway, NJ: Aldine Transaction.

16. Li, X.-D., Sun, W.-Q., & Luo, G.-Z. (2010). 李行道孙文卿罗贯中集 [Collection of Li Xingdao, Sun Wenqing, and Luo Guanzhong]. Shangxi: People's Publishing House.

17. Todd, S. C. A. (2008). *Commentary on Lysias: Speeches 1–11.* Oxford: Oxford University Press.

18. Smith, R. M. (1995). *A new look at the canon of the Ten Attic Orators.* Mnemosyne 48.1.

19. Todd, S. C. A. (2000). *The Oratory of Classical Greece: Volume 2.* Austin: University of Texas Press.

20. Cowell, F. R. (1973). *Cicero and the Roman Republic* (5th ed.). New York: Penguin.

21. Plutarch (2009). *Plutarch's lives of Pericles & Fabius Maximus, Demosthenes & Cicero.* Ann Arbor: University of Michigan Library.

22. Guthrie, W. K. C. (1969). *History of Greek philosophy.* Cambridge: Cambridge University Press.

23. Aristotle (1992). *The art of rhetoric.* New York: Penguin.

24. Four years ago, our son was a sophomore in college and took a course on public speaking. He came home very excited after the first few classes and shared with us the concepts of "ethos," "pathos," and "logos." He showed us every speech he worked on that contained these three principles of persuasive speech.

25. Cicero (1986). *Cicero on oratory and orators.* [Trans. by J. S. Watson]. Carbondale: Southern Illinois University Press.

26. Quintilian (2002). *Orator's education, Volume I: Books 1–2.* [Trans. by D. A. Russell]. Cambridge, MA: Harvard University Press.

27. I am grateful to Becca Goldstein for sharing the Jewish tradition with me and for pointing to the reference of Fox, S., Scheffler, I., & Marom, D. (Eds.). (2003). *Visions of Jewish education.* New York: Cambridge University Press.

28. For example, the university where I teach does not have enough course offerings to freshmen and sophomores, frequently even juniors. Students have to wait until their senior year to get into a public speaking course.

29. Grice, H. P. (1975). Logic and conversation. In P. Cole & J. L. Morgan (Eds.), *Syntax and semantics: Vol. 3. Speech acts* (p. 45). New York: Academic Press.

30. Lucy, J. A. (1992). *Language diversity and thought: A reformulation of the linguistic relativity hypothesis*. New York: Cambridge University Press.

31. Bilbow, G. T. (1997). Cross-cultural impression management in the multicultural workplace: The special case of Hong Kong. *Journal of Pragmatics, 28*, 461–487; Lewis, M. (1993). The development of deception. In M. Lewis & C. Saarni (Eds.), *Lying and deception in everyday life* (pp. 106–125). New York: Guilford; and Lee, K., Cameron, C. A., Xu, F., Fu, G.-Y., & Board, J. (1997). Chinese and Canadian children's evaluations of lying and truth telling: Similarities and differences in the context of pro- and antisocial behaviors. *Child Development, 68*(5), 924–934.

32. See the third reference in note 31 to this chapter; and Lee, K., Xu, F., Fu, G., Cameron, C. A., & Chen, S. (2001). Taiwan and Mainland Chinese and Canadian children's categorization and evaluation of lie- and truth-telling: A modest effect. *British Journal of Developmental Psychology, 19*, 525–542.

33. Yum, J. O. (1991). The impact of Confucianism on interpersonal relationships and communication patterns in East Asia. In L. A. Samovar & R. E. Porter (Eds.), *Intercultural communication: A reader* (pp. 66–78). Belmont, CA: Wadsworth.

34. See the first reference in note 31 to this chapter.

35. See the first reference in note 31 to this chapter.

36. Gottman, J. M. (1993). How children become friends. *Monograph of the Society for Research in Child Development, 48*(3, Serial No. 201).

37. See the first reference in note 31 to this chapter, and note 33 to this chapter.

38. Lam, S.-F., Law, Y.-K., & Shum, M. S.-K. (2009). Classroom discourse analysis and educational outcomes in the era of education reform. *British Journal of Educational Psychology, 79*, 617–641; Gillies, R. M. (2006). Teachers' and students' verbal behaviours during cooperative and small-group learning. *British Journal of Educational Psychology, 76*, 271–287; and Hogan, K., Nastasi, B. K., & Pressley, M. (2000). Discourse patterns collaborative scientific reasoning in peer and teacher-guided discussion. *Cognition and Instruction, 17*, 379–432. Also see Alexander, R. (2000). *Culture & pedagogy: International comparison in primary education*. Oxford: Blackwell for his comprehensive research on classroom discourse across five cultures.

39. See note 38 to this chapter; note 14 to Chapter 4; and Webb, N. M., Franke, M. L., Ing, M., Chan, A., De. T., Freund, D. et al. (2008). The role of teacher instructional practices in student collaborations. *Contemporary Educational Psychology, 33*, 360–381.

40. Hewitt, R., & Inghilleri, M. (1993). Oracy in the Classroom: Policy, pedagogy, and group oral work. *Anthropology & Education Quarterly, 24*(4), 308–317, p. 310. Also see Lisa Delpit calls this learning mastery of the "code of power" in Delpit, L. D. (1995). *Other people's children: Cultural conflict in the classroom*. New York: The New Press.

41. See Tobin, J., Hsueh, Y., & Karasawa, M. (2009). *Preschool in three cultures revisited: China, Japan, and United States.* Chicago: University of Chicago Press for vivid examples in American preschools.

42. See the first reference in note 40 and the last reference in note 38 to this chapter.

43. Interestingly, both White and Afro-Caribbean children were keenly aware that the kind of oracy they were learning in school requiring disagreement and argumentation about a topic was separate from their real-life talk where cooperation and agreement reigned. Even after their formal debate in class, the children would try to "repair" their disagreement and resume the "cooperative" imperative that governed their verbal interaction outside of school.

44. O'Connor, M. C., & Michaels, S. (1993). Aligning academic task and participation status through revoicing: Analysis of a classroom discourse strategy. *Anthropology & Education Quarterly, 24*(4), 318–335.

45. Goodwin, M. H. (1990). *He-said-she-said: Talk as social organization among Black children.* Bloomington: Indiana University Press.

46. See note 9 to this chapter.

47. See note 44 to this chapter, p. 322.

48. See note 44 to this chapter, p. 327.

49. Caudhill, W., & Weinstein, H. (1969). Maternal care and infant behavior in Japan and America. *Psychiatry, 32,* 12–43; Minami, M. (1994). English and Japanese: A cross-cultural comparison parental styles of narrative elicitation. *Issues in Applies Linguistics, 5,* 383–407; and Murase, T., Dale, P. S., Ogura, T., Yamashita, Y., & Mahieu, A. (2005). Mother–child conversation during joint picture book reading in Japan and the USA. *First Language, 25,* 197–218.

50. Heath, S. B. (1983). *Ways with words: Language, life, and work in communities and classrooms.* New York: Cambridge University Press.

51. See note 6 to Chapter 7.

52. See note 6 to Chapter 7; and the third and fourth references in note 7 to Chapter 7.

53. See note 74 to Chapter 2.

54. Liu, Y.-M. (2004). "Nothing can be accomplished if the speech does not sound agreeable": Rhetoric and the invention of classical Chinese discourse. In C. S. Lipson & R. A. Binkley (Eds.), *Rhetoric before and beyond the Greeks* (pp. 147–164). Albany: State University of New York Press.

55. See note 79 to Chapter 2.

56. See note 5 to Chapter 2, 1.3.

57. Xu, G. Q. (2004). The use of eloquence: The Confucian perspective. In C. S. Lipson & R. A. Binkley (Eds.), *Rhetoric before and beyond the Greeks* (pp. 115–130). Albany: State University of New York Press, p. 118.

58. See note 5 to Chapter 2, 16.1 and 15.11.

59. See note 5 to Chapter 2, 17.18.

60. See note 79 to Chapter 2, p. 16.

61. See note 5 to Chapter 2, 16.5.

62. "Chariots" is a reference to the size of a state during the Spring and Autumn and Warring State periods (722–221 BCE). A chariot is a military vehicle with

four horses and three soldiers. "A thousand chariots" indicates a midsize state. Retrieved November 5, 2010 from http://www.cxgjdq.com/cy/ZmZzZm8.html

63. See note 5 to Chapter 2, 11.26.

64. See note 5 to Chapter 2, 11.26.

65. See note 5 to Chapter 2, pp. 46–48. The authors argue that *Heaven* as a traditional translation of *tian* is inaccurate because *Heaven* denotes the Judeo-Christian concept, but this is not the meaning by *tian*. They decided not to translate this term for *the Analects*. I concur with the authors but have chosen to use *Heaven* here for convenience.

66. See note 62 to Chapter 2. Jin Li's translation.

67. See note 5 to Chapter 2, 17.19.

68. See note 5 to Chapter 2, p. 122.

69. Lyon, A. (2004). Confucian silence and remonstration: A basis for deliberation? In C. S. Lipson & R. A. Binkley (Eds.), *Rhetoric before and beyond the Greeks* (pp. 131–145). Albany: State University of New York Press, p. 137.

70. See note 5 to Chapter 2, 2.13, 4.24, and 4.22. Also see 14.27, I.14, 12.3, and 13.20.

71. See note 69 to this chapter.

72. See note 5 to Chapter 2, 12.1.

73. See note 5 to Chapter 2, 8.4, 16.6, and 10.1.

74. See note 69 to this chapter, p. 136.

75. See note 69 to this chapter, pp. 136–137.

76. See the first reference in note 75 to Chapter 2; and Ishii, S., & Bruneau, T. (1994). Silence and silences in cross-cultural perspective: Japan and the United States. In L. A. Samovar & R. E. Porter (Eds.), *Intercultural communication: A reader* (7th ed.) (pp. 246–251). Belmont, CA: Wadsworth for valued silence in contemporary Japanese culture.

77. Cheng, C.-Y. (1987). Chinese philosophy and contemporary human communication theory. In L. Kincaid (Ed.), *Communication theory: Eastern and Western perspectives* (pp. 23–43). San Diego, CA: Academic Press.

78. See note 91 to Chapter 6.

79. Paulhus, D. L., Hendin, H., & Shaver, P. R. (2001). European vs. Asian heritage differences in personality: Narcissism, modesty, and self-construal. Unpublished manuscript; and McCrae, R. R., Yik, M. S. M., Trapnell, P. D., Bond, M. H., & Paulhus, D. L. (1998). Interpreting personality profiles across cultures: Bilingual, acculturation, and peer-rating studies of Chinese undergraduates. *Journal of Personality and Social Psychology, 74*, 1041–1055.

80. See the first reference in note 75 to Chapter 2.

81. Li, J., & Sklar, S. (2011). To speak or not to speak: European American eagerness versus Chinese reluctance. Manuscript in preparation.

82. Gao, G. (1998a). "Don't take my word for it:" Understanding Chinese speaking practices. *International Journal of Intercultural Relations, 22*, 163–186; and Chang, H. C. (1999). The "well-defined" is "ambiguous:" Indeterminacy in Chinese conversation. *Journal of Pragmatics, 31*, 535–556.

83. See the Introduction to the *Analects of Confucius* in note 5 to Chapter 2.

84. See reference in note 47 to Chapter 2.

85. More detailed discussion on Asian listenership in later sections.

86. See note 82 to this chapter.

87. Liu, I.-M. (1986). Chinese cognition. In M. H. Bond (Ed.), *The psychology of Chinese people* (pp. 73–105). Hong Kong: Oxford University Press.

88. See, for example, the second and third references in note 4 to this chapter.

89. Smith, D. (1991). Children of China: An inquiry into the relationship between Chinese family life and academic achievement in modern Taiwan. *Asian Culture Quarterly, 14*(1), 1–29.

90. Sue, D., Sue, D. M., & Ino, S. (1990). Assertiveness and social anxiety in Chinese-American women. *Journal of Psychology, 124,* 155–163.

91. Liberman, K. (1994). Asian student perspectives on American University instruction. *International Journal of Intercultural Relations, 18,* 173–192. Also see Liu, J. (2002). Negotiating silence in American classrooms: Three Chinese cases. *Language and intercultural communication, 2*(1), 37–54 for Chinese graduate students' showing respect toward professors by not speaking in U.S. classrooms.

92. See note 81 to this chapter.

93. Zane, N. W., Sue, S., Hu, L.-T., & Kwon, J.-H. (1991). Asian-American assertion: A social learning analysis of cultural differences. *Journal of Counseling Psychology, 38,* 63–70.

94. See note 81 to this chapter.

95. Triandis, H. C. (1995). *Individualism and collectivism.* Boulder, CO: Westview.

96. See the first reference in note 82 to this chapter and Yang, Y.-Y. (2001). '自己人': 一項有關中國人關系分類的個案研究 ['One of us': A case study on the classification of Chinese guanxi]. *Indigenous Psychological Research in Chinese Societies, 13,* 277–316.

97. See the third reference in note 1 to Chapter 2.

98. Yang, Y.-Y. (2001). 自己人: 從中國人情感格局看婆媳關系 [Zijiren: From Chinese affection pattern to understanding the relation between mother-in-laws and daughter-in-laws]. *Indigenous Psychological Research in Chinese Societies, 16,* 1–39.

99. See note 3 to this chapter.

100. See note 93 to this chapter.

101. See the first reference in note 82 to this chapter.

102. See the second reference in note 51 to Chapter 2; note 93 to this chapter; Ting-Toomey, S. (Ed.) (1994). *The challenge of facework: Cross-cultural and interpersonal issues.* Albany: State University of New York Press; and Gao, G. (1998b). An initial analysis of the effects of face and concern for "other" in Chinese interpersonal communication. *International Journal of Intercultural Relations, 22*(4), 467–482.

103. See note 80 to Chapter 2; and the second reference in note 82 to this chapter.

104. See the first reference in note 82 to this chapter.

105. See note 90 to this chapter.

106. See note 93 to this chapter.

107. See note 3 to this chapter.

108. See note 60 to Chapter 4; and Kim, H. S. (2008). Culture and the cognitive and neuroendocrine responses to speech. *Journal of Personality and Social Psychology, 94* (1), 32–47.

109. Yang, S.-Y., & Sternberg, R. J. (1997). Taiwanese Chinese people's conceptions of intelligence. *Intelligence, 25*(1), 21–29.

110. See note 24 to Chapter 4.

111. See the second reference in note 76 to this chapter; the second reference in note 80 to Chapter 2; and Azuma, H. (1986). Why study child development in Japan? In H. Stevenson, H. Azuma, & K. Hakuta (Eds.), *Child development and education in Japan* (pp. 3–12). New York: Freeman.

112. See note 82 to this chapter; Young, L. W. L. (1982). Inscrutability revisited. In J. J. Cumpez (Ed.), *Language and social identity* (pp. 72–84). Cambridge: Cambridge University Press; and Gudykunst, W. B., & Ting-Toomey, S. (1988). *Culture and interpersonal communication*. Newbury Park, CA: Sage.

113. See note 112 to this chapter.

114. See note 10 to this chapter.

115. See the second reference in note 82 to this chapter.

116. See the first reference in note 29 to Chapter 2; and note 53 to Chapter 5.

117. See notes 33 and 77 to this chapter.

118. See note 10 to this chapter.

119. See the fourth references in note 102 to this chapter; the third reference in note 112 to this chapter; and Young, L. W. L. (1994). *Crosstalk and culture in Sino-American communication*. New York: Cambridge University Press.

120. See note 82 to this chapter.

121. See the first reference in note 82 to this chapter, p. 180. In the third reference in note 111 to this chapter, Azuma discusses that speaking directly and sharply is considered arrogant and rude in Japanese culture.

122. See the second reference in note 82 to this chapter.

123. Fung, H., Miller, P. J., & Lin, L. C. (2004). Listening is active: Lessons from the narrative practices of Taiwanese families. In M. W. Pratt & B. E. Fiese (Eds.), *Family stories and the life course: Across time and generations* (pp. 303–323). Mahwah, NJ: Erlbaum; and Miller, P. J., Fung, H., Lin, S., Chen, E. C.-H., & Boldt, B. R. (2012). How socialization happens on the ground: Narrative practices as alternate socializing pathways in Taiwanese and European-American families. Monographs of the society for research in child development, 77(1, Serial No. 302). Boston, MA: Wiley-Blackwell.

124. See note 33 to this chapter; and the first reference in note 82 to this chapter.

125. See the first reference in note 82 to this chapter, pp. 169–170.

126. Li, J. (1997). Creativity in horizontal and vertical domains. *Creativity Research Journal, 10*, 107–132.

127. This phrase came from Confucius' words from the *Analects*, providing testimony for the enduring influence of Confucius.

128. See the first reference in note 82 to this chapter, pp. 169–170.

129. See note 5 to Chapter 2, p. 75.

130. See the first reference in note 123 to this chapter, pp. 134–135.

131. See note 10 to this chapter.

132. See the second reference in note 29 to Chapter 4; Huang, R.-J., & Leung, K. S. F. (2004). Cracking the paradox of Chinese learners: Looking into the mathematics classrooms in Hong Kong and Shanghai. In L.-H. Fan, N.-Y. Wong, J.-F. Cai, S.-Q. Li, & T.-Y. Tso (Eds.), *How Chinese learn mathematics: Perspectives from insiders* (pp. 348–381). Singapore: World Scientific; and Lopez-Real, F., Mok, A. C. I., Leung, K. S. F., & Marton, F. (2004). Identifying a pattern of teaching:

An analysis of a Shanghai teacher's lessons. In L.-H. Fan, N.-Y. Wong, J.-F. Cai, S.-Q. Li, & T.-Y. Tso (Eds.), *How Chinese learn mathematics: Perspectives from insiders* (pp. 382–412). Singapore: World Scientific.

133. See the second reference in note 29 to Chapter 4.
134. See note 132 to this chapter.
135. See this discussion in the first part of Chapter 3.
136. Winner, E. (1989). How can Chinese children draw so well? *Journal of Aesthetic Education, 23*(1), 65–84.
137. See note 132 to this chapter.
138. See the third reference in note 29 to Chapter 3.
139. See the fifth reference in note 29 to Chapter 4, p. 125.
140. See the fifth reference in note 29 to Chapter 4.
141. See note 49 to this chapter.
142. Kagan, J., Kearsley, R. B., & Zelazo, P. R. (1977). The effects of infant daycare on psychological development. *Evaluation Quarterly, 1*, 109–142; and Swann, Jr., W. B., & Rentfrow, P. J. (2001). Blirtatiousness: Cognitive, behavioral, and physiological consequences of rapid responding. *Journal of Personality and Social Psychology, 81*, 1160–1175.
143. See note 89 to this chapter.

9

Implications for the Changing Landscape of Learning

As the natural flux of human history proceeds, the current world is always different from the one just passed, no matter how people may define the current world and past worlds. All signs indicate, however, that the very current world is not only as much in flux as any prior world, but the pace of change is unprecedentally fast. Change is taking place on many fronts, affecting virtually every aspect of human life. No doubt, with the advent of science and technology, particularly communication technology, the world is experiencing accelerated and often unpredictable change. The term that is used to capture this large-scale change is globalization. Political change is seen in the democratization of nations, social change in everyday life within nations, economic change in the cross-nation interdependency, scientific/technological change in the explosion of knowledge and digitization of the world, and, pessimistically, environmental change in the direction of destruction. It is not surprising that many find this kind of change disorienting and dizzying. The fragility and ephemeral nature of life are felt more than ever before.

GLOBAL MASSIVE MIGRATION

As a result of all these changes, the world is witnessing massive population migration.[1] Two trends of this migration have been observed in recent decades. First is the within-nation migration owing to economic/social/political development. For example, more than 100 million migrant workers in China have been leaving farming to rush to cities to find work, which is visible in all the new construction that has taken place in China over the past thirty years. These migrant workers surely make better wages than they did tilling the land their ancestors have tilled for millennia. Many not only migrate to nearby cities, but travel afar to seek greater economic reward.[2]

The second trend, much more massive, is the cross-nation migration and immigration (the former may not seek to settle down in the new culture but the latter may). The motivation for such massive global migration is driven by the same forces as those within nation.[3]

As part of the second trend, for example, we are seeing a surge of international students coming from many countries, especially newly emerging economies such as China and India, to the West,[4] particularly the United States. These students, now able to afford better education,[5] not only seek traditional graduate training; many forego their countries' undergraduate and even high school education and enroll abroad instead. At the same time, and for the first time in history, an increasing number of students from the West, South America, Africa, and Middle East go to countries such as China to study. Many Western people now work in non-Western countries. Without any doubt, these trends have led to unmatched cultural exchange. As a case in point, the remote town where I took my European-American colleague to study rural Chinese children's cognitive development in late December 2004 was, to our shock, inundated with Christmas decorations and music all over their streets.

Consequently, few children today grow up in a self-contained cultural bubble, or in the same place, speaking the same local tongue and interacting with familiar people. More and more, children are born in one place and then are moved to another. Many reside in multiple places and speak multiple languages before reaching adulthood.[6] Immigrant families represent the highest-growing population group in the United States and Europe, for example. The new U.S. census data show that the nation's Hispanic population has reached more than 50 million (16.3 percent of the total population) – an increase of 43 percent from 2000 to 2010. Although the Asian-American population remains relatively small (about 15 million, or 4.8 percent of the total population), it witnessed the fastest increase of 43.3 percent for the same period. These changes were primarily a result of the influx of new immigrants, compared to increases among nonimmigrant European-American and other ethnic populations.[7] Additionally, we are observing new migration patterns such as "cyclical migrants," including Mexican labor migrants who move across borders between rural and urban residences. Moreover, families may reside in their host culture for a number of years and then return to their home culture, and to continue to alternate their residence between the two cultures. For this reason, they have acquired the label "transnational families."[8] Likewise, adolescent-aged students who "drop" from Asian airplanes to attend Western high schools are the new "parachute children."[9] Of course, there are millions of undocumented, either being shipped into the target land without a legal status or remaining in the land of immigration beyond their visa allowance.[10]

INEVITABLE CULTURAL MERGING

The more frequent and profound exchange among cultures is likely to enable them to borrow ideas, linguistic expressions, aesthetics, strategies, and more effective ways to work and to manage their own lives. Indeed, we see these trends of cultural merging, or hybridization, for example, in food production and consumption (e.g., sushi restaurants now have proliferated across North America and Europe), fashion design (Asian motifs are increasingly noticeable), and fitness programs (e.g., karate studios are just around the corner in practically any U.S. town). Of course, as noted in previous chapters, East Asia for at least the past 150 years has sought with great effort to adopt many aspects of the West. Science and democracy are two main pursuits that not only have never subsided, but actually have intensified. East Asian educational systems were initially eager but clumsy copies of the American and European education systems, which only gave the appearance of Western practice. Today, they are mandating Western-style practice (e.g., emulating Western children's free exploration and creativity on the school ground).[11]

As cultural exchange deepens, we have reasons to believe that cultural differences may one day disappear and that we all will reemerge as one culture under the sun. This is not a far-fetched thought, but was in fact (still is) one that guided the quick assimilation policy (e.g., English-only school instruction for Native-American children and quick transitional bilingual program in school so that children of non-English-speaking backgrounds could be assimilated into American culture).[12] Others have proposed this idea from the perspective of social cohesion that is seen as central to society.[13] Yet, still others see a trend that the world's diverse peoples may soon strive to become all European- and European-American-like,[14] or, to borrow a recent catchy acronym, WEIRD (white, educated, industrialized, rich, democratic) folks.[15]

VARIATIONS REMAIN DESPITE DEEPENING CULTURAL EXCHANGE

Undeniably, all the broadening and deepening cultural exchange will lead to more learning among peoples and cultures as a whole. Doing so is both necessary and advantageous for everyone. However, I join many researchers in believing that the cliché of the salad bowl analogy in the United States is actually not that cliché after all. Perhaps the melting pot is also correct in some way, but only superficially and to the extent that people from different cultures can acculturate quite successfully. But such acculturative success, I venture to say, is *acculturated* change without fundamentally altering people's *enculturated* core if enculturation takes place before acculturation (e.g., adults relocate from one culture to another). Research evidence reviewed in this book suggests that the basic patterns of cultural learning models are tenacious and unlikely to melt in grand unification.

To my mind, the strongest support for this claim comes from two related lines of research. First is the fact that basic values and beliefs are still endorsed and behavior guided thereby in cultures that have gone through much of their political, social, and economic transformation, for example, Japan, Korea, and Taiwan, Hong Kong, Singapore, and now China. These societies enjoy comparably high levels of education of their populace. They are certainly industrialized and commercialized, frequently even more so than the West (one needs only to go to Hong Kong to see the complete dominance of commercial life!). Because they have strong economies, they are consequentially rich, reaping expected benefits from their economic achievement. And finally, many of these societies are democratic, having adopted the Western-style political system. The existence of these societies provides perfect testing sites for the enduring power of culture, because researchers do not even need to worry about comparability. Any confounding effects stemming from the differences in socioeconomic level, length of education, and political systems are naturally controlled for. This means that if two groups share much of their background, but they still differ in thinking, feeling, and behavior, then the shared background cannot be the explanation of differences. Culture must be the explanation. Indeed, despite all these melting characteristics, comparative research on Western and East Asian psychology, child development, and education has overwhelmingly demonstrated very large and persistent cultural variations that show no signs of disappearing.[16] This evidence casts doubt directly on the forecast that all culturally diverse people would one day become alike under one culture, specifically more like Westerners. As a good example, we observe that China now has a national award called the "Award for Moving China," which is granted to people who make great contributions to society, but also to exemplars of filial piety.[17] Chinese applications to UNESCO designed to preserve their tangible (temples, archeological sites) and intangible (dance, music, philosophy) cultural heritage are at a record high. On a more personal level, we also see that more and more Chinese children express their filial piety to their parents through more expensive means such as taking them on Caribbean cruises instead of cooking meals for them. Having more resources may enable people to express their culturally formed desires and values more readily, conveniently, and frequently. Cultural values may, surprisingly, be perpetuated in this fashion.

The second support for the persistence of fundamental cultural values comes from the mosaic nature of societies with high levels of diversity. The United States and other traditional immigrant societies such as Canada and Australia offer good examples. Although their original immigrant population is from European heritage, and still the majority, the rest of their population – particularly the fastest-increasing sector – consists of many ethnicities. However, just because diverse people live together and acquire the same nationality and common language does not mean that they *culturally* and *ethnically* identify themselves with the majority's cultural heritage. In fact, great effort is made by each mosaic group to retain their own unique cultural heritage. For such people, a bicultural existence is the norm.[18]

Relatedly, research on immigrants also overwhelmingly documents the persistence of home cultural heritage.[19] This pertains not only to the current first and second generations, but to those of later generations as the case of fifth and sixth generations of Chinese Americans demonstrate. Research on the learning beliefs of third and fourth generations of Japanese Americans shows strong endorsement of hard work and other related learning virtues despite much acculturation into mainstream social norms (e.g., communication with school).[20] Although most research on immigrant population addresses non-European groups, the same pattern, with little doubt, applies to European immigrants as well. For example, European-American people are more extreme than Europeans in many domains of psychology such as independence, freedom, patriotism, litigation, and philanthropy.[21] These converging research findings clearly show that the European-American people who immigrated to America did not form an entirely different culture by merging with Native Americans, but instead retained much of their European heritage, most emphatically.

Cultural Values Live on in Individual Members

In light of the aforementioned evidence, one is compelled to ask why cultures tend to endure more than to collapse into one another despite such unprecedented and accelerated cultural exchange? As far as I can identify, there are two large, related reasons for cultural endurance. First, as cultural psychologists have theorized and documented, cultural models live on because they enter into the minds of individual cultural members by the process of enculturation/socialization.[22] This process is the one of upbringing. Because of the intense parent–child bonds, these interactions result inevitably in the strong internalized beliefs that individual cultural members hold.[23] So long as cultural members continue to exist from generation to generation, cultural models are likely to survive in the collective.

But the critical efficacy enabling cultural endurance lies in the moment when individual cultural members become *parents*. By assuming the parental role, cultural members gain culturally acknowledged and often explicitly granted (and legally privileged) prerogative to guide/instruct their children. But more importantly, as discussed in Chapter 7, these cultural members become willing and tireless executors of their culture's models. They do so because of their own beliefs and convictions. Although parents are largely unaware of their role in cultural transmission, they are the most effective and successful promoters of their cultural models. In this fashion, cultural reproduction is ensured and perpetuated.

What happens when adults and children encounter different and competing cultural values as globalization is surely to cause? Cultures that have a long history of such challenges may have already built effective fences and strategies to deal with such challenges.[24] These cultures have essentially found a way to retain their core values while accepting the nonthreatening values from the outside. When faced with threats, they may actively reject the directly contradictory beliefs and ideas outright or ignore them altogether. For example, when Western painting was first introduced to China, it was rejected by Chinese ink-and-brush painters because Western aesthetics was totally incommensurable with Chinese aesthetics ("crafty" was the judgment cast on Western painting; thus, Giuseppe Castiglione, 1688–1766 – known in Chinese as 郎世寧 – an Italian missionary, later Chinese court painter, faced rejection for his effort to combine both painting styles).[25] Now, Chinese painting continues to thrive as the traditional form while Western paining is accepted in China as a separate realm of aesthetics. However, the more compatible beliefs may be absorbed, adopted, and modified because they do not pose a threat to the existing cultural models. For example, the Western concept of efficiency in industry sat well with East Asian cultures because the latter have a similar history and inclination to seek better ways to do things. In extreme cases, a culture may decide to adopt life-altering ideas from the outside (e.g., democracy, Marxism). Many East Asian cultures witnessed such transitions during the turn of the nineteenth and twentieth centuries. These undoubtedly painful political and social struggles stood a chance of succeeding only if external influence turned into internal forces that demanded change.[26]

Cultural change notwithstanding, if a foreign idea is only adopted by assimilation (meaning superficial change), it is unlikely to alter the existing belief system fundamentally simply because the new idea is merely assimilated into a large and more established system. Quite the contrary, such absorption may even serve to strengthen the original culture, perfecting it rather than altering it qualitatively. If so, such modifications end up being more peripheral than central, more superficial than profound. These adaptive strategies in the face of cultural exchange are also transmitted to children along with cultural core values. As a result, children are also likely to grow up with defensive capacity. This explains why, despite the destructive forces of Cultural Revolution, today's Chinese children still learn Confucian values because they receive day-to-day Confucian socialization at home. The process also helps explain why despite their long assimilation into American culture, third and fourth generations of Japanese Americans still hold on to their basic learning virtues.[27]

Cultural Values Are Intertwined with Individuals' Identity

The second large reason for persisting cultural values is that individual beliefs are intimately connected to their identity. In a fast-changing world, we observe that some things are indeed shed more willingly and even purposefully by people. Nonetheless, other things are gripped more tightly and guarded well by the same people. Whereas the former is expected, the latter, to many, is surprising. For example, when I first bumped into Amish people in Western rural Pennsylvania in the 1980s, I was in utter disbelief that there are such people in the United States. I thought that I went back almost 1,600 years and treaded into the Land of Peach Blossoms (桃花源記) as a fictitious place, a utopia written by the Chinese poet/writer Tao Yuan-ming in 421 CE.[28] The existence of groups such as the Amish in the deep swirl of globalization attests to the fact that many, if not all, cultural groups hold on to their cultural values tightly.

Those elements of the original culture that are jettisoned are likely to be aspects not fitting their present adaptation. For example, Chinese-style architecture for homes on a large lot with sets of rectangle-shaped courtyards and open space in between simply cannot continue because of rapid population growth, even though its architectural aesthetics is a unique and significant achievement in human history. The Western invention of skyscrapers, with hundreds of apartment units that take much less land and can accommodate many more families, is now the standard home architecture. But even so, the Chinese also strive to preserve their courtyard architecture and other cultural achievements such as Suzhou gardens as a cultural symbol through the official protection of the UNESCO.

Those things that people grip more tightly are a different story. These are the time-tested but also culture-specific values that are indispensible and *dear* to the people. These are likely elements that enter the core of people's cultural and ethnic identity. For example, Taiwan, after decades of not requiring schoolchildren to study Confucian texts (presumably in response of internal struggles of tradition and modernity), recently announced a new educational policy proposal that requires all high school students to take one class per week to read Confucian texts. Part of the reason for such a requirement is for improving Taiwanese children's "declined" moral education, as seen in the deteriorated student–teacher relationships and increasing bullying in school.[29] Even China, after denouncing Confucian values during the Cultural Revolution (1966–1976) and several decades of ambivalent exploration into the past, somewhat clandestinely erected (in early 2011) a large Confucius statue on its Tian An Men Square, the utmost political center of China, both physically and symbolically. They now also confidently put Confucian excerpts in their language arts curriculum for their nine-year compulsory education.[30] Furthermore, they issued national economic and social policies that ring a definitive Confucian tone such as "peaceful and prosperous society" (小康社會), ensuring that every family has sufficient food, shelter, and secure and peaceful life. This was a utopia as envisioned by the great sages of Chinese culture thousands of years ago but was never possible to achieve. Now, after several decades of effort, this utopia (at least as it was outlined by the Chinese government) has been, surprisingly, achieved by China.[31] When China announced this national goal back in 1982, it resonated well with people, and subsequently the whole society engaged in concerted effort to achieve this goal. I argue that this type of concerted effort is possible because the goal strikes a deep harmonious chord with long-held cultural beliefs and desires that individual members share.

The development of children's cultural/ethnic identity in a multicultural or immigrant context offers a further example. It is also a well-known phenomenon that overseas Chinese (and, for that matter, other immigrant groups regardless of their cultural origin) are more traditional in some ways than those living in China proper. How can this be? How can people who live in a culture that demands them to become more assimilated into the host culture, like the United States, for example, wind up being more traditional than folks who continue to live in their native culture and, for the most part, never had a day living abroad? To put this contrast more sharply, Asian people who grow up in the United States, a culture that has very different values that frequently contradict Asian home values, uphold more Chinese traditional values than their fast-changing Chinese contemporaries in China. Yet, it has been repeatedly observed that Asian Americans retain their cultural values in ways that Chinese in Taiwan, Hong Kong, and China may find outdated, kitsch, and tacky (俗氣 or 土氣), particularly among the motherland youth who tend to gravitate toward vogue and break away from tradition.[32]

The answer to this puzzling phenomenon lies in the fact that to the extent that every human being develops and needs to come to terms with his or her identity, cultural models continue to serve as sources and resources for immigrant children's identity development. Those who left their native culture and settled in a new place have nothing to rely on but the cultural models they took with them. Whatever they have is the model they use to cope with their new adaptation and to rear their children (unlike the early waves of immigrants, many current immigrants also maintain ties to their home culture thanks to the advancement of communication technology. Such effort affords them renewed sources and resources from their home cultures). Some cultural elements they brought with them originally may prove to be irrelevant to their new lives, and thus may be abandoned. But what defines who they are, distinguishes them from other groups, connects them back to their ancestral lineage, and what they do best lie at the very core of their sociocultural existence, their identity, and is therefore unlikely to be discarded.

There is a large body of research on human identity and its development. Culture and ethnicity play an unquestionable role in shaping human identity. During psychology's infancy, the great American psychologist William James identified two mutually constitutive perspectives of human self: the "I-self" and the "Me-self."[33] In his theory, the I-self is the knower, the side that does the recognizing, observing, judging, forming goals, and taking action for the self. The Me-self is what is known about the self. It is the content of the self-description and self-characterization. To use a more current metaphor that captures the distinction, the I-Self is the author or storyteller whereas the Me-Self is the character in the story itself.[34]

Clearly, culture influences both sides of self-development. However, culture's role may weigh more heavily on the I-Self within three dimensions: self-continuity, self-distinctness, and self-agency.[35] Self-continuity is the sense that we are the same persons over time, even though we all grow and change throughout our lives. For those who live in a culture that is penetrated by a much larger and powerful culture and faced with difficulties of maintaining their own culture, such as Native Americans living on reservations, their children's challenged sense of self-continuity can lead to grave consequences.[36] Similarly, for those who are enculturated in one culture and then move to another to be further acculturated, their sense of continuity may also face challenges. All ethnic groups strive to maintain their sense of continuity by actively teaching their home culture's values to their children. Retaining one's cultural/ethnic identity is a serious developmental task for such children[37] and has been repeatedly documented to be significant protective factor for them.[38]

Self-distinctness is the sense that, despite commonly shared human characteristics, we strive to retain our unique quality as a cultural group. For this reason, we observe that unique cultural values along with the more visible markers such as language, food, traditional garment, arts, and festivals of a given culture are clear targets of distinctness. Children appropriate such distinctness as their own as they grow up. Finally, self-agency is the sense that we are the cause of our thoughts, actions, effectiveness, and achievement. Things a culture is said to excel at may be the most relevant feedback for self-agency. Children are more likely to be taught such skills, and in turn perpetuate the excellence of that culture. For example, Asian movie makers know that their martial arts movies are recognized throughout the world. It does not surprise anyone that *Crouching Tiger, Hidden Dragon* would be made by a Chinese movie maker, and made well. These three core components of self as shaped by culture give rise to individuals' sense of cultural/ ethnic belonging and pride. Research has shown that this identity-shaping source of cultural/ethnic belonging and pride is essential in the development of minority and immigrant children.[39]

LEARNING BELIEFS AS PART OF ONE'S IDENTITY

Because children develop learning beliefs early on, first under parental socialization and later under the joint socialization of parents and school, culturally informed learning beliefs are part of children's identity. The degree to which learning beliefs are integrated into children's identity should reflect the degree of the overall importance that a given culture attaches to learning. As reviewed in this book, learning beliefs differ from culture to culture, such as purpose of learning, how to self-express in the West, and how not to speak in social contexts in East Asia. We have reason to believe that the more complex the skills children are required to learn in a given culture, the more their learning beliefs matter to their identity. This argument rests on a simple assumption: the more complex skills children are required to learn, the more *time* they will spend on such learning. When a person spends most of his or her time doing one kind of activity, that activity is bound to be of high importance. Currently, owing to compulsory education, school learning in the West, Asia, and most other cultures in the world has reached this level of importance for learning. The relative seriousness is perhaps reflected in the length of the school day and school year, and the amount of homework students are required to complete.

It is true that not all children take school learning as their most important activity, despite the fact that their cultures may hold such a view. But many children do, perhaps not initially, but gradually when they take on their culture's view as their own. They do so also because their learning beliefs serve them well, enabling them to achieve better and consequently receive recognition from their culture. If learning models/beliefs did not have any efficacy and real benefit, they would have been abandoned by the culture. Based on research, learning with a virtue orientation certainly assumes the utmost importance for most East Asian children and families, but the same is also true for many children and families of Western and other cultural groups according to their own cultural heritages. For these children, learning occupies a central place in their identity. Once a part of one's identity, culturally informed learning beliefs will continue to guide that person's thinking, feeling, and behavior throughout his or her life.

Viewed from this perspective, the two large reasons identified for maintaining cultural values are quite related. When children are young, they are socialized by parents and their larger social world in accordance with parental beliefs and convictions that are informed by their cultural learning models. As internalization continues, these values become part of the children's mindset as they are growing up, and are eventually integrated as part of their identity. When they mature and become parents themselves, they repeat the same cycle in childrearing, thus renewing their cultural models.

In sum, although globalization is accelerating and cultural mixing is expanding, cultural learning models are unlikely to disappear or collapse into one grand global consilience.[40] Instead, different learning models will continue to survive and revive across different groups, creating the ever-widening mosaic landscape.

CHALLENGES IN CHILD DEVELOPMENT AND EDUCATION IN EAST ASIA

The force of cultural retention and the force of cultural mixing lead to inevitable tension that confronts childrearing and education. In a fast-changing world, it is unavoidable for children in any culture that is open to the outside world to be exposed to values other than those of their native culture. Many cultures are also actively seeking and borrowing educational concepts and practices from other cultures and intentionally subject their children to such mixed learning. This even happens within cultures with mostly homogenous population, such as China.[41] I recall being asked a few years ago to give workshops to school teachers in China on how to foster creativity in Chinese children. I gave an example of how my own son as an elementary school student in an American private school was asked to pretend to be a plant in the garden. His learning was to document how he as this plant grew and thus to observe the plant everyday to describe its growth. It was a scientific as well as a literary project. My son pretended to be a bitter squash in his grandma's garden, a vegetable beloved by the Chinese (as I discussed in Chapter 4). He did a great job with his project, but admittedly under much nudging and supervision of his mother – me.

Upon hearing this example intended to foster children's creativity in learning science and in writing, the Chinese teachers shook their heads saying, "It is impossible for us to teach like that." It was not the case that they did not have the understanding of such teaching and learning or they lacked ability to do so, but they rejected this way of teaching, for two reasons. First, Chinese children must be prepared for their local and national examinations that determine whether a given student will advance to higher and more competitive schooling, given that their compulsory education promises only nine years. This type of free exploration takes time Chinese teachers and students do not have. Thus, teachers who participated in the workshop regarded inquiry-based learning as a luxury. Second, this type of free-ranging learning struck them as no different from herding sheep (放羊式教育) – that is, letting children roam around aimlessly with no measurable teaching and learning results at the end. How would we know if the child learned anything? What is the difference between this type of learning and growing vegetables as they have been doing before schooling begins? What if children simply do not do it? Who makes sure that each child will actually do it if it is totally up to the child to decide? What if the child does not like it? These teachers asked many questions. To them, this type of teaching is irresponsible and would not sit well with parents most of whom do not have my kind of educational background (PhD) to supervise their children. These teachers felt a responsibility to ensure that *every* child receives the same education, and as such no child should be let loose to wander off without instruction and guidance. If so, they reasoned, they would have an education system of much inequity, because family had to assume more responsibility. To my mind, there was a third objection these teachers did not articulate but nevertheless implicitly expressed: Free-ranging learning would forfeit the development of learning virtues, which, according to the review of this book, is a serious cultural challenge.

It is clear that Chinese and other East Asian educators as well as parents have envied Western educational ideals for 150 long years. This envy has resulted in endless efforts to learn from the West. To be sure, and to their credit, they have learned much that is worthy of learning (e.g., science, democracy, and the whole formal educational system). I would argue that they successfully mastered the *content*. But teaching and learning with the Western approach, particularly free exploration, learning by interest and choice, challenge to authority, and verbal communication – the backbone of Western learning – have proven to be extremely difficult. A case in point is offered by most recent research conducted by Marieke van Egmond.[42] She used my proposed conceptual mind- versus-virtue distinction to study Chinese and German college students. She found that the supposedly more westernized Shanghai college cohort and those Western-minded Chinese students who chose to study in German universities still show more virtue orientation and less mind orientation than their German peers. Given that more than a century has been spent on borrowing Western learning approaches, it seems to be taking an inordinately long time for them to manifest themselves. It would be difficult to argue that East Asia has not tried hard. I would say that they have tried enough, even by the Confucian standard for life-long self-perfection. Peculiarly and surprisingly, much of the Confucian way has prevailed, as if hinting that the more effort is made to eradicate it, the more immune it has become to such effort. It seems, ironically, that a Sisyphus type of effort-failure spell has been cast on this cross-cultural learning.

We are compelled to ask: Why keep trying to change something that has failed to change for 150 years? Or perhaps the question ought be posed in a different way: Is it worth this effort? And to what end? After all, we pity and laugh at Sisyphus, a mythological creation, because in our sane mind we would not do what he does. If this were the behavioral pattern of an individual, few would think that this is normal human behavior. But East Asia does not seem to have any problems with this type of continuously futile effort. I think it is time for them to stop to ponder.

As discussed in this book, the resistance to change is bound to happen first because the basic family relationships continue without much challenge. If the senseless Cultural Revolution did penetrate into the family and managed to dent the family system, it did not destroy it permanently. It would be hard to imagine any force that would succeed in eradicating Confucian family relationships and childrearing practices after they have survived for thousands of years. So long as this system continues, children come to school with home-forged ideas, motivation, and behaviors. Second, this resistance is expected because the tradition serves the people well even in modern and globalized learning. Asian children's repeated high achievement in international education assessment undoubtedly strengthens their confidence, and deservedly so. And the current economic success of China and other East Asian cultures would have been unthinkable if their people had been unwilling to make great efforts or learned only for personal fun or interest. No one denies that much of East Asia's economic achievement reflects the economic processes and standards of the West. However, it is also apparent that East Asia relied on, even in learning to be like the West, their native learning model, namely those learning virtues discussed in this book.

I am not advocating that East Asian educators and parents should not look at the West – or, for that matter, any other culture – in order to borrow ways to help their children learn better. I am of the opinion that East Asia stands to benefit from contemplating ways to foster both models of learning. But this effort requires careful contemplation, design, and practice. Before design and practice, there is an even more basic requirement: a shift in a philosophical outlook. It is important that this learning from the West not pit one model against the other, particularly condemning their own Confucian model as inferior and embracing wholesome importation of the Western model as a panacea for their educational problems. As alluded to before, this way of learning from the West has proceeded in a schizophrenic fashion. On the one hand, there is incessant condemnation of their own tradition, but on the other, their cultural model survives and benefits them, thanks to the tireless home socialization. Such learning for the past 150 years has had heavy liabilities and unintended consequences, and these ought to be analyzed, recognized, and made clear to parents, educators, and children themselves. East Asia is more likely to succeed in finding outside ways to improve their learning if these ways do not end up costing their parent–child relationships, teacher–child relationship, and peer relationships, all of which thrive on Confucian core values.

In the larger scheme of learning, there are plenty of successful learners from East Asia who master both models well as a result of studying in both systems (but such success within East Asia is highly questionable, as discussed previously). They are a good place for education designers to start. On the high end, those Nobel Prize winners and great scientists of East Asia such as C. N. Yang, T. D. Lee, and Y. T. Lee all grew up in East Asian families and went to school there, but they later received Western education and research training. Perhaps this is one way to contemplate how to help children learn both ways. Such exemplars' learning experiences and creativity are usually sequenced from home culture to Western culture, with the former laying a solid foundation and the latter fostering creative breakthrough. Whether their early foundational learning turned out to be an asset or a liability, or a liability stimulating creativity, this process should be studied and documented. Important insights can be gained to guide educational adjustment and parental socialization efforts.

On the ordinary end, millions of East Asian students seeking undergraduate and graduate education in the West for the past decades also offer overwhelming examples of learning both ways. These learning experiences deserve to be studied and analyzed and in turn offer useful practices within East Asian cultures. Regrettably, very little research exists on such a potentially enlightening topic involving such a large group of students. It is intuitively vital to understand how such learners with deeply entrenched learning beliefs from their home cultures encounter Western learning. Do they undergo the same process as I did with my German studies? Do they stumble over their own taken-for-granted cultural beliefs? If so, how does that process unfold? How does it enable them to forge ahead and to achieve creativity, as many ostensibly do? On the negative side, such a cross-cultural reflection may end up eroding their self-confidence, resulting in many deserting their intellectual pursuits altogether. If so, how does their alienation take place? It seems to me that such a research effort will yield significant insights into cross-cultural learning.

Finally, learning both ways well may require designing specific and thoughtful contexts within East Asia. For example, children could be taught that both fun/interest-based learning and must-learn activities regardless of personal interest (e.g., math and languages) are important. Schools can offer contexts in which children's own interests can be the primary propeller for learning, but also contexts in which learning how to exercise virtues is the main goal. Being able to learn both ways is certainly better than being able to learn only one way. But how best to achieve such learning and education will depend, in part, on knowledge backed by research on such experiments and processes. In the absence of reliable research, experimentation is likely to be haphazard and futile.

CHALLENGES IN CHILD DEVELOPMENT AND EDUCATION
FOR EAST ASIAN IMMIGRANTS

Whereas schools in East Asia have some leeway to decide which way, or what combination of ways, to apply, immigrant children from East Asia to the West have no choice but to plunge into the two learning models. East Asians have been settling down in the West for more than a century, particularly in the United States, but very little research on their general acculturation exists. Even less research is available on how children develop and are socialized in developing their learning beliefs at home and school. There is research on Asian Americans, but such research does not typically focus on the immigrant context. Currently, 70 percent of Asians in the United States come from the so-called two-generation families, with parents born and raised in their home cultures and children born and raised in the United States.[43] As it turns out, this immigrant context is full of challenges and risks.

Child development in immigrant context has drawn increasing attention from researchers. In this section, I share some relevant findings from my own research comparing learning beliefs of Chinese immigrant and European-American children at preschool age. For the first set of findings, we examined children's achievement in three domains: oral expression, reading, and math.[44] To our surprise, Chinese immigrant children's oral expression was significantly below that of their European-American peers, despite their often remarkable achievement in reading and math. Moreover, their oral expression was also below the national mean (100). In other words, Chinese immigrant children may know more literacy and math than they are able to express. These research findings are especially troubling against the cultural directive of verbal expression in America. Even at age four, these children are significantly behind their European-American peers in this development.

The second set of research findings also pertain to Chinese immigrant children's self-expression.[45] Recall the large differences in speaking versus not speaking between the West and East Asia as discussed in Chapter 8. My colleagues and I were interested in how Chinese immigrant children are perceived by their teachers given the cultural difference and their low oral expression found earlier. We looked at two groups of Chinese immigrant children in two school contexts in comparison with European-American children. The first group attended Asian-dominant preschools, with 50 percent or more Asian staff and children, commonly found in ethnic enclaves such as Chinatown. The second group of children attended European

American-dominant schools, with few or no Asian staff and children, in the suburbs, typical for Chinese middle-class immigrant children. Needless to say, all European-American children attended European American-dominant schools. We also assessed children's learning engagement, school adjustment, and peer relations as a function of the teacher perceptions of their quietness.

We found that Chinese immigrant children, irrespective of their socio-economic status, their English proficiency, and teachers' own ethnic background, are indeed perceived as less self-expressive and quieter than their European-American peers by their teachers. Sadly, being quiet but in European American-dominant schools, Chinese children showed less learning engagement and suffered worse peer relations. However, being quiet in Asian-dominant schools not only did not predict any negative associations, but also was positively correlated with school adjustment and learning engagement. In comparison, the quietness of European-American children did not impact their learning engagement, school adjustment, or peer relations at all.

Taken together, quiet Chinese immigrant children did not fare well intellectually and socially in European American-dominant schools even when they came from a comparable socioeconomic status and spoke fluent English. They faced these problems because, we suspect, their quietness in the European-American context was regarded as a negative trait. However, their quietness was viewed as positive in learning and peer relations in schools where most adults and children were culturally similar to them. Thus, the traditional view in psychology that quietness somehow is an immutable property, a personality trait, residing only inside the child is questionable. Asian children's quietness may be an oscillating object in the eye of the beholder. Depending on who is looking at them, their quietness can be viewed as positive or negative. Furthermore, it would be strange if immigrant children who grow up in Western cultures that strongly value and cultivate children's self-expression turn out to be *more* quiet than children in East Asia where judicious silence is truly golden. But this strange situation may be surprisingly true with East Asian children in the West. Their home culture's prized reluctance to speak may put them at risk in their host culture.

It is not easy for adults to imagine what it would feel like to be innocent young children but cast in a negative light in a social context that is supposed to help them learn and grow. It is also disheartening to think about these children who step outside their protective home, where they are showered with love and positive regard,[46] into a place where they receive negativity. Worse yet, such negativity is emitted under the false pretence of positivity of loving and caring preschool. Most difficult of all is the fact that neither the immigrant families, nor the schools with their well-meaning teachers and staff, nor the children themselves are cognizant of this deeply hidden but effectual negativity. It is hidden because we did not know about its existence until this research has revealed it. It is effectual because it shows the associated negative impact on their development. Nonetheless, although young and innocent, children are able to perceive the contrast between home's true positive regard and school's perplexing negativity. This kind of daily experience between the positive and negative cannot be harmless to children. Under such school socialization, Asian immigrant children's development is likely to worsen as they grow older.

Unfortunately, there is severe shortage of research on Asian immigrant children, and as a result, Western cultures at large are not well informed about these children's challenges and processes for successful acculturation. Current education policies leave Asian children out because they achieve well on paper.[47] Thus, their quietness may turn into quiet suffering. There are many other areas that also show signs of concern because of East Asian learning models and beliefs. For example, parents' emphasis on academic achievement may be suspected of doing psychological harm to children. As discussed in Chapter 6, peer harassment and bullying is rampant against Asian immigrant children because of their perceived achievement.

THE NEED TO UNDERSTAND DIVERSE CULTURAL LEARNING MODELS

Thus far, I have said little in this chapter about whether the West should and can learn something from East Asia. To be sure, the West has been learning some things from East Asia, such as martial arts and contemplative practice, which is even entering today's Western formal schooling. But I am not aware of the concerted, long-term commitment to learning anything more from East Asia on the part of the West. It is not my goal to entertain in this book why this is the case. But I hope that this book can stimulate thinking on this topic among interested readers.

It is, however, my view that, if childrearing and education are to succeed in our accelerated globalized world, it is imperative that more research be conducted on cultural learning models, children's learning beliefs, and related socialization. Globalization increases rather than reduces the need for us to understand cultural variations. Undoubtedly, such research will, on a more general level, inform cultures that are confronted with the questions of what to treasure and retain and what to reform and discard, what to learn from the outside and what to create on their own. Engaging in such debates can enable cultures not only to find their best ways to navigate through and move along with the globalized world, but also to avoid costly mistakes and irreparable damage.[48]

On a more practical level, such research will certainly inform cultures that receive many international students who seek higher education, such as the United States and many other Western cultures. Students from different cultures bring with them deeply rooted learning beliefs when they come to a culture for undergraduate or graduate education. Yet, if the receiving cultures remain unaware of important cultural differences, or worse yet, only stereotypically aware of superficial "differences," the receiving cultures are bound to offer educational programs and pedagogy that do not serve the students' needs well. If so – and frequently it is the case – both the cultures and international students stand to lose much.

Last but not least, research on cultural learning models and learning beliefs is also urgently needed to inform parents in their home cultures who contemplate immigration to another culture (i.e., voluntary immigrants). Knowing what might be at stake for their children may help them make judicious decisions. For children already immersed in another culture, it is imperative that parents, communities, and schools have full knowledge of potential risks associated with immigration. Such awareness is the only path toward finding possible ways to ease the acculturative stress for families and their children.

There is really no need for a Faustian either-or bargain. It is quite possible to obtain knowledge and to retain one's soul. Perhaps one simply needs to respect and understand one's cultural values and learning beliefs but also venture into those of others. One can grow both with what has been enculturated and assimilated in one's own culture and what has been acculturated in another. As Voltaire once said, we all must cultivate our garden, planting what is useful to us and removing the weeds that stifle growth.

NOTES

1. Portes, A., & Rumbaut, R. G. (2001). *Legacies: The story of the immigrant second generation.* Berkeley: University of California Press; Suárez-Orozco, C., & Suárez-Orozco, M. (2001). *Children of Immigration: The developing child.* Cambridge, MA: Harvard University Press; Suárez-Orozco, C., Suárez-Orozco, M., & Todorova, I. (2008). *Learning a new land: Immigrant students in American society.* New York: Belknap; and Garcia Coll, C. T., & Marks, A.

(2009). *Immigrant stories: Ethnicity and academics in middle childhood*. New York: Oxford University Press.

2. Li, H., & Zahniser, St. (2002). The determinants of temporary rural-to-urban migration in China. *Urban Studies, 39,* 2219–2235, and National Bureau of Statistics of China. (201, March, 11). Rural migrant workers amounted to 225.42 million (16.8% of its total population) at the end of 2008. Retrieved April, 16 2011 from http://www.stats.gov.cn/tjfx/fxbg/t20110310_402710032.htm

3. See note 1 to this chapter.

4. China topped the list of countries sending students to the United States, with 127,628, making up 18.5% of total international students, followed by India (15.2%) and South Korea (10.4%), and the largest increase of all sending countries by 29.9% in academic year 2009–2010; also see Institute of International Education. (n.d.). Retrieved April, 16 2011 from http://www.iie.org/en/Research-and-Publications/Open-Doors. China is also the largest country sending students to Europe, with the United Kingdom the top destination; see UK Council for International Student Affairs. (n.d.). Retrieved from April 16, 2011 from http://www.ukcisa.org.uk

5. As of 2009–2010, 70% of international students were funded by non-U.S. sources, with 62% from personal and family sources. Data from same source as the first reference in note 4 to this chapter.

6. See note 1 to this chapter.

7. U.S. Census Bureau. (2010). Overview of race and Hispanic origin: 2010 (Release No. C2010BR-02). Retrieved from http://www.census.gov/prod/cen2010/briefs/c2010br-02.pdf

8. Mahalingam, R. (Ed.). (2006). *Cultural psychology of immigrants*. Mahwah, NJ: Erlbaum.

9. Zhou, M. (2009). Conflict, coping, and reconciliation: Intergenerational relations in Chinese immigrant families. In N. Foner (Ed.), *Across generations: Immigrant families in America* (pp. 21–46). New York: New York University Press.

10. Yoshikawa, H. (2011). *Immigrants raising citizens: Undocumented parents and their Children*. New York: Sage.

11. See note 41 to Chapter 8 for ethnographic descriptions of how some Chinese preschools are now actively promoting children's critical thinking, exploration, creativity, and verbal expression.

12. Peréa, F. C., & García Coll, C. (2008). The social and cultural contexts of bilingualism. In J. Altarriba & R. Heredia (Eds.), *An introduction to bilingualism: Principles and processes* (pp. 199–241). Mahwah, NJ: Erlbaum.

13. See Putnam, R. D. (2007). E Pluribus Unum: Diversity and community in the twenty-first century: The 2006 Johan Skytte Prize lecture. *Scandinavian Political Science, 30,* 137–174 for his comprehensive research documenting that as American communities become more diverse, people tend to hunker down into their own private lives, resulting in less civic participation and trust of each other.

14. Rozin, P. (2010). The weirdest people in the world are a harbinger of the future of the world. *Behavioral and Brain Sciences, 33,* 108–109.

15. Henrich, J., Heine, S. J., & Norenzayan, A. (2010). The weirdest people in the world? *Behavioral and Brain Sciences, 33,* 61–83.

16. See, for example, Behrens, K. (2004). A multifaceted view of the concept of *amae*: Reconsidering the indigenous Japanese concept of relatedness. *Human Development, 47,* 1–27 for research on the unique concept of *amae* in Japanese parent–child and other relationships; and the third reference in note 51 to Chapter 2 for research on the prominence of shame and shaming techniques used to socialize children among Taiwanese.

17. Baike (n.d.). Retrieved May 22, 2011 from http://baike.baidu.com/view/14280. htm#sub14280

18. See Phinney, J. S., & Baldelomar, O. A. (2011). Identity development in multiple cultural contexts. In L. Arnett Jensen (Ed.), *Bridging cultural and developmental approaches to psychology: New syntheses in theory, research, and policy* (pp. 161–186). New York: Oxford University Press for a summary discussion on this topic.

19. See note 1 to this chapter.

20. Schneider, B., Hieshima, J. A., Lee, S., & Plank, S. (1994). East-Asian academic success in the United States: Family, school, and cultural explanations. In P. M. Greenfield & R. R. Cocking (Eds.), *Cross-cultural roots of minority child development* (pp. 332–350). Hillsdale, NJ: Erlbaum.

21. Lipset, S. M. (1996). *American exceptionalism: A double-edged sword.* New York: Norton, and note 15 to this chapter.

22. See note 52 to Chapter 3; and Bruner, J. (2008). Culture and mind: Their fruitful incommensurability. *Ethos, 36*(1), 29–45.

23. Bornstein, M. (Ed.). (1995). *Handbook of parenting, Vol. 4.* Hillsdale, NJ: Erlbaum.

24. See Wex, M. (2005). *Born to kvetch: Yiddish language and culture in all of its moods.* New York: Harper Collins for the Jewish example.

25. See Song, N. (1995). 鬆年 *(1837–1906)* 頤園畫語 [Song Nian (1837–1906) on painting in the Nurturing Garden (reprint)]. Shanghai: Shanghai Ancient Books for rejection of Western painting techniques by Chinese literati painters.

26. See note 2 to Chapter 1.

27. See note 20 to this chapter.

28. Tao, Y.-M. (1963). 桃花源記, 古文觀止, 上 [The land of peach blossoms in C.-C. Wu & D.-H. Wu (Eds.). *Essence of classical literature, Vol.1*]. Zhonghua Book Company.

29. See Taiwan Center for Chinese Curriculum. (n.d.). Retrieved April 8, 2011 from http://chincenter.fg.tp.edu.tw/cerc/98ke.php for proposal to require high school students to read Confucian texts by Taiwan's Ministry of Education.

30. Hong, Z.-L. (2nd ed.). (2004). 義務教育課程標准實驗教科書:《語文》九年級. 江蘇教育出版社 [Chinese for 9th Grade: Standard experimental textbook for compulsory education] (Ed.). Jiangsu Province: Jiangsu Education Press.

31. The term *xioakang* (小康之家), "every family with sufficient food, shelter, and secure and peaceful life," then extended to a society of such families (小康社會), is the millennia-long aspiration in Confucian political and social thought. This aspiration is not after wealth and luxury, but after contentment with life. It also

hopes for a community where the young are looked after, the old have a sense of belonging, peace and friendship are treasured, and people are worry free. This type of community is the ideal of Chinese people for generations. For Chinese government to set *xioakang* as an economic and social goal for 1.3 billion people, put a dollar figure on it ($800 annually per capita), and achieve it was no small accomplishment.

32. When they visit China, some Chinese-American children receive remarks that their outfit is outdated, kitsch, and tacky (俗氣 or 土氣). Many people initially mistake Chinese-American children for poor kids from the countryside. Only upon hearing them speak flawless English would people believe that they came from the United States. Similarly, when I first came to Boston Chinatown in the 1980s, I thought that it was filled with all kitsch Chinese stuff such as the images of dragon and phoenix, the pompous golden color on restaurants' façades, and other "cheap" symbols of Chinese culture. But after some years in the United States, I find myself endeared to the "kitsch."

33. James, W. (1892, 1963). *Principles of psychology.* New York: Holt.

34. Nakkula & Toshalis, 2006. *Understanding youth: Adolescent development for educators.* Cambridge, MA: Harvard Education Press.

35. Damon, W., & Hart, D. (1988). *Self-understanding in childhood and adolescence.* New York: Cambridge University Press.

36. Chandler, M. J., Lalonde, C. E., Sokol, B. W., & Hallett, D. (2003). Personal persistence, identity development, and suicide: A study of Native and non-Native North American adolescents. *Monograph of the Society for Research in Child Development, 68*(2), vii–130.

37. See note 18 to this chapter.

38. Kulis, S., Napoli, M., & Marsiglia, F. (2002). Ethnic pride, biculturalism, and drug use norms of urban American Indian adolescents. *Social Work Research, 26*, 101–112.

39. Juang, L. P., & Nguyen, H. H. (2010). Ethnic identity among Chinese-American youth: The role of family obligation and community factors on ethnic engagement, clarity, and pride. *Identity: An International Journal of Theory and Research, 10*(1), 20–38.

40. See Wilson, E. O. (1998). *Consilience: The unity of knowledge.* New York: Knopf for a proposal for a grand consilience of all knowledge.

41. See note 40 to Chapter 8.

42. Van Egmond, M. C. (2011). Mind and virtue: A cross-cultural analysis of beliefs about learning. Unpublished doctoral dissertation, Jacobs University, Germany.

43. U.S. Census Bureau. (2004). *We the people: Asians in the United States, Census 2000 Special Report.* Washington, DC: U.S. Census Bureau.

44. Li, J., Yamamoto, Y., Luo, L., Batchelor, A., & Bresnahan, R. M. (2010). Why attend school? Chinese immigrant and European American preschoolers' views and outcomes. *Developmental Psychology, 46*(6), 1637–1650.

45. Yamamoto, Y., & Li, J. (2012). Quiet in the eye of the beholder: Teacher perceptions of Asian immigrant children. In C. Garcia Coll (Vol. Ed.), *The impact of immigration on children's development* (pp. 1–17). *Contributions to Human Development. Human Development.* Basel: Karger.

46. See note 62 to Chapter 3.
47. For example, I spent two years doing research in a high school that was attended by some 400 Asian immigrant children. There was only one guidance counselor of Asian heritage. Yet, much of the school funding came from these Asian families' property tax. It was not much of a surprise that these children did not receive due service from the school district.
48. During the Cultural Revolution, much of China's Confucian tradition of learning was attacked and abandoned. In the zeal of embracing Marxist educational ideology, millions of middle school, high school, and college-educated Chinese youth were sent to the countryside by Mao Zedong to receive so-called re-education from working people. This ten-year-long educational experiment was based on the conviction of one man who held most power in the nation with the largest population on this planet. The economic, social, and health costs to the nation, as well as individuals' psychological suffering cause by this movement, are immeasurable.

BIBLIOGRAPHY

Aeschylus (1996). *The Oresteia trilogy: Agamemnon, the libation-bearers and the furies*. Mineola, NY: Dover.

Alexander, R. (2000). Culture & pedagogy: International comparison in primary education. Oxford: Blackwell.

American heritage dictionary of the English language (3rd ed.). (1992). New York: Houghton Mifflin.

Ames, R. T., & Rosemont, Jr., H. (1999). *The analects of Confucius: A philosophical translation*. New York: Ballantine.

An, S.-H. (2004). Capturing the Chinese way of teaching: The learning-questioning and learning-reviewing instructional model. In L.-H. Fan, N.-Y. Wong, J.-F Cai, S.-Q. Li, & T.-Y. Tso (Eds.), *How Chinese learn mathematics: Perspectives from insiders* (pp. 462–482). Singapore: World Scientific.

Anderson, G. I. A. (Ed.) (1977). *Masterpieces of the Orient* (6th ed.). New York, Norton.

Anglin, J. M. (1977). *Word, object, and conceptual development*. New York: Norton.

Aristotle (1992). *The art of rhetoric*. New York: Penguin.

Arnett, J. J. (2008). The neglected 95%: Why American psychology needs to become less American. *American Psychologist, 63*(7), 602–614.

Asher, S. R., & Coie, J. D. (Eds.) (1990). *Peer rejection in childhood*. New York: Cambridge University Press.

Astington, J. W. (1993). *The child's discovery of the mind*. Cambridge, MA: Harvard University Press.

Atkinson, J. W. (1964). *An introduction to motivation*. Princeton, NJ: Van Nostrand.

Atkinson, J. W., & Rynor, J. O. (1978). *Personality, motivation, and achievement*. New York: Wiley.

Atkinson, J. M., & Heritage, J. (Eds.) (1984). *Structures of social action: Studies in the conversation analysis*. Cambridge: Cambridge University Press.

Au, T. K. F., & Harackiewicz, J. M. (1986). The effects of perceived parental expectations on Chinese children's mathematics performance. *Merrill-Palmer Quarterly, 32*(4), 383–392.

Ayduk, O., May, D., Downey, G., & Higgins, E. T. (2003). Tactical differences in coping with rejection sensitivity: The role of prevention pride. *Personality and Social Psychology Bulletin, 29*(4), 435–448.

Azuma, H. (1986). Why study child development in Japan? In H. Stevenson, H. Azuma, & K. Hakuta (Eds.), *Child development and education in Japan* (pp. 3–12). New York: Freeman.

Baike (n.d.). Retrieved May 22, 2011 from http://baike.baidu.com/view/14280. htm#sub14280

Bakeman, R., & Gottman, J. M. (1986). *Observing interaction: An introduction to sequential analysis.* Cambridge: Cambridge University Press.

Bakeman, R., & Quera, V. (1995). *Analyzing interaction: Sequential analysis with SDIS and GSEQ.* New York: Cambridge University Press.

Bandura, A. (1993). Perceived self-efficacy in cognitive development and functioning. *Educational Psychologist, 28*(2), 117–148.

   (2001). Social cognitive theory: An agentic perspective. *Annual Review of Psychology, 52,* 1–26.

Bandura, A., & Schunk, D. (1981). Cultivating competence, self-efficacy, and intrinsic interest through proximal self-motivation. *Journal of Personality and Social Psychology, 41,* 586–598.

Baumrind, D. (1980). New directions in socialization research. *American Psychologist, 35,* 639–652.

Behrens, K. (2004). A multifaceted view of the concept of *amae*: Reconsidering the indigenous Japanese concept of relatedness. *Human Development, 47,* 1–27.

Berkeley, G. (1713/2006). *George Berkeley: Three dialogues between Hylas and Philonous.* Upper Saddle River, NJ: Prentice Hall.

Berliner, D. C., & Biddle, B. J. (1995). *The manufactured crisis.* Reading, MA: Addison-Wesley.

Berlyne, D. (1966). Curiosity and exploration. *Science, 153,* 25–33.

Berry, J. W. (1969). On cross-cultural comparability. *International Journal of Psychology, 4,* 119–128.

Bertensson, S., Leyda, J., & Satina, S. (2002). *Sergei Rachmaninoff: A Lifetime in music.* Bloomington: Indiana University Press.

Bilbow, G. T. (1997). Cross-cultural impression management in the multicultural workplace: The special case of Hong Kong. *Journal of Pragmatics, 28,* 461–487.

Bishop, J. H., & Bishop, M. M. (2008). An economic theory of academic engagement norms: The struggle for popularity and normative hegemony in secondary schools. Unpublished manuscript.

Boehnke, K. (2008). Peer pressure: a cause of scholastic underachievement? A cross-cultural study of mathematical achievement among German, Canadian, and Israeli middle school students. *Social Psychology of Education, 11*(2), 149–160.

Bornstein, M. (Ed.) (1995). *Handbook of parenting, Vol. 4.* Hillsdale, NJ: Erlbaum.

Bradly, R. H., & Corwyn, R. F. (2005). Caring for children around the world: A view from HOME. *International Journal of Behavioral Development, 29*(6), 468–478.

Brickman, P., & Bulman, R. J. (1977). Pleasure and pain in social comparison. In J. M. Suls & R. L. Miller (Eds.), *Social comparison processes: Theoretical and empirical perspectives* (pp. 149–186). Washington, DC: Hemisphere.

Brophy-Herb, H. E., Schiffman, R. F., Bocknek, E. L., Dupuis, S. B., Fitzgerald, H. E. et al. (2011). Toddlers' social-emotional competence in the contexts of maternal emotion socialization and contingent responsiveness in a low–income sample. *Social Development, 20*(1), 73–92.

Brown, R. (1973). *A first language: The early stages.* Cambridge, MA: Harvard University Press.

Brown, T. (1994). Affective dimensions of meaning. In W. F. Overton & D. S. Palermo (Eds.), *The nature and ontogenesis of meaning* (pp. 167–190). Hillsdale, NJ: Erlbaum.

Bruner, J. (1987). *Actual minds, possible worlds.* Cambridge, MA: Harvard University Press.

(2008). Culture and mind: Their fruitful incommensurability. *Ethos, 36*(1), 29–45.

Bruner, J. S. (1986). Value presupposition of developmental theory. In L. Cirillo & S. Wapner (Eds.), *Value presuppositions in theories of human development* (pp. 19–28). Hillsdale, NJ: Erlbaum.

Buck, R. (1999). The biological affects: A typology. *Psychological Review, 106*(2), 301–336.

Caudhill, W., & Weinstein, H. (1969). Maternal care and infant behavior in Japan and America. *Psychiatry, 32,* 12–43.

Chamberlain, P., & Patterson, G. R. (1995). Discipline and child compliance in parenting. In M. Bornstein (Ed.), *Handbook of parenting, Vol. 4* (pp. 205–225). Hillsdale, NJ: Erlbaum.

Chandler, M. J., Lalonde, C. E., Sokol, B. W., & Hallett, D. (2003). Personal persistence, identity development, and suicide: A study of Native and non-Native North American adolescents. *Monograph of the Society for Research in Child Development, 68*(2), vii–130.

Chang, H. C. (1997). Language and words: Communication in the Analects of Confucius. *Journal of Language and Social Psychology, 16,* 107–131.

(1999). The "well-defined" is "ambiguous:" Indeterminacy in Chinese conversation. *Journal of Pragmatics, 31,* 535–556.

Chang, T. H. (1999). *China during the Cultural Revolution, 1966–1976: A selected bibliography of English language works.* Westport, CT: Greenwood.

Chao, R. K. (1996). Chinese and European American mothers' views about the role of parenting in children's school success. *Journal of Cross-Cultural Psychology, 27,* 403–423.

Cheek, J. M., & Buss, A. H. (1981). Shyness and sociability. *Journal of Personality and Social Psychology, 41,* 330–339.

Chen, C., & Stevenson, H. W. (1989). Homework: A cross-cultural examination. *Child Development, 60,* 551–561.

Chen, F.-N. (2005). Residential patterns of parents and their married children in contemporary China: A life course approach. *Population Research & Policy Review, 24*(2), 125–148.

Chen, X.-Y. (2008, October) at the conference, *Bridging developmental and cultural psychology: New syntheses in theory, research, and policy.* Worcester, MA: Clark University.

Chen, X.-Y., & French, D. C. (2008). Children's social competence in cultural context. *Annual Review of Psychology, 59,* 591–616.

Chen, X.-Y., Lei, C., Liu, H.-Y., & He, Y.-F. (2008). Effects of the peer group on the development of social functioning and academic achievement: A longitudinal study in Chinese children. *Child Development, 79*(2), 235–251.

Cheng, C.-Y. (1987). Chinese philosophy and contemporary human communication theory. In L. Kincaid (Ed.), *Communication theory: Eastern and Western perspectives* (pp. 23–43). San Diego, CA: Academic Press.

Cheng, K.-M. (1996). *The quality of primary education: A case study of Zhejiang Province, China.* Paris: International Institute for Educational Planning.

Child Welfare League Foundation (n.d.). *Report on school bullying.* Retrieved March 15, 2010 from http://www.children.org.tw/database_report.php?typeid=34

Chomsky, N. (1972). *Language and mind.* San Diego, CA: Harcourt.

Cicero (1986). *Cicero on oratory and orators.* [Trans. by J. S. Watson]. Carbondale: Southern Illinois University Press.

Cole, M. (1998). *Cultural Psychology: A once and future discipline.* Cambridge, MA: Harvard University Press.

Cole, M., Cole, S. R., & Lightfoot, C. (2005). *The development of children* (5th ed.). New York: Worth Publishers.

Coley, R. J. (2002). *An uneven start: Indicators of inequality in school readiness.* Princeton, NJ: ETS.

Colvin, G. (2008). *Talent is overrated: What really separates world-class performers from everybody else.* New York: Portfolio.

Conti, R., Amabile, T. M., & Pollack, S. (1995). Enhancing intrinsic motivation, learning, and creativity. *Personality and Social Psychology Bulletin, 21,* 1107–1116.

Cooper, C. (2004). *Sights and sounds of the Athenian Court.* New York: Routledge.

Corriveau, K. H., & Harris, P. L. (2010). Preschoolers (sometimes) defer to the majority in making simple perceptual judgments. *Developmental Psychology, 46*(2), 437–445.

Cortazzi, M., & Jin, L.-X. (2001). Large classes in China: "Good" teachers and interaction. In D. A. Watkins & J. B. Biggs (Eds.), *Teaching the Chinese learner: Psychological and pedagogical perspectives* (pp. 115–134). Hong Kong: Comparative Education Research Centre.

Covington, M. V. (2000). Goal theory, motivation, and school achievement: An integrative review. *Annual Review of Psychology, 51,* 171–200.

Covington, M. V., & Beery, R. (1976). *Self-worth and school learning.* New York: Holt, Rinehart & Winston.

Covington, M. V., & Omelich, C. L. (1979). Effort: The double-edged sword in school achievement. *Journal of Educational Psychology, 71,* 169–182.

Cowell, F. R. (1973). *Cicero and the Roman Republic* (5th ed.). New York: Penguin.

Coyle, D. (2009). *The talent code: Greatness isn't born. It's grown. Here's how.* New York: Bantam Dell.

Crystal, D. S., Chen, C.-S., Fuligni, A. J., Stevenson, H. W., Hsu, C. - C., Ko, H.-J. et al. (1994). Psychological maladjustment and academic achievement: A cross-cultural study of Japanese, Chinese, and American high school students. *Child Development, 65,* 738–753.

Csikszentmihalyi, M. (1990). *Flow: The psychology of optimal experience.* New York: Harper & Row.

Csikszentmihalyi, M., & Rathunde, K. (1998). The development of the person: An experiential perspective on the ontogenesis of psychological complexity. In R. M. Lerner (Ed.), *Handbook of child psychology. Vol 1: Theoretical models of human development* (5th ed., pp. 635–684). New York: Wiley.

Dahlin, B., & Watkins, D. (2000). The role of repetition in the processes of memorizing and understanding: A comparison of the views of Western and Chinese secondary school students in Hong Kong. *British Journal of Educational Psychology, 70,* 65–84.

d'Ailly, H. (2003). Children's autonomy and perceived control in learning: A model of motivation and achievement in Taiwan. *Journal of Educational Psychology, 95*(1), 84–96.

Damasio, A. (2005). *Descartes' error: Emotion, reason, and the human brain.* New York: Penguin.

Damerow, P. (1998). Prehistory and cognitive development. In J. Langer & M. Killen (Eds.), *Piaget, evolution, and development* (pp. 227–270). Mahwah, NJ: Erlbaum.

Damon, W., & Hart, D. (1988). *Self-understanding in childhood and adolescence.* New York: Cambridge University Press.

D'Andrade, R. G. (1992). Schemas and motivation. In R. G. D'Andrade & C. Strauss (Eds.), *Human motives and cultural models* (pp. 23–44). New York: Cambridge University Press.

(1995). *The development of cognitive anthropology.* New York: Cambridge University Press.

Davidson, N., Scherer, K., & Goldsmith, H. (Eds.) (2003). *Handbook of affective science.* New York: Oxford University Press.

de Bary, W. T. (1991). *Learning for one's self.* New York: Columbia University Press.

DeCasper, A. J., & Spence, M. J. (1986). Prenatal maternal speech influences newborn's perceptions of speech sounds. *Infant Behavior and Development, 3,* 133–150.

deCharms, R. (1984). Motivation enhancement in educational settings. In R. Ames & C. Ames (Eds.), *Research on motivation in education: Student motivation* (pp. 275–309). New York: Academic Press.

Deci, E. L., & Ryan, R. M. (1985). *Intrinsic motivation and self-determination in human behavior.* New York: Academic Press.

Delpit, L. D. (1995). *Other people's children: Cultural conflict in the classroom.* New York: The New Press.

Descartes, R. (1637/2007). *Discourse on method.* Miami, FL: BN Publishing.

(1642/2007). *Meditations.* Miami, FL: BN Publishing.

Doi, T. (1981). *The anatomy of dependence* (J. Bester, Trans.). New York: Kodansha International.

Doidge, N. (2007). *The brain that changes itself: Stories of personal triumph from the frontiers of brain science.* New York: Penguin.

Dweck, C. (1975). The role of expectations and attributions in the alleviation of learned helplessness. *Journal of Personality and Social Psychology, 31,* 674–685.

Dweck, C. S. (1999). *Self-theories.* Philadelphia: Psychology Press.

Dweck, C. S., & Leggett, E. (1988). A social-cognitive approach to motivation and personality. *Psychological Review, 95,* 256–273.

Eaton, M. J., & Dembo, M. H. (1997). Differences in the motivational beliefs for Asian-American and Non-Asian students. *Journal of Educational Psychology, 89*(3), 433–440.

Edwards, C., Gandini, L., & Forman, G. (Eds.) (1998). *The hundred languages of children: The Reggio Emilia approach – advanced reflections* (2nd ed.). Westport, CT: Ablex.

Edwards, C. P. (1989). The transition from infancy to early childhood: A difficult transition and a difficult theory. In V. R. Briker & G. H. Gossen (Eds.), *Ethnographic encounters in Southern Mesoamerica: Essays in honor of Evon Z. Vogt, Jr.* (pp. 167–175). Austin: University of Texas Press.

Eid, M., & Diener, E. (2001). Norms for experiencing emotions in different cultures: Inter- and intranational differences. *Journal of Personality and Social Psychology, 81*(5), 869–885.

Eimas, P. D. (1985). The perception of speech in early infancy. *Scientific American, 252*(1), 66–72.

Eisenberg, N., Cumberland, A., & Spinrad, T. L. (1998). Maternal socialization of emotion. *Psychological Inquiry, 9,* 241–273.

Eisenberg, N., Spinrad, T. L., & Cumberland, A. (1998). The socialization of emotion: Reply to commentaries. *Psychological Inquiry, 9*(4), 317–333.

Elliott, J. G., Hufton, N. R., Illushin, L., & Willis, W. (2005). *Motivation, engagement, and educational performance: International perspectives on the contexts of learning.* New York: Palgrave Macmillan.

Ennis, R. (1987). A taxonomy of critical thinking dispositions and abilities. In J. Baron & R. Sternberg (Eds.), *Teaching thinking skills: Theory and practice* (pp. 9–26). New York: Freeman.

Exline, J. J., & Geyer, A. L. (2004). Perceptions of humility: A preliminary study. *Self and Identity, 3,* 95–114.

Facione, P. (1990). Critical thinking: A statement of expert consensus for purposes of educational assessment and instruction. Executive summary of "The Delphi Report." Milbrae: The California Academic Press.

Feather, N. T. (1989). Attitudes towards the high achiever: The fall of the tall poppy. *Australian Journal of Psychology, 41*(3), 239–267.

Fingarett, H. (1972). *Confucius: The secular as sacred.* New York: Harper & Row.

Fischer, H. A., Manstead, A. S. R., & Rodriguez Mosquera, P. M. (1999). The role of honor-related vs. individualist values in conceptualizing pride, shame, and anger: Spanish and Dutch cultural prototypes. *Cognition & Emotion, 13*(2), 149–179.

Fischer, K. W., & Tangney, J. P. (1995). Self-conscious emotions and the affect revolution: Framework and overview. In J. P. Tangney & K. W. Fischer (Eds.), *Self-conscious emotions: The psychology of shame, guilt, embarrassment, and pride* (pp. 3–22). New York: Guilford.

Fisher, C. B., Wallace, S. A., & Fenton, R. E. (2000). Discrimination distress during adolescence. *Journal of Youth & Adolescence, 29,* 679–695.

Fiske, A. P., & Haslam, N. (2005). The four basic social bonds: Structures for coordinating interaction. In M. W. Baldwin (Ed.), *Interpersonal cognition* (pp. 267–298). New York: Guilford.

Fivush, R., & Nelson, K. (2006). Parent-child reminiscing locates the self in the past. *British Journal of Developmental Psychology, 24*(1), 235–251.

Flowerdew, J., & Miller, L. (1995). On the notion of culture in L2 lectures. *TESOL Quarterly, 29*(2), 345–373.

Fordham, S., & Ogbu, J. U. (1986). Black students' school success: Coping with the "Burden of 'Acting White.'" *The Urban Review, 18*, 176–206.

Forster, K. I. (1976). Accessing the mental lexicon. In R. J. Wales & E. Walker (Eds.), *New approaches to language mechanisms* (pp. 257–287). Amsterdam: North Holland.

Fox, S., Scheffler, I., & Marom, D. (Eds.) (2003). *Visions of Jewish education.* New York: Cambridge University Press.

Francis, N. W., & Kucera, H. (1982). *Frequency analysis of English usage: Lexicon and grammar.* Boston, MA: Houghton Mifflin.

Frattaroli, J. (2006). Experimental disclosure and its moderators: A metaanalysis. *Psychological Bulletin, 132*, 823–865.

Frei, J. R., & Shaver, P. R. (2002). Respect in close relationships: Prototype definition, self-report assessment, and initial correlates. *Personal Relationships, 9*, 121–139.

Frijda, N. H. (1986). *The emotions.* Cambridge: Cambridge University Press.

Fukuyama, M. A., & Greenfield, T. K. (1983). Dimensions of aggressiveness in an Asian-American student population. *Journal of Counseling Psychology, 30*, 429–432.

Fülöp, M. (1999). Students' perception of the role of competition in their respective countries: Hungary, Japan, and the USA. In A. Ross (Ed.), *Young citizens in Europe* (pp. 195–219). London: University of North London.

Fung, H. (1999). Becoming a moral child: The socialization of shame among young Chinese children. *Ethos, 27*, 180–209.

Fung, H., & Chen, E. C.-H. (2001). Across time and beyond skin: Self and transgression in the everyday socialization of shame among Taiwanese preschool children. *Social Development, 10*(3), 420–437.

Fung, H., & Liang, C. H. (2008). 越南媽媽,台灣囡仔: 台灣跨國婚姻家庭幼兒社會化之初探 [Vietnamese mothers, Taiwanese children: Socializing practices with young children in Sino-Vietnamese cross-border marriage families in Taipei, Taiwan]. 台灣人類學刊 *[Taiwan Journal of Anthropology]*, 6, 47–88.

Fung, H., Miller, P. J., & Lin, L. C. (2004). Listening is active: Lessons from the narrative practices of Taiwanese families. In M. W. Pratt & B. E. Fiese (Eds.), *Family stories and the life course: Across time and generations* (pp. 303–323). Mahwah, NJ: Erlbaum.

Galton, F. (1869/2006). *Hereditary genius: An inquiry into its laws and consequences.* Amherst, NY: Prometheus.

Gao, G. (1998a). "Don't take my word for it:" Understanding Chinese speaking practices. *International Journal of Intercultural Relations, 22*, 163–186.

(1998b). An initial analysis of the effects of face and concern for "other" in Chinese interpersonal communication. *International Journal of Intercultural Relations, 22*(4), 467–482.

Gao, L.-B., & Watkins, D. (2001). Identifying and assessing the conceptions of teaching of secondary school physics teachers in China. *British Journal of Educational Psychology, 71*, 443–469.

Garcia Coll, C. T., & Marks, A. (2009). *Immigrant stories: Ethnicity and academics in middle childhood*. New York: Oxford University Press.

Gardner, H. (1983). *Frames of mind*. New York: Basic Books.

(1989). *To open minds*. New York: Basic Books.

(1991). *The unschooled mind: How children think and how schools should teach*. New York: Basic Books.

Gardner, H., Csikszentmihalyi, M., & Damon, W. (2001). *Good work: When excellence and ethics meet*. New York: Basic Books.

Gardner, M., & Steinberg, L. (2005). Peer influence on risk taking, risk preference, and risky decision making in adolescence and adulthood: an experimental study. *Developmental* Psychology, *41*(4), 625–635.

Geertz, C. (1973). *The interpretation of culture*. New York: Basic Books.

Gergen, K. J. (2010). The acculturated brain. *Theory & Psychology, 20*(6), 795–816.

Gernet, J., Foster, J. R., & Hartman, C. (1996). *A history of Chinese civilization*. New York: Cambridge University Press.

Gillies, R. M. (2006). Teachers' and students' verbal behaviours during cooperative and small-group learning. *British Journal of Educational Psychology, 76*, 271–287.

Ginsberg, E. (1992). Not just a matter of English. *HERDSA News, 14*(1), 6–8.

Gluckman, M. (2006). *Politics, law and ritual in tribal society*. Piscataway, NJ: Aldine Transaction.

Godes, O. (2009). *The effects of utility value on achievement behavior of two cultures*. Unpublished doctoral dissertation. University of Wisconsin, Madison.

Goffman, E. (1981). *Frames of talk*. Philadelphia: University of Pennsylvania Press.

Goleman, D. (1995). *Emotional intelligence: Why it can matter more than IQ*. New York: Bantam.

Gonzales, P., William, T., Jocylin, L., Roey, S., Kastberg, D., & Brewalt, S. (2008). *Highlights from TISMM 2007*. Washington, DC: National Center for Education Statistics.

Goodwin, M. H. (1990). *He-said-she-said: Talk as social organization among Black children*. Bloomington: Indiana University Press.

Gottfried, A. E., Fleming, J. S., & Gottfried, A. W. (1998). Role of cognitive stimulating home environment in children's academic intrinsic motivation: A longitudinal study. *Child Development, 69*, 1448–1460.

Gottman, J. M. (1993). How children become friends. *Monograph of the Society for Research in Child Development, 48*(3, Serial No. 201).

(1996). *The heart of parenting: How to raise an emotionally intelligent child*. New York: Simon & Shuster.

Gottman, J. M., Katz, L. F., & Hooven, C. (1996). Parental meta-emotion philosophy and the emotional life of families: Theoretical models and preliminary data. *Journal of Family Psychology, 10*(3), 243–268.

Grant, H., & Higgens, E. T. (2003). Optimism, promotion pride, and prevention pride as predictors of qualify of life. *Personality and Social Psychology Bulletin, 29*(12), 1521–1523.

Greene, M. L., Way, N., & Pahl, K. (2006). Trajectories of perceived adult and peer discrimination among Black, Latino, and Asian American adolescents: Patterns and psychological correlates. *Developmental Psychology, 42*(2), 218–238.

Grice, H. P. (1975). Logic and conversation. In P. Cole & J. L. Morgan (Eds.), *Syntax and semantics: Vol. 3. Speech acts.* New York: Academic Press.

Grolnick, W. S., Ryan, R. M., & Deci, E. L. (1991). Inner sources for school achievement: Motivational mediators of children's perceptions of their parents. *Journal of Educational Psychology, 83,* 508–517.

Gudykunst, W. B., & Ting-Toomey, S. (1988). *Culture and interpersonal communication.* Newbury Park, CA: Sage.

Gumperz, J. J., Drew, P., Goodwin, M. H., & Schiffrin, D. (1982). *Discourse strategies.* New York: Cambridge University Press.

Guthrie, W. K. C. (1969). *History of Greek philosophy.* Cambridge: Cambridge University Press.

Han, X.-R. (2006). *Chinese discourses on the peasant, 1900–1949.* Albany: State University of New York Press.

Harkness, S., & Super, C. (1992). The developmental niche: A theoretical framework for analyzing the household production of health. *Social Science and Medicine, 38,* 217–226.

Harkness, S., & Super, C. M. (Eds.) (1996). *Parents' cultural belief systems: Their origins, expressions, and consequences.* New York: Guilford.

Harkness, S. & Super, C. M. (1999). From parents' cultural belief systems to behavior: Implications for the development of early intervention programs. In L. Eldering & P. Leseman (Eds.), *Effective early education: Cross-cultural perspectives.* New York: Falmer.

Hau, K. T., & Salili, F. (1991). Structure and semantic differential placement of specific causes: Academic causal attributions by Chinese students in Hong Kong. *International Journal of Psychology, 26,* 175–193.

He, A. W. (2010). The language of ambiguity: Practices in Chinese heritage language classes. *Discourse Studies, 3,* 75–96.

Heath, S. B. (1983). *Ways with words: Language, life, and work in communities and classrooms.* New York: Cambridge University Press.

Hecht, J. M. (2003). *Doubt, a History: The great doubters and their legacy of innovation from Socrates and Jesus to Thomas Jefferson and Emily Dickinson.* New York: HarperCollins.

Heine, S. J., Kitayama, S., Lehman, D. R., Takata, T., Ide, E., Leung, C., et al. (2001). Divergent consequences of success and failure in Japan and North America: An investigation of self-improving motivations and malleable selves. *Journal of Personality and Social Psychology, 81,* 599–615.

Heine, S. J., Lehman, D. R., Markus, H. R., & Kitayama, S. (1999). Is there a universal need for positive self-regard? *Psychological Review, 106,* 766–794.

Helmke, A., & Tuyet, V. T. A. (1999). Do Asian and Western students learn in a different way? An empirical study on motivation, study time, and learning strategies of German and Vietnamese university students. *Asian Pacific Journal of Education, 19*(2), 30–44.

Hennessey, B. A., & Amabile, T. M. (1998). Reward, intrinsic motivation, and creativity. *American Psychologist, 53,* 674–675.

Henrich, J., Heine, S. J., & Norenzayan, A. (2010). The weirdest people in the world? *Behavioral and Brain Sciences, 33,* 61–83.

Herlitz, A., & Rehnman, J. (2008). Sex differences in episodic memory. *Current Directions in Psychological Science, 17*(1), 52–56.

Hernstein, R. J., & Murray, C. (1994). *The bell curve*. Chicago: Free Press.

Hess, R. D., & Azuma, H. (1991). Cultural support for schooling: Contrasts between Japan and the United States. *Educational Researcher, 20*(9), 2–8.

Hess, R. D., Azuma, H., Kashiwagi, K., Holloway, S. D., & Wenegrat, A. (1987). Cultural variations in socialization for school achievement: Contrasts between Japan and the United States. *Journal of Applied Developmental Psychology, 8*, 421–440.

Hess, R. D., Chang, C.-M., & McDevitt, T. M. (1987). Cultural variations in family belief about children's performance in mathematics: Comparisons among People's Republic of China, Chinese American, and Caucasian-American families. *Journal of Educational Psychology, 79*, 179–188.

Hess, R. D., Kashiwagi, K., Azuma, H., Price, G. G., & Dickson, W. P. (1980). Maternal expectations for mastery of developmental tasks in Japan and the United States. *International Journal of Psychology, 15*, 259–271.

Hewitt, R., & Inghilleri, M. (1993). Oracy in the Classroom: Policy, pedagogy, and group oral work. *Anthropology & Education Quarterly, 24*(4), 308–317.

Heyman, G. D., Fu, G.-Y., & Lee, K. (2008). Reasoning about the disclosure of success and failure to friends among children in the United States and China. *Developmental Psychology, 44*(4), 908–918.

Hidi, S., & Renninger, K. A. (2006). The four-phase model of interest development. *Educational Psychologist, 41*(2), 111–127.

Hill, N. E. (2009). Culturally-based world views, family processes, and family-school interactions. In S. L. Christenson & A. Reschly (Eds.), *Handbook of School-Family Partnerships* (pp. 101–127). New York: Routledge.

Hishino, H. J., & Larson, R. (2003). Japanese adolescents' free time: *Juku, Bukatsu*, and government efforts to create more meaningful leisure. In S. Verma & R. Larson (Eds.). *Examining adolescent leisure time across cultures: developmental opportunities and risks (New Directions for Child and Adolescent Development, No. 99)*. San Francisco: Jossey-Bass.

Ho, I. T. (2001). Are Chinese teachers authoritarian? In D. A. Watkins & J. B. Biggs (Eds.), *Teaching the Chinese learner: Psychological and pedagogical perspectives* (pp. 99–114). Hong Kong: Comparative Education Research Centre.

Hogan, K., Nastasi, B., K., & Pressley, M. (2000). Discourse patterns collaborative scientific reasoning in peer and teacher-guided discussion. *Cognition and Instruction, 17*, 379–432.

Holloway, S. D. (1988). Concepts of ability and effort in Japan and the US. *Review of Educational Research, 58*, 327–345.

Holman, R. L. (1991, December 21). Exam hell linked to depression. *Wall Street Journal, (Eastern ed.)*. New York: Dec. 26, p. 4.

Holton, G. (1973). *Thematic origins of scientific thought*. Cambridge, MA: Harvard University Press.

Hong, Z.-L. (2nd ed.). (2004). 義務教育課程標准實驗教科書：《語文》九年級. 江蘇教育出版社 [Chinese for 9th Grade: Standard experimental textbook for compulsory education] (Ed.). Jiangsu Providence, China: Jiangsu Education Press.

Hsu, F. L. K. (1981). *Americans and Chinese: Passage to difference* (3rd ed.). Honolulu: University of Hawaii Press.

Hsueh, Y. (1999). A day at Little Stars Preschool, Beijing, China. Unpublished video footage.

Hsueh, Y., Zhou, Z.-K., Cohen, R., Hundley, R. J., & Deptula, D. P. (2005). Knowing and showing respect: Chinese and U.S. children's understanding of respect and its association to their friendships. *Journal of Psychology in Chinese Societies*, 6(2), 89–120.

Huang, D. Y., & Peng, H. J. (1992). 三字經 [*Three character classic*]. Taipei, Taiwan: Ruisheng Book & Magazine Publishing House.

Huang, H.-M. (2004). Effects of cram schools on children's mathematics learning. In L.-H. Fan, N.-Y. Wong, J.-F. Cai, S.-Q. Li, & T.-Y. Tso (Eds.), *How Chinese learn mathematics: Perspectives from insiders* (pp. 282–306). Singapore: World Scientific.

Huang, R.-J., & Leung, K. S. F. (2004). Cracking the paradox of Chinese learners: Looking into the mathematics classrooms in Hong Kong and Shanghai. In L.-H. Fan, N.-Y. Wong, J.-F. Cai, S.-Q. Li, & T.-Y. Tso (Eds.), *How Chinese learn mathematics: Perspectives from insiders* (pp. 348–381). Singapore: World Scientific.

Hufton, N., & Elloitt, J. (2000). Motivation to learn: The pedagogical nexus in the Russian school: Some implications for transnational research and policy borrowing. *Educational Studies*, 26, 115–122.

Hume, D. (1740/2008). *A treatise of human nature*. Sioux Falls, SD: NuVision.

Inagaki, K., Hatano, G., & Morita, E. (1998). Construction of mathematical knowledge through whole-class discussion. *Learning and Instruction*, 8, 503–526.

Ishii, S., & Bruneau, T. (1994). Silence and silences in cross-cultural perspective: Japan and the United States. In L. A. Samovar & R. E. Porter (Eds.), *Intercultural communication: A reader* (7th ed., pp. 246–251). Belmont, CA: Wadsworth.

Ishisada, M. (1974). The civil service examination: China's examination hell. *Chinese Education*, 7, 1–74.

Institute of International Education (n.d.). Retrieved April, 16 2011 from http://www.iie.org/en/Research-and-Publications/Open-Doors

Ivanhoe, P. J. (2000). *Confucian moral self cultivation* (2nd ed.). Indianapolis, IN: Hackett.

Iyengar, S. S., & Lepper, M. R. (1999). Rethinking the value of choice: A cultural perspective on intrinsic motivation. *Journal of Personality and Social Psychology*, 76, 349–366.

Jackson, P. W., Boostrom, R. E., & Hansen, D. T. (1993). *The moral life of schools*. San Francisco, CA: Jossey-Bass.

James, W. (1892, 1963). *Principles of psychology*. New York: Holt.

Jameson, K. A. (2005). The role of culture in color naming research. *Cross-Cultural Research: The Journal of Comparative Social Science*, 39(1), 88–106.

Jin, L., & Cortazzi, M. (1998). Dimensions of dialogue: Large classes in China. *International Journal of Educational Research*, 29(8), 739–761.

Johnson, D. (2009, Dec. 7). Attacked Asian students afraid to go to school: 26 Asian students were attacked last week. Retrieved from November, 20, 2010 from http://www.nbcphiladelphia.com/news/local-beat/Attacked-Asian-Students-Fear-Returning-to-Class-78652997.html

Johnson, F. A., & Marsella, A. J. (1978). Different attitudes toward verbal behavior in students of Japanese and European ancestry. *Genetic Psychology Monographs, 97,* 43–76.

Jones, W. H., & Carpenter, B. N. (1986). Shyness, social behavior and relations. In W. H. Jones, J. M. Cheek, & S. R. Briggs (Eds.), *Shyness: Perspectives on research and treatment* (pp. 227–238). New York: Plenum.

Juang, L. P., & Nguyen, H. H. (2010). Ethnic identity among Chinese-American youth: The role of family obligation and community factors on ethnic engagement, clarity, and pride. *Identity: An International Journal of Theory and Research, 10*(1), 20–38.

Juvonen, J., & Gross, E. F. (2005). The rejected and the bullied: Lessons about social misfits from developmental psychology. In W. D. Kipling, J. P. Forgas, & W. von Hippel (Eds.), *The social outcast: Ostracism, social exclusion, rejection, and bullying* (pp. 155–170). New York: Psychology Press.

Juvonen, J., & Murdock, T. B. (1995). Grade-level differences in the social value of effort: Implications for self-presentation tactics of early adolescents. *Child Development, 66*(6), 1694–1705.

Kagan, J., Kearsley, R. B., & Zelazo, P. R. (1977). The effects of infant daycare on psychological development. *Evaluation Quarterly, 1,* 109–142.

Kant, I. (1787/1999). *Critique of pure reason.* New York: Cambridge University Press.

(1803/1960). *Kant on education.* Ann Arbor: University of Michigan Press.

Katriel, T., & Philipsen, G. (1981). "What we need is communication": "Communication" as a cultural category in some American speech. *Communication Monographs, 48,* 301–317.

Kember, D. (2000). Misconceptions about the learning approaches, motivation, and study approaches of Asian students. *Higher Education, 40,* 99–121.

Kim, H. S. (2002). We talk, therefore we think? A Cultural analysis of the effect of talking on thinking. *Journal of Personality and Social Psychology, 83,* 828–842.

(2008). Culture and the cognitive and neuroendocrine responses to speech. *Journal of Personality and Social Psychology, 94*(1), 32–47.

Kim, U., & Park, Y. S. (2008). Cognitive, relational and social basis of academic achievement in Confucian cultures: Psychological, indigenous and cultural perspectives. In R. Sorrentino and S. Yamaguchi (Eds.), *Handbook of motivation and cognition across cultures* (pp. 491–515). New York: Elsevier.

Kindermann, T. (1993). Natural peer groups as contexts for individual development: The case of children's motivation in school. *Developmental Psychology, 29,* 970–977.

Klopf, D. W., Cambra, R. E. (1979). Communication apprehension among college students in American, Australia, Japan, and Korea. *Journal of Counseling Psychology, 102,* 27–31.

Knox, M. M., McGalliard, J. C., Pasinetti, P. M., Hugo, H. E., Spacks, P. M., Wellek, R., Doughlas, K., & Lawall, S. *The Norton anthology of world masterpieces, Vol. 2.* New York: Norton.

Kobayashi, Y. (1994). Conceptual acquisition and change through social interaction. *Human Development, 37,* 232–241.

Kuhn, D. (1991). *Education for thinking.* Cambridge, MA: Harvard University Press.

Kulis, S., Napoli, M., & Marsiglia, F. (2002). Ethnic pride, biculturalism, and drug use norms of urban American Indian adolescents. *Social Work Research, 26,* 101–112.

Kwan, V. S. Y., Bond, M. H., Boucher, H. C., Maslach, C., & Gan, Y.-Q. (2002). The construct of individuation: More complex in collectivist than in individualist cultures. *Personality and Social Psychology Bulletin, 28*(3), 300–310.

Ladd, G. W., & Troop-Gordon, W. (2003). The role of chronic peer difficulties in the development of children's psychological adjustment problems. *Child Development, 74*(5), 1344–1367.

La Greca, A. M., & Harrison, H. M. (2005). Adolescent peer relations, friendships, and romantic relationships: Do they predict social anxiety and depression? *Journal of Clinical Child & Adolescent Psychology, 34,* 49–61.

Lam, S.-F., Law, Y.-K., & Shum, M. S.-K. (2009). Classroom discourse analysis and educational outcomes in the era of education reform. *British Journal of Educational Psychology, 79,* 617–641.

Lao, Tzu (1992). *The Tao of the Tao Te Ching* (M. LaFargue, Trans.). Albany: State University of New York Press.

Lapointe, A. E., Mead, N. A., & Askew, J. M. (1992). *Learning mathematics.* Princeton, NJ: Educational Testing Service.

Lee, A. Y., Aaker, J. L., & Gardner, W. L. (2000). The pleasures and pains of distinct self-construals: The role of interdependence in regulatory focus. *Journal of Personality and Social Psychology, 78*(6), 1122–1134.

Lee, K., Cameron, C. A., & Board, J. (1997). Chinese and Canadian children's evaluations of lying and truth telling. *Child Development, 68,* 924–934.

Lee, K., Xu, F., Fu, G., Cameron, C. A., & Chen, S. (2001). Taiwan and mainland Chinese and Canadian children's categorization and evaluation of lie- and truth-telling: A modest effect. *British Journal of Developmental Psychology, 19,* 525–542.

Lee, T. H. C. (1985). *Government education and examinations in Sung China, 960–1278.* Hong Kong: Chinese University Press.

(1999). *Education in traditional China: A history.* Boston, MA: Brill Academic.

Lee, W. O. (1996). The cultural context for Chinese learners: Conceptions of learning in the Confucian tradition. In D. A. Watkins & J. B. Biggs (Eds.), *The Chinese learner* (pp. 45–67). Hong Kong: Comparative Education Research Centre.

Legge, J. (Trans.) (1960). *The Chinese classics, 5 volumes.* Hong Kong: University of Hong Kong.

LeVine, R. A. (1974). Parental goals: A cross cultural view. In H. J. Leichter (Ed.), *The family as educator* (pp. 52–65). New York: Teachers College Press.

(1990). Enculturation: A biosocial perspective on the development of self. In D. Cicchetti & M. Beeghly (Eds.), *The self in transition: Infancy to childhood* (pp. 99–117). Chicago: University of Chicago Press.

Levy, R. I. (1973). *Tahitians.* Chicago: University of Chicago Press.

Lewis, C. C. (1995). *Educating hearts and minds: Reflections on Japanese preschool and elementary education.* New York: Cambridge University Press.

Lewis, M. (1993). The development of deception. In M. Lewis & C. Saarni (Eds.), *Lying and deception in everyday life* (pp. 106–125). New York: Guilford.

(2007). Self-conscious emotional development. In J. L. Tracy, R. W., Robins, R. W., & J. P. Tangney (Eds.), *The self-conscious emotions: Theory and research* (pp. 134–152). New York: Guilford.

Lewis, M., & Wolan-Sullivan, M. (2005). The development of self-conscious emotions. In A. Elliot & C. S. Dweck (Eds.), *Handbook of competence and motivation* (pp. 185–201). New York: Guilford.

Li, H., & Zahniser, S. (2002). The determinants of temporary rural-to-urban migration in China. *Urban Studies, 39*, 2219–2235.

Li, J. (1997). Creativity in horizontal and vertical domains. *Creativity Research Journal, 10*, 107–132.

(1998). The power of embedding learning beliefs in everyday learning: Language arts texts as a vehicle for enculturation. Unpublished manuscript.

(2001). Chinese conceptualization of learning. *Ethos, 29*, 111–137.

(2002). A cultural model of learning: Chinese "heart and mind for wanting to learn." *Journal of Cross-Cultural Psychology, 33*(3), 248–269.

(2003). U.S. and Chinese cultural beliefs about learning. *Journal of Educational Psychology, 95*(2), 258–267.

(2004). Learning as a task and a virtue: U.S. and Chinese preschoolers explain learning. *Developmental Psychology, 40*(4), 595–605.

(2005). Mind or virtue: Western and Chinese beliefs about learning. *Current Directions in Psychological Science, 14*(4), 190–194.

(2006). Self in learning: Chinese adolescents' goals and sense of agency. *Child Development, 77*(2), 482–501.

Li, J., & Fischer, K. W. (2004). Thoughts and emotions in American and Chinese cultural beliefs about learning. In D. Y. Dai & R. Sternberg (Eds.), *Motivation, emotion, and cognition: Integrative perspectives on intellectual functioning and development* (pp. 385–418). Mahwah, NJ: Erlbaum.

(2007). Respect as a positive self-conscious emotion in European Americans and Chinese. In J. L. Tracy, R. W. Robins, & J. P. Tangney (Eds.), *The self-conscious emotions: Theory and research* (pp. 224–242). New York: Guilford.

Li, J., Fung, H., Liang, C.-H., Resch, J., Luo, L., & Lou, L. (2008, July). When my child doesn't learn well: European American and Taiwanese mothers talking to their children about their children's learning weaknesses. In J. Li & H. Fung (Chairs), *Diverse paths and forms of family socialization: Cultural and ethnic influences.* Symposium paper presented by biannual conference of the International Society for the Study of Behavioral Development, Würzburg, Germany.

Li, J., Fung, H., Liang, C.-H., Resch, J., & Luo, L. (2008, July). Guiding for self-discovery or self-betterment: European American and Taiwanese mothers talking to their children about learning. In A. Bernardo (Chair), *Achievement motivation and achievement attribution among Asian students: Insights from qualitative data.* Invited paper symposium by the International Congress of Psychology, Berlin, Germany.

(2009). Is the glass half-empty or half-full? Emotional responses to children's learning among European American and Taiwanese parents. Manuscript under review.

Li, J., Holloway, S. D., Bempechat, J., & Loh, E. (2008). Building and using a social network: Nurture for low-income Chinese American adolescents' learning. In H. Yoshikawa & N. Way (Eds.), *Beyond families and schools: How broader social contexts shape the adjustment of children and youth in immigrant families* (pp. 7–25). San Francisco, CA: Jossey-Bass.

Li, J., Wang, L.-Q., & Fischer, K. W. (2004). The organization of Chinese shame concepts. *Cognition and Emotion, 18*(6), 767–797.

Li, J., & Wang, Q. (2004). Perceptions of achievement and achieving peers in U.S. and Chinese kindergartners. *Social Development, 13*(3), 413–436.

Li, J., Yamamoto, Y., Luo, L., Batchelor, A., & Bresnahan, R. M. (2010). Why attend school? Chinese immigrant and European American preschoolers' views and outcomes. *Developmental Psychology, 46*(6), 1637–1650.

Li, J.-H. (2004). Thorough understanding of the textbook: A significant feature of [the] Chinese teacher manual. In L.-H. Fan, N.-Y. Wong, J.-F. Cai, S.-Q. Li, & T.-Y. Tso (Eds.), *How Chinese learn mathematics: Perspectives from insiders* (pp. 262–281). Singapore: World Scientific.

Li, X.-D, Sun, W.-Q., & Luo, G.-Z. (2010). 李行道孙文卿罗贯中集 *[Collection of Li Xingdao, Sun Wenqing, and Luo Guanzhong]*. Shangxi, China: People's Publishing House.

Li, Y.-T, & Yan, B.-H. (2003). 梁漱溟先生講孔孟 *[Liang Shuming on Confucius and Mencius]*. Guilin, China: Guangxi Normal University Press.

Liang, C.-H. (2007). Shame and pride: Age, kinship terms and socialization practice in a middle-class Taiwanese preschool. Poster presented at the Biannual Meetings of Society for Research in Child Development, Boston, MA.

Lipset, S. M. (1996). *American exceptionalism: A double-edged sword.* New York: Norton.

Litman, J. A., & Silvia, P. J. (2006). The latent structure of trait curiosity: Evidence for interest and deprivation curiosity dimensions. *Journal of Personality Assessment, 86*(3), 318–328.

Liu, Y.-M. (2004). "Nothing can be accomplished if the speech does not sound agreeable": Rhetoric and the invention of classical Chinese discourse. In C. S. Lipson & R. A. Binkley (Eds.), *Rhetoric before and beyond the Greeks* (pp. 147–164). Albany: State University of New York Press.

Lopez-Real, F., Mok, A. C. I., Leung, K. S. F., & Marton, F. (2004). Identifying a pattern of teaching: An analysis of a Shanghai teacher's lessons. In L.-H. Fan, N.-Y. Wong, J.-F. Cai, S.-Q. Li, & T.-Y. Tso (Eds.), *How Chinese learn mathematics: Perspectives from insiders* (pp. 382–412). Singapore: World Scientific.

Lucy, J. A. (1992). *Language diversity and thought: A reformulation of the linguistic relativity hypothesis.* New York: Cambridge University Press.

Lyon, A. (2004). Confucian silence and remonstration: A basis for deliberation? In C. S. Lipson & R. A. Binkley (Eds.), *Rhetoric before and beyond the Greeks* (pp. 131–145). Albany: State University of New York Press.

Locke, J. (1690/2008). *An essay concerning human understanding.* Oxford: Oxford University Press.

(1693/2007). *Some thoughts concerning education.* Sioux Falls, SD: NuVision.

Luria, A. R. (1981). *Language and cognition.* New York: Wiley.

Mahalingam, R. (Ed.) (2006). *Cultural psychology of immigrants.* Mahwah, NJ: Erlbaum.

Mangan, J. A. (Ed.) (1994). *A significant social revolution: Cross-cultural aspects of the evolution of compulsory education*. London: Woborn.

Marcovitch, S., & Zelazo, P. D. (2009). A hierarchical competing systems model of the emergence and early development of executive function. *Developmental Science, 12*(1), 1–18.

Markus, H. R., & Nurius, P. (1986). Possible selves. *American Psychologist, 41*, 954–969.

Marton, F., Dall'Alba, G., & Beaty, E. (1993). Conceptions of learning. *International Journal of Educational Research, 19*, 277–300.

Marton, F., Dall'Alba, G., & Tse, L. K. (1996). Memorizing and understanding: The keys to the paradox? In D. A. Watkins & J. B. Biggs (Eds.), *The Chinese learner* (pp. 69–83). Hong Kong: Comparative Education Research Centre.

Masataka, N. (1999). Nihonteki ijime no seiritsu to ikuji [The formation of Japanese bullying and child-rearing]. *Japanese Journal of Addiction and Family, 16*(4), 438–444.

Mascolo, M. F., Fischer, K. W., & Li, J. (2003). The dynamic construction of emotions in development: A component systems approach. In N. Davidson, K. Scherer, & H. Goldsmith (Eds.), *Handbook of affective science* (pp. 375–408). New York: Oxford University Press.

Matsushita, K. (1994). Acquiring mathematical knowledge through semantic and pragmatic problem solving. *Human Development, 37*, 220–232.

McBride, R. E., Xiang, P., Wittenburg, D., & Shen, J.-H. (2002). An analysis of preservice teachers' dispositions toward critical thinking: A cross-cultural perspective. *Asian-Pacific Journal of Teacher Education, 30*(2), 131–140.

McClelland, D. C. (1963). Motivational pattern in Southeast Asia with special reference to the Chinese case. *Journal of Social Issues, 19*(1), 6–19.

McGuire, J. (1997). *English as a foreign language in China. Occasional Papers, 48*. University of Southampton: Centre for Language in Education.

McKnight, C. C., Crosswhite, F. J., Dossey, J. A., Kifer, E., Swafford, J. O., Travers, K. J., & Cooney, T. J. (1987). *The underachieving curriculum: Assessing U. S. school mathematics from an international perspective*. Champaign, IL: Stipes.

McLean, B., & Elkind, P. (2004). *The smartest guys in the room: The amazing rise and scandalous fall of Enron*. New York: Portfolio Trade.

Medrich, E. A., & Griffith, J. E. (1992). *International mathematics and science assessment: What have we learned?* Washington, DC: U.S. Department of Education.

Meisner, M. (1999). *Mao's China and after: A history of the People's Republic* (3rd ed.). New York: Free Press.

Mencius (1970). *Mencius* (D. C. Lao, Trans.). Harmondsworth: Penguin Books.

Mesquita, B. (2003). Emotions as dynamic cultural phenomena. In N. Davidson, K. Scherer, & H. Goldsmith (Eds.), *Handbook of affective science* (pp. 871–890). New York: Oxford University Press.

Mesquita, B., & Frijda, N. H. (1992). Cultural variations in emotions: A review. *Psychological Bulletin, 112*, 179–204.

Miller, P. J., Fung, H., Lin, S., Chen, E. C.-H., & Boldt, B. R. (2012). How socialization happens on the ground: Narrative practices as alternate socializing pathways in Taiwanese and European-American families. Monographs of the society for research in child development. 77(1, Serial No. 302). Boston, MA: Wiley-Blackwell.

Miller, P. J., Sandel, T. L., Liang, C.-H., & Fung, H. (2001). Narrating transgressions in Longwood: The discourses, meanings, and paradoxes of an American socializing practice. *Ethos, 29*(2), 159–186.

Miller, P. J., Wang, S.-H., Sandel, T., & Cho, G. E. (2002). Self-esteem as folk theory: A comparison of European American and Taiwanese mothers' beliefs. *Parenting: Science and Practice, 2*(3), 209–239.

Minami, M. (1994). English and Japanese: A cross-cultural comparison parental styles of narrative elicitation. *Issues in Applies Linguistics,* 5, 383–407.

Mishima, K. (1996). Bullying amongst close friends in elementary school. *Japanese Journal of Social Psychology, 19*(1), 41–50.

Moll, L. C. (1995). *Vygotsky and education: Instructional implications and applications of sociohistorical psychology.* New York: Cambridge University Press.

Morris, J. A., Brotheridge, C. M., & Urbanski, J. C. (2005). Bringing humility to leadership: Antecedents and consequences of leader humility. *Human Relations, 58*(10), 1323–1350.

Morton, J. (1969). Interaction of information in word recognition. *Psychological Review,* 76, 165–178.

Moser, P. K., & Nat, A. V. (2002). *Human knowledge: Classical and contemporary approaches* New York: Oxford University Press.

Murase, T., Dale, P. S., Ogura, T., Yamashita, Y., & Mahieu, A. (2005). Mothery-child conversation during joint picture book reading in Japan and the USA. *First Language, 25,* 197–218.

Nakkula, M., & Toshalis, E. (2006). *Understanding youth: Adolescent development for educators.* Cambridge, MA: Harvard Education Press.

National Bureau of Statistics of China (2011, March, 11). Rural migrant workers amounted to 225.42 million (16.8% of its total population) at the end of 2008. Retrieved April, 16 2011 from http://www.stats.gov.cn/tjfx/fxbg/t20110310_402710032.htm

National Center for Education Development Research (2001). *2001 年中國教育綠皮書 [2001 green paper on education in China: Annual report on policies of China's education].* Beijing, China: Educational Science Publishing.

Ng, F. F.-Y., Pomerantz, E., & Lam, S.-F. (2007). European American and Chinese parents' responses to children's success and failure: Implications for children's responses. *Developmental Psychology, 43*(5), 1239–1255.

Nicholls, J. G. (1978). The development of the concepts of effort and ability, perception of academic attainment, and the understanding that difficult tasks require more ability. *Child Development, 49,* 800–814.

Nisbett, R. E. (2003). *The geography of thought.* New York: Simon & Schuster.

Nishina, A., & Juvonen, J. (2005). Daily reports of witnessing and experiencing peer harassment in middle school. *Child Development, 76*(2), 435–450.

Nobel Museum (n.d.). Retrieved from October 5, 2010 from http://nobelprize.org/nobel_prizes/physics/laureates/

(n.d.). Retrieved from October 5, 2010 from http://nobelprize.org/nobel_prizes/medicine/laureates/

Nugent, B. (2007, July 29). Who's a nerd, anyway? *New York Times Magazine*. Retrieved July 28, 2007 from http://www.nytimes.com/2007/07/29/magazine/29wwln-idealab-t.html?_r=1&ref=magazine&oref=slogin

Oakes, J., & Guiton, G. (1995). Matchmaking: The dynamics of high school tracking decisions. *American Educational Research Journal, 32*(1), 3–33.

O'Connor, M. C., & Michaels, S. (1993). Aligning academic task and participation status through revoicing: Analysis of a classroom discourse strategy. *Anthropology & Education Quarterly, 24*(4), 318–335.

Olson, D. R. (1994). *The world on paper: The conceptual and cognitive implications of writing and reading.* New York: Cambridge University Press.

Olson, D. R., & Katz, S. (2001). The fourth folk pedagogy. In B. Torff and R. S. Sternberg (Eds.), *Understanding and teaching the intuitive mind* (pp. 243–263). Mahwah, NJ: Erlbaum.

Organisation for Economic Co-operation and Development. (2003). *Education at a glance: OECD indicators 2003.* Paris: OECD.

(2006). *Education at a glance: OECO indicators 2006.* Paris: OECD.

(2009). *PISA 2009 results: Executive summary.* Retrieved January 5, 2011 from http://www.pisa.oecd.org/dataoecd/34/60/46619703.pdf

Paine, L. W. (1990). The teacher as virtuoso: A Chinese model for teaching. *The Teachers College Record, 92*(1), 49–81.

Paulhus, D. L., Duncan, J. H., & Yik, M. S. M. (2002). Patterns of shyness in East-Asian and European-heritage students. *Journal of Research in Personality, 36,* 442–462.

Paulhus, D. L., Hendin, H., & Shaver, P. R. (2001). European vs. Asian heritage differences in personality: narcissism, modesty, and self-construal. Unpublished manuscript.

Paulhus, D. L., & Morgan, K. L. (1997). Perceptions of intelligence in leaderless groups: Dynamic effects of shyness and acquaintance. *Journal of Personality and Social Psychology, 72,* 581–591.

Pellegrini, A. D., & Long, J. D. (2003). A longitudinal study of bullying, dominance, and victimization during the transition from primary through secondary school. *British Journal of Developmental Psychology, 20,* 259–280.

Peng K.-P., & Nisbett, R. E. (1999). Culture, dialects, and reasoning about contradiction. *American Psychologist, 54,* 741–754.

Peng, S. S. (1998, July). Communication at Meeting of Chinese American Educational Research and Development Association, Chicago, IL.

Peng, S. S., & Wright, D. (1994). Explanation of academic achievement of Asian American students. *Journal of Educational Research, 87*(6), 346–352.

Peréa, F. C., & García Coll, C. (2008). The social and cultural contexts of bilingualism. In J. Altarriba & R. Heredia (Eds.), *An introduction to bilingualism: Principles and processes* (pp. 199–241). Mahwah, NJ: Erlbaum.

Perkins, D. N. (1995). *Smart schools.* New York: Free Press.

Perner, J., Leekam, S. R., & Wimmer, H. (1987). Three year olds difficulty with false belief: The case for a conceptual deficit. *British Journal of Developmental Psychology, 5*(2), 125–137.

Petrie, K. J., Booth, R. J., Pennebaker, J. W., & Davison, K. P. (1995). Disclosure of trauma and immune response to a hepatitis B vaccination program. *Journal of Counseling and Clinical Psychology, 63,* 787–792.

Phinney, J. S., & Baldelomar, O. A. (2011). Identity development in multiple cultural contexts. In L. Arnett Jensen (Ed.), *Bridging cultural and developmental psychology: New syntheses in theory, research and policy* (pp. 161–186). New York: Oxford University Press.

Piaget, J., & Inhelder, B. (1969). *The psychology of the child* (H. Weaver, Trans.). New York: Basic.

Pinker, S. (1994). *The language instinct.* New York: Harper.

Pintrich, P. R., Smith, D. A. F., Garcia, T., & McKeachie, W. J. (1993). Reliability and predictive validity of the motivated strategies for learning questionnaire (MSLQ). *Educational and Psychological Measurement, 53,* 801–813.

Plato (1981). *Five dialogues* (G. M. A. Gruber, Trans.). Indianapolis, IN: Hackett.

(1991). *The republic of Plato* (2nd ed.). (A. Bloom, Trans.). New York: Basic Books.

Plutarch (2009). *Plutarch's lives of Pericles & Fabius Maximus, Demosthenes & Cicero.* Ann Arbor: University of Michigan Library.

Popper, K. (1972/1989). *Objective knowledge: An evolutionary approach.* Oxford: Oxford University Press.

Portes, A., & Rumbaut, R. G. (2001). *Legacies: The story of the immigrant second generation.* Berkeley: University of California Press.

Pratt, D. D., Kelly, M., & Wong, K. M. (1999). Chinese conceptions of "effective teaching" in Hong Kong: Towards culturally sensitive evaluation of teaching. *International Journal of Lifelong Learning, 18,* 241–258.

Purdie, N., & Hattie, J. (1996). Cultural differences in the use of strategies for self-regulated learning. *American Educational Research Journal, 33,* 845–871.

Purdie, N., Hattie, J., & Douglas, G. (1996). Student conceptions of learning and their use of self-regulated learning strategies: A cross-cultural comparison. *Journal of Educational Psychology, 88,* 87–100.

Putnam, R. D. (2007). *E Pluribus Unum*: Diversity and community in the twenty-first century: The 2006 Johan Skytte Prize lecture. *Scandinavian Political Science, 30,* 137–174.

Qin, D. B.-L. (2008). Doing well vs. feeling well: Understanding family dynamics and the psychological adjustment of Chinese immigrant adolescent. *Journal of Youth and Adolescence, 37*(1), 22–35.

(2008). The other side of the model minority story: Understanding psychological and social adjustment of Chinese American students. In G. Li & L. Wang (Eds.), *Model minority myths revisited: An interdisciplinary approach to demystifying Asian American education experiences* (pp. 133–156). Charlotte, NC: Information Age.

Qin, D. B., Way, N., & Mukherjee, P. (2008). The other side of the model minority story the familial and peer challenges faced by Chinese American adolescents. *Youth & Society, 39*(4), 480–506.

Quinn, N., & Holland, D. (1987). Introduction. In D. Holland & N. Quinn (Eds.), *Cultural models in language and thought* (pp. 3–40). New York: Cambridge University Press.

Quintilian (2002). *Orator's Education, Volume I: Books 1–2.* (Trans. by D. A. Russell). Cambridge, MA: Harvard University Press.

Rakoczy, H., Warneken, F., Tomasello, M. (2008). The sources of normativity: Young children's awareness of the normative structure of games. *Developmental Psychology, 44*(3), 875–881.

Ramsden, S. R., & Hubbard, J. A. (2002). Family expressiveness and parental emotion coaching: Their role in children's emotion regulation and aggression. *Journal of Abnormal Child Psychology, 30*(6), 657–667.

Ran, A. (2001). Traveling on parallel tracks: Chinese parents and English teachers. *Educational Research, 43*, 311–328.

Rivas-Drake, D., Hughes, D., & Way, N. (2008). A closer look at peer discrimination, ethnic identity, and psychological well-being among urban Chinese American sixth graders. *Journal Youth Adolescence, 37*, 12–21.

Rogers, C. (1969). *Freedom to learn.* Columbus, OH: Merrill.

Rogoff, B. (1990). *Apprenticeship in thinking: Cognitive development in social context.* New York: Oxford University Press.

(2003). *The cultural nature of human development.* New York: Oxford University Press.

Rosch, E. (1975). Cognitive representations of semantic categories. *Journal of Experimental Psychology: General, 104*, 192–233.

(1978). Principles of categorization. In E. Rosch & B. B. Lloyd (Eds.), *Cognition and categorization* (pp. 27–48). Hillsdale, NJ: Erlbaum.

Rosemont, Jr., H. (1992). Rights-bearing individuals and role-bearing persons. In I. M. Bockover (Ed.), *Rules, rituals, and responsibility: Essays dedicated to Herbert Fingarette* (pp. 71–101). La Sale, IL: Open Court.

(2003). Is there a universal path of spiritual progress in the texts of early Confucianism? In W. M. Tu & M. E. Tucker (Eds.), *Confucian spirituality, vol. 1* (pp. 183–196). New York: Crossroad.

Rosenbloom, S. R., & Way, N. (2004). Experiences of discrimination among African American, Asian American, and Latino adolescents in an urban high school. *Youth & Society, 35*(4), 420–451.

Ross, M., Heine, S. J., Wilson, A. E., & Sugimori, S. (2005). Cross-cultural discrepancies in self-appraisals. *Personality and Social Psychology Bulletin, 31*(9), 1175–1188.

Rothbaum, F., & Wang, Y. Z. (2011). Cultural and developmental pathways to acceptance of self and acceptance of the world. In L. A. Jensen (Ed.), *Bridging cultural and developmental approaches to psychology: New syntheses in theory, research, and policy* (pp. 187–211). New York: Oxford University Press.

Rotter, J. (1966). Generalized expectancies for internal versus external control of reinforcement. *Psychological Monographs, General & Applied, 80*(1), (Whole No. 609).

Rousseau, J. J. (1762/1979). *Emil, or on education* (A. Bloom, Trans.). New York: Basic Books.

Rozin, P. (2010). The weirdest people in the world are a harbinger of the future of the world. *Behavioral and Brain Sciences, 33*, 108–109.

Ruble, D. N., Eisenberg, R., & Higgins, E. T. (1994). Developmental changes in achievement evaluations: Motivational implications of self-other differences. *Child Development, 65*, 1095–1110.

Ruble, D. N., Frey, K. S, & Greulich, F. (1995). Meeting goals and confronting conflicts: Children's changing perceptions of social comparison. *Child Development, 66*, 723–738.

Russell, B. (1975). *A history of western philosophy and its connection with political and social circumstances from the earliest times to the present day.* New York: Simon & Schuster.

Ryan, R. M., & Deci, E. L. (2000). Self-determination theory and the facilitation of intrinsic motivation, social development, and well-being. *American Psychologist, 55*(1), 68–78.

Salili, F., & Hau, K. T. (1994). The effect of teachers' evaluative feedback on Chinese students' perception of ability: A cultural and situational analysis. *Educational Studies, 20,* 223–236.

Schiffrin, D. (1994). *Approaches to discourse: Language as social interaction,* Malden, MA: Blackwell.

Schneider, B., Hieshima, J. A., Lee, S., & Plank, S. (1994). East-Asian academic success in the United States: Family, school, and cultural explanations. In P. M. Greenfield & R. R. Cocking (Eds.), *Cross-cultural roots of minority child development* (pp. 332–350). Hillsdale, NJ: Erlbaum.

Scollon, C. N., Diener, E., Oishi, S., & Biswas-Diener, R. (2005). An experience sampling and cross-cultural investigation of the relation between pleasant and unpleasant affect. *Cognition and Emotion, 19*(1), 27–52.

Seuss, G. T. (1950). *If I ran the zoo.* New York: Random House.

Shaver, P., Schwartz, J., Kirson, D., & O'Connor, C. (1987). Emotion knowledge: Further exploration of a prototype approach. *Journal of Personality and Social Psychology, 52,* 1061–1086.

Shun, K.-L., & Wong, D. B. (2004). *Confucian ethics.* New York: Cambridge University Press.

Shweder, R. A. (1991). *Thinking through cultures.* Cambridge, MA: Harvard University Press.

(2011). Commentary: Ontogenetic cultural psychology. In L. A. Jensen (Ed.), *Bridging cultural and developmental psychology: New syntheses in theory, research and policy* (pp. 303–310). New York: Oxford University Press.

Siu, M. K. (2004). Official curriculum in mathematics in ancient China: How did Candidates study for the examination? In L.-H. Fan, N.-Y. Wong, J.-F. Cai, S.-Q. Li, & T.-Y. Tso (Eds.), *How Chinese learn mathematics: Perspectives from insiders* (pp. 157–185). Singapore: World Scientific.

Sizer, T. R. (1996). *Horace's hope: What works for the American high school.* Boston, MA: Houghton Mifflin.

Smith, D. (1991). Children of China: An inquiry into the relationship between Chinese family life and academic achievement in modern Taiwan. *Asian Culture Quarterly, 14*(1), 1–29.

Smith, R. M. (1995). A new look at the canon of the Ten Attic Orators. Mnemosyne 48.1.

Smits, W., & Stromback, T. (2001). *The economics of the apprenticeship system.* Cheltenham: Elgar.

Sommers, S. (1984). Adults evaluating their emotions: A cross-cultural perspective. In C. Z. Malatesta & C. E. Izard (Eds.), *Emotion in adult development* (pp. 319–338). Beverly Hills, CA: Sage.

Song, N. (1995). 鬆年 *(1837–1906)* 頤園畫語 [Song Nian (1837–1906) on painting in the Nurturing Garden (reprint)]. Shanghai, China: Shanghai Ancient Books.

Spinrad, T. L., Eisenberg, N., Gaertner, B., Popp, T., Smith, C. L., Kupfer, A. et al. (2007). Relations of maternal socialization and toddlers' effortful control to children's adjustment and social competence. *Developmental Psychology, 43*(5), 1170–1186.

St. Augustine. (397/1998). *St. Augustine confessions* (H. Chadwick, Trans.). New York: Oxford University Press.

State Statistics Bureau (SSB). (2005). 新中國55年統計資料匯編 [China's fifty-five years of statistical data]. Beijing, China: China Statistical Press.

Steenbergen-Hu, S.-Y., & Moon, S. M. (2011). The effects of acceleration on high-ability learners: A meta-analysis. *Gifted Child Quarterly, 55*(1), 39–53.

Steinberg, L., Dornbusch, S., & Brown, B. (1992). Ethnic differences in adolescent achievement: An ecological perspective. *American Psychologist, 47*, 723–729.

Sternberg, R. J. (1985). *Beyond IQ: A triarchic theory of human intelligence*. New York: Cambridge University Press.

(1985). Implicit theories of intelligence, creativity, and wisdom. *Journal of Personality and Social Psychology, 49*, 607–627.

Stevenson, H. W., & Stigler, J. W. (1992). *The learning gap*. New York: Simon & Schuster.

Stigler, J. W., & Hiebert, J. (1999). *The teaching gap: Best ideas from the world's teachers for improving education in the classroom*. New York: The Free Press.

Stipek, D. (1998). Differences between Americans and Chinese in the circumstances evoking pride, shame, and guilt. *Journal of Cross-Cultural Psychology, 29*(5), 616–629.

Storch, E. A., & Masia-Warner, C. (2004). The relationship of peer victimization to social anxiety and loneliness in adolescent females. *Journal of Adolescence, 27*, 351–362.

Strayer, F. F. (1991). The development of agonistic and affiliative structures in pre-school play groups. In J. Silverberg & P. Gray (Eds.), *To fight or not to fight: Violence and peacefulness in humans and other primates*. Oxford: Oxford University Press.

Su, Y.-F., & Wu, J.-Y. (2005). 中國新教育的萌芽與成長 *(1860–1928)* [The emergence and development of new Chinese education (1860–1928)]. Taipei, Taiwan: Wunan Publishing.

Suárez-Orozco, C., & Suárez-Orozco, M. (2001). *Children of immigration: The developing child*. Cambridge, MA: Harvard University Press.

Suárez-Orozco, C., Suárez-Orozco, M., & Todorova, I. (2008). *Learning a new land: Immigrant students in American society*. New York: Belknap.

Sue, D., Sue, D. M., & Ino, S. (1990). Assertiveness and social anxiety in Chinese–American women. *Journal of Psychology, 124*, 155–163.

Swann, Jr., W. B., & Rentfrow, P. J. (2001). Blirtatiousness: Cognitive, behavioral, and physiological consequences of rapid responding. *Journal of Personality and Social Psychology, 81*, 1160–1175.

Taiwan Center for Chinese Curriculum (n.d.). Retrieved April 8, 2011 from http://chincenter.fg.tp.edu.tw/cerc/98ke.php

Takeuchi, D. T., Chung, R. C. Y., Lin, K. M. et al. (1998). Lifetime and twelve-month prevalence rates of major depressive episodes and dysthymia among Chinese Americans in Log Angeles. *American Journal of Psychiatry, 155*, 1407–1414.

Tang, T. K. W. (2001). The influence of teacher education on conceptions of teaching and learning. In D. A. Watkins & J. B. Biggs (Eds.), *Teaching the Chinese learner: Psychological and pedagogical perspectives* (pp. 221–238). Hong Kong: Comparative Education Research Centre.

Tangney, J. P. (2000). Humility: Theoretical perspectives, empirical findings and directions for future research. *Journal of Social and Clinical Psychology, 19*(1), 70–82.

(2002). Humility. In C. R. Snyder & S. J. Lopez (Eds.), *Handbook of positive psychology* (pp. 411–419). New York: Oxford University Press.

Tao, Y.-M. (1963). 桃花源記, 古文觀止, 上 [The land of peach blossoms in C.-C. Wu & D.-H. Wu (Eds.). *Essence of classical literature, Vol. 1]*. Zhonghua Book Company.

Tesser, A., Campbell, J., & Smith, M. (1984). Friendship choice and performance: Self-evaluation maintenance in children. *Journal of Personality and Social Psychology, 46*(3), 561–574.

The Economist. (2008, September 11). Huddled classes: How migrants fare in school, and what schools can learn from them (print ed.). http://www.economist.com/world/international/displaystory.cfm?story_id=12208631

Thomaes, S., Reijntjes, A., de Castro, B. O., & Bushman, B. J. (2009). Reality bites – or does it? Realistic self-views buffer negative mood following social threat. *Psychological Science, 3*(2), 1–2.

Ting-Toomey, S. (Ed.) (1994). *The challenge of facework: Cross-cultural and interpersonal issues*. Albany: State University of New York Press.

Tobin, J., Hsueh, Y., & Karasawa, M. (2009). *Preschool in three cultures revisited: China, Japan, and United States*. Chicago: The University of Chicago Press.

Tobin, J. J., Wu, D. Y. H., & Davidson, D. H. (1989). *Preschool in three cultures: Japan, China, and the United States*. New Haven, CT: Yale University Press.

Toch, T. (1991). *In the name of excellence*. New York: Oxford University Press.

Todd, S. C. A. (2008). *Commentary on Lysias: Speeches 1–11*. Oxford: Oxford University Press.

(2000). *The Oratory of Classical Greece: Volume 2*. Austin: University of Texas Press.

Tomasello, M. (1999). *The cultural origins of human cognition*. Cambridge, MA: Harvard University Press.

Tracy, J. L., & Robins, R. W. (2007). The self in self-conscious emotions: A cognitive appraisal approach. In J. L. Tracy, R. W. Robins, & J. P. Tangney (Eds.), *The self-conscious emotions: Theory and research* (pp. 3–20). New York: Guilford.

(2007). The nature of pride. In J. L. Tracy, R. W. Robins, & J. P. Tangney (Eds.), *The self-conscious emotions: Theory and research* (pp. 263–282). New York: Guilford.

Traub, G. S. (1983). Correlations of shyness with depression, anxiety, and academic performance. *Psychological Reports, 52*, 849–850.

Trevarthen, C. (1998). The concept and foundation of infant intersubjectivity. In S. Braten (Ed.), *Intersubject communication and emotion in early ontogeny* (pp. 15–46). New York: Cambridge University Press.

Triandis, H. C. (1995). *Individualism and collectivism*. Boulder, CO: Westview.

Tsai, J. L., Knutson, B., & Fung, H. H. (2006). Cultural variation in affect valuation. *Journal of Personality and Social Psychology, 90*(2), 288–307.

Tsai, J. L., Louie, J. Y., Chen, E. E., & Uchida, Y. (2007). Learning what feelings to desire: Socialization of ideal affect through children's storybooks. *Personality and Social Psychology Bulletin, 33*(1), 17–30.

Tseng, V., & Fuligni, A. J. (2000). Parent-adolescent language use and relationships among immigrant families with East Asian, Filipino, and Latin American Backgrounds. *Journal of Marriage and the Family, 62*, 465–476.

Tu, W. M. (1979). *Humanity and self-cultivation: Essays in Confucian thought.* Berkeley, CA: Asian Humanities Press.

Tweed, R. G., & Lehman, D. R. (2002). Learning considered within a cultural context: Confucian and Socratic approaches. *American Psychologist, 57*(2), 89–99.

Uguroglu, M. E., & Walberg, H. J. (1986). Predicting achievement and motivation. *Journal of Research and Development in Education, 19*, 1–12.

UK Council for International Student Affairs (n.d.). Retrieved from April 16, 2011 from http://www.ukcisa.org.uk

U.S. Census Bureau (2004). We the people: Asians in the United States, Census 2000 Special Report. Washington, DC: U.S. Census Bureau.

(2010). Overview of race and Hispanic origin: 2010 (Release No. C2010BR-02). Retrieved May 20, 2011 from http://www.census.gov/prod/cen2010/briefs/c2010br-02.pdf

U.S. National Survey on Drug Use and Health (2005). *The NSDUH report.* Retrieved July 8, 2009 from http://www.oas.samhsa.gov/2k5/suicide/suicide.htm

Van Abbema, D. L., & Bauer, P. J. (2008). Autobiographical memory in middle childhood: Recollections of the recent and distant past. *Memory, 13*(8), 829–845.

Van Egmond, M. C. (2011). *Mind and virtue: A cross-cultural analysis of beliefs about learning.* Unpublished doctoral dissertation, Jacobs University, Germany.

Vansteenkiste, M., Zhou, M.-M., Lens, W., & Soenens, B. (2005). Experiences of autonomy and control among Chinese learners: Vitalizing or immobilizing? *Journal of Educational Psychology, 97*(3), 468–483.

Vygotsky, L. S. (1978). *Mind in society: The development of higher psychological processes.* Cambridge, MA: Harvard University Press.

Wang, H., Chang, B.-R., Li, Y.-S., Lin, L.-H., Liu, J., Sun, Y.-L., et al. (1986). 現代漢語頻率詞典 [Dictionary of the frequency of vocabulary in modern Chinese]. Beijing, China: Beijing Languages Institute Press.

Wang, Q. (2001). "Did you have fun?" American and Chinese mother-child conversations about shared emotional experiences. *Cognitive Development, 16*, 693–715.

(2004). The emergence of cultural self-constructs: Autobiographical memory and self-description in European American and Chinese children. *Developmental Psychology, 40*(1), 3–15.

Wang, Q., & Leichtman, M. D. (2000). Same beginnings, different stories: A comparison of American and Chinese children's narratives. *Child Development, 71*, 1329–1346.

Wang, T., & Murphy, J. (2004). An examination of coherence in a Chinese mathematics classroom. In L.-H. Fan, N.-Y. Wong, J.-F. Cai, S.-Q. Li, & T.-Y. Tso (Eds.), *How Chinese learn mathematics: Perspectives from insiders* (pp. 107–123). Singapore: World Scientific.

Wang, T., Ruan, Z.-F., Chang, X.-F., Bao, K.-Y., Wang, J.-Y., Li, Z.-Y., et al. (1985). 中國成語大辭典 [Dictionary of Chinese idioms]. Shanghai: Shanghai Dictionary Press.

Wang, Y.-T. (Ed.) (1992). 新現代漢語詞典 [A new dictionary of modern Chinese language]. Hainan, China: Hainan Publishing House.

Watkins, D. A. (2009). Motivation and competition in Hong Kong secondary schools: The students' perspective. In C. Chan & N. Rao (Eds.), Revisiting the Chinese learner: Psychological and pedagogical perspectives (pp. 71–88). Hong Kong: Comparative Education Research Centre (CERC), University of Hong Kong and Springer Press.

Watkins, D. A., & Biggs, J. B. (Eds.) (1996). The Chinese learner: Cultural, psychological, and contextual influences. Hong Kong: Comparative Education Research Centre.

(2001). Teaching the Chinese learner: Psychological and pedagogical perspectives. Hong Kong: Comparative Education Research Centre.

Way, N. (2005). Seeking engagement: Reflections from a qualitative researcher. Journal of Adolescent Research, 20, 531–537.

Webb, N. M., Franke, M. L., Ing, M., Chan, A., De. T., Freund, D., et al. (2008). The role of teacher instructional practices in student collaborations. Contemporary Educational Psychology, 33, 360–381.

Webster's new collegiate dictionary. (1973). Springfield, MA: Merriam.

Weiner, B. (1986). An attributional theory of motivation and emotion. New York: Springer.

Wellman, H. M., Cross, D., & Watson, J. (2001). Meta-analysis of theory of mind development: The truth about false beliefs. Child Development, 72, 655–684.

Wentzel, K. R., & Asher, S. R. (1995). The academic lives of neglected, rejected, popular, and controversial children. Child Development, 66, 754–763.

Wentzel, K. R., & Caldwell, K. (1997). Friendships, peer acceptance, and group membership: Relations to academic achievement in middle school. Child Development, 68, 1198–1209.

Wentzel, K. R., & Wigfield, A. (1998). Academic and social motivational influence on students' academic performance. Educational Psychology Review, 10(2), 155–175.

Wertsch, J. V. (1996). A socio-cultural approach to socially shared cognition. In P. Baltes & U. Staudinger (Eds.), Interactive minds (pp. 85–100). New York: Cambridge University Press.

Westfall, R. (1971). The construction of modern science: Mechanisms and mechanics. New York: Cambridge University Press.

Wex, M. (2005). Born to Kvetch: Yiddish language and culture in all of its moods. New York: Harper Collins.

White, M. I., & LeVine, R. A. (1987). What is an "ii ko" (good child)? In H. Stevenson, H. Azuma, & H. Kenji (Eds.), Child Development in Japan (pp. 55–62). New York: Freeman.

White, S. H. (1998). What do we have to do to create a better social design for adolescence? Paper read in honor of Theodore Sizer at Brown University.

Williams, M. (2001). Problems of knowledge: A critical introduction to epistemology. New York: Oxford University Press.

Wilson, E. O. (1998). Consilience: The unity of knowledge. New York: Knopf.

Wilson, J. Q. (1993). *The moral sense*. New York: Simon & Schuster.

Wilson, R. (1980). Conformity and deviance regarding moral rules in Chinese society: A socialization perspective. In A. Kleinman & T. Lin (Eds.), *Moral and abnormal behavior in Chinese culture* (pp. 117–136). Dordrecht: D. Reidel.

Winner, E. (1989). How can Chinese children draw so well? *Journal of Aesthetic Education, 23*(1), 65–84.

(1996). *Gifted children: Myths and realities*. New York: Basic Books.

Wong, N.-Y. (2004). The CHC learner's phenomenon: Its implications on mathematics education. In L.-H. Fan, N.-Y. Wong, J.-.F Cai, S.-Q. Li, & T.-Y. Tso (Eds.), *How Chinese learn mathematics: Perspectives from insiders* (pp. 503–534). Singapore: World Scientific.

Wong, N.-Y., Han, J.-W., & Lee, P.-Y. (2004). The mathematics curriculum: Toward Globalization or Westernization? In L.-H. Fan, N.-Y. Wong, J.-F. Cai, S.-Q. Li, & T.-Y. Tso (Eds.), *How Chinese learn mathematics: Perspectives from insiders* (pp. 27–64). Singapore: World Scientific.

Wu, C.-X., & Chao, R. K. (2005). Intergenerational cultural conflicts in norms of parental warmth among Chinese American immigrants. *International Journal of Behavioral Development, 29*(6), 516–523.

Wu, D. Y. H. (1996). Chinese childhood socialization. In M. Bond (Ed.), *The handbook of Chinese psychology* (pp. 143–154). Hong Kong: Oxford University Press.

Wu, J.-Y. (1990). 中華民國教育政策發展史(國民政府時期 1925-1940) [History of the development of education policy during 1925–1940 under the China's Nationalist government]. Taipei, Taiwan: Wunan Publishing.

Wu, S.-P., & Lai, C.-Y. (1992). 白話四書五經全譯本 [Complete translations of the four books and five classics into modern Chinese]. Beijing, China: International Culture Press.

Xu, G. Q. (2004). The use of eloquence: The Confucian perspective. In C. S. Lipson & R. A. Binkley (Eds.), *Rhetoric before and beyond the Greeks* (pp. 115–130), Albany: State University of New York Press.

Yamamoto, Y., & Li, J. (2012). Quiet in the eye of the beholder: Teacher perceptions of Asian immigrant children. In C. Garcia Coll (Vol. Ed.), *The impact of immigration on children's development* (pp. 1–17). *Contributions to human development: Human Development*. Basel, Switzerland, Karger.

Yang, C.-L. (1995). 論兒童讀經的淵源及從理想層面探討兩種讀經法的功能 [Reciting or listening to the origin and ideal of children's classics training]. 高雄國文學報 *[Bulletin of Chinese]* (National Kaohsiung Normal University), *8*, 1–50.

Yang, K. S. (Ed.) (1988). 中國人的心理學 *[Chinese people's psychology]*. Taipei, Taiwan: Gwei Gwan Tu Shu.

Yang, S.-Y., & Sternberg, R. J. (1997). Taiwanese Chinese people's conceptions of intelligence. *Intelligence, 25*(1), 21–29.

Yang, Y.-Y. (2001a). '自己人': 一項有關中國人關系分類的個案研究 ['One of us': A case study on the classification of Chinese guanxi]. *Indigenous Psychological Research in Chinese Societies, 13*, 277–316.

(2001b). 自己人: 從中國人情感格局看婆媳關係 [Zijiren: From Chinese affection pattern to understanding the relation between mother-in-laws and daughter-in-laws]. *Indigenous Psychological Research in Chinese Societies, 16,* 1–39.

Yao, E. (1985). A comparison of family characteristics of Asian-American and Anglo-American high achievers. *International Journal of Comparative Sociology, 26*(34), 198–208.

Yoshikawa, H. (2011). *Immigrants raising citizens: Undocumented parents and their children.* New York: Sage.

Young, L. W. L. (1982). Inscrutability revisited. In J. J. Cumpez (Ed.), *Language and social identity* (pp. 72–84). Cambridge: Cambridge University Press.

(1994). *Crosstalk and culture in Sino-American communication.* New York: Cambridge University Press.

Yu, Y.-S. (1992). 中國文化與現代變遷 *[Chinese culture and modern evolution].* Sanmin Publishing House.

(2003). 士與中國文化 *[Intellectuals and Chinese culture].* Shanghai: Shanghai People's Press.

Yum, J. O. (1991). The impact of Confucianism on interpersonal relationships and communication patterns in East Asia. In L. A. Samovar & R. E. Porter (Eds.), *Intercultural communication: A reader* (pp. 66–78). Belmont, CA: Wadsworth.

Zane, N. W., Sue, S., Hu, L.-T., & Kwon, J.-H. (1991). Asian-American assertion: A social learning analysis of cultural differences. *Journal of Counseling Psychology, 38,* 63–70.

Zhang, D.-Z., Li, S.-Q., & Tang, R.-F. (2004). The "two basics": Mathematics teaching and learning in Mainland China. In L.-H. Fan, N.-Y. Wong, J.-F. Cai, S.-Q. Li, & T.-Y. Tso (Eds.), *How Chinese learn mathematics: Perspectives from insiders* (pp. 189–207). Singapore: World Scientific.

Zhou, M. (2009). Conflict, coping, and reconciliation: Intergenerational relations in Chinese immigrant families. In N. Foner (Ed.), *Across generations: Immigrant families in America* (pp. 21–46). New York: New York University Press.

Zhou, M., & Kim, S. S. (2006). Community forces, social capital, and educational achievement: The case of supplementary education in the Chinese and Korean immigrant communities. *Harvard Educational Review, 76,* 1–29.

INDEX